MULTICULTURAL EDUCATION 98/99

Editor

Fred Schultz

University of Akron

Fred Schultz, professor of education at the University of Akron, attended Indiana University to earn a B.S. in social science education in 1962, an M.S. in the history and philosophy of education in 1966, and a Ph.D. in the history and philosophy of education and American studies in 1969. His B.A. in Spanish was conferred by the University of Akron in May 1985. He is actively involved in researching the development and history of American education with a primary focus on the history of ideas and social philosophy of education. He also likes to study languages.

Annual Editions
A Library of Information from the Public Press
Dushkin/McGraw·Hill
Sluice Dock, Guilford, Connecticut 06437

Visit us on the Internet—http://www.dushkin.com/

The Annual Editions Series

ANNUAL EDITIONS, including GLOBAL STUDIES, consist of over 70 volumes designed to provide the reader with convenient, low-cost access to a wide range of current, carefully selected articles from some of the most important magazines, newspapers, and journals published today. ANNUAL EDITIONS are updated on an annual basis through a continuous monitoring of over 300 periodical sources. All ANNUAL EDITIONS have a number of features that are designed to make them particularly useful, including topic guides, annotated tables of contents, unit overviews, and indexes. For the teacher using ANNUAL EDITIONS in the classroom, an Instructor's Resource Guide with test questions is available for each volume. GLOBAL STUDIES titles provide comprehensive background information and selected world press articles on the regions and countries of the world.

VOLUMES AVAILABLE

ANNUAL EDITIONS

Abnormal Psychology
Accounting
Adolescent Psychology
Aging
American Foreign Policy
American Government
American History, Pre-Civil War
American History, Post-Civil War
American Public Policy
Anthropology
Archaeology
Astronomy
Biopsychology
Business Ethics
Canadian Politics
Child Growth and Development
Comparative Politics
Computers in Education
Computers in Society
Criminal Justice
Criminology
Developing World
Deviant Behavior
Drugs, Society, and Behavior
Dying, Death, and Bereavement

Early Childhood Education
Economics
Educating Exceptional Children
Education
Educational Psychology
Environment
Geography
Geology
Global Issues
Health
Human Development
Human Resources
Human Sexuality
International Business
Macroeconomics
Management
Marketing
Marriage and Family
Mass Media
Microeconomics
Multicultural Education
Nutrition
Personal Growth and Behavior
Physical Anthropology
Psychology
Public Administration
Race and Ethnic Relations

Social Problems
Social Psychology
Sociology
State and Local Government
Teaching English as a Second
   Language
Urban Society
Violence and Terrorism
Western Civilization, Pre-Reformation
Western Civilization, Post-Reformation
Women's Health
World History, Pre-Modern
World History, Modern
World Politics

GLOBAL STUDIES

Africa
China
India and South Asia
Japan and the Pacific Rim
Latin America
Middle East
Russia, the Eurasian Republics, and
   Central/Eastern Europe
Western Europe

Cataloging in Publication Data
Main entry under title: Annual editions: Multicultural Education. 1998/99.
   1. Intercultural education—Periodicals. I. Schultz, Fred, comp. II. Title: Multicultural education.
ISBN 0–697–39177–9   370.19'341'05   ISSN 1092–924X

Fifth Edition

Cover image © 1998 PhotoDisc, Inc.

Printed in the United States of America   1234567890BAHBAH901234098

Printed on Recycled Paper

Editors/Advisory Board

Members of the Advisory Board are instrumental in the final selection of articles for each edition of ANNUAL EDITIONS. Their review of articles for content, level, currentness, and appropriateness provides critical direction to the editor and staff. We think that you will find their careful consideration well reflected in this volume.

EDITOR

Fred Schultz
University of Akron

ADVISORY BOARD

Staff

Ian A. Nielsen, Publisher

To the Reader

In publishing ANNUAL EDITIONS we recognize the enormous role played by the magazines, newspapers, and journals of the *public press* in providing current, first-rate educational information in a broad spectrum of interest areas. Many of these articles are appropriate for students, researchers, and professionals seeking accurate, current material to help bridge the gap between principles and theories and the real world. These articles, however, become more useful for study when those of lasting value are carefully *collected, organized, indexed,* and *reproduced* in a *low-cost format*, which provides easy and permanent access when the material is needed. That is the role played by ANNUAL EDITIONS. Under the direction of each volume's *academic editor*, who is an expert in the subject area, and with the guidance of an *Advisory Board*, each year we seek to provide in each ANNUAL EDITION a current, well-balanced, carefully selected collection of the best of the public press for your study and enjoyment. We think that you will find this volume useful, and we hope that you will take a moment to let us know what you think.

There probably has not been a time of greater need for serious consideration of intercultural relations and multicultural realities in the field of education. We have much in common as human beings and as the heirs of great civilizations, yet we must cherish those cultural values and heritages that make us unique and diverse. An education for transformative intellectual and social development should focus on those things that liberate us from cultural stereotypes. No voices should be excluded from the dialogue regarding how to achieve such educational goals. How we help our students develop their voices and be heard is a major question for concerned teachers.

The concept of multicultural education evolved and took shape in the United States out of the social travail that wrenched the nation in the late 1960s, through the 1970s and 1980s, and into the present decade. The linkages between diverse and coexisting ethnic, racial, and socioeconomic heritages need to be explored. There has been enthusiastic support for the idea of a volume in this series exclusively devoted to multicultural education. Having taught and studied multicultural education for 29 years, it is a pleasure to serve as editor of *Annual Editions: Multicultural Education 98/99*.

The critical literature on gender, race, and culture in educational studies increases our knowledge base regarding the multicultural mosaic that so richly adorns North American culture. When the first courses in multicultural education were developed in the 1960s, the United States was in the midst of urban and other social crises, and there were no textbooks available. Educators who taught in this area had to draw heavily from academic literature in anthropology, sociology, social psychology, social history, sociolinguistics, and psychiatry. Today, there are textbooks available in the field, but there is also a need for a regular, annually published volume that offers samples from the most recent journal literature in which the knowledge bases for multicultural education are developed. This volume is intended to address that need.

The National Council for the Accreditation of Teacher Education (NCATE) in the United States has national standards requiring that accredited teacher education programs offer course content in multicultural education. A global concept of the subject is usually recommended in which prospective teachers are encouraged to develop empathetic cultural sensitivity to the demographic changes and cultural diversity that continue to develop in the public schools.

In this volume we first explore the national and global social contexts for the development of multicultural education. Its role in teacher education is then briefly defined in the essays in unit 2. In unit 3 the nature of multicultural education as an academic discipline is discussed by James Banks and others, and several issues related to this topic are explored. The readings in unit 4 look at multicultural education from the perspective of people in the process of developing their own unique personal identities in the context of their interactions with their own as well as others' cultural heritages and personal life experiences. The readings in unit 5 focus on curriculum and instruction in multicultural perspective. Unit 6 addresses special topics relevant to development of multicultural insight, and the essays in unit 7 explore alternative visions for multicultural education and the need for a conscious quest for emancipatory educational futures for people of all cultural heritages.

New to this edition are *World Wide Web* sites that can be used to further explore article topics. These sites are cross-referenced by number in the *topic guide*.

This year I would like to acknowledge the very helpful contributions of the advisory board members in finding useful sources. I would also like to acknowledge Dr. Stephen H. Aby, research librarian at the University of Akron, whose assistance is greatly valued.

This volume will be useful in courses in multicultural education at the undergraduate and graduate levels. It will add considerable substance to the sociocultural foundations of education, educational policy studies, and leadership, as well as to coursework in other areas of preservice and inservice teacher education programs. We hope you enjoy this volume, and we would like you to help us improve future editions. Please complete and return the *article rating form* at the back of the book. We look forward to hearing from you.

Fred Schultz

Fred Schultz
Editor

Contents

UNIT 1

The Social Contexts of Multicultural Education

Seven articles discuss the importance of a multicultural curriculum in sensitizing students to an integrated world society.

The concepts in bold italics are developed in the article. For further expansion please refer to the Topic Guide and the Index.

UNIT 2

Teacher Education in Multicultural Perspective

Six selections examine some of the major issues being debated on how to effectively integrate the multicultural dynamic into teacher education programs.

The concepts in bold italics are developed in the article. For further expansion please refer to the Topic Guide and the Index.

UNIT 3

Multicultural Education as an Academic Discipline

Four selections examine the dynamics of integrating multicultual education into the discipline of education.

The concepts in bold italics are developed in the article. For further expansion please refer to the Topic Guide and the Index.

UNIT 4

Identity and Personal Development: A Multicultural Focus

Five articles consider the interconnections between gender, social class, racial and ethnic heritage, and primary cultural values.

The concepts in bold italics are developed in the article. For further expansion please refer to the Topic Guide and the Index.

viii

UNIT 5

Curriculum and Instruction in Multicultural Perspective

Eight articles review how curriculum and instruction must be formulated to sensitize young people to the multicultural reality of a national civilization.

The concepts in bold italics are developed in the article. For further expansion please refer to the Topic Guide and the Index.

ix

UNIT 6

Special Topics in Multicultural Education

Five articles explore some
of the ways that students
succeed or fail in culturally
pluralistic school settings.

The concepts in bold italics are developed in the article. For further expansion please refer to the Topic Guide and the Index.

UNIT 7

For Vision and Voice: A Call to Conscience

Three selections address the concerns that must be kept in mind for the future improvement of our educational system.

The concepts in bold italics are developed in the article. For further expansion please refer to the Topic Guide and the Index.

1

Topic Guide

This topic guide suggests how the selections in this book relate to topics of traditional concern to students and professional educators involved with the study of education. It is useful for locating articles that relate to each other for reading and research. The guide is arranged alphabetically according to topic. Articles may, of course, treat topics that do not appear in the topic guide. In turn, entries in the topic guide do not necessarily constitute a comprehensive listing of all the contents of each selection. **In addition, relevant Web sites, which are annotated on pages 4 and 5, are noted in bold italics under the topic articles.**

TOPIC AREA	TREATED IN	TOPIC AREA	TREATED IN
Affirmative Action	4. Challenge of Affirmative Action *(8, 19, 33, 39)*	**Curriculum and Instruction (cont.)**	27. Success for Hispanic Students 28. Creating Positive Cultural Images 29. Early Childhood Education 30. NAEYC Position Statement 31. Of Kinds of Disciplines and Kinds of Understanding 32. Disappearance of American Indian Languages *(9, 10, 11, 12, 13, 23, 28, 33)*
Bias	18. Acquisition and Manifestation of Prejudice in Children 19. Race and Class Consciousness 31. Of Kinds of Disciplines and Kinds of Understanding *(7, 13, 19, 27, 28, 29, 32, 34)*		
Bilingual Education	24. Meeting the Needs of Hispanic Immigrants 25. Is English in Trouble? 27. Success for Hispanic Students 30. NAEYC Position Statement 32. Disappearance of American Indian Languages *(9, 14, 23, 33, 37, 39)*	**English as a Second Language**	24. Meeting the Needs of Hispanic Immigrants 25. Is English in Trouble? 27. Success for Hispanic Students 30. NAEYC Position Statement 32. Disappearance of American Indian Languages *(23, 25, 28, 29, 33)*
Cultural Stereotypes	1. Moving from an Obsolete Lingo to a Vocabulary of Respect *(10, 20)*	**Ethnicity**	29. Early Childhood Education *(22, 23, 24, 25, 27, 28, 29, 33)*
Cultures	1. Moving from an Obsolete Lingo to a Vocabulary of Respect 3. Melting Pot, Salad Bowl, Multicultural Mosaic, Crazy Quilt . . . 7. Home Was a Horse Stall 10. Faculty Fear 18. Acquisition and Manifestation of Prejudice in Children 19. Race and Class Consciousness 20. Decentering Whiteness 22. Making of a Hip-Hop Intellectual 23. Becoming Multicultural 24. Meeting the Needs of Hispanic Immigrants 26. "Let Me Take You Home . . ." 27. Success for Hispanic Students 28. Creating Positive Cultural Images 29. Early Childhood Education 30. NAEYC Position Statement 31. Of Kinds of Disciplines and Kinds of Understanding 32. Disappearance of American Indian Languages 34. Confronting White Hegemony 35. Family and Cultural Context *(10, 15, 16, 23, 24, 25, 27, 32, 33)*	**Families and Education**	24. Meeting the Needs of Hispanic Immigrants 33. Parents as First Teachers 35. Family and Cultural Context *(30, 31)*
		Gay, Lesbian, and Trans-Gendered Students	21. Opening the Closet
		Hispanics	24. Meeting the Needs of Hispanic Immigrants 27. Success for Hispanic Students *(24, 28, 29, 30, 31, 32, 33)*
		Holocaust	31. Of Kinds of Disciplines and Kinds of Understanding *(34)*
		Identity Development	3. Melting Pot, Salad Bowl, Multicultural Mosaic, Crazy Quilt . . . 18. Acquisition and Manifestation of Prejudice in Children 19. Race and Class Consciousness 20. Decentering Whiteness 21. Opening the Closet 22. Making of a Hip-Hop Intellectual *(7, 8, 9, 19, 20, 21, 22, 23, 32, 33)*
Curriculum and Instruction	5. How to Teach Our Children Well 6. New Vision for City Schools 23. Becoming Multicultural 24. Meeting the Needs of Hispanic Immigrants 25. Is English in Trouble? 26. "Let Me Take You Home . . ."	**Japanese Americans**	7. Home Was a Horse Stall

Selected World Wide Web Sites for
Annual Editions: Multicultural Education

All of these Web sites are hot-linked through the *Annual Editions* home page:
http://www.dushkin.com/annualeditions (just click on this book's title). In addition, these sites are
referenced by number and appear where relevant in the Topic Guide on the previous two pages.

Some Web sites are continually changing their structure
and content, so the information listed may not always
be available.

General Sources

1. Educational Resources Information Center—*http://www.aspensys.
com/eric/index.html*—This invaluable site provides links to all ERIC
sites: clearinghouses, support components, and publishers of ERIC
materials. You can search the ERIC database, find out what is
new, and ask questions about ERIC.

2. Education Week on the Web—*http://www.edweek.org/*—At this *Education Week* home page, you will be able to open archives, read special
reports, keep up on current events, look at job opportunities, and access a variety of articles of relevance in multicultural education.

3. Global SchoolNet Foundation—*http://www.gsn.org/*—Access this site
for multicultural education information. The site includes news for
teachers, students, and parents; as well as chat rooms, links to educational resources, programs, and contests and competitions.

4. Multicultural Publishing and Education Council—*http://www.mpec.
org/*—This is the home page of the MPEC, a networking and support organization for independent publishers, authors, educators,
and librarians fostering authentic multicultural books and materials. It has excellent links to a vast array of resources related to
multicultural education.

5. National Education Association—*http://www.nea.org/*—Something—
and often quite a lot—about virtually every education-related
topic can be accessed at or through this site of the 2.3-million-
strong National Education Association.

6. Phi Delta Kappa—*http://www.pdkintl.org/home.htm*—This important organization publishes articles about all facets of education.
By clicking on the links at this site, for example, you can check
out the journal's online archive.

The Social Contexts of
Multicultural Education

7. American Psychological Association—*http://www.apa.org/psychnet/*—
By exploring the APA's "PsychNET," you will be able to find links
to an abundance of articles and other resources that are useful in
understanding the factors that are involved in the development
of prejudice.

8. Association for Moral Education—*http://www.wittenberg.edu/ame/*—
AME is dedicated to fostering communication, cooperation, training, curriculum development, and research that links moral theory
with educational practices. From here it is possible to connect to
several sites on ethics, character building, and moral development.

9. Center for Innovation in Education—*http://www.educenter.org/*—
This is the home page of the Center for Innovation in Education,
self-described as a "not-for-profit, non-partisan research organization" focusing on K–12 education reform strategies. Click on its
links for information about and varying perspectives on various
reform initiatives.

Teacher Education in
Multicultural Perspective

10. Awesome Library for Teachers—*http://www.neat-schoolhouse.org/
teacher.html*—Open this page for links and access to teacher information on many topics of concern to multicultural educators.

11. Education World—*http://www.education-world.com/*—Education
World provides a database of literally thousands of sites that can
be searched by grade level, plus education news, lesson plans,
and professional-development resources.

12. PREPnet—*http://prep.net/*—This site contains Web sites for educators. It covers a wide range of topics dealing with K–12 resources
and curricula. Its links will prove useful for examining issues that
pertain to multicultural education.

13. Teacher Talk Forum—*http://education.indiana.edu/cas/tt/tthmpg.
html*—Visit this site for access to a variety of articles discussing
life in the classroom. Clicking on the various links will lead you
to electronic lesson plans, covering a variety of topic areas, from
Indiana University's Center for Adolescent Studies.

Multicultural Education
as an Academic Discipline

14. Canada's Schoolnet Staff Room—*http://www.schoolnet.ca/adm/
staff/*—Here is a resource and link site for anyone involved in education, including bilingual education teachers, parents, volunteers, and administrators.

15. Carfax—*http://www.carfax.co.uk/subjeduc.htm*—Look through this
superb index for numerous articles as well as links to education
publications such as *Journal of Beliefs and Values, Educational Philosophy and Theory, European Journal of Intercultural Studies,* and
Race, Ethnicity, and Education.

16. Goals 2000: A Progress Report—*http://www.ed.gov/pubs/goals/
progrpt/index.html*—Open this site to survey a progress report by
the U.S. Department of Education on the Goals 2000 reform initiative. It provides a sense of what goals that educators are
reaching for as they look toward the future.

17. Teachers Helping Teachers—*http://www.pacificnet.net/~mandel/*—
This site provides basic teaching tips, new teaching-methodology
ideas, and forums for teachers to share their experiences. Down-
load software and participate in chat sessions. It features educational resources on the Web, with new ones added each week.

18. Washington (State) Commission on Student Learning—*http://csl.
wednet.edu/*—This Washington State educational site is designed
to provide access to information about the state's new academic
standards, assessments, and accountability system, but it is useful
to teachers from other regions as well. Many resources and Web
links are included.

Identity and Personal Development:
A Multicultural Focus

19. Ethics Updates/Lawrence Hinman—*http://ethics.acusd.edu/*—This is
Professor Hinman's consummate learning tool. The site provides

both simple concept definition and complex analysis of ethics, original treatises, and sophisticated search engine capability. Subject matter covers the gamut, from ethical theory to applied ethical venues. There are many opportunities for user input.

20. Kathy Schrock's Guide for Educators—*http://www.capecod.net/schrockguide/*—This is a classified list of sites on the Internet found to be useful for enhancing curriculum and teacher professional growth. It is updated daily.

21. The National Academy for Child Development—*http://www.nacd.org/*—This international organization is dedicated to helping children and adults reach their full potential. This page presents links to various programs, research, and resources in a variety of topics.

22. Nurturing Kid's Seven Ways of Being Smart—*http://place.scholastic.com/instructor/classroom/organizing/smart.htm*—Open this page for Kristen Nelson's discussion of ways in which teachers can help to develop children's multiple intelligences. She provides a useful bibliography and resources.

Curriculum and Instruction in Multicultural Perspective

23. American Indian Science and Engineering Society—*http://spot.colorado.edu/~aises/aises.html*—This is the AISES "Multicultural Educational Reform Programs" site. It provides a framework for learning about science, mathematics, and technology by which minority students and their teachers can make meaningful cultural connections to teaching and learning. There are links to teacher and curriculum programs for Native American education.

24. Child Welfare League of America—*http://www.cwla.org/*—The CWLA is the United States' oldest and largest organization devoted entirely to the well-being of vulnerable children and their families. This site provides links to information about issues related to the process of becoming multicultural.

25. STANDARDS: An International Journal of Multicultural Studies—*http://stripe.colorado.edu/~standard/*—This fascinating site provides access to a seemingly infinite number of archives and links to topics of interest in the study of multiculturalism.

Special Topics in Multicultural Education

26. American Scientist—*http://www.amsci.org/amsci/amsci.html*—Investigate this site to access a variety of articles and to explore issues and concepts related to race and gender.

27. American Studies Web—*http://www.georgetown.edu/crossroads/asw/*—This eclectic site provides links to a wealth of resources on the Internet related to American studies, from gender studies to race and ethnicity. It is of great help when doing research in demography and population studies.

28. Early Intervention Solutions—*http://www.earlyintervention.com/library4.htm*—EIS presents this site to address concerns about child stress and reinforcement. It suggests ways to deal with negative behaviors that may result from stress and anxiety among children.

29. National Institute on the Education of At-Risk Students—*http://www.ed.gov/offices/OERI/At-Risk/*—The At-Risk Institute supports a range of research and development activities designed to improve the education of students at risk of educational failure due to limited English proficiency, race, geographic location, or economic disadvantage. Access its work and links at this site.

30. National Network for Family Resiliency—*http://www.nnfr.org/nnfr/*—This organization's home page will lead you to a number of resource areas of interest in learning about resiliency: General Family Resiliency, Violence Prevention, and Family Economics.

31. National Parent Information Network/ERIC—*http://ericps.ed.uiuc.edu/npin/npinhome.html*—This is a clearinghouse of information on education. Browse through its links for information for parents and for people who work with parents.

32. Patterns of Variability: The Concept of Race—*http://www.as.ua.edu/ant/bindon/ant101/syllabus/race/race1.htm*—This site provides a handy, at-a-glance reference to the prevailing concepts of race and the causes of human variability since ancient times. It can serve as a valuable starting point for research and understanding into the concept of race.

33. U.S. Department of Education—*http://www.ed.gov/pubs/TeachersGuide/*— Explore this government site for examination of institutional aspects of multicultural education. National goals, projects, grants, and other educational programs are listed here as well as many links to teacher services and resources.

34. U.S. Holocaust Memorial Museum—*http://www.ushmm.org/*—This site provides insights into the many causes and results of prejudice.

For Vision and Voice: A Call to Conscience

35. Classroom Connect—*http://www.classroom.net/*—This is a major Web site for K–12 teachers and students, with links to schools, teachers, and resources online. It includes discussion of the use of technology in the classroom.

36. EdWeb/Andy Carvin—*http://edweb.cnidr.org/*—The purpose of EdWeb is to explore the worlds of educational reform and information technology. Access educational resources around the world, learn about trends in education policy and information infrastructure development, examine success stories of computers in the classroom, and much more.

37. Hypertext and Ethnography—*htthp://www.umanitoba.ca/faculties/arts/anthropology/tutor/aaa_presentation.html*—This site, presented by Brian Schwimmer of the University of Manitoba, will be of great value to people who are interested in culture and communication. He addresses such topics as multivocality and complex symbolization, among many others.

38. Online Internet Institute—*http://www.oii.org/*—A collaborative project among Internet-using educators, proponents of systemic reform, content-area experts, and teachers who desire professional growth, this site provides a learning environment for integrating the Internet into educators' individual teaching styles.

39. SchoolHouse Talk—*http://wworks.com/~pieinc/index.htm*—The strong opinions and diverse viewpoints about issues in multicultural education reproduced or expressed through this Web site are guaranteed to generate heated debate among educators and the citizenry.

We highly recommend that you review our Web site for expanded information and our other product lines. We are continually updating and adding links to our Web site in order to offer you the most usable and useful information that will support and expand the value of your Annual Editions. You can reach us at: *http://www.dushkin.com/annualeditions/*.

The Social Contexts of Multicultural Education

The power of culture cannot be ignored in shaping peoples' conceptions of social reality and the phenomenology of their visions of their own lives and the lives of others around them. Every person needs to develop his or her own social vision of life as it relates to actual cultural realities in society.

The United States is becoming an ever more multicultural nation. Canada is also experiencing major changes in its cultural composition due to its generous immigration policies. Some demographic projections indicate that within 5 years a majority of the total American elementary and secondary school student body will be composed of people of color, the children of the rainbow coalition—Native American, African American, Asian American, and Latino American.

Multicultural national communities face special challenges in daily life among the diverse cultural groups that comprise them. Such societies also have unique opportunities to develop great culturally pluralistic civilizations in which the aesthetic, artistic, literary, and moral standards of each cultural group can contribute to the creation of new standards. Groups can learn from one another; they can benefit from their respective strengths and achievements; and they can help one another to transcend problems and injustices. Furthermore, there are several major multicultural national social orders worldwide, and they can learn from and help each other even more than they have in the past. We ought, therefore, to see the multicultural national fabric that is our social reality as a circumstance of promise, hope, and pride.

However, social conditions exist that are yet to be rectified. Students must be empowered with a constructive sense of social consciousness and a will to transcend the social barriers to safety, success, and personal happiness that confront, in one form or another, almost one-third of them.

Certain very important questions must be asked about children and young adults. Are they hungry? Are they afraid? Are they angry? Do they have a sense of angst; are they filled with self-doubt and uncertainty as to their prospects in life? For far too many children and adolescents from all socioeconomic strata, social classes, and cultural groups, the answer is "yes." Far greater numbers of children from low-income minority cultural groups answer "yes" to at least some of these questions than do children from higher socioeconomic groups.

Having done this, educators and civic leaders should consider a few questions. What are the purposes of schooling? Are schools limited to their acknowledged mission of intellectual development? Or are schools also capable of advancing, as did classical Greek and Roman educators, the traits of honor, character, courage, resourcefulness, civic responsibility, and social service? This latter concept of the mission of schooling is still today the brightest hope for the full achievement of our great promise as a multicultural society in an interdependent world community of nations.

What are the obstacles to achieving this end? Each child must be able to advance intellectually in school as far as possible. As educators, we need to help students develop a sense of honor, self-respect, and pride in their own cultural heritages that will lead them in their adult years to want to serve, help, and heal the suffering of others. We need to produce intellectually curious and competent graduates who know and care about their own ethnic heritages and are committed to social justice for all—in their own nation and in the community of nations.

The problems that go along with achieving such intellectual and social ends are significant. Developing multicultural curriculum materials for schools and integrating them throughout the course content and activities of the school day and year can help sensitize all students to the inherent worth of all persons. All youth deserve the opportunity to learn about their own cultural heritages, and they deserve to understand that heritage from an objective, scientific perspective that cannot be seen through the cultural lenses of a Eurocentric perspective.

Many believe that all people must understand the interdependence of humanity and the interests and concerns that all human cultures embrace. North American nations have qualitative issues to face in the area of intercultural relations. Problems differ because of diverse national experiences and school systems. Around the world other nations have to wrestle with providing adequate opportunity for minority populations while maintaining high intellectual standards.

There have been dramatic changes in the characteristics of the world's population and in the interdependence of the world's nations in a global economy. We must reconsider how we develop human talent in our schools, for young people will be our most basic resource for the future.

Young adults should be aware that the struggle for freedom, and against tyranny, is not over everywhere in the world despite the great advances that democratic forces have made in recent years. They should know the history of the civil rights movement in the United States as well as the origins of many racial and cultural stereotypes. Young people need to be able to accept and to value cultural diversity. This essay has sought to discuss the nature of the social context in which efforts to expand multicultural education have occurred.

The unit essays are relevant to courses in cultural foundations of education, educational policy studies, multicultural education, social studies education, and curriculum theory and construction.

Looking Ahead: Challenge Questions

What should every student learn about cultural diversity and her or his own cultural heritage?

What facets of the history of the human struggle for civil rights should be taught to students?

What should students learn about other nations and other democratic traditions?

How can the mass media more effectively inform the public on issues related to cultural diversity?

What can educators do to help students better understand the social contexts in which they live?

What should every student know about cultural diversity and equality of opportunity?

What should everyone know about our common humanity?

Moving from an Obsolete Lingo
to a Vocabulary of Respect

by Zoë Anglesey

anguage creates community. Or words, unlike sticks and stones, may endure for centuries as weapons aimed at the psyche to injure not only individuals, but whole societies as well. Words carry the cargo of etymological history in their meanings, and when we use them, we communicate what we may or may not intend. In short, we cannot remain complicitous or naive when it comes to a labeling vocabulary that generalizes, stereotypes, or demeans others.

Presently, the term "post-colonial" refers generally to a consciousness that contests the imposition of colonial terms of identity, politics, or economics. The word means "after colonialism," to designate an era when national and cultural integrity are to be respected. Post-colonial discourse opposes and re-envisions the practice of domination, starting with language itself. If in principle we believe in equality, if we also understand how inequality affects people sometimes after the moment of birth, we can communicate our belief via word choices that promote peace and respect. Based on these principles, citizens of the global community have the right to name themselves, define their histories, and live according to their culture.

For example, Columbus and the Europeans who subjugated the indigenous inhabitants first in the Caribbean and later throughout the Americas, depended on a dehumanizing lexicon of inaccurate, illusory, or abusive terms. When Columbus encountered the Tainos, Arawaks, and Caribs, he referred to them as "Indians" to deny their authority in identifying themselves. Ultimately, he continued to use the term to justify his miscalculation that he had encountered people on islands in the

> *Or words, unlike sticks and stones, may endure for centuries as weapons aimed at the psyche to injure not only individuals, but whole societies as well*

seas surrounding India or the archipelago of Asian islands rimming the Pacific. Columbus and other Europeans had inherited the word from the Greeks, for which "Indian" referred to "others" in the east who rode elephants.

It's often argued that some admittedly pejorative, obsolete, or inaccurate terms with origins in the colonial past enjoy common usage if not acceptance among the very cultural groups they attempt to label, such as "Indians," "Caucasians," "mulattoes," or "blacks." The word "tribe," even in its original usage to designate regional language and cultural groups forced to submit to the hegemony of Rome, provides another case in point. Frantz Fanon wrote, "Colonialism does not simply state the existence of tribes; it also reinforces it and separates them" (p. 94). To their benefit, colonizers insisted on such lingo to divide and conquer. Professionals in an array of disciplines still rely on such terms, and the outcome remains the same. When questioned about the accuracy or social consequences of such language, the final resort is to state that it's too troublesome to use alternatives. This is an admission that the internalizing of colonial domination began with language and unfortunately continues.

Fanon spoke of the "Third World" to relay the unity of interests that the colonized world shared. The concept of this term, while positive in the 1960s and 1970s, has evolved with discourse and changing geopolitics into its negative connotation today. Alternatively, naming nations, citing geographical locations, specifying language groups and cultures, particularly identifies the subjects of discussion. What most stratifies people is their

From *MultiCultural Review,* September 1997, pp. 23-28. © 1997 by Greenwood Publishing Group, Inc. (Greenwood Subscription Publications), Westport, CT. Reprinted by permission.

economic status and whether or not they live within exploited economies. Racial terms, usually based on perceptions, persist in labeling complex cultural, social, and economic groups. Besides being generally harmful, they are obsolete in light of current archaeological evidence as well as DNA technology, which verifies our common ancestry as a species. Scientifically speaking, people are of mixed heritages and have been mixing since their migrations out of Africa maybe three million to as late as 60,000 years ago.

Acknowledging this scientific and historical reality, contemporary Caribbean writers seem to be the most willing to call into question this archaic language. Edouard Glissant, Patrick Chamoiseau, Derek Walcott, Jamaica Kincaid, and Edwidge Danticat, for example, critique terms of domination—especially simple racialisms—and instead subscribe to the concept of Creolity that acknowledges the indigenous, European, African, and Asian matrix of contemporary life. Strikingly, Jamaica Kincaid, in *The Autobiography of My Mother*, relies on geographical terms that identify the predominant heritages of a character, like "Scotsman," "African," "English," and "Carib." This provides the reader with specific geographical bearings within a history that the easy labels like "black" and "white" do not provide.

The chart below questions further usage of obsolete, inaccurate, or dehumanizing terms, with the hope that an alternative vocabulary will emerge to communicate more precisely our post-colonial consciousness and to acknowledge everyone on the planet as human and worthy of respect. Following the chart is a bibliography of classic and recent writings that explore the issues of language and identity.

INTERDISCIPLINARY WORKS CONSULTED

Anglesey, Zoë. "Double Tonguing: Or, The Meaning of It All." *The Voice Literary Supplement.* (November 1994): 21. English terms re: Spanish-Speaking Cultures in the U.S.

Appiah, K. Anthony and Gutman, Amy. *Color Conscious: The Political Morality of Race.* Princeton, N.J.: Princeton University Press, 1996.

Appiah, Kwame Anthony and Gates, Henry Louis, Jr. *The Dictionary of Global Culture.* Michael Colin Vasquez, ed. New York: Knopf, 1997.

Ards, Burgher, Dauphin, Poerter, Reeves, Suggs, "Color Me Multiracial," *The Village Voice.* (Feb. 11, 1997): 36ff.

Ashdown, Peter. *Caribbean History in Maps.* 5th ed. Harlow, England: Longman, 1988.

Belford, Robert James, ed. *A History of the United States in Chronological Order from A.D. 432 to the Present Time.* New York: The World, 1886.

Berreby, David. "Arrogance, Order, Amity and Other National Traits." *The New York Times* (May 26, 1996): Section 4, p.1.

Bhabha, Homi K., ed. *Nation and Narration.* London: Routledge, 1990.

Boland, Eavan. *Object Lessons: The Life of the Woman and the Poet in Our Time.* New York: W. W. Norton, 1995.

Brown, Tony. *Black Lies, White Lies.* New York: Quill/William Morrow, 1995.

Carew, Jan. *Fulcrums of Change: African Presence in the Americas.* Trenton, N.J.: Africa World Press, 1988.

Cavalli-Sforza, L. Luca; Menozzi, Paolo; and Piazza, Alberto. *The History and Geography of Human Genes.* Abridged paperback ed. Princeton, N.J.: Princeton University Press, 1994.

Cesaire, Aimé. *Discourse on Colonialism.* New York: Monthly Review Press, 1972.

Dasgupta, Partha S. "Population, Poverty and the Local Environment." *Scientific American* (February 1995): 40-45. Example of economic but bias-free vocabulary.

Dash, Michael J. *Edouard Glissant.* New York: Cambridge University Press, 1995.

Dirlik, Arif. *After the Revolution: Waking to Global Capitalism.* Hanover, N.H.: University Press of New England, 1994.

——. *The Postcolonial Aura: Third World Criticism in the Age of Global Capitalism.* Boulder, Colo.: Westview, 1997.

Eagan, Timothy. "Tribe Stops Study of Bones that Challenge History." *The New York Times* (September 30, 1996): A12.

Eagleton, Terry. *The Illusions of Postmodernism.* Cambridge, Mass.: Blackwell, 1996.

Fanon, Frantz. *The Wretched of the Earth.* Trans. by Constance Farrington. New York: Grove Press, 1963.

Fischer, Claude S.; Hout, Michael; Sánchez Jankowski, Martín; Lucas, Samuel R.; Swidler, Ann; and Voss, Kim. *Inequality by Design: Cracking the Bell Curve Myth.* Princeton, N.J.: Princeton University Press, 1996.

Forbes, Jack D. *Africans and Native Americans: The Language of Race and the Evolution of Red-Black Peoples.* Urbana: University of Illinois Press, 1993.

Galeano, Eduardo. *We Say No: Chronicles 1963-1991.* New York: W. W. Norton, 1992.

——. "A Tale of Ambiguities." *Index of Censorship* 3 (1995): 34-36.

Gilroy, Paul. *Small Acts: Thoughts on the Politics of Black Cultures.* London: Serpent's Tail, 1993.

Glissant, Édouard. *Poetics of Relation.* Translated by Betsy Wing. Ann Arbor: University of Michigan Press, 1997. Multiforms of culture, transformative history, creolization.

Goldberg, Carey. "Hispanic Households Struggle Amid Broad Decline in Income." *The New York Times* (January 30, 1997): 1, 16.

Gould, Stephen Jay. "The Dodo in the Caucus Race." *Natural History* 105/11 (November 1996): 22-33.

Greene, Sandra E. *Gender, Ethnicity, and Social Change on the Upper Slave Coast: A History of the Anglo-Ewe.* Portsmouth, N.H.: Heinemann, 1996.

Hannaford, Ivan. "The Idiocy of Race." *The Wilson Quarterly* (Spring 1994): 8-35.

Hoxie, Frederick E., ed. *Encyclopedia of North American Indians: Native American History, Culture, and Life from Paleo-Indians to the Present.* Boston, Mass.: Houghton Mifflin, 1996.

Incer, Jaime, ed. *Toponimas Indigenas de Nicaragua.* San Jose, Costa Rica: San Pedro de Montes de Oca/Libro Libre, 1985.

James, C.L.R. *The Black Jacobins: Toussaint L'Ouverture and the San Domingo Revolution.* 1963. Reprint. London: Allison & Busby, 1980, p. 283.

Johnson, Charles. *Being and Race: Black Writing Since 1970.* Bloomington: Indiana University Press, 1988.

Kim, Elaine H. and Alarcón, Norma, eds. *Writing Self, Writing Nation: Essays on Theresa Hak Kyung Cha's* Dictee. Berkeley, Calif.: Third Woman Press, 1994.

Kincaid, Jamaica. *The Autobiography of My Mother.* New York: Plume/Penguin, 1997.

Klor de Alva, J. Jorge. "The Postcolonization of the (Latin) American Experience: A Reconsideration of 'Colonialism,' 'Postcolonialism,' and 'Mestizaje.'" In *After Colonialism* (p. 241-275). Princeton, N.J.: Princeton University Press, 1995.

Larick, Roy, and Ciochon, Russell L. "The African Emergence and Early Asian Dispersals of the Genus *Homo.*" *American Scientist* 84/6 (Nov.-Dec. 1966): 538-551.

Leone, Mark P., and Silberman, Neil Asher. *Invisible America: Unearthing Our Hidden History.* New York: Henry Holt, 1995.

Lewontin, Richard. "Of Genes and Genitals." *Transition* 69:186 (Spring 1996): 192-193. Review of J. Phillip Rushton, *Race, Evolution, and Behavior: A Life History Perspective.*

Maggio, Rosalie. *The Bias-Free Word Finder: A Dictionary of Nondiscriminatory Language.* Boston: Beacon Press, 1991.

Marable, Manning. *Beyond Black & White: Transforming African American Politics.* New York: Verso, 1997.

———. *Speaking Truth to Power: Essays on Race, Resistance, and Radicalism.* Boulder, Colo.: Westview, 1996.

Marriott, Michel. "Multiracial Americans Ready to Claim Their Own Identity." *The New York Times* (July 20, 1996): 1, 7.

Mertz, Henriette. *Pale Ink.* Chicago: The Swallow Press, 1972.

Morley, Sylvanus G. *The Ancient Maya.* Stanford, Calif.: Stanford University Press, 1946. (Plate 50, Uaxactun)

Nieto, Sonia. *Affirming Diversity: The Sociopolitical Context of Multicultural Education.* White Plains, N.Y.: Longman, 1996.

Olds, Bruce. *Raising Holy Hell: A Novel of John Brown.* New York: Penguin, 1997.

Prakash, Gyan, ed. *After Colonialism: Imperial Histories and Postcolonial Displacement.* Princeton, N.J.: Princeton University Press, 1995.

Said, Edward. "Secular Interpretation, the Geographical Element, and the Methodology of Imperialism." In *After Colonialism,* ed. by Gyan Prakash (pp. 21-39). Princeton, N.J.: Princeton University Press, 1995.

———. *Culture and Imperialism.* New York: Knopf, 1993.

———. "The Splendid Tapestry of Arab Life." In *The Politics of Dispossession: The Struggle for Palestinian Self-Determination 1969-1994.* New York: Pantheon, 1994.

Salgado, Sabastião. *An Uncertain Grace.* Photographs and captions by Salgado; Essays by Eduardo Galeano and Fred Ritchin. New York: Aperture Foundation/Farrar Straus Giroux, 1990. See photos of 50,000 miners of Brazil's Serra Pelada gold mine.

Sardar, Zia; Nandy, Ashis; and Davies, Merryl Wyn. *Barbaric Others: A Manifesto on Western Racism.* Boulder, Colo.: Westview, 1994.

Stephens, Julie. "Cultural Dominance at Its Most Benevolent: An Interview with Gayatri Chakravorty Spivak." *Arena Jounal* 6 (1996): 35-50.

"Study Bolsters Theory of Early Humans." *The New York Times* (March 3, 1996): C1. Sarah Tishkoff study, Yale University)

Trouillot, Michel-Rolph. *Silencing the Past: Power and the Production of History.* Boston, Mass.: Beacon Press, 1995.

Tucker, William H. *The Science and Politics of Racial Research.* Urbana: University of Illinois Press, 1994.

Vélez-Ibáñez, Carlos G. *Border Visions: Mexican Cultures of the Southwest United States.* Tucson: University of Arizona Press, 1996.

West, Cornel. "The New Cultural Politics of Difference." *October* (Summer 1990): 53, 93.

Wilford, John Noble. "Bones in China Put New Light on Old Humans." *The New York Times* (Nov. 16, 1995): 8.

Zoë Anglesey compiled and edited the multilingual book *Ixok Amar Go—Central American Women's Poetry for Peace* (1987), *!Word Up! Hope for Youth Poetry* (El Centro de la Raza, 1992), and the bilingual *Stone on Stone/Piedra Sobre Piedra: Poetry by Women of Diverse Heritages* (Open Hand, 1994). Her forthcoming anthology features ten emerging poets from the Brooklyn Moon Cafe/Nuyorican Poets Cafe scene. Besides teaching college writing, she reviews books about jazz.

(Continued on next page)

MOVING FROM AN OBSOLETE LINGO TO A VOCABULARY OF RESPECT

Instead of	Preferred term{s}	Reason, source
African	. Country name of origin or specific indigenous culture or heritage, e.g. Ibo from Nigeria, Fon of Dahomey	Africa refers to a huge continent with many nations and cultures. One hundred twenty indigenous languages are spoken in Nigeria, for example. Each language represents an ancient culture. History, geography, present-day nations inform accurate depictions of people and their home cultures. A general rule of thumb is to be as specific as possible in identifying nationality, place, place names, or place and culture of origin.
Afro	. African	Refers to a hairstyle. As an abbreviation or prefix, diminishes the term "African."
Afro-Cuban	. Cuban of African descent . Cuban rhythms from the Yoruba	Our public language, written and spoken, conveys respect and dignity by usage of a vocabulary that relays specific, accurate information in standard English.
Alien	. Nationality, immigrants from ____ . Displaced workers from _____ . Undocumented worker	"Alien" means "others," "foreigners," "outsiders." Immigrants or displaced workers from Mexico, for example, may be indigenous to the border area whether in the U.S. or Mexico with roots that go back hundreds or thousands of years. "Illegal alien" conveys bias; legal terms should be precise and bias-free.
America	. United States . When referring to the Americas, use North, Central, and South America	Confusing outside of the United States. Immigrants use the word as shorthand for a nation that has a name--the United States of America. Recent historians have traced the origin of the continent's name from indigenous sources outside of the United States. Amac-Ric, according to Jan Carew, is an indigenous Mayan-Carib word that means "strong wind," associated with gold fields of Amerrique Mountains close to Nicaragua's Caribbean coast. Amac-Roc also means "strong life force."
Anglo	. English, of English descent . European American, or be specific about national or cultural group	Germanic Ingwinian people (Angles, Saxons, Jutes) who preceded Normans from France. "Anglo" now refers to the English. "Anglo" is an appropriate prefix for some words like Anglophile--someone fond of English customs and manners. Refer to specific family name of settlers who migrated west in early U.S. history. "Anglos" might be a shorthand way to say "English-speaking," but say "English-speaking" to distinguish this group from people, especially in areas of the southwestern U.S., where the majority speak Spanish and/or indigenous languages.
Biracial	. Multicultural, of diverse heritages . Multinational, e.g. of African and Italian descent . Be specific or use bicultural, dual citizenship	Given that "race" is an unscientific term invented to typify pseudo criteria for racist policies and ideas, it's preferable to select a word with a different "root" for its basic meaning. To be specific, a person's heritage from two parents or families can be characterized by saying "of Senegalese and French descent." When people investigate the family trees of parents, it becomes apparent that both sides are usually and recently from multiple heritages or various nationalities. For example, a second-generation Puerto Rican born in New York may be of Puerto Rican, Dominican, Spanish, Irish, Arawak and Yoruba descent.
Black	. African American . Nationality, e.g. Liberian, Venezuelan of African descent . People of African descent	Africa is one place of origin for most people of African descent in the Americas. Especially in the beginning, the majority of slaves brought to the Americas were men. They in turn started families with indigenous women and others who were already in the Americas. "Black" refers to a perceived physical description that does not accurately indicate heritage, origins, culture, or nationality.
Caucasian	. European, European American . Of European descent . Specific nationality, e.g. Swedish	Mountainous area in Russia, the Caucasus is between the Black and Caspian Seas, inhabited by Moslems mainly. Blumenbach first used the term in 1800 to designate "white race" with skull features, etc.
Colored, coloreds	. People of diverse heritage or be specific--e.g. people of Zulu, Indian, and Dutch heritage, or of African, Muskogee, and English heritage	"Colored" and "coloreds" refer to people's complexions, which really diminishes them to an identity that the perceiver decides on. Rather, we must ask those being perceived who they are, what their family roots are, or what is the history of their family--maternal and paternal sides. These are terms based on perception, that fail to connect people with their distinct histories and communities.
East Indian	. Name specific place, nation, island	Vague reference to places in region of India or Malay archipelago from the perspective of European colonizers.

Instead of	Preferred term{s}	Reason, source
Ethnic	. Cultural group, nationality, heritage, community, language group, usually displaced, nomadic, or immigrants	Original meaning of "ethnic"--heathen, "others"--other than Christians and Jews, conquered and converted on behalf of Roman Empire. This word refers to distinct communities that share culture, customs, history, religion, or nationality but live within another nation because of displacement or migration. According to sociologist Arif Dirlik, these communities may be reconstituted differently under different circumstances.
Hispanic / Latino	. Continent of origin . South American . Central American . Name of island nation in Caribbean . Specific nation of origin--e.g. Mexican . Of Spanish-speaking cultures	"Hispanic," (Spanish) or "Latino"--language of Latin roots too vague: A person may be of indigenous heritage speaking any number of ancient languages formerly under Spanish control (22 in Guatemala alone), may be multilingual, speak English, or, for example, Garifuna--a creole spoken by Hondurans of Caribbean African descent. If someone comes from a Spanish-speaking culture, in the U.S., he/she may no longer speak Spanish but still identify with the culture. Filipinos and Salvadorans are from distinct Spanish-speaking cultures, but they have Spanish colonial history in common.
Indian	. Indigenous--generic term, kin groups and progeny in and associated with a locale for thousands of years . Use proper name of a people or specific name people call themselves . Use indigenous "peoples," "population," "inhabitants," "nations" instead of "tribes"	Columbus's term for aboriginal peoples who introduced themselves as Arawaks or Caribs to convince Spanish royalty he had been in the "Indies" via the Indian Ocean or Asian subcontinent. It's not helpful to say "the Choctaw Indians"; say "the Choctaw" just as you'd say "the French." No one says the "French Europeans." The root "gen(s)" in "indigenous" means a "family group whose exfoliation in time generates history." See Edward W. Said, *Essays on Postmodern Culture*. All of our ancestors have indigenous history associated with a specific locale. "Indian" might refer to the national citizenship of a person from India, but as with any hugely populated nation state, it is populated by people of various traditions, cultures and heritages as well. There is nothing homogenous about "Indian" except citizenship.
Jungle	. Accurate description of terrain . Precise terms of geography or vegetation	Uncultivated forest occupied by wild animals, meaning "dry" or "desert," "wasteland" from Sanskrit "jangala." British depiction of land which justified their taking of land, turning it into plantations to exploit. In urban jargon, a site of ruthless behavior which relates a subjective judgement about the social life in a particular part of a city.
Minority	. Recent immigrant populations . Political sector . Disenfranchised . Populations competing for political power	Recent immigrants will always be fewer in number than the resident population. A "majority" may only be so under certain circumstances. Power relationships are created and manipulated, and democracies depend on "majorities" in votes and polls. The term "minority" legitimizes powerlessness in the face of a majority with legalized powers. For example, people of indigenous heritage outside cities in Central and South America outnumber the populations in cities--they are the "majority" in real terms but when they move to cities, they become the "minority." "Minority" and "majority" distort and obscure political relationships among language, cultural, and national groups.
Mulatto	. Of multicultural origin . Heritage of diverse origin . Of African and _____ descent	Means "mule"--sterile hybrid of a male ass and female horse, beast of burden, conveys associations of "stupid," and "stubborn." Perpetuates racist caste labels based again on perception without reference to origins
Multiracial	. Multicultural . Of diverse heritages . multinational background	Given that "race" is an unscientific term that was invented to typify pseudo criteria for racist policies and ideas, it's preferable to select words with a different root for basic meaning. Given the long history of the human species, we all have ancestry in common, and yet a unique heritage if we think of the last five to ten thousand years.
Native American	. Be specific in name or region of indigenous people . Use "indigenous" as a generic term	Confusing because "native" means to be born in a place; this literally means to be born somewhere in the Americas (North, Central, or South).
Natives	. Indigenous population, proper names of a people, inhabitants, the population of _____	Means "born of the place" but meaning conveys "uncivilized," "savages" as in Tarzan movies, media. Use place names and names of people as they call themselves. We are "native" to the place, the state, or country where we were born.

Instead of	Preferred term{s}	Reason, source
Orient, orientals	. Asia, Asians . Asian Americans	Means "east" from Europe's perspective, east of the Mediterranean
People of color	. Be specific with origins, heritage, nationality, culture(s)	Relies on perception of melanin, one physical characteristic. Vague; all of human species inherit melanin except albinos with mutant gene.
Race	. Heritage, culture, nationality, origins	A nonscientific, pseudo social term that invents identities for purposes of domination. Based on arbitrary perceptions of physical attributes. Henry Louis Gates, Jr. characterizes "race" as a metaphor or arbitrary linguistic category; racism as a real social phenomena makes this arbitrary category seem natural and fixed.
Spanish	. Refer to people of Spain, direct descendants of Spanish	People who speak Spanish are of many nationalities because of Spanish colonialism. Be specific with nationality or geographic origins.
Third World	. Poor nations, impoverished populations . postcolonial areas of the world, economically colonized	Within a global elitist hierarchy considering the wealth of nations, the implication is that "Third World" people and nations rank less than the wealthier countries and inhabitants of the planet."Third World" people are deemed second-class citizens of the world by virtue of their nationality and impoverished economic status. This term is used for populations who need aid for subsistence, who are illiterate or bound to agricultural systems that serve the "First World" as determined by elites that enact international economic deals and policies. Their political and economic destinies are determined beyond their borders. The wealth of nations comes from a long historical and economic process originating in feudal and colonial controls. The phrase "economically colonized" acknowledges that independence may have ended political colonialism, but economic power is exerted over nations and peoples from abroad.
Tribe	. Inhabitants, population of nation . specific name of group . indigenous to _____ (name of locale)	"Tribe" comes from Latins, Sabines, and Etruscans from Etruria--originally people from Asia Minor who occupied central Italy before Rome took control of them and their territory. Connotation: "uncivilized," non-nation culture, unsophisticated, of the "jungle." A particularly sensitive issue when referring to the peoples of Africa. It's easy to say the Yoruba of Nigeria, the Hausa people, the Makah of the Olympic Peninsula in Washington State, or the Iroquois nation. When we use the specific name and locale, we are conveying information and knowledge.
WASP	. Refer to class, origins, state, family history	Acronym for "white Anglo-Saxon [meaning, of English descent] Protestant." This term usually does not fit the described accurately. Find economic terms or family lineage that specifies people being described. Be specific, e.g., from a long-established New England family of wealth who maintained familial ties in England.
The West	. Refer to nations and global relationships	Terms like "the West" and "the East" are holdovers from a Eurocentric perspective.
Western Civilization	. Name cultures, geography, e.g., Greco-Roman period of history	Implies "civilization" resides in the West. If someone was looking eastward from Asia, like Hwui Shan did in the year 464, it's unlikely that a term like "Eastern Civilization" would have been coined. Rather, place names or descriptions identify better. Further, this phrase implies a duality of "East" and "West" that does not accommodate the plurality of cultures and nations within an ever-evolving past and present.
West Indian	. Caribbean	"West Indian" is the term devised by Columbus, whereas "Caribbean" is derived from the ancient indigenous word naming the pre-Columbian inhabitants, sea, and islands.
White	. European American . Refer to specific nationality or religious group	"White" is a perceived physical description that does not adequately reflect the origins of European-American people.

PROGRESSIVE EDUCATORS EXPLAIN WHAT IT WILL TAKE TO GET BEYOND THE GIMMICKS.

Saving Public Education

President Clinton's inaugural address envisioned a "land of new promise" in which "the knowledge and power of the information age will be within reach...of every classroom." Clinton's proposals for getting there have featured school uniforms and think tank clichés. We thought we'd help out by asking several progressive educators to consider briefly what we could do if we really wanted to improve our schools.

Their responses assess the currently fashionable solutions, examine the cultural and ideological roots of our neglect of schools, especially city schools, and propose a host of changes. Underlying them all is a respect for children and a determination to elicit every young person's potential.

They share another conviction as well: that no reform—no national standard, no charter school, no parent participation, no breakup of large schools—can ultimately succeed in a system in which some schools are short on desks, classrooms, textbooks, qualified teachers and working plumbing, while others boast a computer on every desk and a senior class trip to Cancun.

The fight for educational equity is being waged in legislatures and courts. And equity itself is not enough: An urban school filled with new immigrants requires more money than one in a wealthy suburb, not the same amount. Of all the notions the right wing has sold Americans, the idea that money cannot improve education may be the most dangerous.

Jonathan Kozol

Jonathan Kozol's newest book, Amazing Grace, *was recently released in paperback by HarperCollins.*

Recycled slogans sometimes seem to be the curse of education policy discussion in this nation, and there is no set of slogans more neurotically reiterated these days than "the need for goals and standards" and "criteria" and "measurements of outcome" in our public schools.

The ritualistic repetition of these phrases started under George Bush when a list of manifestly insincere objectives was advanced and codified under the pretentious banner of "America 2000." All children, we were told, would enter school "ready to learn." All children would be given skills required for participation in "the workplace of the future," and all would graduate from high school fully literate. Best of all, we were assured, these goals would be attained not by such seemingly essential strategies as spending money to deliver preschool education to poor children, lowering class size or rebuilding the decrepit schools in which so many inner-city children are concealed, but solely by the cost-free exercise of "raising expectations," holding children and their teachers "more accountable" and penalizing those who measurably fail.

As the eighties ended with no evidence that goals like these were ever going to be reached, there was a noticeable panic in some quarters; but politicians and the pundits who advise them seem to grow addicted to their lists and incantations. Instead of revising them in light of evident defeat, they decorate their lists and add new promises, new "instruments of measurement" and

new demands. It is not surprising, therefore, that the White House now has added several fashionable buzzwords from the world of cyberspace to modernize the rhetoric of insincerity—but once again, with not the faintest whisper about equity.

To speak of national standards and, increasingly, of national exams but never to dare speak of national equality is a transparent venture into punitive hypocrisy. Thus, the children in poor rural schools in Mississippi and Ohio will continue to get education funded at less than $4,000 yearly and children in the South Bronx will get less than $7,000, while children in the richest suburbs will continue to receive up to $18,000 yearly. But they'll all be told they must be held to the same standards and they'll all be judged, of course, by their performance on the same exams.

Slogans, standards and exams do not teach reading. Only well-paid and proficient teachers do, and only if they work under conditions that do not degrade their spirits and demean their students. Education Secretary Richard Riley is a thoughtful and sophisticated man who understands this just as well as any teacher in New York who has to struggle to get forty kids to pay attention in a classroom that has only thirty books and thirty chairs, or any teacher in Ohio working with her pupils in a basement corridor because the district lacks the money to build schools. The President surely understands this too. If political considerations silence him from saying what he knows, they need not silence those of us who teach and work with children.

Money, as the rich and powerful repeatedly remind us, may not be "the only way" to upgrade education, but it seems to be the way that they have chosen for their own kids, and if it is good for them—and for the daughter of the President—it is not clear why it is not of equal worth to children of poor people. A useful strategy for activists, therefore, would be to take the rhetoric of goals and standards at face value but to insist that it be wrapped in the same package as the equity agenda. "If all our kids are to be judged by equal standards," we might reasonably say, "then every one of them deserves an equal opportunity to meet them. Anything less will merely add humiliation to defeat and further stigmatize those who were cheated in the first place."

This argument, we may assume, will not be heard from anyone in Congress; but at the state and local levels it could fuel the efforts of a growing number of determined organizers who are now in court attempting to compel their legislatures to rewrite the funding formulas that rig the game of education almost everywhere in favor of the children of the orchestrating class. That class will never willingly give up the power it possesses to defend its children against honest competition from the children of the poor; but a grass-roots struggle for equality in education finance has been percolating now for several years, and advocates and lawyers may decide that this is a good time to seize upon the rhetoric of standards to put teeth at last into the fight for simple justice. As odious as it may seem to use the language of our adversaries, it may be the best weapon we have.

Amy Stuart Wells
Amy Stuart Wells, an associate professor at U.C.L.A.'s Graduate School of Education and Information Studies, is author (with Robert L. Crain) of Stepping Over the Color Line *(forthcoming from Yale).*

There is at least one domestic policy issue on which President Clinton has remained consistent—an issue he has used as a bridge, if you will, to his second term: charter schools. Now passed in twenty-five states and the District of Columbia, charter school laws allow groups of parents, educators, community activists and entrepreneurs to start publicly funded schools free of most state and local regulations. From Boston to San Diego, approximately 450 charter schools have begun operating since 1991.

Charter schools in themselves do not have a clear political agenda. With diverse roots—from the urban community activism of the sixties to the conservative pro-market reform rhetoric of the eighties and nineties—charter schools promise to be all things to all people by granting disparate groups the power to create schools distinct from the traditional public education system. As a result, a wide range of activists—from born-again Christians to civil rights leaders—who are dissatisfied with public schools have embraced the charter school concept. Policy-makers from both sides of the political aisle have vaulted onto the charter school bandwagon, for very different reasons.

Pro-voucher conservatives, for instance, see charter school legislation as a way to shake up public education by forcing competition into a "monopolistic" and over-regulated system. They see charter schools as one step down the road toward dismantling the public system and funding schools (public or private) based on per-pupil calculations, or vouchers.

For progressives, charter school reform promises to empower poor communities to wrestle control of their schools from the uncaring and hegemonic state. Publicly funded Afro-centric and Chicano-centric charter schools are the left's answer to the myth that equal opportunity exists within the current public system. Moderate Democrats like Clinton applaud charter schools for providing divergent groups with autonomy while holding all schools accountable to high academic standards.

Thus the definition of charter school reform—what it stands for and its implications for the future of public education—will be contested in the next few years. To the extent that Clinton wants to leave his imprint on this popular reform, he needs to go beyond his call for 3,000 charter schools by the year 2000. He also needs to help clarify the purpose and the promise of these schools.

He could, for instance, argue that a certain percentage of the $51 million in federal charter school grants to states must be earmarked specifically for transportation costs for students from low-income communities who want to cross school district lines and attend a charter school in a more affluent area. If the President really believes the assertion in his inaugural speech that "great rewards will come to those who can live together, learn together, work together, forge new ties that bind together," why not target federal funds specifically to charter schools that are racially and socioeconomically diverse—that help lessen the vast chasm between the ethnic groups and social classes that our housing patterns reinforce? Including state-funded urban-suburban transfer programs as a component of charter school reform would help alleviate racial segregation while providing greater educational opportunities. And targeting federal funds toward the lowest-income and most disadvantaged communities would help realize the goal of community empowerment through charter school reform.

Currently, the federal guidelines for state applications for charter school grant money and the President himself have not addressed these critical issues, allowing voices on the right to dominate the national policy debate. Government has a role to play in standing up for our values and our interests and giving Americans the power to make a difference in their lives, Clinton tells us. He can demonstrate that by working to shape the charter school reform movement to democratic ends.

Lisa D. Delpit
Lisa D. Delpit, a professor of urban education at Georgia State University, is the author of Other People's Children: Cultural Conflicts in the Classroom *(New Press).*

On Dr. King's birthday, I watched, riveted, the PBS special on the civil rights movement. The filmmakers accomplished an amazing feat: The smooth-skinned, bright-eyed, idealistic faces of the young civil rights workers, Bob Moses and Endesha Mae Holland among them, faded into the same faces, forty years older—lined, deeper-eyed, voices less strident but somehow more intensely determined—reminiscing about the past and talking about the present. I was moved to tears by the commitment that these heroes have kept alive so long, as well as by the powerful struggle that occurred when I was too young to participate.

How strong these young people were, but how little the nation cared. Those valiant boys and girls in Mississippi were humiliated, beaten, even killed. The local "law" was the evil killing machine that tore their flesh and offered their spirits to snarling dogs. The federal government said there was nothing it could do. Before the media arrived citizens throughout the nation watched *Ed Sullivan* and *Leave It to Beaver* in their suburbs, with little thought given to those polite black children who were stirring up so much trouble.

Coming to terms with this sobering reality led the civil rights workers to a unique strategy. They could be spared only if they brought young white people into their struggle, young white people whose well-heeled families could call senators and judges—and get their calls returned. Young white people whom the nation watched and fretted over, ready to usher them into their rightful futures as doctors, lawyers and nuclear scientists. The black children were so despised, so hated, so...unnecessary, that nothing could protect them except the presence of the young white "freedom riders" from the North.

So often I feel that the African-American children of poverty today are in similar straits. No one cares about them, really. They are viewed as despised "others" whose families are pathological, whose mothers want to bilk the system, whose language is termed "guttural ghetto speak," whose intelligence is constantly questioned. And who are stuffed away in forgotten neighborhoods into ramshackle buildings called schools, with faulty plumbing, malfunctioning heating systems, peeling paint and questionable electricity—reminiscent of the sharecropper shacks in Mississippi. Pizza Hut won't even deliver to the "dangerous communities" in which these schools are located. As I visit many of these urban schools, I cannot but wonder, Who cares? Who can protect them? There are no more white children to ride in and force the nation's attention.

There is one difference between today's children and the children of Mississippi's past. Despite the nation's neglect, the Mississippi children knew who they were. They knew that their work was important, that they were right and righteous and, whether they lived or died, their actions would be writ large on history's pages. Today's children, like Pecola Breedlove in Toni Morrison's *The Bluest Eye*, look at themselves with the loathing of the nation that despises them. But unlike Pecola, not only do they turn the hatred inward but their rage bursts forth as they seek to snuff out the lives of those who provide mirror images of themselves in an effort to obliterate their own perceived ugliness and unworthiness. You cannot seek to kill your image if you value yourself.

But why has this country heaped neglect and hatred upon these children? Why do middle-class white audiences give standing ovations to the author of *The Bell Curve* when he insists that black children are genetically inferior to white, when he recommends limiting the schooling of poor black children to menial job training, when he suggests that poor black children be taken from their parents to be raised in state institutions? Why is it so popular to deny children food stamps or housing or medical treatment? Why do I so often see fear or only thinly veiled stares of hatred when groups of boisterous African-American youngsters enter a store or restaurant or bus?

I don't know why America still finds its brown children so despicable and dispensable. And I don't know what to do about it. Somehow the thousands of African-American children who failed to dodge successfully one of the bullets regularly fired in their neighborhoods fade into oblivion. But when one white child dies horribly from a gunshot because her parents turned into the "wrong" street one night, the entire nation is in an uproar. Why is it that so many people in this country don't care about children who look like mine? How can I make them?

What can Bill Clinton do? Still haunted by the civil rights documentary, I'm tempted to ask for a public service campaign to value African-American children. I see brown children's bright-eyed faces with disheveled hair and unkempt clothes fade into the adults they can become if we allow it—doctors, lawyers, ministers, teachers. I want to shove in a resistant nation's face the humanity, the vulnerability, the neediness of those babies who need our protection, who need us to hold visions for their futures so they do not destroy themselves and one another as they bask in our, at best, "benign neglect."

But I know that will serve no purpose. What I want of Bill Clinton is that he value black children—or at least act as though he does. There should be a law that says no children should have to live in a neighborhood deemed "too dangerous" for pizza delivery. He can push policy to insure that all children are fed, have shelter and receive medical attention. He should insure funding to repair the school buildings falling down on our children's heads, and insist that state and local authorities make them welcoming havens. He can push for systems that reward teachers who are willing to teach those children who are least well served, and who do so in ways that the children, their parents and their communities value.

What can I say? He can value the children. He can protect them. He can care. We all can.

Mike Rose

Mike Rose is a professor at U.C.L.A.'s Graduate School of Education and Information Studies. His Possible Lives: The Promise of Public Education in America *was recently released in paperback by Penguin.*

I have been thinking a lot lately about the way we talk about school—public school in particular. What do we hear on talk-radio, see on the evening news, read in the paper? How do education issues get shaped in legislative debates? How is school depicted in popular culture and how is it characterized in "high-brow" media, of left, right or center persuasion? I think it's fair to say that, with some exceptions, the talk and imagery about public school tends to be negative, bleak, often cynical, at times vicious. Here are some examples that I read or heard in a two-day period: "America's schools are the least successful in the Western world"; "Face it, the public schools have failed"; "The kids in the Los Angeles School District are garbage."

God knows, there is a lot wrong with our schools—from the way we educate teachers to the often patronizing curriculums we offer our students, the tangles of school politics and the terrible things we assume about the abilities of kids from poor communities. I don't dispute that, have taught in the middle of it, have tried to write about it. And I surely don't dispute the legitimate anger of people who have been betrayed by their schools. But the scope and sweep of the negative public talk is what concerns me, for it excludes the powerful, challenging work done in schools day by day across the country, and it limits profoundly the vocabulary and imagery available to us, constrains the way we frame problems, blinkers our imagination. This kind of talk fosters neither critique nor analysis but rather a grand dismissiveness or despair. It plays into equally general and troubling—and equally unexamined—causal claims about the schools' responsibility for our economic woes and social problems. And this blend of crisis rhetoric and reductive models of causality yields equally one-dimensional proposals for single-shot magic bullets: Standards will save us, or charter schools, or computer technology, or the free market. Each of these can have merit, but careful, nuanced reflection about education gets lost in such fall-from-grace/redemption narratives.

When was the last time you heard extensive, deliberative public talk that places school failure in the context of joblessness, urban politics, a diminished tax base, unequal funding, race and class bias? Or heard a story of achievement that includes discussion of curiosity, reflectiveness, uncertainty, a willingness to take a chance, to blunder? How about accounts of reform that present change as alternatively difficult, exhilarating, ambiguous, promising—and that find reform not in a device, technique or structure but in the way we think about teaching and learning? And that point out how we need a language of schooling that, in addition to economy, offers a vocabulary of respect, decency, aesthetics, joy, courage, intellect, civility, heart and mind, skill and understanding? For that matter, think of how rarely we hear of a commitment to public education as the center of a free society. We need a richer public discussion than the one we have now.

Deliberation about school funding and teachers' salaries, about charter schools and national standards, about multicultural education and school-to-work programs and which method of reading instruction to adopt—all take place within a discourse of decline. This language has been with us for so long—at least since the publication of *A Nation at Risk* in 1983—that we accept it as natural and miss the ways it affects our thinking about what public schools should accomplish in a democracy and why and how they fail.

An important project for the left—and though I focus on schools, this applies to a range of social issues—will be to craft a language that is critical without being reductive, that frames this critique in nuance and possibility, that honors the work good teachers do daily and draws from it broader lessons about ability, learning and opportunity, that scrutinizes public institutions while affirming them.

Norm Fruchter

Norm Fruchter, the director of N.Y.U.'s Institute for Education and Social Policy, was an elected school board member in Brooklyn.

The critical task for urban education is to improve our poorly performing city schools. In contrast to conservative strategies that trickle down resources or cream the best students, raising the floor of academic performance in city school systems can improve outcomes for all our students.

How prevalent are poorly performing urban schools? The Chicago Schools C.E.O. recently put 20 percent of that city's schools on probation. The New York State Commissioner and New York City Schools Chancellor have identified 100 city schools that desperately need improvement. If, as the Chancellor has indicated, another hundred could easily be added, at least 20 percent of New York City schools need immediate intervention.

Since most city schools serve poor students of color, these lowest 20 percent serve the poorest students. In many cities, newspapers publish school rankings based on standardized test scores. If those newspapers ranked schools on a poverty index, the results would be substantially the same. As a nation, we get the schooling results we pay for, and we don't pay enough for the education of poor kids of color in cities.

How can urban systems improve the schools that fail to serve these students? Unfortunately, there are no magic bullets. Poorly performing schools are cultures of failure developed over many years. Richard Elmore, in a recent *Harvard Educational Review* article, argues that successful reform must change "the core of educational practice," the deep structure of how teachers think about knowledge and how students learn, as well as how teachers organize their classrooms, group and assess students, work with other teachers and effectively communicate student outcomes. If this deep structure of belief and practice needs to change in at least 20 percent of our urban schools, radical intervention is required. Yet most urban systems' bureaucratic response is to require poorly performing schools to design their own improvement.

Changing the core structures of belief and practice in failing schools depends on new leadership and the support of other professionals skilled at helping failing cultures change. (For how to recruit, prepare and support such professionals, see the recent report of the National Commission on Teaching and America's Future, directed by Linda Darling-Hammond.) Such change also needs time for the change processes to develop, as well as funding to support the collaborations and professional development involved. Where will the necessary resources come from?

Protracted political struggles in New Jersey, Texas, Alabama and Connecticut demonstrate both the potential and the difficulties of one approach to resource provision—attacking school financing through the courts. (As the current challenge by the Campaign for Fiscal Equity against funding inequity for New York City schools gathers momentum, New York State will become another site for fierce school finance struggle.) If such efforts do not ultimately resolve urban funding shortfalls, they do reduce the inequalities, produce more funding for the entire state system and force confrontation about how much we are prepared to tolerate public schooling that underfunds other people's children.

Parents are another resource for improving poorly performing schools. In spite of all the pieties about parental involvement, parents are still marginalized in most urban schools. Yet contrary to the relentless national press assault on the Chicago reform that mandated significant parent decision-making through local school councils, research indicates much promise in such efforts. Studies by the Consortium on Chicago School Research demonstrate that Chicago schools with strong democratic councils also generate deep structures of schoolwide reform, and that such reform efforts eventually produce significant academic improvement.

Local organizations could provide other crucial resources. Community development corporations, neighborhood improvement associations and youth-serving organizations are increasingly realizing that school failure limits the effectiveness of their own work. These organizations have strong neighborhood roots, active memberships, full-time staffs and well cultivated political connections. Such organizations have often been viewed with suspicion by urban systems; if collaboration could replace hostility, critical new support for school improvement could result.

Improving the lowest-performing schools in urban public systems can help to improve academic achievement in all our city schools. Investing the necessary resources is not impossible; what's required is the political will to transform the life chances of our nation's most imperiled children.

Herbert Kohl

Herbert Kohl is the author of I Won't Learn From You *and* Should We Burn Babar? *(both New Press).*

President Clinton will soon formally announce a national literacy program, calling for more than a million volunteers to teach reading to underachieving children from poor communities. The emphasis will be on catching the children when they're young, before the third grade. This is an instance of the Administration recognizing the right problem while proposing the wrong solution.

There is no doubt that an outrageous number of poor and particularly African-American and Latino children never learn to read on a fundamental level. This failure begins to show up dramatically in the fourth and fifth grades. Despite *Sesame Street*, Head Start, Upward Bound and volunteer reading programs, not to mention the efforts made by teachers and reading specialists, the problem remains intractable. There is some disconnection between children and texts that takes place at school, and there is no reason to believe that sending volunteers into the early grades on an episodic basis will be more useful than any of the other efforts made at increasing literacy among the poor.

However, there is another approach to tackling the problem that might, if implemented on a large scale and in a qualitative way, make a difference in developing literacy and at the same time lead to a partial solution to other social problems that the Administration and the legislature created during the last session of Congress. At this point there are no literacy workers in the schools—people whose sole purpose is to develop and implement reading programs based on continuous personal contact with children over their entire school careers. In fact, the teaching of basic reading skills disappears from the classroom after the fourth grade, and there is certainly no direct reading instruction in high school other than in specifically remedial classes. However, adult literacy programs have succeeded throughout the world, and it is clear that it is never too late to learn how to read well. The actual skills needed to teach reading are no more complex than the skills needed to repair a car or renovate a house.

A new category of school workers whose specialty is literacy can be created. The prerequisites for such people might be as simple as decent reading skills, a sensitive knowledge of the culture and strengths children bring to school, and a level of comfort within poor communities that would allow literacy workers to function in parks, apartments, churches and social service centers, as well as within the relative security of the school building.

Many people who live in poor communities have these skills and, more to the point, many people about to be required to work have them. I suggest that the President propose a federally developed, state- and federally supported program lodged at junior colleges to train people to become literacy workers, with a special emphasis on reaching out to people currently on welfare. This would provide dignified work with the potential for future advancement. A new Associate of the Arts degree in literacy education could lead to work within schools and community organizations. Clinton's volunteers can also have a role. Since they have time to donate, they can use it to raise funds to create permanent jobs for this new category of teachers.

The President should also offer two additional years of college free for five years of literacy work in the schools and put such people on a fast track to getting B.A.s and full teaching credentials. This would create a pool of potential African-American and Latino teachers, solving a major problem facing public schools these days—a decline in the number of teachers of color at the same time as an increase in the number of students of color.

Looking to the volunteer sector to improve education is like looking to the generosity of corporate leaders to keep their workers employed. What we need is new people in the schools, committed not so much to the world-class standards mouthed by educational professionals as to world-class children.

Deborah W. Meier

Deborah W. Meier, the author of The Power of Their Ideas *(Beacon), has worked in public schools for the past thirty years.*

Contrary to popular wisdom, America's schools are not an utter failure. When I was a kid in the thirties, fewer than half our fellow citizens even started high school, much less finished it. The United States still ranks at the top in international tests of literacy. And we remain one of the world's most productive nations.

But our schools are not good enough. Most of them are far too big, impersonal and factorylike; they're too standardized—trying to satisfy everyone by never taking a stand on anything—and they leave too little power in the hands of the families and teachers who know the kids best. The most sought-after schools defy all three of these—they're mostly small, self-chosen and self-governing.

Meanwhile, the more we complain about our schools the bigger, more standardized and less powerful they become! Every complaint produces a new level of bureaucracy, a new mandate. Policy-makers from left to right want to make sure that all schools teach their brand of truth, and academics have always wished kids came to them already knowing more about their particular speciality. Between them they are busy designing high-stakes national tests to make us all more like them. What they can't seem to tolerate is that there isn't a single definition of being smart and never will be—especially in a democratic society.

The policy-makers also forget that education depends on relationships between people, and nothing they invent in their ivory towers will work if we don't get those right. We won't grow thoughtful adults in thoughtless schools. And thoughtful adults don't all subscribe to the same version of the perfect school.

There are five things we need to do immediately to turn our schools around:

1. We need schools that are human-sized—a few hundred kids in each. Small enough for everyone to know and be known well; for adults to gather together to make decisions that they agree on. Where families and teachers can get to trust one another, over time. We don't have to get rid of all the big buildings. Big buildings can house separate small schools. The cost? Minimal.

2. As far as possible, parents, kids and staff should have choices among schools. No two schools should or can be alike. Even where they start alike, over time they develop different styles, priorities and ways of organizing themselves. Some have mixed age groups, emphasize phonics, have put their resources into instrumental music instead of camping, are more or less formal, etc. To parents and teachers these differences are matters of importance. Not having a choice means people waste precious time fighting over such matters or water down their ideas to get a consensus.

3. If we want schools to be responsible for results, they need to have sufficient power over the factors that help produce success—like staffing, spending money, scheduling, curriculum and assessment. There's no point in knowing one another well if we don't have the power to make decisions based on that knowledge.

4. Small, self-governing schools of choice are necessary but not sufficient. We need to design ways for parents, teachers and the public to have access to credible and user-friendly information and to create places for them to talk. This takes time and access to expertise. It can be helped by enlightened public policy, for example, requiring employers to give parents time off, encouraging teachers to visit other schools, using public television to share public stories, developing peer and school accountability.

5. Finally, it takes a fair distribution of resources. Having advantages is an advantage; we're fooling ourselves if we ignore the inequalities it produces. But to make matters worse, we provide less public funding for those already in communities of poverty. The resource gap is shameful—whether we're talking personnel, technology, books or physical facilities. Changing people takes money just as much as changing machinery.

Two currently popular nostrums, school vouchers and a national testing system, head us in precisely the wrong direction. Vouchers will subsidize the abandonment of public education, mostly in ways that will hurt the most needy. National testing—sometimes called national standards—will take away even more authority from local school communities. Teachers and communities shorn of the capacity to use their own ideas, judgments and initiative in matters of importance can't teach kids to do so.

Producing responsible citizens is best done in places where responsible citizenship is at the heart of the school's life.

Randall Cole

Randall Cole works at the Hetrick-Martin Institute in New York City, a social service, education and advocacy organization serving lesbian, gay, bisexual and transgender youth.

Today's youth face social problems ranging from substance abuse, violence and poverty to H.I.V./AIDS. These problems are compounded for gay and lesbian youth, many of whom live in fear and secrecy. Without role models and support networks, 80 percent of gay, lesbian and bisexual youth report severe isolation. In addition, gay and lesbian young people face violence in school perpetrated by both students and teachers. Frequently, they drop or are pushed out of school. Most alarming is the study conducted by the Health and Human Services Department that found that gay and lesbian youth are two to three times more likely to attempt suicide than other young people, and that approximately one-third of youth suicides are carried out annually by gay youth.

Of the estimated 20,000 youths who find themselves without a permanent residence in New York City, more than a third self-identify as gay, lesbian or bisexual. Many of them are kicked out by their families or flee because of abuse. Moreover, gay and lesbian youth are at a higher risk for contracting H.I.V. because of their isolation and lowered sense of self-esteem.

Since the founding in 1985 of the Harvey Milk School, the nation's first high school designed specifically for gay and lesbian youth, sponsored by the New York City Board of Education, the number of applicants has steadily increased. We can now accept only about 30 percent of the 100 students who apply each year. The school was founded in recognition of the fact that many students drop out rather than face abuse from teachers and classmates. However, our objective is not to segregate gay and lesbian students from their straight peers, but to change the way we all think about education. Hetrick-Martin staff and youth educators go to classrooms from kindergarten to high school to educate students and their teachers about the issues faced by gay and lesbian youth. This sets up a model for dialogue both in the classroom and at home that helps to combat homophobia.

From the President to the local school boards to families, we must demonstrate our commitment to educating all young people regardless of class, gender, race, sexual orientation and language or cultural background. We must make our schools places where all children feel safe and valued. Until then, the need for organizations such as the Hetrick-Martin Institute and its Harvey Milk School program will continue. Our goal is to one day make ourselves obsolete.

Melting pot, salad bowl, multicultural mosaic, crazy quilt, orchestra or Indian stew: For Native peoples, it's your choice! Or is it?

By Cornel Pewewardy

Special to *Today*

Introduction

Does the term "melting pot" express the nature of the American national culture much more accurately than metaphors like "salad bowl" or "multicultural mosaic" or "crazy quilt" or "orchestra?" Where do American Indians and Alaska Natives fit into these models? What choices(s) do we have in the upcoming U.S. census? For those of us who are "mixed bloods" or "mixed blood/full bloods," do we check the census box labeled "multi-racial," as proposed by the Office of Management and Budget? What about "Americans of Indian descent?" Do Native people have the choice to decide who we are, or are we forced to choose one box in the race category? Choosing your race category is a paradox for many American Indians and Alaska Natives.

The common culture of the United States is a blending of many ethnic groups, including recent and past immigrants with the indigenous peoples of North America. The early history of American Indian education is about assimilation whereby American Indians accepted the importance of understanding multiple beliefs, but it had as a primary goal the amalgamation of all groups into the American mainstream.

The glory of America was denied to many who already lived here. Those whose appearance and cultural traits set them apart found that they were excluded from the benefits of being American. There were, for example, Native peoples and some Spanish-speaking citizens who had been defeated in many battles and, unlike the "immigrant minorities," "involuntary minorities" had no wish to become American. On one hand there is a group of Africans, enslaved, who over time wanted to be a part of American public policy, but the door to that opportunity was slammed in their face. On the other hand there is a group of Indians who never wanted to be a part of American public policy, and the American plan was to assimilate them into the homogenized American society.

Turtle Island

America is not a nation of immigrants as many early writers and educators would like for us to believe. Many indigenous people still "walk the talk" of their traditional ways and speak the tribal languages, which the Creator blessed them with. There is still much truth in traditional knowledge and the wisdom of Native people. Many tribal elders and Indian scholars warn coming generations of scientists, both Indians and white, not to repeat the ethnocentric omissions of the past by ignoring Indian oral tradition (i.e., inaccurate scientific theories of evolution, radiocarbon dating techniques and the Bering Strait migration hoax.) They continue to tell their creation stories from Turtle Island, not the Ellis Island concept of America as a nation of immigrants or a Euro-American melting pot. Only after Ellis Island was shut down was it and the Statue of Liberty transformed into an idealized symbol of a European-American "melting pot."

Language

The melting pot theory was one of the first politically correct phrases that monolingual speakers invented, thereby creating the framework for xenophobic-coded language in America. Assimilationists value bilingual education as the quickest way for non-English-speaking Americans to become literate in English—to speak English only. The English Only movement represents a threat to American Indians and Alaska Natives because it would seem to outlaw the official use of Native Indigenous languages just at a time when many tribal languages are being saved through written materials for educational and tribal government usage. Although it is not intended as such, the English Only movement is a reminder of a history of prejudice toward speakers of foreign tongues. If you recall, many Indians were prohibited and punished for speaking their own tribal languages in U.S. government-run Indian boarding schools.

The loss of language is one of the most critical problems facing Indian people today. The loss of language leads to a breakdown in communication between children and their grandparents and causes them to be cut off from their past and their heritage. Tribal heritage is not outdated in modern society as it provides a sense of group belonging (tribalism) that is badly needed in today's American schools which are mainly Eurocentric, competitive, individualistic and materialistic. Therefore, elevating English as an icon has appeal for the insecure and the resentful. Do we live in the United States of America or the "United States of Europe?" These inquir-

ies provide a clear response to the question: Who belongs in America?

Melting Pot

Speaking about who belongs in America, the original American melting pot was actually designed to address European diversity and was truly Eurocentric from its beginning. Its conclusion was the best way to address diversity was to eliminate it. If you eliminate diversity by culture, it means that you have to be taken out of your group. So in America we don't have a model that says that ultimately something should be normal for people who are not supposed to be here in this country like American Indians and Alaska Natives.

Israel Zangwill's 1909 play "The Melting Pot" worked for most White Anglo-Saxon Americans because this idealistic, vaguely egalitarian (for whites only) melting-pot nationalism was the consensus of the times. The idea of cultural fusion and ethnic amalgamation was popularized by this play, which Mr. Zangwill dedicated to President Theodore Roosevelt. As a result, European immigrants and Anglo-Americans were slowly amalgamating in a true melting-pot fashion. The melting pot worked first in popular culture and even introduced this philosophy into early Bureau of Indian Affairs boarding schools.

The melting pot of the United States omitted the spice of the Native people. The idea of assimilation which mixes culture, race, language and political identity into a common culture never became an accepted value for American Indians. Native peoples never were invited nor wanted to be a part of the melting pot. Only acculturated as assimilated Indians participated fully in this myth.

Early American immigrants who were not of exclusively English origin had already found it easy to slip into the prevailing Anglo-Saxon rhetoric and beliefs that Theodore Roosevelt was to see his heritage and name as no obstacle in defending a full-scale Anglo-Saxon interpretation of American and world history. The Anglo-Saxon interpretation of the last half-century was no benign expansionism although it used the rhetoric and language of redemption because it assumed that one race was destined to lead and others were to serve—that one race was to flourish and many to die. The world was to be transformed not by the strength of better ideas but by the power of a so-called superior race.

The melting pot as a metaphor for the emergence of a new American type from the fusion of immigrant groups has been

replaced by different symbols: the mosaic and the crazy quilt. Multiculturalists believe that the melting-pot concept of American identify has been, or should be, repudiated in favor of a new understanding of American society as a mosaic of five races—whites, African Americans, Hispanics or Latinos, Asian and Pacific Islanders and American Indians/Alaska Natives. Sometimes a salad bowl metaphor is used as an alternative rather than the metaphor of a mosaic or a quilt—allegedly discrediting the melting-pot ideal. The idea behind the salad bowl concept is that different ethnic and racial groups in America can retain their own distinct identities when tossed together. Still, if the salad dressing works in giving it flavor, the overall taste should be better. The crazy quilt metaphor is a quilting of many cultures pieced together to make one larger quilt. There is much richness in its designs printed in colors of the threads. The orchestra metaphor represents the collective whole playing music in harmony from one musical song sheet.

American Indians/Alaska Natives will soon have another model from which to choose their identity. The Office of Management and Budget (OMB) and the Census Department started to formulate in 1994 a plan to identify individuals of multiracial ethnicity and create a new multiracial race category. Apparently, by the year 2000, the census will contain questions that will aid in the identification of Native Americans, Hispanic, Asian and black populations that are a product of more than one race. The individuals who are identified as a mixed race population will then be excluded from the race with which they identify, (i.e., Native American) and be included in the count for the multiracial population.

Responding to this proposal, Barbara Warner, executive director of the Oklahoma Indian Affairs Commission in 1994, said, "In Oklahoma and, I am sure all across Indian country, this manipulation of ethnicity would have a devastating effect. One possible reason OMB's involvement in this is because populations currently targeted for funding would decrease in number and, thus, less funding would be required." The concern that Barbara Warner expressed to OMB were that "first of all, sovereign nations determine their population by their own definition and enrollment. Secondly, this plan would exclude all Native people with the exception of full bloods, of which there are a decreasing number. I also pointed out that some Native Americans were not, for reasons of adoption, undocumented paternity, the Dawes Act etc., able to establish their blood lines and these individuals, also, would be classified as multiracial, even though, by tribal definition, they were Native American." Ultimately, this proposal threatens again the tribal sovereignty of American Indians/Alaska Natives.

Multiculturalism and Tribalism

In the past multicultural education often attempted to assimilate new and old cultural groups into a single American culture. Now, tradition has two rivals: tribalism and multiculturalism. One form of cultural pluralism for Native peoples is to embrace multiculturalism while exercising tribal sovereignty is affirming tribalism. The fundamental contrast between European America and Native America is likely to remain. We might think of it as a contrast between territorially grounded ("tribal") and groundless ("multicultural") difference. Therefore, the "Indian stew" metaphor is synonymous with tribal sovereignty for Native people—"separate but equal tribes living in harmony." In July 1831 in his second effort to define the status of Indian tribes, Chief Justice John Marshall elaborated on his vague characterization of the Cherokee of Georgia as "domestic dependent nations." Preserving the right to self-government and the attributes of Indian sovereignty has always been a challenge since Marshall's decision for Indian nations within—"nations-within-a-nation."

Manifest Destiny and the Doctrine of Discovery

As most of you already know, particularly if you have experience working in Indian education, Native people have become the most devastated people in this country—knowing all too well humiliation, degradation and denigration. Through four centuries of conquest, cultural extermination, genocide and coercive assimilation, the American Indian has borne the brunt of the most pervasive physical, economic, political and cultural discrimination in this country's history. That over 500 tribes have survived is remarkable indeed. As a result, most tribes are trying to heal their wounds from a century of cultural disruption. Tribes have been altered by the Doctrine of Discovery if not shattered by conquest of the Manifest Destiny ideology. It is part of a continuing legacy of an enduring colonist mentality that denies the very existence of Native peo-

ples of North America. The best way to keep a people down is to deny them the means of improvement and achievement and cut them off from the opportunities of national life. Everything is taken away from us. We have to demand curriculum change, and multicultural education is that umbrella for change.

It is the legacy that is built upon the Doctrine of Discovery that gave Europeans a God-given right to claim lands occupied by American Indians and Alaska Natives. By 1850, the story of America was the myth of the Manifest Destiny and Doctrine of Discovery of Anglo-Saxon Protestants, fulfilling a mission from God to create a new citadel for true Christianity and republican government that stretched from the Atlantic to the Pacific. During this period most white Americans assumed that the only method to spread American democracy throughtout the country was to conquer and settle it. Indeed, America is a "gun-fighter nation," leaving behind a bloody trail of the system of mythic and ideological formations that constitute the significance of the Frontier Myth in American history.

For whites, especially those who trace their ancestry back to the early years of the Republic, the American heritage is a source of pride. In under-represented groups in this country, it is more likely to evoke anger and shame. The place where hope is shared is the future. Demographer Ben Watterberg, formerly perceived as a resister to social change, says, "There's a nice chance that the American myth in the 1990s and beyond is going to rachet another step toward this idea that we are the universal nation. That rings the bells of manifest destiny. We're a people with a mission and a sense of purpose, and we believe we have something to offer the world."

American racism, as we see it today, began in this country for economic reasons that spread into the societal aspects of colonial America. For slavery to exist and hence to continue as a source of free labor, a concerted effort had to take place to dehumanize Native peoples and the African. The fact the perpetrators of slavery went to great lengths to disprove our humanity with bogus scientific fact, religious teaching, media, gross misconceptions and illustrations and rumors proves the point.

Monocultural Perspective

Assimilationists believe that one's identification with an ethnic group should be short-lived and temporary because it

presents an obstacle to an individual's long-term interests and needs. Assimilationists believe that, for a society to advance, individuals must give up their ethnic identities, languages and ideologies in favor of the norms and values of the larger, national society. The goal of the school, from an assimilationist perspective, should be to socialize individuals into the society at large so all can function in an "appropriate" manner, that is, in a manner that supports the goals of the nation as expressed through its leaders. Ethnic group identification, if it is to be developed, should be confined to small community organizations. In short, the goal for assimilationists is to make it possible for everyone to be "melted" into a homogeneous whole.

The assimilationist view, however, is referred to as a monocultural perspective and shares an Anglo-conformity model of American culture." This model "Angloconformity" later termed "assimilationist" was further popularized as "Americanization." All in all, it's a sort of "Europeanization of America." It originated in an ideology of Northern and Western European superiority which maintained that groups not from these areas threatened American society and should either be restricted from immigrating to the United States or be compelled to conform. The dominant group's values were accepted as the values everyone should assume so the burden for change rested with the immigrant group. Has there ever been a more destructive force in the world than Western culture with its obsessive pursuit of dominance, and its manifest racism which has repeatly led to genocide? A historic monoculturalists do not want to know and do not want others to know that side of Western culture. In ideas of superior and inferior races that permeated American thinking about continental and world mission also often permeated the thinking of the English and of Western Europeans in general by the mid-nineteenth century. In 1942 Felix Cohen (Needs to be identified.) tried to warn non-Indian policymakers about their "nihilism" toward Native peoples in his classic thesis "Americanizing the White Man."

America's immigrant communities have a radically different character. Each of them has a center of active participants, some have even been "born again" into a generic American or hyphenated American. Most of their communities are without boundaries, shadowing off into a residual mass of people who think of themselves simply as Americans. In the United States, people call themselves Americans but most of them actually behave not as Americans but rather as Europeans-in-America because of a history that has viewed Americans as European in ancestry. Therefore, can we instead fashion an authentic American identity which is inclusive of all ethnic groups as "We the people" as addressed in the The Great Law of Peace Kaianerekowa of the Haudenausaunee, Iroquois Confederacy (from the 10th to the 15th century)?

In America "race" has been used as a metaphor in constructing the Melting Pot Theory. It also constructed the phrase "Americanization." The evolution of our national identity as "American" has been mainly defined as "white." Once multicultural America moves beyond denial, hostility and guilt, we will be able to revise our national history (which includes tribal nations) from different cultural perspectives because there is more than one perspective on the interpretations of facts and events in this country. The history of America—the truth—is too big to be bound up in just one culture.

Conclusion

Issues related to national identity and the content of our national curriculum fuel the debate between multiculturalist and monoculturalist. This continued debate is America's intensifying racial crisis. Placing ideas within a conceptual approach encourages students to think critically and make connections among a variety of world views and perspectives. As we engage in such discussions and analyses, we may ultimately come to a clearer understanding of what multicultural education really means for American Indians and Alaska Natives.

As far as I can see, the only thing that ever melted in the Melting Pot Theory was the "pot." Even as we enter the 21st century, a multicultural discussion of a new racial melting pot starts to bubble—a "Trans-racial Melting Pot." Many multiculturalists believe that the cultural melting pot can, and should, become a racial melting pot. For Native peoples, however, maintaining their cultural identity is still the issue. Many Native peoples still affirm their cultural identity by exercising tribal sovereignty, thus, choosing to remain themselves. Therefore, I say thanks, but no thanks to the offer of claiming "multiracial" as an OMB proposal in the next U.S. Census Bureau count. Quite frankly, as sovereign Native people, we have a choice and my choice is to affirm and enjoy my (tribal sovereignty) frybread dipped in "Indian stew!"

Editor's Note: Dr. Cornel Pewewardy, Comanche-Kiowa, teaches multicultural education in the School of Education at the University of Kansas in Lawrence, Kan.

The Challenge
of Affirmative Action

By Valerie Ooka Pang,
David Strom,
& Russell L. Young

Affirmative action has been and continues to be a complex social issue that demands courageous and difficult decisions. Many questions arise in the discussion: Is it best to be color-conscious or color-blind? How can a nation ensure equity for all people? Though Supreme Court Justices like Sandra Day O'Connor, Antonin Scalia, and Clarence Thomas have ruled that the Constitution protects individuals and not groups, the United States is clearly not a color-blind society, and many individuals have been and continue to be discriminated against due to their membership in groups based on race, ethnicity, religion, gender, class, and sexual orientation.

The purpose of this paper is to look at the challenge of using affirmative action programs when there are competing groups of underrepresented people struggling for limited school resources. We view affirmative action as actions that address past and current patterns of discrimination and promote the goal of diversity in society. Many people believe these programs represent preferential treatment primarily based on race and gender, while others see affirmative action programs as crucial means to be inclusive of the diversity in society.

In this paper we present the case study of a San Francisco high school where sev-

Valerie Ooka Pang, David Strom, and Russell L. Young are faculty members in the School of Education at San Diego State University, San Diego, California.

eral Asian-American students did not feel they were treated fairly because of their ethnicity. The students are an example of a group within the underrepresented community who feel they are being discriminated against because they have done well. The case of Lowell High School brings to the surface conflicting values. The challenge is how to balance competing goals. Several tensions have emerged. In this situation, the goals of affirming diversity and addressing historical patterns of discrimination are in conflict with the goal of equal treatment of each person.

The Case of Lowell High School in San Francisco

In San Francisco at Lowell High School, Chinese-American students are finding themselves in the middle of a fierce discussion on affirmative action. Last year, 94 Chinese Americans were denied admissions to the school.[1] These students had scores that were comparable or higher than other students admitted from other ethnic groups. The year before, 90 Chinese-American students were turned away under the same conditions. The debate has fueled dialogue over the importance of academic opportunities and quotas.

In 1994, three Chinese-American students, Brian Ho, Patrick Wong, and Hilary Chen, and their parents filed a federal class-action lawsuit against this school and its desegregation plan, which does not allow more than 40 percent of students to come from one ethnic group. This suit challenges a 1983 court desegregation decision limiting the number of Chinese Americans who can enroll in the school. Every year, 1,800 students apply for about 700 new freshman positions in the ninth grade class.[2] For the fall of 1995, Chinese Americans had to score a minimum of 63 on the school's admission index of 69, while Whites and other Asians had to score at least 60, and Latinos and Blacks had to have scores of at least 55. There is also an affirmative action category that admits Blacks and Latinos who score in the range of 50 to 54.

Lowell High School is one of the most coveted public schools in the Bay Area and many students would like the opportunity to attend. The case study provides students the opportunity to discuss how affirmative action goals clash in real life. Discussions may help students understand that group and individual goals can be sources of tension, especially when trying to be equitable.

In a democracy, it is crucial for students, teachers, and parents in our communities to work together to solve problems. The challenge is not only to define equity, but also to get people to work together toward a common goal that may not seem to benefit the individual directly or immediately.

From *Multicultural Education*, Summer 1997, pp. 4-8. © 1997 by Caddo Gap Press, Inc. Reprinted by permission of *Multicultural Education*, the magazine of the National Association for Multicultural Education.

Strategies for Promoting the Goal of Diversity in Society

What Should Be Done at Lowell High?

As the debate over the admissions policy continues, the following simulated conversation among the Chinese-American parents and the children who filed the lawsuit, the school personnel, and other Lowell High School parents about the admissions policy presents some of the perspectives in the controversy:

School Personnel: We're sorry, but your children will not be allowed to go to Lowell. You will have to send your children to another school because our school is already 40 percent Chinese American and we need more diversity at Lowell.

Chinese American Parent 1: That's not fair. Our children have done what you told them to do. They have earned mostly A's and they have also been leaders in the community volunteering many hours in hospitals, nursing homes, and recreation centers. They have also gotten high scores on their standardized tests, and their scores are higher than other students you are admitting. We don't understand why our children can't get in. If we send them to another school, our kids will not get as good of an education.

Other Parents: We know you want your children to go to the best schools. We do too, but there are already many Chinese Americans going to the school. For us to ever achieve equity in society, we need spaces for other students.

Chinese-American Students Filing Suit: Quotas are unfair. Quotas always discriminate against someone. We know what it is to be called "Chink" or "Chinaman." We do not oppose affirmative action, but we have worked hard and it is not fair to exclude us while other less qualified students are allowed into Lowell High School.

Chinese-American Parent 2: We don't want to stick out in this lawsuit. Our kids didn't get in either and they were qualified. We know your kids didn't get in and were also qualified. So why don't we work together.

Chinese-American Parent 1: What can we do?

Non-Chinese-American Parent: Let's get together and ask the district why there aren't more opportunities for all these qualified students.

Another Parent: Why can't other schools be as outstanding as Lowell? Why isn't the district doing something to help other schools become excellent?

Before discussing the alternative of creating other excellent schools, the next section presents the new admissions policies at Lowell High School.

Lowell High School: New Admissions Policies

San Francisco Unified School District has revised their admissions policies for Lowell High School.[3] The new policies are similar to the earlier ones. Under the new proposal

. . . approximately 80 percent of the 9th grade Lowell class for the 1996–7 school year will be admitted using the same point criteria for all students. The process for point determination remains unchanged. The remaining approximately 20 percent will be admitted on a "value added" diversity basis open to all ethnic groups who meet socio-economic disadvantage criteria and high academic achievement performance. Students who qualify for this "value added" pool to Lowell will be required to attend a special six-week summer session prior to their freshman year. This summer session will also be open to all incoming Lowell students.[4]

The new 20 percent "value diversity" category differs little from past affirmative action practices. The suit that was filed by the Chinese American students and their parents has not been settled.[5]

Since the class action suit involves a high school, students may be able to relate to this issue and it may be a meaningful case study of equity for them to address through an issues-centered approach.

Using an Issues-Centered Approach with Students: Raising the Issue of Affirmative Action in the Classroom

An issues-centered approach is consistent with our national ideals as an exercise in democratic values. It fosters examination, discussion, and resolution of public issues in a multicultural society. The approach encourages students to consider other perspectives, develop their own "voice" without the filters of others, respect and listen to others, and foster a sense of community through dialogue and collaborative solutions. It is an effective way to teach controversial topics like affirmative action.

When engaged in the process, students develop critical-thinking skills by sorting through their competing and conflicting values and arriving at a thoughtful decision after considering alternatives and their consequences. Students must develop the ability to engage in discussion of controversial issues which are sources of tension so they can become informed participants in society.[6] Since this approach is open-ended, teachers usually take a neutral role during the discussion, though they also must make sure that the discussion does not stop. Teachers may ask students questions to keep the momentum of the dialogue moving.

Following are several components of an issues-centered unit.[7]

- Teachers introduce students to the issue. The teacher can begin by presenting the case of Lowell High School. Additional resources can be provided for students to read, such as newspaper articles from the *San Francisco Examiner* or other articles on affirmative action.
- Students review information and define the major issue. The teacher may ask the following questions and write the responses on the board. In addition, it may help students to focus by having them write their answers quickly on a sheet of paper before they

are asked to share their perspectives with the class orally.
- What is the main issue at Lowell High School?
- Who are the main participants in the problem?
- Students clarify terms and share information. Students may be asked:
- How would you define affirmative action?
- What is a level playing field?
- What are the important points being made?
- What tensions do you see?
- Students examine their values. These questions can help students to identify what their own conflicting values are in this situation:
- What values are conflicting in this issue?
- Which values do you think are most important?
- In the final segment of the approach, students come to a decision and give an analysis of how they came to their final position. The teacher may ask:
- What are possible solutions at Lowell?
- What are the consequences to each alternative suggested?
- What do you think should be done at Lowell? What policies should be adopted? Why?

To extend the approach, after students discuss what they think should be done, they can form teams where the group role-plays the solutions by choosing various roles like the Chinese-American students who filed the suit, other Asian-American students, African-American, Anglo-American, and Latino students, parents, teachers, and the school board.

A teacher can also have students get involved in a mock trial where the state supreme court is hearing the case brought to them by the Chinese-American students. Students would take on the roles of lawyers, plaintiffs, parents, school boards, teachers, and judges. This would actively involve students in the process and stimulate further discussion.

Background Information for Teachers

Affirmative action is a complex issue. Before teachers have students grapple with the issue in class, teachers are advised to examine the issue themselves. Students may need teachers to provide some direction, because the issue is like an onion with many layers. There are many issues at the core of this situation as indicated by the following questions:

- What is equity?

- What is the purpose of affirmative action?
- What protections does the fourteenth amendment provide individuals? groups?
- What is the responsibility of society towards its members: equality of opportunity or equality of results?
- How can minority interests be protected from the majority?
- Should affirmative action be implemented? Is so, how? If not, why?
- What policies should be implemented at Lowell?
- Why aren't there more Lowells?
- There is only one Lowell High School. How can school districts be encouraged to create more excellent schools?

In preparation for class discussions, the teacher should examine the issue of why there aren't more schools like Lowell.

Why Aren't There More Lowells?

One of the questions that arose in the simulated discussion was why aren't there more Lowell High Schools. Many skeptics would say, "Because it can't be done."

Skeptics often think of a pie as an analogy for resources. There is one pie and a set number of pieces to go around. With this perception, it becomes necessary to fight for a slice of the pie, rather than work together to build more bakeries that could produce more pies. Often people's viewpoints are based upon the economic assumption that there just isn't enough money. However, a long-term goal can have a longer impact, but often it is more difficult to implement.

Using another example, when two people love each other, they may have or adopt a child. They do not love their partner any less because they now share their love with a child. Instead, their capacity to love grows. In terms of the pie analogy, the pie becomes twice as large, it does not shrink.

Excellent schools can be a model for others. If one school is successful, the others can be successful too. In fact, Deborah Meier has shown that affirming schools can be built for all children.[8] Meier is the director of schools that have been extremely successful in school reform. With the help of teachers, parents, and students, she reinvented schools by creating a group of four Central Park East schools (CPESS) in East Harlem. The secondary school graduates 95 percent of its students and 90 percent of those students go on to college. Most of the students are Latinos and African Americans who come from low-income families.

The number of students in the Central Park East schools ranges from 250 to 400.

The small size of the schools allows faculty to respond to the needs of the students more quickly: for example, a class schedule for the entire school can be changed in a week. In addition, one of the most important philosophical aspects of the school is respect:

A good school for anyone is a little like kindergarten and a little like a good post-graduate program—the two ends of the educational spectrum, at which we understand that we cannot treat any two human beings identically, but must take into account their special interests and styles even as we hold all to high and rigorous standards. . . . The main difference between the advantaged and the disadvantaged is that the latter need such flexible schools even more. When people think "those kids' need something special, the reply we offer at CPESS is, Just give them what you have always offered those who have the money to buy the best, which is mostly a matter of respect. (p. 49)[9]

The Manhattan Center for Math and Science was also created using the Central Park East model. It houses an elementary school, a junior high, and high school. Franklin High had previously served the area, but was closed when the Manhattan school opened. It had only a seven percent graduate rate and 44 percent of the students attended class on any given day.[10] Principal Cole Genn and his assistant principal, Gene Brown, wanted to change the community's feeling of hopelessness about the school to one of success.

The administrators involved community people from institutions and businesses such as Columbia Teachers College and General Electric at the Manhattan Center. Parents also became involved. Within four years, all but four of 154 students graduated from High School and went on to college.[11] Parents beamed with pride because their young people were being admitted to prestigious universities like M.I.T., Harvard, Amherst, Cornell, Trinity, and Wesleyan. The Manhattan class of 1986 was featured on the cover of *The New York Times*. Although many had said that these schools could not be created, parents, students, community people, and school personnel believed in the potential of each student. Together they worked to provide students with skills, confidence, and opportunities. Meier and Genn are revolutionary educators. Their vision was not limited. They made the pie larger and this gave many more students the opportunity to go to excellent schools.

Affirmative Action Addresses Past Patterns of Discrimination

In the case of Lowell High School, the goal of the district is to address past patterns of discrimination by encouraging broad representation of diverse students in the school. It is difficult to respond to Chinese-American students who believe they have not been treated equally. They are members of a group which has been and continues to be subjected to discrimination and social oppression. However, in this particular context, they are not victims of a pattern of exclusion. Since 40 percent of the school is Chinese American, there is little to suggest a conspiracy to keep the Chinese Americans as a group out of the school. The issue of providing access to students from all groups is the most pressing issue at the school. Students from all groups should have the opportunity to attend the Lowell.

> In order to fight racial oppression, it may be necessary for individuals, at particular times, to place the collective good before their own personal needs.

While it may appear that the rights of individual Chinese-American students are being denied, the rights of Chinese Americans as a group are not being denied. In this particular case, the primary goals of Lowell should be to have an integrated population and to address the past pattern of exclusion. Race does matter and has since the beginning of our nation. To argue that we live in a color-blind society, and thus the Chinese-American students should be allowed into Lowell, denies that race matters. People are not the same, nor are they treated the same. In order to fight racial oppression, it may be necessary for individuals, at particular times, to place the collective good before their own personal needs.

In addition to competing values, there are many myths in society. These myths serve to keep the status quo and do not encourage an inclusionary society. The following are myths that act as obstacles to addressing and finding ways to solve our equity issues, and the comments that follow are responses to those myths.

- Preferences need to be done away with. William H. Gray III, President of the United Negro College Fund, remarked: "Our society has been loaded with preferences. Preferences for veterans, preferences for senior citizens, preferences for farmers. Government contracting has had preference for small business—small white business—that far exceeds the preferences for [businesses owned by] minorities. I don't see anyone saying let's stop that preference. . . . The only one they want to get rid of is race."[12]
- Merit can be objectively measured. Merit is a subjective measure and is judged by the person who is doing the measuring. That person will determine what is valuable.
- The resource pie is limited and each person must fight to get their share. Our nation does not have limited resources, rather the problem is limited visions. Communities can create more excellent schools like what Deborah Meier and Cole Genn have accomplished in New York City.
- Admission quotas are a major tool in affirmative action programs. Quotas can be used to allow people to get in, but they also can be used to exclude others. When quotas are used to encourage more diversity in our institutions, they are only a short-term answer to social discrimination.
- The Supreme Court ruled against racial preference in the *Bakke* case. Though the Supreme Court ruled that the use of quotas was unlawful in this case, there have been numerous cases where courts have upheld the use of quotas in cases where there is evidence of discrimination. In addition, the Supreme Court ruled in the *Bakke* case that race could be considered in admissions programs created to increase the participation of underrepresented groups.[13]

Today there is a great deal of racism, sexism, homophobia, and classism in society. Children must be taught to include people rather than exclude them. Society will not change without the participation of a diversity of citizens. In order to have equal opportunity and equal results, we must have programs like affirmative action that create an equitable playing field and affirm our diversity as a nation.

Conclusion

Harvard Professor Randall Kennedy's following remarks point to the core issue: "What is required is to create political institutions that address the needs and aspirations of all Americans, not simply whites, who have long enjoyed racial privilege, but people of color who have long suffered racial exclusion from policy making forums."[14] Students need to understand that though the affirmative action debate is often seen from a winners and losers perspective, this is a limiting perception. Rather, affirmative action is really about encouraging all people to participate in society.

Lani Guinier suggests an alternative to the winner-take-all majoritarianism; she recommends through dialogue, compromise, and consensus "the principle of taking turns."[15] Guinier believes that when all citizens are empowered to participate in society, the majority does not lose, rather they "simply learn to take turns" which is a "positive-sum solution that allows all . . . to feel that they participate" in a meaningful way.[16]

Sherman Schwartz reiterates Guinier's viewpoint and explains how the majority may not understand that its actions are limiting the abilities of others to participate in society. He states:

Affirmative-action hiring plans . . .are not intended to deny jobs to whites but to make jobs available to blacks. Any harm to whites [or Asians] is entirely unintentional. . . . Centuries of discrimination are so embedded in institutions and attitudes that whites are often unaware of their impact. . . . Affirmative-action plans that allocate a relative handful of business or other opportunities for qualified minorities are thus nothing like the racist laws that subjected human beings to brutality, poverty, and powerlessness. Only the most willful blindness fails to see this.[17]

What are the goals of schools? Are they intended only to provide children with reading, writing, mathematics, and computer skills? Or are they also intended to transmit American values like equality, freedom, democracy, and diversity. Today, few would argue against racial equality; however, racial equality is an ideal. When confronted with affirmative action in one's personal life, individuals may feel they are being threatened and treated unfairly. For example, when a qualified person from an underrepresented group is hired, many individuals may resent her because they do not understand that this person is bringing with her not only skills and knowledge needed for the position, but also a different set of experiences and information that enrich the organization. Students need to struggle with the complexities and dilemmas that are aspects of affirmative action programs. What happened at Lowell is a good example.

People from all groups feel that they have struggled and been victims of discrimination; the historical record of discrimination towards groups like African-Americans is shameful. Many European-American groups like the Irish, Italians, and Polish also faced severe discrimination. However European Americans have been able to assimilate more easily into the macroculture, while people of color continue to face the barrier of discrimination. We must look at the historical context of discrimination and its impact on society when everyone does not have the opportunity to develop her/his talents and interests. Stanley Crouch wrote, "Unless Americans begin to assert the commonality of their fates, . . .and are convinced that a superb work force can include people from many backgrounds through fair practices, the squabble will continue and the bitterness will deepen in all directions."[18]

As Cornel West has stated, race does matter.[19] Gender, class, and social orientation also matter in our society. One of the questions we have asked Non-African-American teachers in our classes is "Would you rather be Black?" Most say no, because they realize that African Americans face myriad social stigmas. People discriminate against African Americans because of color. Would you rather be rich or poor? Would you rather be male or female? By posing these questions, teachers can attempt to confront social oppression by bringing the issues to students on a personal level. Dialogue in a supportive and trusting atmosphere is crucial to moving forward.

As John Dewey explained, democracy is a social process where we dialogue and live together, rather than a form of government.[20] Democracy should provide us with the tools to change our institutions so that they are more fair and just. Even though the need for community is inherent in the human condition, it does not occur automatically, nor does it come about when people live in the same neighborhoods; communities are formed because of shared interests and a willingness to work for common issues.[21] This process is often challenging and difficult. Tensions will arise just as they did at Lowell High School; however, in a place where community is important, members will work to find solutions that strengthen the community rather than tear it apart.

Affirmative action refers to programs that are affirming, affirming our interconnections and diversity with each other.[22] Taking turns and encouraging a broad participation of the community are two critical aspects of our democratic values. More Lowell High Schools must be created because every child must have an opportunity to attend a school which is dedicated to and effective with all its students.

Injustice anywhere is a threat to justice everywhere. We are caught in an inescapable network of morality, tied in a single garment of destiny. What affects one directly, affects all indirectly.

—Martin Luther King, Jr.

Notes

1. Elaine Woo, "Caught on the Wrong Side of the Line? The Los Angeles Times, Thursday, 13 July 1995, pp. A1, A15; and "Suit Allowed Over Race Quotas in S. F. Schools," San Diego Union-Tribune, Saturday, 30 September, 1995, p. A3.
2. Woo., A15.
3. Waldemar Rojas, "Letter to Parents, Lowell High School Admissions Process," January 20, 1996, pp. 1–2.
4. Ibid., p. 1.
5. Venise Wagner, "Elite S. F. School Faces new Policy," San Francisco Examiner, December 21, 1995, Newsbank 1995 EDU 101:A5.
6. James Shaver, "Rationales for Issues-Centered Social Studies Education," The Social Studies, 83, 3, 95–99.
7. Shirley Engle & Anna Ochoa. Education for Democratic Citizenship: Decision-making 'in the Social Studies. New York: Teachers College Press, 1988.
8. Deborah Meier. 1995. The Power of Their Ideas. Boston, MA: Beacon Press, p. 49.
9. Ibid., p. 49.
10. Seymour Fliegel & James MacGuire, 1993. Miracle in East Harlem. New York: Random House.
11. Ibid., p. 151
12. Voices, Los Angeles Times, Sunday, April 30, 1995, p. A24.
13. Peter Irons & Stephanie Guitton (Eds.) May It Please The Court. New York: New Press, 1993, p. 318.
14. Lani Guinier. The Tyranny of the Majority. New York: Free Press, 1994, p. 6.
15. Ibid.
16. Guinier, p. 6–7.
17. Sherman Schwartz, "The Blind Spot in Strict Scrutiny." The Los Angeles Times, Sunday, 18 June 1995, p. M1.
18. Stanley Crouch, "Someone Ate My Bowl of Privilege," The Los Angeles Times, Sunday, 18 June 1995, pp. M1, M6.
19. Cornel West. Race Matters. Boston, MA: Beacon Press, 1993.
20. John Dewey, Democracy and Education: An Introduction to the Philosophy of Education. New York: Macmillan, 1916.
21. Valerie Ooka Pang, Geneva Gay & William B. Stanley, 1995. "Expanding Conceptions of Community and Civic Competence for a Multicultural society," Theory and Research in Social Studies Education 23(5), pp. 302–331.
22. Geneva Gay. Private Interview. April, 1995, San Francisco, Ca.

H OW TO

Teach Our Children Well

(It can be done)

By STEVE WULF

O N A BEAUTIFUL FALL AF-
ternoon not long ago, all 120
eighth-grade students and four
of their teachers at the Olson
Middle School in Minneapo-
lis, Minn., walked across a grassy playing field down to nearby Shingle Creek.
For the past five weeks, they had been
raising monarch butterflies—from caterpillar through chrysalis—and now 30 of
them were ready for release.

Raising butterflies isn't all that easy,
as the Olson eighth-graders discovered.
Every other day, the students would gather
milkweed pods for their charges to eat.
They kept journals, which they took home
to their parents for evaluation. They
rushed in on Mondays to see how their
monarchs were doing, but they also
struggled with large issues when one of
them died.

After the butterflies were relocated to
long tubes of bridal-veil material, the kids
gingerly placed them on sponges filled
with honey and water, then took delight as
the creatures learned to go to the nectar on
their own. Two days before their release,
the students ever so carefully attached

tiny tags to their hind wings—tags that a
University of Kansas professor would use
to monitor their migration to Mexico.

RAISING CHILDREN ISN'T EASY EITHER, AS
we all know. The task becomes even more
difficult when we don't give them the education they deserve. We send them off to
school every day, hoping for the best but
often settling for less. Teachers are usually overworked and underpaid. Public
schools are often overcrowded and un-
derfunded. We begrudge tax hikes for
schooling, then bemoan low test scores.

Our concern for education, well in-
tentioned though it may be, has lately
manifested itself in an insistence on such
standards as test scores or dress codes or
class size. But like the tag on a wing of a
butterfly, such mandates must be applied
gently. Too much testing will cut into the
work that teachers and students should be
doing; uniforms should not stifle efforts to
bring out the individuality in each student; a large class with an inspiring leader
is far better than a small class with a mediocre teacher.

What makes a good school? There are
no stock answers, like wardrobe or testing
or size. But there are some universal
truths. A good school is a community of
parents, teachers and students. A good
school, like a good class, is run by someone with vision, passion and compassion.
A good school has teachers who still enjoy
the challenge, no matter what their age
or experience. A good school prepares its
students not just for the SATS or ACTs but
also for the world out there.

To better illustrate what makes a good
school, TIME has chosen three as shining
examples—two of them middle schools,
the third a secondary school combining
Grades 7 through 12. They were selected
in part because middle schools are an especially tough test for educators who have
to swim upstream against the changes of
adolescence and the customary disappearance of parental involvement at that
stage. These three have also succeeded
despite a profile that seems to predict failure or mediocrity: a majority of minority
students, limited resources and membership in a large school system. They, and
thousands of other outstanding public

From *Time*, October 27, 1997, pp. 62-65, 68-69. © 1997 by Time Inc. Magazine Company. Reprinted by permission.

schools we might have mentioned, are the good news in American education.

OF THE 1,256 STUDENTS WHO ATTEND THE Stanford Middle School in the Los Altos

LESSON #1

AFTER SCHOOL

Good after-school programs, those that engage the interests of both students and staff, can bring dazzling results.

■ **It's all in the execution. Tired teachers who take on kids at the end of a full day in the classroom are little more than baby sitters. But when these programs are done right, they can do much more than safeguard at-risk children from the dangers of the streets and of the television. They can both extend and improve upon a regular school day's learning, making magic after the last bell rings.**

neighborhood of Long Beach, Calif., 34% are Hispanic, 22% Asian, 23% Caucasian, 17% African American, 3% Filipino and 2% either Pacific Islander or Native American. More than 75% qualify for the free or reduced-cost lunch program, thus enabling Stanford to receive federal funding under Title I. Because the district allows parents to choose their children's schools, only about one-third of the students reside in the neighborhood; the others arrive on 16 buses. When Stanford's rainbow coalition gets off those buses, it is a vision in white and black: white-collared shirts and black pants for the boys, white blouses and black skirts or pants for the girls.

Four years ago, the Long Beach Unified School District, the third largest in California, decided to change over to "standards-based" education and to initiate a mandatory school-uniform policy. At the same time, Stanford principal Judi Gutierrez embarked on a program to restructure and reform her school. She created schools within the school, one for each of the three grades, with a "learning director" heading a core group of teachers. She allowed the students to pick their own mottoes—in the sixth grade, it's "Begin the Journey ... Stride into Excellence." Gutierrez also stressed staff development, sending teachers to seminars and workshops using Title I funds.

Little changes can mean a lot. Each classroom has a nameplate with the educational background of the teacher. Kids with a grade-point average of 2.0 or better get T shirts and patches that designate their achievements. A special grant pays

for eight college students to monitor 50 kids considered "at risk."

The big change that means the most to critics of education is that Stanford's test scores are on the rise—particularly in mathematics, where the sixth-, seventh- and eighth-graders were, respectively, in the state's 77th, 74th and 66th percentile rank. Another measure of the school's success is its desirability: four years ago, the school accepted every student who applied; this year 200 students had to be turned away.

While almost all the teachers share a common passion, one Stanford staff member fairly pants at the opportunity to help students. She is Apache Rose, a four-year-old German shorthaired pointer and a licensed therapy dog belonging to physical-education teacher Monica Havelka. Apache was brought to school for the seventh-grade programs in health, science and phys ed, but she has become so popular that she now has kids of diverse backgrounds talking about her. She even has her own program to train older kids to handle therapy dogs—Apache Rose and Friends, or simply and cutely, ARF.

The other day at Stanford, a tall Hispanic boy and a small, autistic Cambodian boy walked Apache Rose through the halls together. The students had nothing in common but a leash to this dog, yet a visitor could sense their mutual pride— the older child in befriending a member of the Stanford family he might never have known about, the younger child in facing his fear and discovering the joys of companionship. Apache Rose, not unlike middle school, is a bridge.

EVERY FRIDAY AT OLSON MIDDLE SCHOOL, the adults—not the children—are in uniform. Principal Shannon Griffin, her staff

and faculty all wear crimson T shirts that read, OLSON MIDDLE SCHOOL—DREAM MAKERS. "Educators crush dreams all the time," explains Griffin. "Here we want to make them."

Six years ago, Griffin was brushing her teeth one night when ... "Bam! It all came together." Of course, she had 30 years of experience teaching in public schools, but in that instant, she saw the way a school should work: teams of teachers helping students learn by themselves, a thematic curriculum, extended days, classes without bells, a three-year relationship between the students and their advisers. At the time, Griffin was working for a school that spurned her ideas. But in April 1995 she was hired to take over Olson, a 30-year-old building on Minneapolis' north side that was being converted from an elementary school into a middle school. Because it was a start-up, Griffin was able to hire without regard to seniority. "If you want high expectations for students," she now says, "you have to have high expectations for your teachers."

Olson has 720 students who reflect the changing face of Minneapolis: a third of them are "European American," a third of them are African American and almost a third are Asian American— mostly Hmong from Southeast Asia. With 78% of the students eligible for free or reduced-cost lunch, Olson is one of the city's poorer middle schools, but in last year's state reading tests, Olson came in third among the seven middle schools.

When the eighth-graders settled into their classrooms on the first week of school this year, they found plastic boxes with mesh tops and one or two caterpillars in them. English teacher Kay Pfaffendorf and social studies teacher Cindy Farmer

LESSON #2

TECHNOLOGY

All kids, not just ones from families that can afford a home computer, should grow up with a mouse in their hand.

■ **As a learning tool, computers make kids adventurers and avid learners, taking them beyond the traditional walls of the schoolhouse. The exorbitant price of wiring classrooms is only one hurdle, however. Teachers must be properly trained to integrate technology into the curriculum if the costly machines are to be more than fancy typewriters.**

LESSON #3

CLASS SIZE

Smaller classes allow for more personal interaction between teachers and students, and they tend to reduce paperwork so teachers can spend more time planning lessons.

■ **While there is no ideal number of students per class, studies show that small classes work best—especially for reading and math in the early primary grades. They are expensive, however, requiring an expanded teaching staff and more classroom space per student.**

LESSON #4

TEACHER PREP

Nearly 2 million new teachers will be entering classrooms over the next decade. The system that prepares them for the job needs to improve.

■ **To raise the quality of teaching and increase respect for the profession, many colleges of education are instituting higher standards, creating extended internships and developing partnerships with public schools. Once on the job, teachers must have greater opportunities to continue their own education.**

had taken a course on raising monarchs at the University of Minnesota in order to present a project involving not only their subjects but also math, science and art.

As the kids found out, the project wasn't just about raising butterflies. It was about emerging from a summer cocoon, sharing their excitement with their parents and bonding with one another in their last year before high school.

CENTRAL PARK EAST SECONDARY SCHOOL IS an experiment that has withstood the test of time. A few years ago, it was one of the most celebrated alternative schools in the country. Deborah Meier, its founder in 1985, was the first public school teacher ever awarded a MacArthur Foundation fellowship, and she wrote a book about her experience, *The Power of Their Ideas*.

Her own idea had been to create a secondary school in New York City's East Har-

lem in which less was more. Smaller and fewer classes meant increased individual attention and a deeper understanding of subjects. She built the school a grade at a time, starting with the seventh in '85, until the school had a Division I for seventh- and eighth-graders, a Division II for ninth- and 10th-graders and a Senior Institute for 11th- and 12th-graders—546 students in all this year, with 41 full-time staff members.

Each of the divisions has a two-year curriculum devoted to the two core subjects, humanities and math-science, keeping the students with the same pair of teachers two years in a row. In the Senior Institute, students assemble portfolios demonstrating mastery in 14 subjects (seven majors and seven minors). Those portfolios are judged by a graduation committee on the basis of how well they satisfy the five "habits of mind" that form the basis for the curriculum: evidence, perspective, connections, supposition and relevance. It sounds New Agey, but students understand. As Lohattis Hayden, a 12th-grader interested in sociology, says, "The way we learn is totally different. We read a lot of articles and literature, but we don't have to take a load of textbooks home. This school is more than just studying—it's looking inside yourself."

Meier, who has since moved on to start a school in Boston, has had her mainstream critics. But she put up numbers that were astonishing, given the secondary school's impoverished surroundings: 90% of the graduates went on to college, some of them to Ivy League schools.

As befits its daring mission, Central Park East Secondary School is situated in the Jackie Robinson Educational Complex at the corner of Madison Avenue and 106th Street in East Harlem. The building is stark on the outside, but inside it turns

friendly, with colorful student-made ceramic tiles leading people to class.

Indeed, the whole school seems a wonderful mosaic of activities and classes and inquiries. In the library, the Tech Scouts, a group of computer-savvy students, show off their Website and online magazine. Up in the Girls Inc. room, students replay a "feminized" skit, based on Snow White and Cinderella, that they performed at a conference. In Brent Duckor's "Democracy, State and Society" class, Senior Institute students openly and persuasively challenge his assertion that they are being cynical. ("You win," he says. "You're not at all cynical.")

Teachers say the school has actually got better in some ways since Deborah Meier left. "Pioneering is exhilarating," said one, "but it is also exhausting." David Smith, a former humanities teacher, now director of the school, brings a sense of calm to the hallways. (The kids, as they do with all of their teachers, call him by his first name.) "Every so often," says Smith, "a student will tell me, 'I don't know how to do that.' And my reply is, 'You don't know how to do that—yet.' That's an empowering word: yet. Our purpose, you see, is not to provide them with the answers but with the tools they'll need to find the answers for themselves."

The teachers at Central Park East Secondary School have something in common with the eighth-graders at Olson Middle School. When the butterflies were finally released on that warm fall afternoon, the kids openly wondered which ones would reach Mexico, and how long it would take. One thing they were certain of: they knew they had done all they could for the butterflies. *—Reported by Deborah Edler Brown/ Long Beach, Emily Mitchell/Minneapolis and Megan Rutherford and Rebecca Winters/New York City*

A new vision for city schools

DIANE RAVITCH & JOSEPH VITERITTI

Diane Ravitch is a senior research scholar at the School of Education of New York University. Joseph Viteritti is a research professor at NYU's Robert F. Wagner Graduate School of Public Service.

YES, there is hope for urban education. A wave of reform is spreading from city to city and state to state. Rather than aiming to alter isolated practices or to fix one piece of a jerry-built system, these changes are meant to transform the basic character of public schooling. When taken together, the ambitious range of initiatives currently under way can be structured into an integrated program for reforming urban education—one that shifts from a bureaucratic system that prizes compliance to a deregulated system that focuses on student performance.

A century ago, progressive reformers reshaped big-city schools according to the era's widely shared vision of efficient administration. To get schools "out of politics," they created tightly controlled bureaucracies. At the apex of authority were "professional experts," who managed a top-down system designed to impose uniform rules on teachers and students alike. The model for this system was the factory, which, at that time in history, was considered the acme of scientific management. The raw materials for these educational factories were the children of immigrants, who were pouring into American cities in unprecedented numbers, in need of instruction in literacy, hygiene, and basic Americanization. The workers in these factories were teachers, whose views about what or how to teach were not solicited. Nor did the experts see any need to consult parents about anything regarding their children, since many of them were barely literate.

These turn-of-the-century efforts to create what historian David Tyack called "the one best system" were remarkably effective for at least the first half of the century. Big-city schools offered unparalleled educational opportunity to millions of children and helped to generate a vast middle class. At mid-century, the nation's urban schools were considered to be a great success. But no more. The system that transformed an earlier generation of impoverished children into prosperous adults has become sclerotic; the bureaucratic organization created to impose efficiency and order has grown tired and inefficient, tangled helplessly in rules and regulations devised by the courts, state governments, federal government, union contracts, and its own minions.

In city after city, reports of corruption, disorder, neglect, and low educational achievement are legion. Urban education is in deep trouble, in part because of inept big-city bureaucracies inherited from the past, but also because the public's expectations for the schools are higher now than they were earlier in the century. Fifty years ago, the public was neither surprised nor alarmed by the large numbers of young people who did not graduate from high school; they believed that the numbers would continually improve over time. Today, the public expects a large majority of students to complete high school, especially since the jobs available for high-school dropouts are diminishing.

Convinced that the structure of public education contributes to its ineffectiveness in educating a larger proportion of students, imaginative leaders in cities and states across the country are implementing systemic changes. The new reforms proceed on the conviction that the century-old bureaucratic structures of urban education cannot succeed in today's society. The century-old system of schools cannot work today because it was designed to function in a very different society, with different social mores and different problems, where supervisors instructed teachers, teachers instructed students, and parents expected their children to mind what they were told.

The factory is no longer a useful model for urban education; teachers and children are not interchangeable parts to be moved around to fit the requirements of administrators. The reforms that are now being enacted in many cities incorporate such

 Reprinted with permission from *The Public Interest*, Winter 1996, pp. 3-16. © 1993 by National Affairs, Inc.

principles as diversity, quality, choice, and accountability. Instead of a system that regulates identical schools, reformers seek a system in which academic standards are the same for all but where schools vary widely. In the new reform vision, the schools are as diverse as teachers' imagination and will; students and their families choose the school that best meets their needs and interests; and central authorities perform a monitoring and auditing function to assure educational quality and fiscal integrity. In such a reconfigured system, the role of the local superintendent shifts from regulating behavior to auditing results. The bottom line is not whether everyone has complied with the same rules and procedures but whether children are learning.

Charter schools

Not since the beginning of the twentieth century has there been such a burst of bold experimentation in the organization and governance of schools as there has been in just the last half decade. Among the most notable initiatives on the current scene are charter schools, the contracting of instructional services, and a variety of school-choice programs. These innovations are driven by demands from parents and elected officials for higher levels of educational success. However, few of these innovations are based on hard evidence that they will succeed. But that is the nature of innovation: one purpose of these experiments is to identify what will work and what will not. Most of these initiatives, however, are based on well-documented evidence that the current institutional arrangement does not work very well for large numbers of children.

One of the most promising ideas to appear on the national horizon is charter schools. Charter schools are semi-autonomous, public entities that are freed from most bureaucratic rules and regulations by state and local authorities in return for a commitment to meet explicit performance goals. They are established under a contract between a group that manages a school and a sponsoring authority that oversees it. The contractor might consist of parents, teachers, a labor union, a college, a museum, or other nonprofit or for-profit entities. The sponsor might be a school board, a state education department, a state university campus, or a government agency. In Arizona, the legislature has created a special governing body authorized to grant or deny a request for a charter; thus such power is not limited to the state or local school boards, which may have a stake in restricting the number of these institutions.

Charter schools may be either new schools or existing ones. Their development will contribute to both the number and variety of quality institutions.

In Detroit, the Drug Enforcement Administration is creating a residential school for 200 at-risk students; a school called Metro Deaf serves the hearing impaired in St. Paul. In Wilmington, Delaware, five corporations and a medical center have cooperated in a joint venture to run a new high school for math and science. Boston University runs a school for homeless children in Massachusetts; and the Denver Youth Academy was created for at-risk, middle-school children and their families in Colorado. The possibilities seem endless.

A charter serves as a negotiated, legal agreement that sets standards and expectations for the school. School professionals are authorized to manage their own budget and to choose their own staff, but the degree of autonomy varies from state to state. The Education Commission of the States, in conjunction with the Humphrey Institute at the University of Minnesota, recently completed a survey of 110 charter schools in seven states. It found that educators at these schools are quite willing to be held more accountable for improved student performance, so long as they are permitted to enjoy more autonomy. A majority of these schools focus their attention on at-risk populations.

Presently 19 states have charter-school laws. Minnesota passed the first one as recently as 1991, with eight schools participating; there are now 40 participating. California approved the establishment of 100 charter schools in 1992. Michigan has 30. Among the states that grant the most autonomy to charter schools are Arizona, California, Colorado, Delaware, Massachusetts, Michigan, Minnesota, New Hampshire, and Texas. (The other states with charter laws are Alaska, Arkansas, Georgia, Hawaii, Kansas, Louisiana, New Mexico, Rhode Island, Wisconsin, and Wyoming.)

Charter schools are public schools. They are accountable to a public authority. In fact, the charter, which defines academic expectations and other legal responsibilities, often serves as a more powerful instrument for accountability than anything that exists for most ordinary public schools. If a charter school fails educationally or misuses its funds, the charter can be revoked, as was the case with one Los Angeles school last year. Most charter schools must accept any student who applies, or they select students by lottery if there are more applicants than places. All are bound by the usual state laws and regulations requiring schools to be nondiscriminatory and protective of civil rights.

Contracts for performance

Unlike charter-school laws, which begin as state initiatives, contracting-out arrangements usually originate with a local school board. It is not unusual for school boards to contract with private vendors for the performance of non-instructional functions—e.g., transportation, food, supplies, facilities, and custodial and administrative services. What is novel about recent developments is for school boards to arrange to have instructional programs provided by outsiders. This approach has given rise to new entrepreneurial organizations on the education scene. Educational Alternatives, Inc. (EAI), for example, is under contract to run nine public schools in Baltimore, as well as a single school in Duluth. It will also overhaul six schools in Hartford (eventually all 32) and assume general responsibility for the management of that district. The Edison Project has contracted to operate individual schools in Wichita, Kansas, Mt. Clemens, Michigan, Sherman, Texas, and Boston. Washington, D.C., has recently contracted with Sylvan Learning Systems to offer remedial reading for a limited number of students; and Sabis, an International group, runs a school in Springfield, Massachusetts.

These arrangements are similar to charter schools in that they are brought into being by a performance agreement between a school organization and a public authority. Some contracts allow more autonomy than others. EAI, for instance, ran into great difficulty implementing changes in Baltimore after it agreed to hire all the existing teachers in what were supposed to be reconstituted schools; moreover, the teachers' union was antagonistic to the project from the beginning. And some argue that EAI committed a major strategic error when it took on general responsibility for running the entire Hartford school district. The approach adopted by the Edison Project, involving the development of new schools, one at a time, with a staff that it has hired and trained, seems to hold more promise.

As with most innovations in public education, the more profound changes exacted through contracting tend to generate the strongest opposition. Wilkinsburg, Pennsylvania, a working-class suburb of Pittsburgh, where 78 percent of the children qualify economically for a free-lunch program, is a case in point. It became the scene of an intense political and legal battle when a newly elected, reform-minded school board announced its intention to contract with Alternative Public School Strategies to operate one of its three elementary schools. The local teachers' union and the National Education Association fiercely opposed its reform proposals: an extended school year, new after-school programs, merit pay for teachers.

Some observers have confused the contracting approach with privatization. Contract schools are public institutions, supported with public funds, accountable to a public authority—usually a local school board. As is the case with charter schools, they are expected to meet specific standards of academic performance defined in a legal agreement. If they do not perform adequately, they can be put out of business. When Baltimore Mayor Kurt Schmoke became dissatisfied with student performance at EAI-operated schools in Baltimore, he said he would rethink the contract. It is a rare occurrence for a city public school to be shut down for poor performance, regardless of its record over time. Contracting arrangements, whether they result from state charter laws or local initiatives, mark a new threshold of aspiration and accountability for public education.

Dimensions of choice

Choice programs are designed to enhance the options made available to parents in selecting a school for their children. The most common form of choice program allows parents to choose a public school that lies outside the ordinary range of geographical options. The objective is to improve the chances for students to be placed in settings that suit their needs. It is also assumed that giving parents choice will induce competition among schools. Minnesota adopted the first statewide inter-district choice program in 1985. By 1991, 10 states had approved some form of open-enrollment program; and now, more than two-thirds of the states have enacted public school-choice programs. The first city-wide choice program was developed in 1981 in Cambridge, Massachusetts; perhaps the most celebrated success story at the local level is found in District 4 of East Harlem.

The basic shortcoming of public school-choice programs is that those jurisdictions that have the greatest need for expanding opportunities usually offer the fewest number of satisfactory options. For example, in Massachusetts, where voluntary inter-district choice has existed since 1991, only 25 percent of the districts participate, and none of the 29 on the suburban rim of Boston is included in this group. Supposedly, New York City has had a city-wide choice program since 1992; but, in reality, choice is permitted in only six of 32 districts, and the availability of space is extremely limited. Without measures designed to increase the total number of quality institutions, public school choice promotes competition among parents and children, not educators. It raises expectations but often leads to disappointment.

In 1990, Wisconsin passed innovative legislation that would expand parental choice among low-income parents in Milwaukee. Families who met income criteria ($18,000 or less) were given a state voucher for $2,987, which they might use in either a public school or a participating private school. By the end of the 1994–1995 school year, there were 1,500 children participating in the program that involved 12 nonpublic schools. Last spring, the legislation was amended to increase the value of the voucher to $3,600 and to permit schools with religious affiliations to participate. By next year, 15,000 low-income students are expected to take advantage of this unusual opportunity.

Similarly, last spring, the Ohio legislature enacted a law that will permit up to 2,000 low-income students in Cleveland to use a $2,500 state voucher in a school of choice—public, private, or sectarian. As in Wisconsin, the law was passed at the urging of minority parents dissatisfied with the quality of education in inner-city public schools. Like parents in Milwaukee, they had been frustrated with court-imposed integration plans that led to longer bus rides, rather than better schools. For the first time, many poor children whose life chances would have been determined by assignment to a failing public school were given the opportunity for real choices that gave them access to quality institutions (choices that were formerly available only to the middle class). In the meantime, the Milwaukee program is being challenged in state court, and a legal contest is expected in Cleveland.

Opponents of these programs claim that they violate requirements for the Constitutional separation of church and state. But there is nothing in the First Amendment of the Constitution that prohibits parents who want to send their children to religious schools from receiving public support. Since 1983, rulings by the Supreme Court have held that such support is legally permissible provided that aid goes directly to the parents (not the school), that the choice of school is freely made by parents, and that the system of funding is neutral. Cognizant of these rulings, opponents of choice have resorted to legal arguments based on provisions found in state law, many of which may be incompatible with federal Constitutional standards.

Some critics of choice fear that providing families with private-school options will spell the doom of public education. They predict a mass exodus of children and dollars from public schools. This is highly unlikely, indeed impossible, since the number of children permitted to participate has been limited. Let us keep in mind that every choice program that has gotten serious consideration by policy makers thus far—including those in Wisconsin and Ohio—has targeted a limited portion of the school population, those on the lowest rung of the economic ladder. Most public-school children were not even eligible according to these criteria.

Traditionally, school reformers have asked how we can improve the existing system; today, many ask, instead, what we can do that is in the best interest of students who are at risk of failing. Since the ground-breaking work by the late sociologist James S. Coleman and his colleagues at the University of Chicago in 1982,[1] there is evidence that private and parochial schools are more educationally effective than public schools. Some scholars have attributed the difference to the selectivity of private schools. However, more recent research on Catholic schools by Bryk, Lee, and Holland[2] indicates that the differences are more the result of characteristics identified within the schools themselves, e.g., high standards, a strong academic curriculum, autonomy, an orderly environment, and a sense of community. Other studies by Coleman, Greeley, and Hoffer[3] have demonstrated rather persuasively that Catholic schools have been particularly effective in educating at-risk, inner-city students who have performed poorly in public schools.

An agenda for change

In light of the wide range of reforms currently under way in cities across the country, we propose a six-point agenda to improve educational opportunities for all children. Some of these proposals will require strong legislative action at the state level. Implementation will require an "hourglass strategy," allowing schools to escape one by one from the bureaucratic system. The best schools would function as charter schools and the worst schools would be replaced by institutions with performance contracts. Over time, more and more schools will seek the autonomy and performance agreements that charter schools have, and educational authorities will incrementally replace ineffective schools with new schools that have committed themselves to meet performance goals. The net effect of this approach would be to increase the number of desirable schools that children can attend.

1. Setting Standards. What matters most is whether children are learning, and this can only be assured by having real accountability at the school level. Each school district should establish clear performance standards and administer regular assessments to determine whether students are learning what they should at each grade level. By standards, we mean objective outcome measures that prescribe what should be expected from every school at regular intervals. For example, we would focus on such items as test scores in reading and math, attendance rates, and dropout rates. We would be especially interested in measuring "value added" or "gain scores"—the progress made over a given academic year—rather than unfairly comparing schools with children from vastly different social circumstances. We would not involve district-level administrators in defining basic inputs like instructional approaches or building specifications beyond code requirements designed to protect safety.

2. School Closings. The public school that once served as a gateway of opportunity for immigrant populations now serves as a custodial institution for disadvantaged children. Even as national achievement-test scores creep slowly upward, the gap between black and white students' scores remains shamefully wide, and those of Hispanic children are actually declining. As a matter of public policy, no child should be forced to go to a failing school. We cannot ask parents of children who are trapped in floundering institutions to be patient while we work things out. Educators and political leaders should not expect poor parents to accept educational standards for their children that the middle class would not tolerate for their own.

Any school that shows a consistent record of failure over several years should be a candidate for closure. The first step must be to define objective standards for placing a school on probation. Most school systems already have the basic data needed to develop appropriate criteria. A combination of attendance rates, test scores, dropout rates, improvement ratings, and similar markers will identify those schools that must be placed on probation or eventually closed.

3. School Autonomy. Schools that are working well should receive a performance contract and control over their budget and personnel. Subject to due process, principals should be able to select and remove staff. They should be allowed to purchase supplies and support services of their choosing, though central authorities will audit these purchases.

All schools, whether autonomous or not, should be liberated from unnecessary and cumbersome mandates. In New York, the state Education Department recently identified more than 120 regulations that are not related to health, safety, or civil rights. California, Michigan, and Florida have taken the lead on regulatory reform; their governors have called for sunsetting the entire education code and starting over, enacting only those regulations that are essential. Illinois is one of 10 states that has set up a procedure where local school districts can request waivers from outdated requirements. School superintendents should conduct a top-to-bottom review of local regulations to eliminate those that are not necessary. The goal should be to minimize the burden on teachers and principals. and to grant schools greater independence in providing education.

Many school systems in the United States are experimenting with site-based management that moves decision making out of the administrative structure of the bureaucracy down to the school level. When implemented seriously, site-based management can improve both flexibility and accountability. However, a key question is whether central school authorities will actually concede the power to which they have become accustomed. A recent evaluation of the Los Angeles autonomy program by McKinsey & Company identified significant delays at the district level in implementing the reforms. Several years ago, New York City launched a modest experiment in school-based management without reducing the power of the central bureaucracy. It resulted in neither real autonomy for participating schools nor increased accountability for student performance.

Worth consideration is the city of London's opt-out program, in which a majority of parents in a school can vote to remove the school from the supervision of the local school district. Independence means that the school gets control over its own budget and a portion of the administrative overhead, so long as it continues to meet well-defined performance standards based on the national curriculum and national tests. All big-city school districts should have a similar plan, enabling schools to "opt out" of the present bureaucratic structure. We would propose, however, that approval require a majority vote of both parents and teachers. Teachers are important members of the school community, and their support is essential for success.

Not all schools are ready for such autonomy. But, if the parents and professionals at a school apply for approval as a charter school, then such a request should be evaluated by the local superintendent, the state education commissioner, or by an independent chartering agency on the basis of established criteria. In exchange for autonomy, the school administration would be required to sign a contract defining educational and financial standards to which the school would be held accountable. Greater autonomy would permit the school to hire staff, choose its teaching materials, set its fiscal priorities, and decide where it wants to purchase supplies and support services. Decisions about what to buy and where to buy it would be made by educators at the school level, not bureaucrats at central headquarters.

4. New Schools. If we intend to close failing schools, we need to provide alternatives to students who attend them. School superintendents should be given the power to solicit proposals for new institutions, either to replace failing schools or to grant contracts for increasing the total number of quality institutions. Proposals would be received from groups of teachers or parents, universities, libraries or museums, nonprofit organizations, or private entrepreneurs who demonstrate a professional capacity to administer a school. They may be progressive schools, family-style schools, Outward Bound schools, single-sex schools, back-to-basics schools, classical academies: The range is as vast as the imagination of creative educators.

These should, of course, be schools of choice. If they attract enough students, they will succeed; if they don't, they won't. These new schools would be established under the same terms as the charter schools described above. They would be granted autonomy in exchange for signing a compact outlining the educational and financial standards to which they would be held accountable. But, if the marketplace prevails, parents will become the ultimate judges of success or failure at the school level.

5. Central Administration. In a recent article in the *Wall Street Journal*, Peter Drucker predicts that in 10 to 15 years, most organizations will be "outsourcing" all of their support activities to specialist groups, thus allowing executives to avoid distractions and focus on functions that are directly related to their central mission. We share a similar vision for public education, where the role of central authorities will be transformed. Over time, the central administrative institution will significantly reduce its role as a provider of support services to schools. It would not be in charge of supplies, leasing, meals, building repairs, transportation, personnel, and other functions that can be performed better by others. Depending on the outcome of the competitive market, support services will either be provided by a private vendor or administered by an appropriate municipal agency. Marriot, for example, already provides food services to schools in Baltimore and Salt Lake City; and most municipal governments are well equipped to assume responsibility for such functions as personnel administration, procurement, transportation, or building maintenance.

According to our plan, the central school administration will become a monitoring agency with clearly focused and limited responsibilities. It will be responsible for educational standards, city-wide assessments, fiscal accountability, capital improvements, the authorization of new schools, and negotiation of union contracts that are specific enough to protect members' rights but flexible enough to permit school-by-school variations. The school system's chief executive should concentrate on setting standards, monitoring performance, and identifying those schools that either should be put on probation or closed. The chief executive would also be responsible for financial monitoring to protect against corruption and malfeasance. In a system where every school has its own budget, this is a formidable task, and it will probably require some form of administrative decentralization.

6. Real Choice for the Poor. Parents whose children attend the worst schools—those targeted for closure—should be given scholarships on a means-tested basis to use in any accredited school, be it public, private, or religious. Middle-class parents exercise such options for their children all the time; poor children should have the same. Priority for financial aid should go first to children in failing institutions whose families are on public assistance. The amount of a scholarship should not exceed the per capita cost of sending a child to public school. Schools receiving scholarship students should accept the award as a full fee for tuition. Students who get public scholarships should be regularly tested to assess their progress, in order to assure accountability and to exclude inadequate schools from participation.

Schools for the twenty-first century

We believe that these proposals, taken together, will strengthen and energize public education—freeing professionals and students from counterproductive regulations, shifting resources from the district level to the schools, providing alternative means for the delivery of vital support services, assuring choice for the students who now receive the least educational opportunity, rewarding success, encouraging creativity, requiring accountability for results, phasing out schools that are not conducive environments for teaching or learning, and placing institutions on the line by putting students first.

The public education system as currently structured is archaic. It cannot reform itself, nor can it be reformed by even the most talented chief executive. Trying to do so would be like trying to convert an old-fashioned linotype machine into a word-processor: It can't be done. They perform the same function, but their methods and technologies are so different that one cannot be turned into the other. Instead of a school system that attempts to impose uniform rules and regulations, we need a system of schools that is dynamic, diverse, performance based, and accountable. The school system that we now have may have been right for the age in which it was created; it is not right for the twenty-first century.

Notes

1. James S. Coleman, Thomas Hoffer, and Sally Kilgore, *High School Achievement: Public, Catholic, and Private Schools* (New York: Basic Books, 1982).
2. Anthony B. Bryk, Valerie E. Lee, and Peter B. Holland, *Catholic Schools and the Common Good* (Cambridge: Harvard University Press, 1993).
3. Andrew M. Greeley, *Catholic High Schools and Minority Students* (Rutgers: Transaction, 1982); Thomas Hoffer, Andrew M. Greeley, and James S. Coleman. "Achievement Growth in Public and Catholic Schools," *Sociology of Education* 58 (1985): 74–97.

Home Was A Horse Stall

Jim Carnes

Yumi Ishimaru was used to picking up and moving on. In 1905, at the age of 20, she left Yamaguchi, Japan, for San Francisco to marry a man she had only seen in a picture. After being detained with other "picture brides" for medical tests at Angel Island, Yumi reached the mainland, met Masajiro Kataoka, and found him shorter than she had expected.

Masajiro, also from Yamaguchi, operated a restaurant off Fillmore Street. After they were married, Yumi went to work as a housekeeper for an American family. Before long, she was expecting her first child. The Kataokas' prospects looked good.

But the great earthquake of April 1906 destroyed Masajiro's restaurant and left the young couple homeless. They lived for a while in a tent in Sacramento Park, then later in a succession of small apartments. Yumi gave birth to a daughter that summer.

Masajiro decided not to rebuild his restaurant. He was tired of city life, of the mobsters who pressured honest businessmen to pay for "protection." He and Yumi and their new baby left San Francisco, and Masajiro made a fresh start as a tenant farmer. He saw a bright future in strawberry farming and hoped one day to own some land.

In 1913, the state of California dashed Masajiro's hope of ever owning his own farm. A new law denied the right of land ownership to anyone who was not eligible to become a U.S. citizen. And, according to the federal Naturalization Law of 1790, only white immigrants were permitted to become naturalized citizens. Although the California alien land law didn't mention the Japanese or any other group by name, its intent was obvious. Ever since the Gold Rush of 1849, white workers in the Western states had seen Asians arrive in increasing numbers to find a place in the American economy. During hard times, competition for jobs brought racial tensions to the surface.

Only white immigrants were permitted to become naturalized citizens.

In 1906, the San Francisco school board segregated all Japanese, Chinese and Korean children into an "Oriental" school. When the Japanese government protested, Pres. Theodore Roosevelt offered a deal: He would reverse the school policy if Japan agreed to let only professionals of certain categories emigrate to the United States. The so-called Gentlemen's Agreement prevented an international confrontation, but bias against the Japanese in California increased. The 1913 alien land law was designed to make people like Yumi and Masajiro Kataoka permanent outsiders.

Farm life was hard work for the Kataokas. Yumi and Masajiro eventually had six children, and all of them had chores to do before and after school. Tsuyako, the youngest daughter, was born in 1918. She got her nickname, "Sox," from white friends who couldn't pronounce her real name. The nickname made her feel more American. Sox remembers that there was no Saturday or Sunday or Monday in the strawberry business, only Workday. And she remembers that no matter how difficult and tiring the labor, her mother was usually singing.

In 1932 Masajiro began renting farmland from a Mrs. Perkins, a strong-willed pioneer rancher whose family owned one of the largest rose nurseries in the world. Mrs. Perkins didn't make Masajiro sign a contract for the land. She even let him build his own house on it. She hired Sox's older sister, Nobuko, to work in her big ranch house. Nobuko got her nickname, "Nee," from the Perkins children, who were tall for their ages and considered her tiny. Nee cooked and cleaned and performed many more tasks than were expected of her, such as chopping firewood. In fact, she was such a vigorous worker that after she married and moved away, everyone else Mrs. Perkins hired seemed lazy by comparison.

Masajiro Kataoka died in late 1940. In keeping with Buddhist tradition, Yumi had his body cremated. Since he had always wanted to see Japan again, Yumi and Nee decided to take his ashes back for burial in Yamaguchi. They went in the late fall of 1941. At that time, World War II was raging in Europe, and many feared that conflict would soon erupt between the U.S. and Japan. Nee and her mother got back to California just before that fear came true.

On Sunday morning, December 7, 1941, Sox, her sister Lillian and their mother were riding in the car. A special bulletin on the radio announced that the Japanese had mounted a surprise air attack on the U.S. Naval base at Pearl Harbor, Hawaii. The girls translated the news for Yumi. "This is terrible," Yumi said to them in Japanese. Because she was an Issei ("first generation" Japanese immigrant), she was not a U.S. citizen. Her native country was now the enemy.

Sox and Lillian knew that their lives were about to change. They were Americans, born on American soil. They listened to the same music, followed the same fashions, pledged allegiance to the same flag as everyone else. But now they wondered how other Americans would treat them. They wondered if the storekeepers would still sell them food. Over the next few weeks, shops in towns around the area began posting signs telling Japanese customers to stay away. Old hostilities found new expression in the name of patriotism. There were scattered incidents of violence against Japanese Americans and their property.

The Kataokas had a mailbox at the post office in Centerville. Every morning, Sox went in to pick up the mail. After the Pearl Harbor attack, the postmaster began holding the family's mail at the window instead of putting it in the box, so that Sox had to come and ask him for it. This way, he could ask her questions, such as "How do you feel about the bombing?" or "What do you think is going to happen to you people?" Sox hated this daily confrontation. She kept her answers short and left as quickly as possible.

The question about what was going to happen was partially answered on February 19, 1942. Pres. Franklin D. Roosevelt on that day issued Executive Order 9066, establishing "military areas" along the West Coast and limiting the activities of "any or all persons" within them. Two months later, Civilian Exclusion Order No. 27 narrowed the focus of the restrictions by announcing that "all persons of Japanese ancestry, both alien and non-alien," would be "excluded" from the West Coast. Even Nisei ("second generation"), or those born in America to Japanese parents, were now unwelcome. The order disrupted the lives of 112,000 people, two-thirds of them U.S. citizens.

Evacuation orders posted on telephone poles and public buildings declared that Japanese Americans had one week to prepare to leave their homes. In the meantime, they had to abide by an 8 p.m. curfew and get permits to travel.

The instructions didn't tell people where they would be going, but they did tell them what to bring: only the bare necessities, like clothing and linens and soap. When someone said they could take what they could carry in two hands, the Kataokas took this literally. They had never owned suitcases, so they got a permit to go to a nearby town and buy two each—flimsy cardboard ones, outrageously priced.

Deciding what to pack was easy; getting rid of the rest was not. Anything obviously Japanese could be interpreted as a sign of collaboration with the enemy. Yumi Kataoka burned her family's Japanese books and letters, advertising calendars from Japanese businesses, even her certificates from a Japanese bank. Many people burned family keepsakes such as photographs and antique kimonos.

As for their other possessions, the evacuees had two choices: either leave them to be stolen or sell them at the going rate. One of Yumi's sons sold two cars, a long-bed truck and a Caterpillar tractor for a fraction of their worth. The Kataokas got $15 for their piano, and Sox was so happy to see it going home with someone that she gave the buyer all her sheet music and even threw her tennis racket into the bargain. Some people in the valley refused to trade their brand new stoves or refrigerators for pocket change, so they stored them in the Japanese school building, in hopes of retrieving them when the war was over.

May 9, 1942, was leaving day. A few days beforehand, Mrs. Perkins got in touch with Nee and told her to bring her whole family to the ranch house for a farewell breakfast. The invitation meant a lot to the Kataokas because most of the other white people they knew had shunned them. That morning, Mrs. Perkins ushered them into her beautiful formal dining room. The long table was set with her best

china and crystal and silver. She usually had someone to cook and serve meals for her, but this time she did everything herself. When Nee and Sox offered to help her bring the food out, she told them that now it was her turn to serve.

After breakfast, Mrs. Perkins drove the Kataokas in her Oldsmobile to the grounds of the Japanese school, where buses were waiting. The fellow who ran the local hamburger stand was the only other white person who came to say goodbye. It hurt Sox's feelings that her close friends didn't show up, but she decided the reason was that they were afraid.

Yumi Kataoka had moved her family many times, but never like this. The bus let them out at Tanforan Racetrack in San Bruno, Calif. No one knew what to expect. None of the Kataokas had even been to a racetrack before. Inside, military policemen searched each person. All suitcases were opened and ransacked. A nurse peered into every eye and down every throat.

On the infield of the track stood new, army-style barracks. Sox said that she wanted to stay in those, but the officer said they were for mothers with infants. He led the Kataokas around back to the stables: Their new home was a horse stall.

The building contained two back-to-back rows of 10 stalls each. Five adults—Sox and her three brothers and their mother—had a 9- by 20-foot enclosure to share. Manure littered the dirt floor. The walls had been recently whitewashed, but carelessly, so that horsehair and dirt were smeared in. And the walls reached only halfway to the roof—there were no ceilings. The nearest bathroom was a long walk away.

Sox worried about how her mother would take such humiliation. She was proud of Yumi for keeping the hurt hidden, for acting as if this were just another move. She knew that keeping the family together was Yumi's biggest concern.

The officers passed out cloth sacks for everyone to fill with hay for mattresses. In the dark stall that night, listening to the noises of all the other people, Sox couldn't fall asleep. She couldn't stop wondering what any of them had done to deserve being penned up like animals. She couldn't believe this was happening in America.

It didn't take Sox long to learn the local routine, including how early she had to get up to find an empty tub in the laundry shed. Her brothers washed dishes in the mess hall. There were long lines everywhere—for the toilets, for the laundry, for food. As clothing wore out, people shopped by mail from the Sears Roebuck catalog.

Occasionally, Mrs. Perkins came to visit. When she saw the damp dirt floor of the drafty stall, she went home and ripped up the linoleum from the Kataokas' kitchen and brought it to them. She didn't want Yumi's rheumatism to get worse. Another time, she took Sox's broken wristwatch to have it repaired.

For four long months, daydreams and small acts of kindness made their internment bearable. Every night, Sox wondered what the next day would bring. There was very little official news about the government's plans, so rumors were the main source of information. Late in the summer a rumor went around that the Japanese were going to be moved inland, to a concentration camp in the desert. Everyone started ordering high-top boots from the catalog—there were scorpions and snakes out there. According to some people, once they got to the new location, the government was going to drop a bomb on them.

Some of the rumors turned out to be true. At the end of the summer, Sox, Yumi and the other Japanese were packed into buses and driven east into the desert. Sox had never seen a place as dry and dusty and lifeless as Topaz, Utah. It looked like the surface of the moon. But when she saw the rows and rows of new barracks, some of them still unfinished, she could have kissed the ground. She reasoned that if the government was spending the time and money to build housing for her people, then it must not be planning to kill them.

The Kataokas' new quarters measured 20 by 24 feet—a little roomier than the horse stall and a lot cleaner. A single naked light bulb hung from the ceiling. In the corner stood a pot-bellied stove. By stringing up a few sheets, family members could carve out the illusion of privacy. The communal bathroom had six toilets and no doors.

There were no chairs or tables. People scoured the construction site for materials. In just a short time, many families skillfully fashioned whole sets of furniture from orange crates and scrap lumber. Later, some residents laid out beautiful rock gardens on the barren ground.

Even in this strange new environment, much about camp life was familiar—the crowded living space, the boredom, the long lines for every necessity. But Sox began to notice changes in the people around her. In the dining hall, children made friends quickly and sat together in groups. The family meal—a central part of Japanese life—was losing its importance. A deeper toll resulted from unemployment: Fathers, no longer breadwinners, began to lose their self-respect and, sometimes, the respect of their families. Everyone was aimless now. Everyone was a small step from stir-crazy.

Camp residents had to pull together to avert despair. They formed social clubs and choirs and sports teams. They started newsletters to share information and ideas.

Sox had the good fortune to get a job as assistant block manager. She was responsible for looking after about 200 people in 72 rooms. The managers met every morning to discuss the needs of their residents. Extremes of climate caused many problems, since temperatures often reached well below zero in the winter and over 100 in the summer months. Food was another source of complaint. The animal innards such as liver, gizzard, tongue, brains and chitterlings that made up much of the meat ration were foreign to the Japanese diet. Sox found them sickening. When the quality of meat improved after a while, Sox decided

DOCUMENT

CONFIDENTIAL

After some Japanese Americans attempted to challenge the internment policy in the courts, the War Relocation Authority included the following statements in a confidential internal memo on August 12, 1942.

The action taken with respect to Japanese in this country is justifiable on the grounds of military necessity for several reasons.

1. All Japanese look very much alike to a white person — it is hard for us to distinguish between them. It would be hard to tell a Japanese soldier in disguise from a resident Japanese. The danger of infiltration by Japanese parachutists, soldiers, etc. is, therefore, reduced and the chances of detecting any attempt at infiltration are increased.

2. The Japanese Government has always tried to maintain close ties with and control over Japanese people in this country with the result that many of them have never really been absorbed into American life and culture. Many Japanese-Americans have been educated in Japan. Many, believers in Shintoism, worship the Emperor and regard his orders as superior to any loyalty they may owe the United States. Therefore, the action has reduced the danger of successful invasion by removing an element of the population which had never been assimilated and which might not successfully withstand the strong emotional impulse to change loyalties or give way to their true feelings in the event that Japanese troops should land on our shores.

DOCUMENT

"A GRAVE INJUSTICE"

On August 10, 1988, Congress enacted a law granting restitution payments for civilians interned during World War II.

SECTION. 2. Statement of the Congress

(a) With Regard to Individuals of Japanese Ancestry. — The Congress recognizes that, as described by the Commission on Wartime Relocation and Internment of Civilians, a grave injustice was done to both citizens and permanent resident aliens of Japanese ancestry by the evacuation, relocation, and internment of civilians during World War II. As the Commission documents, these actions were carried out without adequate security reasons and without any acts of espionage or sabotage documented by the Commission, and were motivated largely by racial prejudice, wartime hysteria, and a failure of political leadership. The excluded individuals of Japanese ancestry suffered enormous damages, both material and intangible, and there were incalculable losses in education and job training, all of which resulted in significant human suffering for which appropriate compensation has not been made. For these fundamental violations of the basic civil liberties and constitutional rights of these individuals of Japanese ancestry, the Congress apologizes on behalf of the Nation.

that the project director must have figured out that her people were human.

The block manager meetings gave Sox and the others some sense of value. But everywhere they looked, barbed wire and police patrols and curfews and watchtowers with armed guards constantly reminded them of their status.

"Americanism is not, and never was, a matter of race or ancestry."

The word around camp was "Don't go near the fence." Most of the military policemen were fresh out of combat duty, and they did not hesitate to use their weapons. At Topaz one day, a man was picking some wild-flowers along the barbed wire. A guard yelled "Halt!" but the man was hard of hearing. He kept on picking and was shot. And once, a grandfather playing catch with his grandson went to retrieve the ball from just beyond the fence. The guard who killed him told authorities that the old man had tried to escape.

As the war in Europe and the Pacific intensified, the government realized that many potentially able soldiers were sitting idle in the camps. In early 1943 Pres. Roosevelt wrote to the Secretary of War and contradicted his earlier Executive Order: "Americanism is not, and never was, a matter of race or ancestry. Every loyal American citizen should be given the opportunity to serve this country . . . in the ranks of our armed forces."

By means of a "loyalty questionnaire," Uncle Sam began recruiting Nisei. In all, more than 30,000 Japanese Americans joined the service during the war. Others protested that they wouldn't serve until their families were allowed to return to the West Coast. About 300 so-called "no-no

boys" refused to pledge their loyalty and were jailed for draft resistance. The questionnaire was also used as a means of releasing internees into the work force. In the camps, this process—however objectionable—stirred the first hopes of freedom.

On November 11, 1944, Pres. Roosevelt lifted the Civilian Exclusion Order. A month later, the government announced that the internment camps would be closed within a year.

Sox married a young man named Tom Kitashima in August 1945, just as the bombing of Hiroshima and Nagasaki brought the war to its conclusion. The camp supervisor offered her a job helping to process the closure of the camp. But since he didn't have a job for Tom, Sox said she couldn't stay. Even so, the supervisor found her a good position in San Francisco.

A few nights before Sox and Tom were set to leave Topaz, the supervisor and his wife invited them out for dinner and a cowboy movie in the town of Delta, 16 miles from the camp. There were rules against this kind of socializing, but the white couple didn't seem to care. The supervisor also gave them a blanket for the cold train ride to San Francisco—the government was using old dilapidated railroad cars to relocate the internees. On an October morning in 1945, Sox repacked the suitcase she had been living out of for three years and four months.

Yumi Kataoka, now 60 years old, prepared to move one more time. People were heading in all directions—there was nothing left to go back to. Yumi joined a large group headed for a housing center at Richmond, Calif. In time, Yumi and her scattered children heard reports from the valley that used to be their home. The Japanese school building had been emptied of all the stored appliances. The house that Masajiro had built on Mrs. Perkins' place was gone now, along with all the little things the family had left behind.

Teacher Education in Multicultural Perspective

At a time when minority students are approaching 50 percent of the national student body, few minority students are preparing to be teachers. At the college level, fewer persons of color are choosing teaching as a career. This social reality within teacher education programs in the United States only underscores the need for multicultural education, as well as for course work in specific cultural study areas in the education of American teachers.

Multicultural education of some sort is now an established part of teacher education programs, but debate continues on how it can be integrated effectively into these programs. The National Council for the Accreditation of Teacher Education (NCATE) has established a multicultural standard for the accreditation of programs for teacher education in the United States. Many educators involved in teaching multicultural education have wondered why such course work is so often a segregated area

of teacher education curricula. And many believe that all teacher educators should become knowledgeable in this area. Teaching preservice teachers to respect cultural diversity can enhance their ability to respect individual students' diversity in learning styles and beliefs. All persons who become teachers need to be sensitized to cultural diversity and to the need to learn about the values and beliefs of their students. The demographic changes in Canada and the United States ensure that many North American teachers will have students from a wide array of cultural heritages.

There is still much misunderstanding within the teacher education establishment as to what multicultural education is. This will continue as long as opponents consider it a political rather than an intellectual or educational concept. If all children and young adults are to enjoy school experiences that nourish and respect

their heritages, all teachers must learn those skills that can empower them to study and to learn about diverse cultures throughout their careers. Multicultural education course content in teacher education programs is about both cultural diversity and about individual students from different cultures.

Teachers will have to consider how each student's development is shaped by the powerful force of those values prevailing in his or her home and community. In a civilization rapidly becoming more culturally pluralistic, resistance to overwhelmingly Eurocentric domination of social studies and language arts curricula will continue. By the year 2000 about 5 billion of the projected 6 billion people on Earth will be persons with a non-Eurocentric conception of the world. Scholars in the social sciences, humanities, and teacher education in North America who study minority-majority relations in the schools now realize that the very terms "minority" and "majority" are changing when we speak of the demographic realities in most major urban and suburban educational systems. This is also true when we consider minority-majority relations in vast isolated rural or wilderness areas where those of western or northern European descent are minorities in the midst of concentrations of indigenous peoples. Many teachers will teach students whose values and views of the world are very different from their own, hence the relevance of teachers learning how to learn about human cultures and belief systems in order to study the lives and heritages of their students.

Many teachers of European heritage are having difficulty understanding the importance of the fact that North American society is becoming more culturally pluralistic. From a multicultural perspective, one of the many things course content seeks to achieve is to help prospective teachers realize the importance of becoming lifelong learners. The knowledge base of multicultural education is further informed by the history of the struggle for civil rights in North American societies. Multicultural education in teacher education programs seeks to alter how prospective teachers perceive society as a whole, not just its current minority members. Culturally pluralistic themes need to be apparent throughout teacher education programs and integrated into the knowledge bases of teacher education. Broadly conceived, multicultural education seeks to help members of all ethnic, cultural backgrounds to appreciate one another's shared human concerns and interrelationships; it should not be conceived as simply the study of minority cultural groups. Teachers need to

be prepared in such a manner that they learn genuine respect for cultural as well as personal diversity.

Teachers should be prepared to take a global perspective of the world and to think critically about the issues confronting them, their students, and society as a whole (seen as part of an interdependent community of nations). Multicultural education should not be politicized. It should be a way of seeing the world as enriched by cultural and personal diversity. Preservice teachers should learn from case studies that exemplify and report on how different traditions in childrearing, entry into adulthood (rites of passage), and styles of child-adult interaction in school settings influence the learning styles of different cultures.

The essays in this unit explore why it is important not to see multicultural education as just a political concept, but rather as an area of critical inquiry from which we can all learn alternative styles of teaching appropriate to the learning styles and cultural backgrounds of students. The articles stress the importance of teachers sharing in social interaction in classroom settings and seeing the impact of race, gender, and social class in teachers' formation of their ideas about themselves as teachers, how they perceive other teachers, and how they perceive their students.

This unit's articles are relevant to courses that focus on introduction to the cultural foundations of education, educational policy studies, history and philosophy of education, and curriculum theory and construction, as well as methods courses in all areas of teacher education programs.

Looking Ahead: Challenge Questions

Why is multicultural education so frequently seen as an isolated, segregated part of teacher education programs?

What are the reasons for so much resistance to course work in the area of multicultural education in teacher education programs?

What can we learn about teaching styles and methods from case studies of teachers from cultures other than our own?

Why can it be said that our understanding of the relevance of multicultural perspectives on teacher education emerged from the struggle for human rights in general?

What seem to be the major points of disagreement about the role of multicultural education in teacher education programs?

What attitudes need to change regarding multicultural education?

Multicultural Education Requirements in Teacher Certification:

A National Survey

By Elizabeth D. Evans, Carol C. Torrey,
and Sherri D. Newton

The demographics within the United States have changed dramatically during the past century, and future projections include even greater diversity in the general population. By the beginning of the next century, it is anticipated that the population will include one-fourth to one-third African-Americans, Asians, or Hispanics (Allen & Turner, 1990; Barrett, 1993; Williams, 1992). Minority cultures continue to increase while the majority Euro-American population decreases (Bountress, 1993; Ramirez, 1988: Wrigley, 1992). Due to the changing demographics, minority school enrollment has increased in 44 states during the past decade. Thirty-three states reported minority enrollment that is 20 percent or greater in grades K-12, and 25 of the largest city school systems indicated majority minorities in their school systems (Dana & Floyd, 1993).

While the percentage of minority

Elizabeth D. Evans is a professor, Carol C. Torrey is an assistant professor, and Sherri D. Newton is a graduate student, all with the Department of Special Education at Southeastern Louisiana University, Hammond, Louisiana.

teachers has not significantly increased, the teaching force throughout the school systems in the United States remains predominantly (85 percent) Euro-American, middle class, and female (Burstein & Cabello, 1989; Grant & Sleeter, 1989). In addition, it has been noted that teachers prefer to teach students from their own cultural orientation, because they share common values, expectations, and experiences. Further research findings suggest that most teachers have concerns about working with diverse student populations (Ladson-Billings, 1991; Marshall, 1993; Moore & Reeves-Kazelskis, 1992) and need to examine beliefs, broaden their knowledge and develop abilities for relating to students from diverse cultures (Burstein & Cabello, 1989).

Given the changing demographics and the concerns of teachers, a priority in teacher education programs should be to prepare teachers to work with students from culturally diverse backgrounds (Burstein & Cabello, 1989). The purpose of the study is to investigate multicultural education requirements by the State Departments of Education for issuance of teaching credentials or teacher certification.

Method

A three-part questionnaire was designed to identify State Department of Education requirements in multicultural education. Each State Department of Education was requested to indicate whether or not they required a multicultural education component as part of their certification/credentialing process in elementary, secondary and special education. They were further requested to provide a printed copy of their credentialing requirements for each of the three areas, identifying specific courses or other information on multicultural education. The remaining sections requested the names of contact people responsible for multicultural training at the State Department of Education, and at universities and colleges.

The National Association of State Directors of Teacher Education and Certification Directory was utilized to generate a current list of contact persons for this study. The questionnaire was mailed to the certification offices in the Departments of Education of all 50 states and the District of Columbia. A second mailing and follow-up telephone calls were completed in 1994.

A graduate student tabulated the responses and reviewed the printed materials to provide clarification and additional information. The principal investigators reviewed the responses for consistency and established subcategories within the responses from the State Departments of Education.

Results

Data from 51 (100 percent) questionnaires were analyzed for this study. The responses from the State Departments of Education on whether or not they required courses in multicultural education are found in Table 1. Thirty-two states (62.7 percent) reported that they did not require courses in multicultural education for teacher credentialing or certification, while 19 (37.3 percent) indicated that coursework was required.

Of the 19 responses indicating that coursework was required in multicultural education, two states reported that a specific number of semester hours was required. Alaska required a 3 semester hour course, and North Dakota required a 2 semester hour course in North Dakota Native American studies. Seventeen states identified the coursework as part of the teacher certification process or the university program approval process. The coursework requirement was mandated through various options in different states. States identified their requirements as part of the human relation standards (Iowa, Minnesota, Nebraska), in the professional studies standards (California, Georgia, Indiana, Kentucky and New York), in the general education standards (Kansas), or interspersed throughout the teacher education program standards (Illinois, North Dakota, Massachusetts, Michigan, Oregon, and Washington). One state (South Dakota) reported that each college or university developed coursework for their specific program. In addition, The District of Columbia and Delaware reported that coursework in multicultural education was required; however, specific information was not provided.

Further investigation was completed on the responses from the 32 states which indicated courses were not required for credentialing or certification. Sixteen of the states provided information for clarification of their responses. Five of these states (Hawaii, Missouri, New Mexico, Tennessee, and Virginia) indicated that multicultural education was required only as part of the English as a Second Language program. Two states, Mississippi and New Jersey, reported that inclusion of multicultural education coursework was determined by each university. Nevada,

South Carolina, and Wyoming reported they were revising and strengthening multicultural requirements in teacher certification due to National Council for Accreditation of Teacher Education (NCATE) standards. The remaining six states (Alabama, North Carolina, Ohio, Texas, Vermont, and Wisconsin) reported no requirement in multicultural education. However, upon further investigation of the printed materials sent by these six states, each required a multicultural component as a part of the teacher certification process or the university program approval process.

The questionnaire asked for additional information regarding variation in multicultural education coursework requirements in elementary, secondary, and special education. Only two states (New York and Delaware) indicated variation in requirements for credentialing or certification. Delaware reported a course requirement for secondary education, but not for elementary education or special education. New York reported a course requirement for elementary and secondary education, but not for special education. However, by 1996, certification in special education will be contingent on a valid New York elementary or secondary education certificate, thus ensuring a multicultural education component for all teachers.

A specific contact person for multicultural education training at the State Departments of Education was reported by 26 states. Only 17 of the respondents identified a specific university(ies) or a specific university contact person.

Discussion

The results of this study indicated that 19 states reported requirements for multicultural education. Upon further investigation of materials sent by State Departments of Education, six additional states had criteria similar to these 19 states. Therefore, it can be concluded that 25 of the 51 respondents (49 percent) had state requirements for multicultural education. While this study gathered information from the State Departments of Education, at least one state, California, had an outside agency with responsibility for credentials.

Upon examination of the responses from the State Departments of Education, variations among requirements for certification were noted. This may have resulted from the multiplicity of criteria for state teacher certification, non-issuance of credentials by some states at the preservice level, or the university program development process. Each State Department of

Table 1
State Department of Education Course Requirements in Multicultural Education

YES	NO
Alaska	Alabama
California	Arizona
Delaware	Arkansas
District of Columbia	Colorado
Georgia	Connecticut
Illinois	Florida
Indiana	Hawaii
Iowa	Idaho
Kansas	Louisiana
Kentucky	Maine
Massachusetts	Maryland
Michigan	Mississippi
Minnesota	Missouri
Nebraska	Montana
New York	New Hampshire
North Dakota	New Jersey
Oregon	New Mexico
South Dakota	Nevada
Washington	North Carolina
	Ohio
	Oklahoma
	Pennsylvania
	Rhode Island
	South Carolina
	Tennessee
	Texas
	Utah
	Vermont
	Virginia
	West Virginia
	Wisconsin
	Wyoming

Education has its own systems for developing teacher certification requirements and competencies. This is a continual process that involves change depending on current educational trends. Universities have their own processes and systems to include these state competencies in courses and curricula at their own discretion. Due to time constraints, these two processes often are not working in tandem. Furthermore, it appeared from this survey that few State Departments of Education were aware of personnel at the university level involved in teacher training in multicultural education.

In addition, different interpretations of multicultural education may occur because of the complexity of the definition and the lack of consistency in the identified competencies. It was not part of this study to impose a specific definition of multicultural education, but to allow each State Department of Education to utilize their own concept of multicultural education. Furthermore, most states did not report having a multicultural education contact person at the state department level; thus, the respondent to the questionnaire may have had limited knowledge or interest in the area of multicultural education.

In this study, some states categorized and identified a specific area of their state requirement for inclusion of multicultural education. These areas included competencies in professional studies, general education, field experiences, or human relations. It appears that these were attempts to incorporate multicultural education. This is encouraging, but it appeared that most requirements were isolated with little infusion throughout the teacher education program. The lack of infusion is problematic because experience and research suggest that a specific course in multicultural education is insufficient to change attitudes and beliefs of teachers (Evans, Torrey, & Richardson, in press; Grottkau & Nickolai-Mays, 1989; Larke, 1990). For teachers to accept, value and respect diversity, multicultural education must be integrated and infused in the teacher training program (Larke, 1990; Wahlstrom & Clarken, 1992). This will facilitate an educator's global perspective of multicultural education.

Criteria which were vague and difficult to measure provided a further explanation of the variance in responses. Such phrases as "exposure to cultural diversity" and awareness of "cultural sensitivity" were not defined, but were identified in several state regulations as fulfilling the multicultural education requirement for teacher education credentialing or certification. This exacerbated the complex task of analyzing the criteria established by the State Departments of Education.

Many professionals are beginning to recognize the complex issues involved in the inclusion of multicultural education concepts in teacher education. The National Council for Accreditation of Teacher Education (NCATE) provides an initial impetus to many universities to include multicultural education in their teacher education programs. Professional organizations support the inclusion of multicultural education in teacher education programs. The National Association for Multicultural Education (NAME) contributes to the awareness and importance of multicultural education, and has developed a cadre of professionals that can be utilized by university personnel as resources. However, there are limited means and incentives available for university personnel to strengthen their awareness and knowledge in multicultural education. Yet, it is a critical issue within our profession that needs to be addressed.

Teacher training programs have the responsibility to develop and incorporate requirements for multicultural education, and to further identify specific competencies related to the multicultural content. Ultimately, teacher education programs must provide the tools and knowledge to enable students to learn about their own and other cultural realities (Erdman, 1991; Moore & Reeves-Kazelskis, 1992; Nell, 1993). If this is achieved, teachers will be better prepared to work successfully in a multicultural environment. University faculty must begin the dialogue with State Department of Education personnel to increase requirements and heighten awareness of the importance for multicultural education competencies. It is ultimately the responsibility of the State Departments of Education to ensure inclusion of multicultural education competencies in teacher training programs.

References

Barrett, M.B. (1993). Preparation for cultural diversity: Experiential strategies for educators. *Equity and Excellence in Education*, 26(1), 19-26.

Bountress, N.G. (1993). Cultural-Linguistic issues: Past, present, and future challenges facing teachers. *Preventing School Failure*, 37(2), 26-30.

Burstein, N. D., & Cabello, B. (1989). Preparing teachers to work with culturally diverse students: A teacher education model. *Journal of Teacher Education*, 40(5), 9-16.

Dana, N.F., & Floyd, D.M. (1993, February). Preparing preservice teachers for the multicultural classroom: A report on the case study approach. Paper presented at the annual meeting of the Association of Teacher Educators, Los Angeles, CA. (ERIC Document Reproduction Service No. ED 355 225)

Erdman, K. (1991, November 27). Universities find multiculturalism no simple task. *The Chronicle of Higher Education*, pp. 1, 16, 17.

Evans, E.D., Torrey, C.C., & Richardson, R.C., (in press). A pre-service teacher training module on multicultural education. *Eastern Education Journal*.

Grant, C. A., & Sleeter, C. E. (1989). *Turning on learning*. Columbus, OH: Merrill.

Grottkau, B.J., & Nickolai-Mays, S. (1989). An empirical analysis of a multicultural education paradigm for preservice teachers. *Educational Research Quarterly*, 13(4), 28-33.

Ladson-Billings, G. (1991). Coping with multicultural illiteracy: A teacher education response. *Social Education*, 55(33), 186-194.

Larke, P. J. (1990). Cultural diversity awareness inventory: Assessing the sensitivity of preservice teachers. *Action in Teacher Education*, 12(3), 23-30.

Marshall, P. L. (1993). Concerns about teaching culturally diverse students. *Kappa Delta Pi Record*, 29(3), 73-75.

Moore, T., & Reeves-Kazelskis, C. (1992, November). Effects of formal instruction on preservice teachers' beliefs about multicultural education. Paper presented at the annual meeting of the Mid-South Educational Research Association, Knoxville, TN. (ERIC document reproduction service No. ED 354 231)

Nell, J. (1993). Preservice teachers' perceptions of minority students. *Educational Horizons*, 71, 120-125.

Ramirez, B.A. (1988). Culturally and linguistically diverse children. *Teaching Exceptional Children*, 20(4), 45-51.

Wahlstrom, M. A., & Clarken, R. H. (1992, April). Preparing teachers for education that is multicultural and global. Paper presented at the annual meeting of the American Educational Research Association, San Francisco, CA. (ERIC document reproduction service No. ED 346 033)

Williams, B.F. (1992). Changing demographics: Challenges for educators. *Intervention*, 27(3), 157-163.

Wrigley, J. (1992). Demographic changes in education. In M. Alkin, M. Linden, J. Noel, & K. Ray (Eds.), *Encyclopedia of Educational Research* (pp. 303-309). New York: McMillan.

Cultural Diversity and the NCATE Standards:

A Case Study

Recognition and full accreditation by the National Council for Accreditation of Teacher Education (NCATE) is a goal for most, if not all, university-based teacher education programs. The NCATE standards represent consensus of the professional community regarding the standards for quality in delivery of teacher education at both preservice and graduate levels. The importance of this recognition is clearly evident in the time invested by the institutional candidates both before and after the visit by the accreditation team. While the accreditation process is not without critics (Sutton, 1993; Watts, 1989), meeting the NCATE standards for accreditation is one way a teacher education unit can communicate that its programs have been judged as meeting the state of the art objectives in preparation of teachers.

For many institutions, there is a particular problem associated with two of the NCATE standards. Standard II.B deals with composition of candidates for licensure. To be in compliance, there must be evidence that the unit recruits, admits, and retains a diverse student body. Standard III.B deals with the composition of the faculty. To be in compliance, there must be evidence that the unit recruits, hires, and retains a diverse faculty.

It is not unusual, and in fact may be the norm, for most public state supported institutions of higher education to have an identified weakness in regard to each of these standards. Often neither the student body nor the education faculty represent a culturally diverse population.

While specific percentages will vary according to the data source, the pattern during the first half of this decade indicates a marked discrepancy between the population distribution and the ethnic distribution in the education profession. For example, Table 1 displays selected data from the 1995 edition of the Digest of Educational Statistics. These data indicate that in public elementary and secondary schools, the fall 1993 total enrollment percentages in categories of White/Non Hispanic, Black/Non Hispanic, Hispanic, Asian/Pacific Islander, and American Indian/Alaskan Native were 66, 17, 13, 4, and 1, respectively (p. 60). In contrast, the ethnic distribution percentage of public school teachers in these categories for the same period was 87, 7, 4, 1, and 1 (p. 77). This is a dramatic difference. Approximately one out of every three students is not in the category of White/Non Hispanic.

The chances of a student having a teacher who is not in the category of White/Non Hispanic is closer to one out of ten.

This same discrepancy is evident in data on ethnicity in university faculties. For the combined fields of study, the percentage distributions in the fall of 1992 for White/Non Hispanic, Black/Non Hispanic, Hispanic, Asian/Pacific Islander, and American Indian/Alaskan Native were 87, 5, 3, 5, and 1, respectively (USDE, 1995, p. 237). Comparable data were evident in the education faculty with corresponding percentages of 85, 9, 3, 2, and 1, respectively.

Table 2 displays comparable data for the state served by our institution. The fall 1993 public school percentage distribution for the categories of White/Non Hispanic, Black/Non Hispanic, Hispanic, Asian/Pacific Islander, and American Indian/Alaskan Native were 71, 9, 14, 4, and 2, respectively (USDE, 1995, p. 60). The percentages for ethnic representation in categories of White/Non Hispanic, Black/Non

Table I

	Public School Students	Public School Teachers	University Faculty	Education Faculty
White/Non Hispanic	66	87	87	85
Black/Non Hispanic	17	7	5	9
Hispanic	13	4	3	3
Asian/Pacific Islander	4	1	5	2
Am Indian/Alaskan Nat	1	1	1	1

The data in this table are drawn from the *1995 Edition of the Digest of Educational Statistics*. Public school student and teacher data are for the fall 1993 semester, pages 60 and 77, respectively. University faculty and college of education faculty data are for the fall of 1992, page 237.

From *Multicultural Education*, Spring 1997, pp. 9-11. © 1997 by Caddo Gap Press, Inc. Reprinted by permission of *Multicultural Education*, the magazine of the National Association for Multicultural Education.

Hispanic, Hispanic, Asian/ Pacific Islander, and American Indian/Alaskan Native in our college of education faculty were 92, 3, 2, 3, and 0, respectively. Comparable percentages for the undergraduate students enrolled in the college of education were 83, 5, 6, 2, and 1 respectively.

Even granting that these statistics are imprecise with potential for error associated with self-report and estimation, the contrast between the public school population and the faculty which serve them is stark. A significant proportion of the elementary and secondary students, approximately 1/3 are in categories other than White/Non-Hispanic. These students are very likely, however, to have teachers whose ethnic identification is White/Non-Hispanic, and that teacher is very likely to have been prepared by a teacher educator whose ethnic identification is White/Non-Hispanic. Percentages for both are in the neighborhood of 85 percent.

The data above are, of course, a surprise to no one. The need for increased evidence of diversity in public school teachers led NCATE (Hawkins, 1994) to initiate a two-year support program to reinforce teacher education in historically black colleges and universities. A college of education faculty could argue that the ethnic distribution among faculty in colleges of education is not particularly different from that of other areas in the university, and it would be thus unfair for accreditation standards to require a higher standard of cultural diversity. It would be possible to attempt to make a case that this is a societal problem, not a problem that should be focused on teacher educators. There are, however, significant flaws in such arguments. As teacher educators we should be proactive in problem solving, not content to simply wait for others to respond. The problem of lack of diversity is everyone's responsibility. It is a problem each institution must address.

The similarity in ethnic distributions between college of education faculty and public school teachers would, at the very least, suggest that failure to address the issue of underrepresentation in colleges of education serves to per-

petuate a problem. It may also be significant that statistics on undergraduate enrollment indicate a much higher proportion in categories other than White/Non-Hispanic than is evident in the university faculties. Table 3 displays national university data for the fall of 1992. The undergraduate percentages in the categories of White/Non Hispanic, Black/Non Hispanic, Hispanic, Asian/Pacific Islander, and American Indian/Alaskan Native were 77, 10, 8, 4, and 1, respectively (USDE, 1995, p. 212). Even the comparable data for graduate students (81, 6, 4, 8, 1) suggests that the ethnic distributions among faculty are not representative of the students being served.

Looking at these data in another way, the national percentage of White/Non-Hispanic students enrolled in the public elementary and secondary schools is 66 percent. At the undergraduate level, the enrollment percentage is 77 percent. At the graduate level, the percentage is 81 percent. Of the graduates who become public school teachers or university professors, the national percentage is 87 percent. The pattern is clear.

Identification of the problem is, of course, much easier than solving it. Neither affirmative action programs or minority scholarship programs have proven sufficient to change the pattern. It would appear instead that reducing the ethnic

discrepancy will require a comprehensive approach focused simultaneously on a number of fronts.

This paper is a description of such a program, a comprehensive initiative at a public university in a western state. The individual elements to be described are not unique, but the breadth of approach may warrant replication in other institutions.

The approach to be described below has three major components. First, there is the program designed to enhance the sensitivity of college of education faculty regarding cultural issues; second, there is the effort to provide a strong support system for underrepresented populations enrolled in the teacher education program, and we have initiated in our local public schools a program aimed at solving the problem.

Our university is located in one of the fastest growing metropolitan areas in this country. The metropolitan area is served by a single, unified school district with a total enrollment among the largest of U.S. school districts. We serve approximately 1,600 undergraduate students and 800 graduate students with more than 60 full-time faculty. More than half of the students are in programs seeking initial teacher licensure or advanced training. The college offers Bachelor's, Master's, Specialist's and Doctoral degrees.

Enhancing Sensitivity

There are a number of available resources (Banks, 1994; Baptiste & Archer, 1994; Bowers & Flinders, 1990) with content which could help college of education faculty incorporate multicultural and global perspectives in their programs. Smith (1991) at the annual conference of the American Association for Colleges of Teacher Education presented a particularly comprehensive model. This model, "Toward Defining Culturally Responsible and Responsive Teacher Education," identified and expanded 14 individual knowledge bases with areas of specific objectives for each.

Such resources, however, presume an interested, involved, and motivated faculty. After the NCATE accreditation team called specific atten-

Table 2

	Public School Students	Teacher Education Students	Education Faculty
White/Non Hispanic	71	83	92
Black/Non Hispanic	9	5	3
Hispanic	14	6	2
Asian/Pacific Islander	4	2	3
Am Indian/Alaskan Nat	2	1	0

Public school data in this table are drawn from the *1995 Edition of the Digest of Educational Statistics*, page 60. The percentages in the column of teacher education students column have total of less than 100; the remainder self-reported as "other."

Table 3

	Undergraduate Students	Graduate Students	University Faculty
White/Non Hispanic	77	81	87
Black/Non Hispanic	10	6	5
Hispanic	8	4	3
Asian/Pacific Islander	4	8	5
Am Indian/Alaskan Nat	1	1	1

The data in this table are drawn from the *1995 Edition of the Digest of Educational Statistics*. Student data are for the fall 1992 semester, page 212. University faculty data are for the fall of 1992, page 237.

tion to the weakness of our program in reference to diversity of the faculty and student populations, it seemed evident that attention to motivational and sensitivity factors should precede specific curricular activity. The NCATE visit was in the spring of 1992. With support and en-couragement from the dean of the college, a two-day workshop designed to address this need was planned to coincide with the beginning of the fall 1992 semester.

A team from the National Conference of Christians and Jews was contracted to present the workshop under the heading "Multicultural School: Challenge for the Workplace and the Classroom." To add further credibility to the importance of this activity, the workshop was conducted in the context of an off-campus retreat. All college of education faculty were informed that attendance at the workshop was expected as a part of the faculty requirements during the week preceding the beginning of classes.

The conference was conducted by two trainers who were not associated with the university. A variety of activities were provided including experiential exercises, small group case-study problem solving, attitude surveys, and some content presentation. The college of education was at that time comprised of 63 faculty, the majority of whom participated in the process.

The response of the faculty to the activity was, as expected, mixed. The overall evaluations conducted at the close suggested a satisfactory experience. Some faculty members reported the typical reactions to inservice activities (*i.e.* unnecessary, could have used time better, don't need outsiders to help with this problem). In isolation, a workshop of this type is insufficient to address the larger need. In concert with the other planned activities, however, the workshop was a critical element in the overall plan. All faculty, regardless of their reported reaction, inevitably exited the workshop with a greater sensitivity to the problem and increased awareness that this was a priority in our college of education. Thus, for an institution desiring to address this issue, we recommend beginning with this type of activity. Significantly, each announcement of the activity, and each reminder about attendance, along with the workshop, emphasized that there was a problem which necessitated attention.

As that fall semester began, there was followup to the workshop via memo and faculty meetings. These served as ongoing reminders that while continuing to require a course in multicultural education was important, there was expectation also to infuse it into other curriculum areas as well.

The extent to which this resulted in increased multicultural study is difficult to assess. Clearly though, there was an increase in the extent to which course syllabi were revised to include multicultural education, and a reasonable expectation that this was also reflected in actual course delivery.

It is important to emphasize that the activities described in this paper were not implemented in a program where there was a vacuum regarding the importance of diversity. The specific required course noted above was already in the degree plans. The university had demonstrated commitment to equal opportunity/affirmative action in employment of faculty. University publications included language suggesting the desire for diversity, and there were specific recruiting efforts to increase the extent of diversity in student and faculty. The problem, described in the statistics that began this paper, was that the tactics were not working. Despite the best efforts at remediation, the problem was not going away, and the fact that it was not unique to our college or university was not a sufficient excuse to ignore it.

Increasing sensitivity of the faculty to multicultural issues and increasing the extent to which these were evident in course delivery served more than one purpose. On the one hand, over time, it is reasonable to hope that when these teacher education students completed their programs and entered their own classrooms, they would take with them a perspective they would impart to their students, eventually leading to more non-majority students with a desire to enter the teaching profession. That is an important part of this initiative, recognizing that it will be a long process involving years before the outcome may be evident in actual student enrollment. Concurrent with was a second focus to retain the students already enrolled or contemplating enrollment in the college of education.

Minority Mentoring

Student advisement in the college of education was problematic in delivery of information to students. Recognizing that the system of individual advisors was not working effectively, the college began to use a central advising center for all undergraduate teacher licensure programs. There is no doubt that the central advising center has resulted in a dramatic improvement in the accessibility and accuracy of advising for all students in the college. Missing, however, in such a process is the individual attention of the mentor.

This seems an especially critical feature in assisting the student identified as "at-risk." The data, unfortunately, indicate that a disproportionate number of such students are from minority populations. Special attention was needed to insure that the group of students targeted to help solve the diversity problem received the best possible assistance in negotiating the system. Accurate and rapid information through the central system was only part of the need. To address other aspects of this need, the college of education in the fall of 1992 initiated a special program to provide mentoring for minority students.

The intent of the Minority Mentoring Program was to establish and maintain rapport between the faculty mentors and the culturally diverse students with the specific goal of enhancing their retention and success in the college of education. The program sought to accomplish this through the creation of friendships, networking among the students and faculty, and through peer tutoring. The specific objectives included: (1) providing academic advisement, (2) assisting students in the identification, location, and utilization of support services at the university, (3) helping students feel that they belonged, and (4) instilling in students the belief that they could succeed in attaining a degree.

College of education faculty members were asked to volunteer to serve as faculty mentors. Approximately 39 percent of the college faculty responded to the request. The faculty mentor was asked to meet with the one or more of the 44 students who signed up for the program once every two weeks. The purpose of the meeting was to discuss the student's academic progress, career interests, current work, and any other issues or concerns the student might have. Monitoring the student's academic progress was central to insuring the student's success, so the faculty mentors were asked to keep a journal, documenting and describing each student contact.

Formal evaluation of the effects of the mentoring program is in process. Informal data, however, clearly suggest that the program has successfully personalized the advisement and support offered to the targeted group and increased the feelings of belonging. The latter is well illustrated in a comment by one of the students served, "Having someone I can go to who understands what it's like to feel different really helps a lot."

Project Multicultural Education

While each of the activities described above is an important element in attaining the goal of increasing diversity, the probable outcomes of these two alone would only be incremental. To truly attain the goal of proportional representation of diverse groups in the population of preservice teachers, public school teachers, and university faculty, requires a long-range commitment beginning in the public school experience of the targeted groups. Faculty in our college of education, in partnership with this school district, embarked on an ambitious project to bring a multicultural perspective to the classrooms in the school district.

The goals of this project, of course, go far beyond simply increasing the evident diversity in the student and faculty populations in the college of education. It is our belief, however, that it is only in projects of this scope that there is hope of eventually attaining the desired representation. The attitudes of students about their teachers and thus the profession of teaching are shaped early in the public school experience. As teachers become more knowledgeable about and more sensitive to the value of diversity, non-majority students begin to see themselves as integral, not separate. A teacher who projects a multicultural perspective is more likely to be seen as a role model for previously neglected students. Those students are more likely to perceive the teaching profession as a potential career and more likely to experience motivation toward such career. This, of course, will not and in fact should not happen with each student. But, in the language of Nevada's primary industry, gambling, the "odds" are much higher.

This project involved an ambitious inservice commitment to eventually reach each teacher in the district's elementary and middle schools. From the period of September 8, 1994 through May 2, 1995, the staff development workshop was presented at 116 different schools. Goals for the workshop were to assist the teachers to: (1) recognize the role of self and culture values, personal feelings, attitude, and beliefs in fostering and inhibiting cultural interactions and awareness, (2) promote positive attitudes about cultural differences, (3) identify levels of racism as it relates to cultural differences, (4) explore strategies for understanding and learning about cultural differences, and (5) develop an awareness action plan for the schools/classrooms. A variety of activities were included to facilitate attainment of these objectives during the one-day period. Included were presentation, role playing case studies, improvisations, and simulation activities.

A total of 2,656 teachers participated in this series of workshops, with an average of 23 participants in each workshop. At the conclusion of each workshop the evaluation instrument requested each participant to evaluate the quality of the presentation and to also indicate whether the topic was perceived as important, if something new was learned, whether the information presented would be useful in the classroom, and if the information would be useful in other ways.

Ninety-six percent of the participants were in agreement or strong agreement that multicultural awareness was an important topic. Ninety-one percent of the participants strongly agreed or agreed that something new was learned. Ninety percent reported agreement or strong agreement that the information would be useful in the classroom. Eighty-four percent expressed agreement or strong agreement that the information would be useful in other ways.

These data suggest that the workshops reached a large number of teachers in the district and that overall the teachers responded positively to the experience. Of particular significance may be that more than half of the respondents expressed strong agreement that this information related to multicultural awareness would be useful in their classrooms. Even with the likelihood that not all teachers would follow through with actual change in classroom behavior, these numbers suggest reason for optimism about changes in the classroom atmosphere which eventually will directly and indirectly positively influence diversity in the student body and faculty of teacher education programs.

Summary

This case study is, of course, a "story in process." Following, and influenced by, the identification by an NCATE accreditation team of insufficient diversity in both the student population and college faculty, a major initiative was undertaken. The initiative was designed to bring both a short-term remedy and eventual long-term resolution.

Our first step was to create a workshop to insure that faculty were aware of the importance of solving the problem and increase faculty sensitivity to the issues involved. Behaviorally, this step led to an increase in the extent to which multicultural issues were included in course syllabi and hopefully in course delivery.

With recognition that some students in the targeted emphasis groups could easily lose a central advising system, a special minority mentoring program was implemented. The desired outcome of this program was increased retention of such students in the teacher education program.

With a view toward a long-range solution, a heavy emphasis was placed on a project in conjunction with the local school district. The project was based on the premise that better delivery of multicultural education in the public schools can lead to more proportional representation of diverse groups in all areas of the university, including the teacher education programs.

Our experience with these three facets of our overall initiative is sufficiently positive to suggest that it may provide a useful model for other institutions. This is a multi-faceted problem which clearly will require multi-faceted approaches for resolution. It is our belief that the activities described in this paper along with periodic addition of new initiatives to keep the need in sharp focus can ultimately lead to success. If we are correct, and given that some of the impetus came from the desire to meet NCATE standards, we can echo the sentiments of Coombs and Allred (1993) that the accreditation process contributed significantly to the enhancement of our teacher education program.

—By Porter Troutman, W. Paul Jones,
and Maria G. Ramirez,
College of Education,
University of Nevada, Las Vegas.

References

Banks, J.A. (1994). *An introduction to multicultural education.* Boston, MA. Allyn & Bacon.

Baptiste, H.P., & Archer, C. (1994). A comprehensive multicultural teacher education program: An idea who time has come. In M.M. Atwater, K. Radzik-Marsh, & M. Strutchens (Eds.), *Multicultural education: Inclusion of all* (pp. 63-90). Athens, GA: The University of Georgia.

Bowers, C.A., & Flinders, D.J. (1990). *Responsive teaching: An ecological approach to classroom patterns of language, culture, and thought.* New York: Teachers College Press.

Coombs, C.G., & Allred, R.A. (1993). NCATE accreditation: Getting the most from the self-study. *Journal of Teacher Education, 44,* 165-169.

Hawkins, B.D. (1994). Tradition gives way to change. *Black Issues in Higher Education, 11,* 12-15.

Smith, G.P. (1991). Toward defining a culturally responsible pedagogy for education: The knowledge base for educating teachers of minority and culturally diverse students. Paper presented at the annual conference of the American Association for Colleges of Teacher Education, Atlanta, GA.

Sutton, J.H. (1993). Undermining a profession. *Phil Delta Kappan, 75,* 158-162.

U.S. Department of Education (1995). *Digest of Educational Statistics, 1995* (NCES Publication Number 95-029). Washington, D.C.: U.S. Government Printing Office.

Watts, D. (1989). NCATE and Texas eyeball to eyeball: Who will blink? *Phi Delta Kappan, 71,* 311-318.

FACULTY FEAR:

BARRIERS TO EFFECTIVE MENTORING ACROSS RACIAL LINES

By Andrea Ayvazian

TODAY IN OUR COLLEGES and universities it is both appropriate and necessary that White faculty members engage in active mentoring relationships with students of color. In this article, I want to examine what I believe are some of the barriers to effective mentoring across racial lines, and discuss concrete approaches for dealing with sensitive issues that often arise in the course of the mentoring relationship.

My interest in mentoring across racial lines grows out of my experiences as a faculty member at the Smith College School for Social Work, where for five years I have taught a graduate course on racism and its implications for clinical social work practice, as well as my teaching on the undergraduate level at Mount Holyoke College. It also reflects the comments, stories, and questions I have heard as I have traveled around the country over the last decade with my colleague, Beverly Daniel Tatum of Mount Holyoke College, conducting workshops and seminars on anti-racism for faculty and administrators at colleges and universities.

Faculty members—especially White faculty—are often eager to discuss with me their own experiences teaching and mentoring across racial lines. This seldom happens in public: I hear the most emotional stories and get the thorniest questions in private settings away from colleagues. It is often in the women's room or while walking me to my car that people tell me what is really on their minds, and reveal the concern,

Andrea Ayvazian has been an anti-racism educator since 1985. She is currently the Protestant Chaplain at Mount Holyoke College in South Hadley, Massachusetts.

confusion, and anxiety they have experienced.

In my discussion, I will focus on the feedback and concerns I have heard from **White** faculty. As a legacy of our country's racist past, the overwhelming majority of professors in higher education today are White; consequently, most faculty attempting to be mentors across racial lines are White. In addition, because I too am White, White faculty members have felt particularly comfortable talking to me about their anxieties *vis a vis* these mentoring relationships.

This is not to say that many White faculty members are not enthusiastic about working with students of color. On the contrary, many have expressed excitement about their roles as mentors. But just as men often approach the mentoring relationship with women with particular caution, Whites also bring special concerns and questions to their mentoring relationships with students of color. While I believe that many of my findings apply—with perhaps some subtle twists—to faculty of color mentoring White students, I will leave it to others to explore those relationships as they grow in number.

Finally, while I zero in on relationships between faculty and the students they mentor, I believe that these barriers and approaches may apply to settings beyond the mentoring relationship, or even in all-White situations. As our communities and our classrooms become increasingly multiracial, the issue of race arises more and more frequently in our teaching. Faculty members have told me that they experience an awkward self-consciousness in both racially mixed and all-White classes when racial content emerges

in the course material or in students' questions. If the barriers seem familiar, the actions I suggest for change may prove helpful.

FEAR AS A STUMBLING BLOCK

From my years of teaching and listening, I have become convinced that, for White faculty, the number one stumbling block to effective mentoring across racial lines is **fear**. Whether expressed or denied, I believe that White faculty harbor considerable fear about how well equipped they are to deal with race issues with their students—White students or students of color.

What are we afraid of? I think we fear that we will make a mistake, and, as a result, will be publicly embarrassed or humiliated. We fear that we will reveal to students and colleagues that we don't know all that there is to know about this highly-charged topic. We fear being misunderstood. And then there is the really **big** fear: the fear that we will be labeled racist because of something we say or imply. The sub-set of that fear is that we **are** in fact racist and that it will show.

In other words, White faculty fear that in some way or another we will do badly on the issue of race. In attempting to cope with our anxiety, we choose to do nothing at all. We retreat into that never-never land of colorblindness: "I don't see color." "I'm just colorblind when it comes to my students." This strategy is tempting, and provides some measure of safety, but it has serious drawbacks.

The first is that it simply is not true. Unless one is actually colorblind, one notices color in objects, in nature, and in people—just as one notices gender or height or other physical attributes.

The second problem is that pretending to be colorblind denies an important part of a person's identity. In effect, White people's discomfort with racial difference strips people of color, of a key aspect of their identity—an aspect about which they may have considerable pride. Furthermore, it denies that one's color is of significance in one's daily life—which of course we know it is.

Drawing upon Janet Helms' and William Cross' stages of racial identity development, we know that many students of color are in "Immersion" during their college years—the stage in which they actively explore their racial identity. Assume for a moment that a student of color in this stage is studying with a White professor who is carefully avoiding all references to race and ethnicity. The faculty member may be in one of the very early stages of White racial identity development, possibly "Contact," maybe "Disintegration." The student in Immersion wants to have his or her racial group membership noticed and affirmed, while the faculty member, intent on promoting a colorblind approach, is deliberately not noticing or affirming anything having to do with race. The result is a painful collision of stages—and the student is the one who will suffer. He or she may end up feeling invisible, or may subtly disassociate from the material being studied or from the mentor.

The third problem with pretending to be colorblind is that it signals to our students of color that we are not available for discussions about academic or campus life that involve race content. The students will know—either consciously or unconsciously—that they should cross those topics off the list of the possible discussions they can have with us. It encourages a student to resort to the unfortunate process of "compartmentalization"—that is, in **some** settings, and with some people, it is okay to be "out" as a Black person or a Latino, while in other settings or with other people, it is not.

So what are we to do? We cannot be colorblind, pretending to never notice race, and yet we may be reluctant to push forward and actually initiate dialogue about this sensitive topic. What alternatives are we left with?

MOVING BEYOND OUR FEAR

There is no single, all-encompassing solution; however, there are a number of strategies we can try. In each case, trying requires that we be willing to take risks and to attempt behaviors that probably were not modeled for us in graduate school. It means being self-confident enough to go out on a limb—to initiate dialogue or respond to questions in ways that may at first seem uncomfortable to us—recognizing that precisely what makes us feel uncomfortable may in fact be increasing the comfort level for our students.

I think that the first step in conquering our fear that we are going to do badly when it comes to the issue of race is to recognize that yes, in fact, we probably will.

WHITE FACULTY FEAR THAT IN SOME WAY OR ANOTHER WE WILL DO BADLY ON THE ISSUE OF RACE. IN ATTEMPTING TO COPE WITH OUR ANXIETY, WE CHOOSE TO DO NOTHING AT ALL.

When Whites tell me that they are beginning to actively build close mentoring relationships with students of color, I know they will experience rewards and mutually fulfilling exchanges, but I can only vaguely imagine the specifics. I **can** predict with some certainty that they will make some mistakes. They will say insensitive things. They will say things that they will later regret.

I have yet to meet anyone in America who has perfect clarity on issues of race equity. These issues are too deep, too complicated, and too painful for anyone to have the right response in every dialogue. I assume that the only White people who are **not** experiencing some awkward and sensitive moments with people of color are those Whites who are **avoiding** close personal and professional connections with people of color.

I don't think our fears about making mistakes are causing us to avoid mentoring relationships with students of color; rather, what seems to happen is that we engage in those relationships, but we hold them at arms length. White faculty admit that while they often find that their mentoring relationships with White students become more informal over time, their relationships with students of color remain formal and distant. The students deal with the implications when it comes time to request reference letters, or assistance with professional networking and contacts, or just get support.

How to rectify this? We can recognize again that race is a charged issue in this country. Meaningful cross-racial relationships are multilayered, gratifying, complicated, and often difficult. Pretending that they are not complicated is not real. We can accept that being a **good** mentor does not have to be synonymous with being a **perfect** mentor. We can accept the fact that we will make mistakes in our mentoring relationships with students of color. But when that happens, the world will not implode, we will not have a heart attack on the spot, and our students and colleagues of color will not abandon us.

I speak from experience on this matter. I talk about race all the time, and I have said things that have turned out to be awkward, insensitive, and embarrassing. But life goes on. And I have found that students and colleagues of color can be quite forgiving **when** (maybe I should say **if**) White people's blunders are made in the context of sincerely demonstrating a commitment to anti-racism in our personal and professional lives.

When Whites mentor students of color I propose we assume two roles. The first is "mentor as mentor," the role we usually think of; the second is "mentor as learner," in which we learn from our students, just as they learn from us.

John Dividio, a social scientist at Colgate University, points out that one can make a long list of the reasons why well-intentioned White people carry prejudices and stereotypes in their mental baggage. Given the pervasive nature of personal, cultural, and institutional racism, it is inevitable that we absorb considerable prejudice—not only in our childhood, but also through innumerable images and messages that reenforce the notion that White is attractive, credible, superior: in other words, the standard in contemporary American society.

Dividio says that the other side of the list—the one that indicates how well-meaning Whites may **not** pick up biases—is remarkably short, limited, he says, to lofty principles and abstractions. And so it is necessary to commit and re-commit ourselves to working out of an active, anti-racist agenda.

From my work I am convinced that people really learn when genuine examples are shared and when one allows oneself to be somewhat vulnerable or transparent. And so, to model the fact that we can be committed anti-racists and not be perfect, I want to share a particularly difficult experience that occurred two years ago at a dismantling racism workshop in Albany, New York.

I was co-leading an intensive three-day experience with an African-American man. Twenty of the 48 participants were people of color. During the very first morning, while I was facilitating report backs from a small group exercise, an African-American woman talked about her pain about how people don't understand the history of the slave trade, the "Slave Castles" in West Africa, the Middle Passage, the auction block. The woman became emotional as she recounted pieces of history that she feels are little-known, misunderstood, and undervalued in American history. When she was done, I told her that I thought I understood or could relate to her pain because I am Armenian-American, and because so many people in this country do not know about or acknowledge the genocide of the Armenian people during the early part of this century. And I went on and on about the genocide.

When I was finished, the woman looked at me and said: "Do you know what you just did?" I said no. She said: "You just did what White people do all the time. Rather than sitting with the pain and intensity I had just shared, you shifted all attention to you...your story, your history, your pain. My stories, my pain were just overshadowed while we all focused on you. And White people do that all the time."

Needless to say, I felt badly. All the things I had ever said in workshops about really listening to and honoring people of color washed over me, I understood that stories about Armenian genocide are important and need to be told. But I realized my timing was wrong. I wanted to diminish the messenger so I could discount the message. I wanted to lash back and say that my pain deserved air time too and blah blah blah...but my own words, words I had said so many times before about making mistakes and moving forward, came back to me. And rather than save face, I tried to practice what I preach. I looked at the woman, who was flushed, angry, and empowered, and said the two words that are hard to say but extremely useful in these situations: "Say more." She paused, and then she did say more. She talked about how tired she was of White people always having the last word, and White people being the center of attention like spoiled children, and how she had high hopes for this workshop but now she wanted to leave.

I asked her to come up to the front of the room and dialogue with me in front of the entire group. She came up front, said more

about her feelings and I listened. We all listened. Then I asked her what, if anything, could be done that would make her want to stay in the workshop. She said she was now ready to hear me talk about her reaction to what I did and what I intended to do with her feedback. I told her that I try hard to be a strong anti-racist in all the ways I have found do-able in my family life, my community life, my church life, and my professional life. But

> **NONE OF US HAVE REACHED THE PROMISED LAND WHERE WE ARE FREE OF STEREOTYPES AND PREJUDICES... FOR ME, IT HAS BEEN MORE USEFUL TO PLEDGE CONTINUALLY TO MOVE FORWARD ON THIS JOURNEY RATHER THAN TO BE CRIPPLED WITH SHAME OR TO BE TIED IN KNOTS WITH DEFENSIVENESS OR DENIAL.**

I am still a work-in-progress and I make mistakes that I regret. I told her I understood what I had just done and I felt badly about it. I told her I was willing to grow. I asked her to remain part of the workshop. She agreed to stay. We talked openly about how most groups—including African Americans, Asian Americans, and Armenian Americans—are often self focused, and how those behaviors do not promote inter-group dialogue.

When I say that I have made mistakes over the years I mean **many**—while teaching, while advising and mentoring students, and in workshops. That was just one example. What is important is that we are out there trying, and learning, and stretching ourselves to be active anti-racists, and not hiding from these issues in the safety of non-involvement.

None of us have reached the promised land where we are free of stereotypes and prejudices. And none of us, of any color, need be paralyzed by guilt for absorbing the negative stereotypes and biases that are prevalent in society, or learning unhelpful behaviors that we saw modeled around us. For me, it has been more useful to pledge continually to move forward on this journey rather than

to be gripped with shame or to be tied in knots with defensiveness or denial.

ACTION STEPS: CHANGING OUR BEHAVIOR

Once we begin to move beyond our fear of making mistakes, we can take action. I have found four concrete changes in behavior helpful in mentoring across racial lines.

Change #1. Break the sound barrier—initiate dialogue about race issues. We cannot wait for students of color to talk with us about race issues, or about the ways that racism effects their lives in college or graduate school. Given the power imbalance between students and professors, it may simply be too difficult for them to broach the subject even when they are eager to express thoughts or feelings. It is our responsibility to initiate the dialogue with Latino/a, Asian American, and African American students. As anti-racists we need to defy the old taboo, the non-useful polite tradition that says we don't discuss issues of race and prejudice—including inter-group tensions.

This means that we need to ask students of color direct questions about race-related issues and open the door for honest dialogue. One question I have often used is: "How is it to work with me, a White professor, as your mentor?"

I have also said: "You may have hoped for an advisor who was a person of color. I want you to know I am open to conversations about your thoughts and feelings about race-related issues if, at any time, you want to talk about them."

And: "Issues of race equity are important to me. I try to bring an anti-racist perspective to my teaching and mentoring. Should you want to talk about these issues, please know that I would welcome that dialogue."

I have found that when students hear that they have an invitation to discuss issues involving race with me, including issues arising from the racial difference between the two of us, there is a freedom, an ease, and an avenue for dialogue that is valuable to both of us.

Faculty members have asked me with concern: What if the student is not in the stages of Immersion or Autonomy? What if we initiate dialogue about race issues with a student in Pre-encounter? A person of color in that stage is not going to be delighted with a professor noticing his or her racial group membership and pointing out that dialogue about race issues is legitimate and welcome.

I have had this experience. Several years ago, when I initiated a conversation about race issues with one of my Black students at Smith, she was taken aback. Because of her circle of friends, I made the assumption that she was further along in her racial identity development than, in fact, she was. She was not anticipating me to notice her race and did not think there was anything we needed to discuss.

I did not intend to surprise this student but I don't regret what I said. It seems to me that she had not yet begun to grapple with her racial identity, but it is likely that she would during her college years. What I tried to model for her is a positive acknowledgment of herself as a Black woman, a fact about her that could be a source of pride and empowerment. She may have wanted to deny the significance of being Black in a White world, but I know that her African-American heritage had an impact on her life every single day on a predominately White campus in a predominantly White town.

Did she avoid me entirely after my remark? No. Did she seem cautious and uncomfortable with me for a long while after that? Yes. But, in general, I have decided that I would rather err on the side of talking about race **too much** than not talking about it enough. I think we all need to engage in more open, honest, respectful, and caring dialogue about race, not less.

Change #2. Welcome criticism and feedback. Although it seems antithetical to our very natures (for most of us) it is true that we grow most rapidly with the greatest clarity and authenticity if we welcome feedback—including difficult, hard-to-hear feedback—about our behavior. We love praise and compliments. Tell us that we are good teachers and we cannot hear enough. But when it comes to tough criticism about how we are doing as anti-racist professors, we tend to fortress ourselves against hearing anything negative. When confronted with manifestations of our own racism, we want to shoot the messenger rather than hear the message. "She is hyper-critical. He didn't understand my point. She is too politically correct. He didn't give me a chance."

But we should welcome this feedback and the opportunity it provides for us to move further along a difficult but tremendously important journey. While we want to be continually open to receiving feedback, I believe that we can maintain an attitude of openness and still critique the viability of the feedback we are receiving. I am not indiscriminate about accepting all feedback I receive. But when I know it is useful, I thank people for their criticisms and let them know that my gratitude is sincere. I have been known to say: "Truthfully, this is

hard to hear. But it is important for me to let it in, and it will influence my behavior in the future." Sure, there is a sting. But with a sincere commitment to doing our best for students of all colors, we can welcome information that helps makes the next encounter with a student more fruitful.

As I mentioned earlier, many Whites in our culture are socialized to feel superior to people of color. Consequently, it is hard for most White people to receive any feedback—especially feedback from people of color—that suggests that our prejudices or biases are showing or that we have done something discriminatory. I know that it is hard for any of us to hear critical feedback; however, I believe that we must assume that the feedback we receive as Whites on the issue of race and racism is true until clearly and unequivocally proven to be incorrect. Rather than jump to a ready defense, we need to practice our Lamaze breathing and open our minds and hearts to listen.

It has been a fairly radical step in my own life to counter the subtle training I received growing up and, as an adult, to try to listen attentively to what people of color are telling me about their lives and my behavior and believe that it is true. Sounds simple. It has actually taken quite a bit of self-discipline to put into practice.

Three years ago in a class at Smith, an African American woman raised her hand—about two weeks into the course—and told me in front of some 25 students that although it was hard for her to say this, she had observed that I called on the White students more often than I called on the students of color. This was not good news. It was not an easy moment. My first impulse was to deny that this could possibly be true and to find a way to discredit the student. But I remembered my little pledge to myself about listening to and believing people of color and I took a deep breath.

Of course I would have sworn that I was long past such inappropriate behavior. Unfortunately, my behavior was completely congruent with the findings of researchers like David and Myra Sadker. In fact, the student was right and she had been keeping a score card to prove it. With the entire class in a hushed state of tension, I told my student that her feedback was hard for me to hear but important nevertheless. We had some discussion back and forth, and after a few minutes I was able to honestly thank her and also to say that I promised I would not overcompensate and call on the students of color when they were simply scratching their nose or reaching for their purse. After a laugh, we went on with the class.

Change #3. Take off the rose-colored glasses. Our friends, colleagues, and stu-

dents who are of color are experiencing a world each day that White people cannot relate to. We certainly have made strides in this country in reducing the overt and ugly forms of racism that were prevalent prior to the 1950s and 60s. However, "neo-racism"—the racism of the 80s and 90s—is still painful, limiting, grinding, and (usually) far more subtle than in years past. As mentors or advisors to students of color, we must remember that they are probably confronting both overt and subtle forms of racism frequently, not only in the wider world but also on the campus and in their classrooms.

Students of color have told me repeatedly that when they recount to White friends or professors some of the comments, incidents, or interactions they have experienced, their stories are met with disbelief and denial. Whites tend to wear rose-colored glasses around race issues, and not see the scope or breath of the problem as it exists in contemporary American society. Furthermore, White people tend to blame the victim for their own racial targeting.

Students of color tell me that their White professors regularly jump to the defense of other professors—even those they have never met—when the student recounts what she or he believes is a racist incident. We have a tendency to explain away colleagues' racial insensitivity. A mentee, who is of color, tells you confidentially that Dr. So-and-So in class XYZ has made demeaning comments, or has an all White reading list that he or she defends tooth and nail, or has missed two consecutive appointments with your mentee, or whatever. Your mentee believes that these incidents have racial content. And then you tell your mentee that Dr. So-and-So doesn't have a prejudiced bone in his or her body.

For some reason, some faculty members are seized by hyper-loyalty when they hear about a colleague's prejudicial behavior. I am reminded of Christine Sleeter's discussion of "White racial bonding": the unspoken ties, loyalties, and assumed understanding that passes between White people. I think this phenomenon helps to explain this tendency to over-defend White colleagues accused of discriminatory behavior. And yet again, the basic principles of listening to and believing people of color become essential. If we listen to and believe our students, we will not silence them by over-protecting our peers.

Change #4. Avoid the temptation of "over-identification" with our students. As mentors, we often have the impulse to smooth the road ahead for our mentees and to relate our successful problem-solving techniques to them for their guidance and support. This is well-meaning and may be useful, but I have been brought up short by offering what I considered tried and true problem-solving skills to students I was mentoring—only to be told later that my advice was only moderately helpful. In fact, the students of color with whom I work have different experiences each day because of their race than I had in college or graduate school. I have learned that it is best for me not to assume that **their** experiencees on campus, in large introductory courses, in labs, in the dorm, and so on is anything like **mine** 25 years earlier. As a White person at predominately White schools, I experienced numerous privileges unavailable to the students of color whom I mentor.

I had a minor but revealing incident two years ago at Smith. I was working with three Asian-American students who were discussing literature by and about Asian-American women in an independent study course. During one of our sessions, one of the women told us that she wanted to share with her mother some of the literature she had read and some insights. I launched into what I thought was a helpful, certainly a lengthy explanation of how she might approach this.

Soon afterwards, fairly quiet, she left my office.

Shortly after she was gone, realizing I had said too much, I set up another meeting with her. When we met, I told her that I thought perhaps I had talked too much and listened too little—and that I had given her excellent advice if she were an Armenian woman in her forties who had my mother as one of her parents. She thought that maybe that was true. I asked her to tell me about the challenge she felt she was facing. She talked, I listened. And after a while, convinced that she would take a quite different approach than the one I had elaborated the day before, she thanked me for my help and left. As I said earlier, our students can be quite forgiving!

CONCLUSION

I believe that strengthening our skills to mentor students across racial lines is one of the small but important steps we can take on the continuing journey toward equity in academia. Striving to be effective and caring mentors, whatever the race of our students, is a process that involves being open, proactive, willing to make mistakes, and both brave and humble.

It is a journey. It's a difficult process but it's worth it. We are not required to be perfect in our efforts, but we do need to try new behaviors and be prepared to stumble and then to continue. As I have tried to model throughout this essay, mistakes are tremendous opportunities for growth.

REFERENCES

Helms, J. E., ed. (1990). *Black and White Racial Identity: Theory, Research and Practice*. Westport, CT: Greenwood Press.

Cross, W. (1991). *Shades of Black: Diversity in African-American Identity*. Philadelphia, PA: Temple University Press.

Cross, W. (1978). "The Cross and Thomas Models of Psychological Nigrescence," *Journal of Black Psychology*, vol. 5, no. 1.

Sleeter, C. (1994). "White Racism," *Multicultural Education*, Spring.

Tatum, B. D. (1992). "Talking About Race, Learning About Racism: The Application of Racial Identity Development Theory in the Classroom," *Harvard Educational Review*, vol. 62, no. 1, Spring.

What Matters Most

A Competent Teacher for Every Child

BY LINDA DARLING-HAMMOND

The report of the National Commission on Teaching and America's Future offers a blueprint for recruiting, preparing, supporting, and rewarding excellent educators in all of America's schools, according to Ms. Darling-Hammond. For the details, read on.

We propose an audacious goal . . . by the year 2006, America will provide all students with what should be their educational birthright: access to competent, caring, and qualified teachers.[1]

WITH THESE words, the National Commission on Teaching and America's Future summarized its challenge to the American public. After two years of intense study and discussion, the commission—a 26-member bipartisan blue-ribbon panel supported by the Rockefeller Foundation and the Carnegie Corporation of New York—concluded that the reform of elementary and secondary education depends first and foremost on restructuring its foundation, the teaching profession. The restructuring, the commission made clear, must go in two directions: toward increasing teachers' knowledge to meet the demands they face and toward redesigning schools to support high-quality teaching and learning.

The commission found a profession that has suffered from decades of ne-

LINDA DARLING-HAMMOND is William F. Russell Professor of Education at Teachers College, Columbia University, New York, N.Y., and executive director of the National Commission on Teaching and America's Future. She is a member of the Kappan *Board of Editorial Consultants.*

glect. By the standards of other professions and other countries, U.S. teacher education has historically been thin, uneven, and poorly financed. Teacher recruitment is distressingly ad hoc, and teacher salaries lag significantly behind those of other professions. This produces chronic shortages of qualified teachers in fields like mathematics and science and the continual hiring

From *Phi Delta Kappan*, November 1996, pp. 193-200. © 1996 by the National Commission on Teaching and America's Future. Reprinted by permission.

of large numbers of "teachers" who are unprepared for their jobs.

Furthermore, in contrast to other countries that invest most of their education dollars in well-prepared and well-supported teachers, half of the education dollars in the United States are spent on personnel and activities outside the classroom. A lack of standards for students and teachers, coupled with schools that are organized for 19th-century learning, leaves educators without an adequate foundation for constructing good teaching. Under these conditions, excellence is hard to achieve.

The commission is clear about what needs to change. No more hiring unqualified teachers on the sly. No more nods and winks at teacher education programs that fail to prepare teachers properly. No more tolerance for incompetence in the classroom. Children are compelled to attend school. Every state guarantees them equal protection under the law, and most promise them a sound education. In the face of these obligations, students have a right to competent, caring teachers who work in schools organized for success.

The commission is also clear about what needs to be done. Like the Flexner report that led to the transformation of the medical profession in 1910, this report, *What Matters Most: Teaching for America's Future*, examines successful practices within and outside the United States to describe what works. The commission concludes that children can reap the benefits of current knowledge about teaching and learning only if schools and schools of education are dramatically redesigned.

The report offers a blueprint for recruiting, preparing, supporting, and rewarding excellent educators in all of America's schools. The plan is aimed at ensuring that all schools have teachers with the knowledge and skills they need to enable all children to learn. If a caring, qualified teacher for every child is the most important ingredient in education reform, then it should no longer be the factor most frequently overlooked.

At the same time, such teachers must have available to them schools and school systems that are well designed to achieve their key academic mission: they must be focused on clear, high standards for students; organized to provide a coherent, high-quality curriculum across the grades; and designed to support teachers' collective work and learning.

We note that this challenge is accompanied by an equally great opportunity; over the next decade we will recruit and hire more than two million teachers for America's schools. More than half of the teachers who will be teaching 10 years from now will be hired during the next decade. If we can focus our energies on providing this generation of teachers with the kinds of knowledge and skills they need to help students succeed, we will have made an enormous contribution to America's future.

The Nature of the Problem

The education challenge facing the U.S. is not that its schools are not as good as they once were. It is that schools must help the vast majority of young people reach levels of skill and competence that were once thought to be within the reach of only a few.

After more than a decade of school reform, America is still a very long way from achieving its educational goals. Instead of all children coming to school ready to learn, more are living in poverty and without health care than a decade ago.[2] Graduation rates and student achievement in most subjects have remained flat or have increased only slightly.[3] Fewer than 10% of high school students can read, write, compute, and manage scientific material at the high levels required for today's "knowledge work" jobs.[4]

This distance between our stated goals and current realities is not due to lack of effort. Many initiatives have been launched in local communities with positive effects. Nonetheless, we have reached an impasse in spreading these promising efforts to the system as a whole. It is now clear that most schools and teachers cannot produce the kind of learning demanded by the new reforms—not because they do not want to, but because they do not know how, and the systems they work in do not support their efforts to do so.

The Challenge for Teaching

A more complex, knowledge-based, and multicultural society creates new expectations for teaching. To help diverse learners master more challenging content, teachers must go far beyond dispensing information, giving a test, and giving a grade. They must themselves know their subject areas deeply, and they must understand how students think, if they are to create experiences that actually work to produce learning.

Developing the kind of teaching that is needed will require much greater clarity about what students need to learn in order to succeed in the world that awaits them and what teachers need to know and do in order to help students learn it. Standards that reflect these imperatives for student learning and for teaching are largely absent in our nation today. States are just now beginning to establish standards for student learning.

Standards for teaching are equally haphazard. Although most parents might assume that teachers, like other professionals, are educated in similar ways so that they acquire common knowledge before they are admitted to practice, this is not the case. Unlike doctors, lawyers, accountants, or architects, all teachers do not have the same training. Some teachers have very high levels of skills—particularly in states that require a bachelor's degree in the discipline to be taught—along with coursework in teaching, learning, curriculum, and child development; extensive practice teaching; and a master's degree in education. Others learn little about their subject matter or about teaching, learning, and child development—particularly in states that have low requirements for licensing.

And while states have recently begun to require some form of testing for a teaching license, most licensing exams are little more than multiple-choice tests of basic skills and general knowledge, widely criticized by educators and experts as woefully inadequate to measure teaching skill.[5] Furthermore, in many states the cutoff scores are so low that there is no effective standard for entry.

These difficulties are barely known to the public. The schools' most closely held secret amounts to a great national shame: roughly one-quarter of newly hired American teachers lack the qualifications for their jobs. More than 12% of new hires enter the classroom without any formal training at all, and another 14% arrive without fully meeting state standards.

Although no state will permit a person to write wills, practice medicine, fix plumbing, or style hair without completing training and passing an examination, more than 40 states allow districts to hire teachers who have not met basic requirements. States pay more attention to the qualifications of the veterinarians treating America's pets than to those of the people educating the nation's youngsters. Consider the following facts:

- In recent years, more than 50,000 people who lack the training required for their jobs have entered teaching annually on emergency or substandard licenses.[6]

- Nearly one-fourth (23%) of all secondary teachers do not have even a minor in their main teaching field. This is true for more than 30% of mathematics teachers.[7]
- Among teachers who teach a second subject, 36% are unlicensed in that field, and 50% lack a minor in it.[8]
- Fifty-six percent of high school students taking physical science are taught by out-of-field teachers, as are 27% of those taking mathematics and 21% of those taking English.[9] The proportions are much greater in high-poverty schools and lower-track classes.
- In schools with the highest minority enrollments, students have less than a 50% chance of getting a science or mathematics teacher who holds a license and a degree in the field in which he or she teaches.[10]

In the nation's poorest schools, where hiring is most lax and teacher turnover is constant, the results are disastrous. Thousands of children are taught throughout their school careers by a parade of teachers without preparation in the fields in which they teach, inexperienced beginners with little training and no mentoring, and short-term substitutes trying to cope with constant staff disruptions.[11] It is more surprising that some of these children manage to learn than that so many fail to do so.

Current Barriers

Unequal resources and inadequate investments in teacher recruitment are major problems. Other industrialized countries fund their schools equally and make sure there are qualified teachers for all of them by underwriting teacher preparation and salaries. However, teachers in the U.S. must go into substantial debt to become prepared for a field that in most states pays less than any other occupation requiring a college degree.

This situation is not necessary or inevitable. The hiring of unprepared teachers was almost eliminated during the 1970s with scholarships and loans for college students preparing to teach, Urban Teacher Corps initiatives, and master of arts in teaching (MAT) programs, coupled with wage increases. However, the cancellation of most of these recruitment incentives in the 1980s led to renewed shortages when student enrollments started to climb once again, especially in cities. Be-

tween 1987 and 1991, the proportion of well-qualified new teachers—those entering teaching with a college major or minor and a license in their fields—actually declined from about 74% to 67%.[12]

There is no real system for recruiting, preparing, and developing America's teachers. Major problems include:

Inadequate teacher education. Because accreditation is not required of teacher education programs, their quality varies widely, with excellent programs standing alongside shoddy ones that are allowed to operate even when they do an utterly inadequate job. Too many American universities still treat their schools of education as "cash cows" whose excess revenues are spent on the training of doctors, lawyers, accountants, and almost any students other than prospective teachers themselves.

Slipshod recruitment. Although the share of academically able young people entering teaching has been increasing, there are still too few in some parts of the country and in critical subjects like mathematics and science. Federal incentives that once existed to induce talented people into high-need fields and locations have largely been eliminated.

Haphazard hiring and induction. School districts often lose the best candidates because of inefficient and cumbersome hiring practices, barriers to teacher mobility, and inattention to teacher qualifications. Those who do get hired are typically given the most difficult assignments and left to sink or swim, without the kind of help provided by internships and residencies in other professions. Isolated behind classroom doors with little feedback or help, as many as 30% leave in the first few years, while others learn merely to cope rather than to teach well.

Lack of professional development and rewards for knowledge and skill. In addition to the lack of support for beginning teachers, most school districts invest little in ongoing professional development for experienced teachers and spend much of these limited resources on unproductive "hit-and-run" workshops. Furthermore, most U.S. teachers have only three to five hours each week for planning. This leaves them with almost no regular time to consult together or to learn about new teaching strategies, unlike their peers in many European and Asian countries who spend between 15 and 20 hours per week working jointly on refining lessons and learning about new methods.

The teaching career does not encourage teachers to develop or use growing expertise. Evaluation and tenure decisions often lack a tangible connection to a clear vision of high-quality teaching, important skills are rarely rewarded, and—when budgets must be cut—professional development is often the first item sacrificed. Historically, the only route to advancement in teaching has been to leave the classroom for administration.

In contrast, many European and Asian countries hire a greater number of better-paid teachers, provide them with more extensive preparation, give them time to work together, and structure schools so that teachers can focus on teaching and can come to know their students well. Teachers share decision making and take on a range of professional responsibilities without leaving teaching. This is possible because these other countries invest their resources in many more classroom teachers—typically constituting 60% to 80% of staff, as compared to only 43% in the United States—and many fewer nonteaching employees.[13]

Schools structured for failure. Today's schools are organized in ways that support neither student learning nor teacher learning well. Teachers are isolated from one another so that they cannot share knowledge or take responsibility for overall student learning. Technologies that could enable alternative uses of personnel and time are not yet readily available in schools, and few staff members are prepared to use them. Moreover, too many people and resources are allocated to jobs and activities outside of classrooms, on the sidelines rather than at the front lines of teaching and learning.

High-performance businesses are abandoning the organizational assumptions that led to this way of managing work. They are flattening hierarchies, creating teams, and training employees to take on wide responsibilities using technologies that allow them to perform their work more efficiently. Schools that have restructured their work in these ways have been able to provide more time for teachers to work together and more time for students to work closely with teachers around more clearly defined standards for learning.[14]

Goals for the Nation

To address these problems, the commission challenges the nation to embrace a set of goals that will put us on the path to serious, long-term improvements in teaching and learning for America. The commission has six goals for the year 2006.

- All children will be taught by teachers who have the knowledge, skills, and commitment to teach children well.
- All teacher education programs will meet professional standards, or they will be closed.
- All teachers will have access to high-quality professional development, and they will have regularly scheduled time for collegial work and planning.
- Both teachers and principals will be hired and retained based on their ability to meet professional standards of practice.
- Teachers' salaries will be based on their knowledge and skills.
- High-quality teaching will be the central investment of schools. Most education dollars will be spent on classroom teaching.

The Commission's Recommendations

The commission's proposals provide a vision and a blueprint for the development of a 21st-century teaching profession that can make good on the nation's educational goals. The recommendations are systemic in scope—not a recipe for more short-lived pilot and demonstration projects. They describe a new infrastructure for professional learning and an accountability system that ensures attention to standards for educators as well as for students at every level: national, state, district, school, and classroom.

The commission urges a complete overhaul in the systems of teacher preparation and professional development to ensure that they reflect current knowledge and practice. This redesign should create a continuum of teacher learning based on compatible standards that operate from recruitment and preservice education through licensing, hiring, and induction into the profession, to advanced certification and ongoing professional development.

The commission also proposes a comprehensive set of changes in school organization and management. And finally, it recommends a set of measures for ensuring that only those who are competent to teach or to lead schools are allowed to enter or to continue in the profession—a starting point for creating professional accountability. The specific recommendations are enumerated below.

1. Get serious about standards for both students and teachers. "The Commission recommends that we renew the national promise to bring every American child up to world-class standards in core academic areas and to develop and enforce rigorous standards for teacher preparation, initial licensing, and continuing development."

With respect to student standards, the commission believes that every state should work on incorporating challenging standards for learning—such as those developed by professional bodies like the National Council of Teachers of Mathematics—into curriculum frameworks and new assessments of student performance. Implementation must go beyond the tautology that "all children can learn" to examine what they should learn and how much they need to know.

Standards should be accompanied by benchmarks of performance—from "acceptable" to "highly accomplished"—so that students and teachers know how to direct their efforts toward greater excellence.

Clearly, if students are to achieve high standards, we can expect no less from teachers and other educators. Our highest priority must be to reach agreement on what teachers should know and be able to do in order to help students succeed. Unaddressed for decades, this task has recently been completed by three professional bodies: the National Council for Accreditation of Teacher Education (NCATE), the Interstate New Teacher Assessment and Support Consortium (INTASC), and the National Board for Professional Teaching Standards (the National Board). Their combined efforts to set standards for teacher education, beginning teacher licensing, and advanced certification outline a continuum of teacher development throughout the career and offer the most powerful tools we have for reaching and rejuvenating the soul of the profession.

These standards and the assessments that grow out of them identify what it takes to be an effective teacher: subject-matter expertise coupled with an understanding of how children learn and develop; skill in using a range of teaching strategies and technologies; sensitivity and effectiveness in working with students from diverse backgrounds; the ability to work well with parents and other teachers; and assessment expertise capable of discerning how well children are doing, what they are learning, and what needs to be done next to move them along.

The standards reflect a teaching role in which the teacher is an instructional leader who orchestrates learning experiences in response to curriculum goals and student needs and who coaches students to high levels of independent performance. To advance standards, the commission recommends that states:

- establish their own professional standards boards;
- insist on professional accreditation for all schools of education;
- close inadequate schools of education;
- license teachers based on demonstrated performance, including tests of subject-matter knowledge, teaching knowledge, and teaching skill; and
- use National Board standards as the benchmark for accomplished teaching.

2. Reinvent teacher preparation and professional development. "The Commission recommends that colleges and schools work with states to redesign teacher education so that the two million teachers to be hired in the next decade are adequately prepared and so that all teachers have access to high-quality learning opportunities."

For this to occur, states, school districts, and education schools should:

- organize teacher education and professional development around standards for students and teachers;
- institute extended, graduate-level teacher preparation programs that provide yearlong internships in a professional development school;
- create and fund mentoring programs for beginning teachers, along with evaluation of teaching skills;
- create stable, high-quality sources of professional development—and then allocate 1% of state and local spending to support them, along with additional matching funds to school districts;
- organize new sources of professional development, such as teacher academies, school/university partnerships, and learning networks that transcend school boundaries; and
- make professional development an ongoing part of teachers' daily work.

If teachers are to be ready to help their students meet the new standards that are now being set for them, teacher preparation and professional development programs must consciously examine the expectations embodied in new curriculum frameworks and assessments and understand what they imply for teaching and for learning to teach. Then they must develop effective strategies for preparing teachers to teach in these much more demanding ways.

Over the past decade, many schools of education have changed their programs to incorporate new knowledge. More than 300 have developed extended programs that add a fifth (and occasionally a sixth) year of undergraduate training. These programs allow beginning teachers to complete a degree in their subject area as well as to acquire a firmer grounding in teaching skills. They allow coursework to be connected to extended practice teaching in schools—ideally, in professional development schools that, like teaching hospitals in medicine, have a special mission to support research and training. Recent studies show that graduates of extended programs are rated as better-prepared and more effective teachers and are far more likely to enter and remain in teaching than are their peers from traditional four-year programs.[15]

New teachers should have support from an expert mentor during the first year of teaching. Research shows that such support improves both teacher effectiveness and retention.[16] In the system we propose, teachers will have completed initial tests of subject-matter and basic teaching knowledge before entry and will be ready to undertake the second stage—a performance assessment of teaching skills—during this first year.

Throughout their careers, teachers should have ongoing opportunities to update their skills. In addition to time for joint planning and problem solving with in-school colleagues, teachers should have access to networks, school/university partnerships, and academies where they can connect with other educators to study subject-matter teaching, new pedagogies, and school change. The benefit of these opportunities is that they offer sustained work on problems of practice that are directly connected to teachers' work and student learning.

3. Overhaul teacher recruitment and put qualified teachers in every classroom. "The Commission recommends that states and school districts pursue aggressive policies to put qualified teachers in every classroom by providing financial incentives to correct shortages, streamlining hiring procedures, and reducing barriers to teacher mobility."

Although each year the U.S. produces more new teachers than it needs, shortages of qualified candidates in particular fields (e.g., mathematics and science) and particular locations (primarily inner city and rural) are chronic.

In large districts, logistics can overwhelm everything else. It is sometimes the case that central offices cannot find out about classroom vacancies, principals are left in the dark about applicants, and candidates cannot get any information at all.

Finally, it should be stressed that large pools of potential mid-career teacher entrants—former employees of downsizing corporations, military and government retirees, and teacher aides already in the schools—are for the most part untapped.

To remedy these situations, the commission suggests the following actions:

- increase the ability of financially disadvantaged districts to pay for qualified teachers and insist that school districts hire only qualified teachers;
- redesign and streamline hiring at the district level—principally by creating a central "electronic hiring hall" for all qualified candidates and establishing cooperative relationships with universities to encourage early hiring of teachers;
- eliminate barriers to teacher mobility by promoting reciprocal interstate licensing and by working across states to develop portable pensions;
- provide incentives (including scholarships and premium pay) to recruit teachers for high-need subjects and locations; and
- develop high-quality pathways to teaching for recent graduates, mid-career changers, paraprofessionals already in the classroom, and military and government retirees.

4. Encourage and reward knowledge and skill. "The Commission recommends that school districts, states, and professional associations cooperate to make teaching a true profession, with a career continuum that places teaching at the top and rewards teachers for their knowledge and skills."

Schools have few ways of encouraging outstanding teaching, supporting teachers who take on the most challenging work, or rewarding increases in knowledge and skill. Newcomers who enter teaching without adequate preparation are paid at the same levels as those who enter with highly developed skills. Novices take on exactly the same kind of work as 30-year veterans, with little differentiation based on expertise. Mediocre teachers receive the same rewards as outstanding ones. And unlicensed "teachers" are placed on the same salary schedule as licensed teachers in high-demand fields such as mathematics and science or as teachers licensed in two or more subjects.

One testament to the inability of the existing system to understand what it is doing is that it rewards experience with easier work instead of encouraging senior teachers to deal with difficult learning problems and tough learning situations. As teachers gain experience, they can look forward to teaching in more affluent schools, working with easier schedules, dealing with "better" classes, or moving out of the classroom into administration. Teachers are rarely rewarded for applying their expertise to the most challenging learning problems or major needs of the system.

To address these issues, the commission recommends that state and local education agencies:

- develop a career continuum linked to assessments and compensation systems that reward knowledge and skill (e.g., the ability to teach expertly in two or more subjects, as demonstrated by additional licenses, or the ability to pass examinations of teaching skill, such as those offered by INTASC and the National Board);
- remove incompetent teachers through peer review programs that provide necessary assistance and due process; and
- set goals and enact incentives for National Board certification in every district, with the aim of certifying 105,000 teachers during the next 10 years.

If teaching is organized as are other professions that have set consistent licensing requirements, standards of practice, and assessment methods, then advancement can be tied to professional growth and development. A career continuum that places teaching at the top and supports growing expertise should 1) recognize accomplishment, 2) anticipate that teachers will continue to teach while taking on other roles that allow them to share their knowledge, and 3) promote continued skill development related to clear standards.

Some districts, such as Cincinnati and Rochester, New York, have already begun to develop career pathways that tie evaluations to salary increments at key stages as teachers move from their *initial license* to *resident teacher* (under the supervision of a mentor) to the designation of *professional teacher*. The major decision to grant *tenure* is made after rigorous evaluation of performance (including both administrator and peer review) in the first several years of teaching. Advanced certification from the National Board for Professional Teaching Standards may qualify teachers for another salary step and/or for the position of lead teacher—a role that is awarded to those who have demonstrated high levels of competence and want to serve as mentors or consulting teachers.

One other feature of a new compensation system is key. The central importance of teaching to the mission of schools should be acknowledged by having the highest-paid professional in a school system be an experienced, National Board-certified teacher. As in other professions, roles should become less distinct. The jobs of teacher, consultant, supervisor, principal, curriculum developer, researcher, mentor, and professor should be hyphenated roles, allowing many ways for individuals to use their talents and expertise without abandoning the core work of the profession.

5. Create schools that are organized for student and teacher success. "The Commission recommends that schools be restructured to become genuine learning organizations for both students and teachers: organizations that respect learning, honor teaching, and teach for understanding."

Many experts have observed that the demands of serious teaching and learning bear little relationship to the organization of the typical American school. Nothing more clearly reveals this problem than how we allocate the principal resources of school—time, money, and people. Far too many sit in offices on the sidelines of the school's core work, managing routines rather than improving learning. Our schools are bureaucratic inheritances from the 19th century, not the kinds of learning organizations required for the 21st century.

Across the United States, the ratio of school staff to students is 1 to 9 (with "staff" including district employees, school administrators, teachers, instructional aides, guidance counselors, librarians, and support staff). However, actual class size averages about 24 and reaches 35 or more in some cities. Teaching loads for high school teachers generally exceed 100 students per day. Yet many schools have proved that it is possible to restructure adults' use of time so that more teachers and administrators actually work in the classroom, face-to-face with students on a daily basis, thus reducing class sizes

while creating more time for teacher collaboration. They do this by creating teams of teachers who share students; engaging almost all adults in the school in these teaching teams, where they can share expertise directly with one another; and reducing pullouts and nonteaching jobs.

Schools must be freed from the tyrannies of time and tradition to permit more powerful student and teacher learning. To accomplish this the commission recommends that state and local boards work to:

- flatten hierarchies and reallocate resources to invest more in teachers and technology and less in nonteaching personnel;
- provide venture capital in the form of challenge grants that will promote learning linked to school improvement and will reward effective team efforts; and
- select, prepare, and retain principals who understand teaching and learning and who can lead high-performing schools.

If students have an inalienable right to be taught by a qualified teacher, teachers have a right to be supervised by a highly qualified principal. The job began as that of a "principal teacher," and this conception is ever more relevant as the focus of the school recenters on academic achievement for students. Principals should teach at least part of the time (as do most European, Asian, and private school directors), and they should be well prepared as instructional leaders, with a solid understanding of teaching and learning.

Next Steps

Developing recommendations is easy. Implementing them is hard work. The first step is to recognize that these ideas must be pursued together—as an entire tapestry that is tightly interwoven.

The second step is to build on the substantial work of education reform undertaken in the last decade. All across the country, successful programs for recruiting, educating, and mentoring new teachers have sprung up. Professional networks and teacher academies have been launched, many teacher preparation programs have been redesigned, higher standards for licensing teachers and accrediting education schools have been developed, and, of course, the National Board for Professional Teaching Standards is now fully established and beginning

to define and reward accomplished teaching.

While much of what the commission proposes can and should be accomplished by reallocating resources that are currently used unproductively, there will be new costs. The estimated additional annual costs of the commission's key recommendations are as follows: scholarships for teaching recruits, $500 million; teacher education reforms, $875 million; mentoring supports and new licensing assessments, $750 million; and state funds for professional development, $2.75 billion. The total is just under $5 billion annually—less than 1% of the amount spent on the federal savings-and-loan bailout. This is not too much, we believe, to bail out our schools and to secure our future.

A Call to Action

Setting the commission's agenda in motion and carrying it to completion will demand the best of us all. The commission calls on governors and legislators to create state professional boards to govern teacher licensing standards and to issue annual report cards on the status of teaching. It asks state legislators and governors to set aside at least 1% of funds for standards-based teacher training. It urges Congress to put money behind the professional development programs it has already approved but never funded.

Moreover, the commission asks the profession to take seriously its responsibilities to children and the American future. Among other measures, the commission insists that state educators close the loopholes that permit administrators to put unqualified "teachers" in the classroom. It calls on university officials to take up the hard work of improving the preparation and skills of new and practicing teachers. It asks administrators and teachers to take on the difficult task of guaranteeing teaching competence in the classroom. And it asks local school boards and superintendents to play their vital role by streamlining hiring procedures, upgrading quality, and putting more staff and resources into the front lines of teaching.

If all of these things are accomplished, the teaching profession of the 21st century will look much different from the one we have today. Indeed, someone entering the profession might expect to advance along a continuum that unfolds much like this:

For as long as she could remember, Elena had wanted to teach. As a peer tutor in middle school, she loved the feeling she got whenever her partner learned something new. In high school, she served as a teacher's aide for her community service project. She linked up with other students through an Internet group started by Future Educators of America.

When she arrived at college she knew she wanted to prepare to teach, so she began taking courses in developmental and cognitive psychology early in her sophomore year. She chose mathematics as a major and applied in her junior year for the university's five-year course of study leading to a master of arts in teaching. After a round of interviews and a review of her record thus far, Elena was admitted into the highly selective teacher education program.

The theories Elena studied in her courses came to life before her eyes as she conducted a case study of John, a 7-year-old whom she tutored in a nearby school. She was struck by John's amazing ability to build things, in contrast with his struggles to learn to read. She carried these puzzles back to her seminar and on into her other courses as she tried to understand learning.

Over time, she examined other cases, some of them available on a multimedia computer system that allowed her to see videotapes of children, samples of their work, and documentation from their teachers about their learning strategies, problems, and progress. From these data, Elena and her classmates developed a concrete sense of different learning approaches. She began to think about how she could use John's strengths to create productive pathways into other areas of learning.

Elena's teachers modeled the kinds of strategies she herself would be using as a teacher. Instead of lecturing from texts, they enabled students to develop and apply knowledge in the context of real teaching situations. These frequently occurred in the professional development school (PDS) where Elena was engaged in a yearlong internship, guided by a faculty of university- and school-based teacher educators.

In the PDS, Elena was placed with a team of student teachers who worked with a team of expert veteran teachers. Her team included teachers of art, language arts, and science, as well as mathematics. They discussed learning within and across these domains in many of their assignments and constructed interdisciplinary curricula together.

Most of the school- and university-based teacher educators who made up the PDS faculty had been certified as accomplished practitioners by the National Board for Professional Teaching Standards, having completed a portfolio of evidence about their teaching along with a set of rigorous performance assessments. The faculty members created courses, internship experiences, and seminars that allowed them to integrate theory and practice, pose fundamental dilemmas of teaching, and address specific aspects of learning to teach.

Elena's classroom work included observing and documenting the learning and behavior of specific children, evaluating lessons that illustrated important concepts and strategies, tutoring and working with small groups, sitting in on family conferences, engaging in school and team planning meetings, visiting homes and community agencies to learn about their resources, planning field trips and curriculum segments, teaching lessons and short units, and ultimately taking major responsibility for the class for a month at the end of the year. This work was supplemented by readings and discussions grounded in case studies of teaching.

A team of PDS teachers videotaped all their classes over the course of the year to serve as the basis for discussions of teaching decisions and outcomes. These teachers' lesson plans, student work, audiotaped planning journals, and reflections on lessons were also available in a multimedia database. This allowed student teachers to look at practice from many angles, examine how classroom situations arose from things that had happened in the past, see how various strategies turned out, and understand a teacher's thinking about students, subjects, and curriculum goals as he or she made decisions. Because the PDS was also wired for video and computer communication with the school of education, master teachers could hold conversations with student teachers by teleconference or e-mail when on-site visits were impossible.

When Elena finished her rich, exhausting internship year, she was ready to try her hand at what she knew would be a demanding first year of teaching. She submitted her portfolio for review by the state professional standards board and sat for the examination of subject-matter and teaching knowledge that was required for an initial teaching license. She was both exhilarated and anxious when she received a job offer, but she felt she was ready to try her hand at teaching.

Elena spent that summer eagerly developing curriculum ideas for her new class. She had the benefit of advice from the district mentor teacher already assigned to work with her in her first year of teaching, and she had access to an on-line database of teaching materials developed by teachers across the country and organized around the curriculum standards of the National Council of Teachers of Mathematics, of which she had become a member.

Elena's mentor teacher worked with her and several other new middle school mathematics and science teachers throughout the year, meeting with them individually and in groups to examine their teaching and provide support. The mentors and their first-year colleagues also met in groups once a month at the PDS to discuss specific problems of practice.

Elena met weekly with the other math and science teachers in the school to discuss curriculum plans and share demonstration lessons. This extended lunch meeting occurred while her students were in a Project Adventure/physical education course that taught them teamwork and cooperation skills. She also met with the four other members of her teaching team for three hours each week while their students were at community-service placements. The team used this time to discuss cross-disciplinary teaching plans and the progress of the 80 students they shared.

In addition to these built-in opportunities for daily learning, Elena and her colleagues benefited from the study groups they had developed at their school and the professional development offerings at the local university and the Teachers Academy.

At the Teachers Academy, school- and university-based faculty members taught extended courses in areas ranging from advances in learning theory to all kinds of teaching methods, from elementary science to advanced calculus. These courses usually featured case studies and teaching demonstrations as well as follow-up work in teachers' own classrooms. The academy provided the technologies needed for multimedia conferencing, which allowed teachers to "meet" with one another across their schools and to see one another's classroom work. They could also connect to courses and study groups at the university, including a popular master's degree program that helped teachers prepare for National Board certification.

With the strength of a preparation that had helped her put theory and practice together and with the support of so many colleagues, Elena felt confident that she could succeed at her life's goal: becoming—and, as she now understood, always becoming—a teacher.

1. *What Matters Most: Teaching for America's Future* (New York: National Commission on Teaching and America's Future, 1996.) Copies of this report can be obtained from the National Commission on Teaching and America's Future, P.O. Box 5239, Woodbridge, VA 22194-5239. Prices, including postage and handling, are $18 for the full report, $5 for the summary report, and $20 for both reports. Orders must be prepaid.

2. *Income, Poverty, and Valuation of Non-Cash Benefits: 1993* (Washington, D.C.: U.S. Bureau of the Census, Current Population Reports, Series P-60, No. 188, 1995). Table D-5, p. D-17. See also *Current Population Survey: March 1988/March 1995* (Washington, D.C.: U.S. Bureau of the Census, 1995).

3. *National Education Goals Report: Executive Summary* (Washington, D.C.: National Education Goals Panel, 1995).

4. National Center for Education Statistics, *Report in Brief: National Assessment of Education Progress (NAEP) 1992 Trends in Academic Progress* (Washington, D.C.: U.S. Department of Education, 1994).

5. For reviews of teacher licensing tests, see Linda Darling-Hammond, "Teaching Knowledge: How Do We Test It?," *American Educator,* Fall 1986, pp. 18–21, 46; Lee Shulman, "Knowledge and Teaching: Foundations of the New Reform," *Harvard Educational Review,* January 1987, pp. 1–22; C. J. MacMillan and Shirley Pendlebury, "The Florida Performance Measurement System; A Consideration," *Teachers College Record,* Fall 1985, pp. 67–78; Walter Haney, George Madaus, and Amelia Kreitzer, "Charms Talismanic: Testing Teachers for the Improvement of American Education," in Ernest Z. Rothkopf, ed., *Review of Research in Education, Vol. 14* (Washington, D.C.: American Educational Research Association, 1987), pp. 169–238; and Edward H. Haertel, "New Forms of Teacher Assessment," in Gerald Grant, ed., *Review of Research in Education, Vol. 17* (Washington, D.C.: American Educational Research Association, 1991), pp. 3–29.

6. C. Emily Feistritzer and David T. Chester, *Alternative Teacher Certification: A State-by-State Analysis* (Washington, D.C.: National Center for Education Information, 1996).

7. Marilyn M. McMillen, Sharon A. Bobbitt, and Hilda F. Lynch, "Teacher Training, Certification, and Assignment in Public Schools: 1990–91," paper presented at the annual meeting of the American Educational Research Association, New Orleans, April 1994.

8. National Center for Education Statistics, *The Condition of Education 1995* (Washington, D.C.: U.S. Department of Education, 1995), p. x.

9. Richard M. Ingersoll, *Schools and Staffing Survey: Teacher Supply, Teacher Qualifications, and Teacher Turnover, 1990–1991* (Washington, D.C.: National Center for Education Statistics, 1995), p. 28.

10. Jeannie Oakes, *Multiplying Inequalities: The Effects of Race, Social Class, and Tracking on Opportunities to Learn Mathematics and Science* (Santa Monica, Calif.: RAND Corporation, 1990).

11. *Who Will Teach Our Children?* (Sacramento: California Commission on Teaching, 1985); and Linda Darling-Hammond, "Inequality and Access to Knowledge," in James Banks, ed., *Handbook of Research on Multicultural Education* (New York: Macmillan, 1995), pp. 465–83.

12. Mary Rollefson, *Teacher Supply in the United States: Sources of Newly Hired Teachers in Public and Private Schools* (Washington, D.C.: National Center for Education Statistics, 1993).

13. *Education Indicators at a Glance* (Paris: Organisation for Economic Cooperation and Development, 1995).

14. Linda Darling-Hammond, "Beyond Bureaucracy: Restructuring Schools for High Performance," in Susan Fuhrman and Jennifer O'Day, eds., *Rewards and Reform* (San Francisco: Jossey-Bass, 1996), pp. 144–94; Linda Darling-Hammond, Jacqueline Ancess, and Beverly Falk, *Authentic Assessment in Action: Studies of Schools and Students at Work* (New York: Teachers College Press, 1995); Fred Newman and Gary Wehlage, *Successful School Restructuring: A Report to the Public and Educators by the Center on Organization and Restructuring of Schools* (Madison: Board of Regents of the University of Wisconsin System, 1995); and Ann Lieberman, ed., *The Work of Restructuring Schools: Building from the Ground Up* (New York: Teachers College Press, 1995).

15. For data on effectiveness and retention, see Michael Andrew, "The Differences Between Graduates of Four-Year and Five-Year Teacher Preparation Programs," *Journal of Teacher Education,* vol. 41, 1990, pp. 45–51; Thomas Baker, "A Survey of Four-Year and Five-Year Program Graduates and Their Principals," *Southeastern Regional Association of Teacher Educators (SRATE) Journal,* Summer 1993, pp. 28–33; Michael Andrew and Richard L. Schwab, "Has Reform in Teacher Education Influenced Teacher Performance? An Outcome Assessment of Graduates of Eleven Teacher Education Programs," *Action in Teacher Education,* Fall 1995, pp. 43–53; Jon J. Denton and William H. Peters, "Program Assessment Report: Curriculum Evaluation of a Nontraditional Program for Certifying Teachers," unpublished report, Texas A & M University, College Station, 1988; and Hyun-Seok Shin, "Estimating Future Teacher Supply: An Application of Survival Analysis," paper presented at the annual meeting of the American Educational Research Association, New Orleans, April 1994.

16. Leslie Huling-Austin, ed., *Assisting the Beginning Teacher* (Reston, Va.: Association of Teacher Educators, 1989); Mark A. Smylie, "Redesigning Teachers' Work: Connections to the Classroom," in Linda Darling-Hammond, ed., *Review of Research in Education, Vol. 20* (Washington, D.C.: American Educational Research Association, 1994); and Linda Darling-Hammond, ed., *Professional Development Schools: Schools for Developing a Profession* (New York: Teachers College Press, 1994).

Teaching teachers

Graduate schools of education face intense scrutiny

Almost a century after they began popping up on America's burgeoning university campuses, graduate schools of education still labor in a shadowland. Although they award more than a quarter of all the advanced degrees conferred each year in the United States, they remain at the bottom of academia's pecking order. As Prof. John Goodlad, director of the Center for Educational Renewal at the University of Washington, puts it: "The only enterprise with lower status than teaching is the enterprise of teacher education."

Yet the issue of how America teaches its teachers to teach is becoming increasingly crucial. A few years from now, the biggest generation of pupils in history will enter the nation's schools, and they will represent the widest imaginable mix of cultures and socioeconomic backgrounds. To deal with this challenge, the nation will need an estimated 2 million new classroom teachers in the coming decade. Linda Darling-Hammond, professor of education at Teachers College at New York's Columbia University, says the nation has reached "a critical moment for transforming the capacity of the American teaching force."

This past January, 87 leading schools of education—known as the Holmes Group after former Harvard Education Dean Henry W. Holmes—demonstrated that they grasped the importance of the moment. They issued a bluntly worded report in which they warned that unless America's schools of education institute real reforms, they should "surrender their franchise" in teacher training.

Certainly, the challenges facing education schools are extraordinary. Among them: attracting a different breed of prospective teacher; elevating teaching to a true profession; forging stronger intellectual ties to other parts of the academic community; developing new links with the real world of education; turning more research into practice; absorbing the lessons of the cognitive revolution that is rapidly altering what we know about how we learn; and most important, restoring the confidence of citizens despairing over conditions in public schools. In short, can the teaching profession emerge from what Goodlad has called a state of "chronic prestige deprivation" by rejuvenating an educational system that needs a transforming overhaul?

Team teaching. So far, the answer is "Maybe." As the Holmes report indicates, "a few institutions already have stirred the winds of change." Some have forged promising links between the campus and public schools. One of the most important of these experiments is at Teachers College, long an intellectual wellspring for graduate teacher education but infrequently involved directly with the schools. Each week a group of Teachers College students in the first year of their graduate program take the subway to Intermediate School 44, a middle school on Manhattan's gentrifying Upper West Side. The visiting students spend 15 to 30 hours weekly team teaching sixth to eighth graders and being mentored by classroom veterans and TC faculty. Then, in January, the three groups join together full time as a team, breaking up the sense of isolation teachers often feel and apparently enriching the educational experience of IS 44's pupils. Says one enthusiastic student: "I felt I was in a new world for four weeks."

The Teachers College experiment is part of what graduate schools of education call "professional development" programs, the counterpart in education of teaching hospitals in medicine. About 200 institutions have established such programs, which provide real-world settings in which prospective teachers and experienced teachers, too, can hone their professional skills, especially classroom techniques. The extended immersion in professional development is a far cry from the traditional training of most of the nation's 2.8 million teachers and most teachers-to-be. Often, seasoned teachers get their only contact with ongoing professional training from "in-service education," which often consists of little more than quickie workshops.

Extended learning. Another reform designed to improve teaching: five-year academic programs that allow undergraduates to major in a liberal arts discipline and then switch to specialized education courses at the graduate level. Five-year teaching programs are becoming the norm, and about 25 percent of newly hired teachers hold master's degrees.

Surprisingly, some of the nation's most respected schools of education—among them the Harvard Graduate School of Education, top ranked in this year's *U.S. News* survey—believe that training teachers is not their primary function. Although even Harvard is making programmatic changes to increase the prominence of teacher-training, research remains the academic lodestar for the most prestigious institutions. As these institutions see it, their main mission is to build the base of research that educators need to make the wisest decisions in day-to-day practice.

Meanwhile, advances in cognitive-science research are spurring new teaching methods. John Bruer, head of the St.

From *U.S. News & World Report*, April 3, 1995, pp. 69-71. © 1995 by U.S. News & World Report. Reprinted by permission.

GRADUATE SCHOOLS OF EDUCATION

WITH THE HIGHEST SCORES IN THE *U.S.* NEWS SURVEY

Rank/School	Overall score	Reputation rank by academics	Rep. rank by school super-intendents	Student selectivity rank	Research activity rank	Facility resources rank	'94 total enrollment	'94 ed. school research	'94 doctoral student/ faculty ratio	'94 acceptance rate
1. Harvard University	100.0	3	1	4	12	1	1,102	$7,100,000	17.3	47.2%
2. Stanford University	99.3	1	2	8	7	9	401	$7,370,982	5.08	39.2%
3. University of California at Berkeley	98.8	6	10	2	2	11	367	$14,000,000	8.35	30.3%
4. Columbia University Teachers College (N.Y.)	98.5	3	10	6	19	2	3,972	$11,498,000	5.36	39.9%
5. University of Wisconsin at Madison	96.2	3	14	9	14	12	1,396	$10,867,641	2.95	37.3%
6. Vanderbilt University (Peabody College) (Tenn.)	95.4	9	8	12	1	29	658	$16,753,048	2.71	53.8%
7. University of Illinois at Urbana-Champaign	92.1	2	19	14	27	24	702	$7,301,000	3.07	37.5%
7. Michigan State University	92.1	6	9	15	5	51	999	$13,295,094	1.29	48.2%
9. Ohio State University	90.8	9	4	70	3	10	2,629	$15,361,911	3.35	59.2%
10. University of California at Los Angeles	89.4	9	13	36	6	44	509	$7,990,520	6.29	44.4%
10. University of Pennsylvania	89.4	25	27	25	15	16	537	$6,999,000	1.71	58.0%
12. NorthwesternUniversity (Ill.)	87.3	25	19	1	59	21	274	$2,386,953	6.11	22.2%
13. Indiana University at Bloomington	86.8	15	15	41	41	17	1,469	$5,284,225	7.17	77.7%
13. University of Virginia	86.8	9	15	18	73	14	906	$2,089,491	2.76	36.7%
15. University of Georgia	86.2	19	46	54	11	4	1,539	$14,522,374	2.92	59.4%
16. Boston College	86.1	52	17	21	30	15	977	$4,429,897	1.88	59.1%
17. University of Kansas	85.2	36	62	16	10	18	1,502	$10,219,861	1.59	60.1%
18. University of Washington	84.9	19	40	19	20	47	511	$5,653,623	2.00	53.4%
19. University of Chicago	84.0	6	11	5	46	84	129	$3,250,000	6.87	66.9%
20. University of Iowa	83.0	24	26	52	18	40	976	$6,197,740	1.96	45.6%
21. University of Maryland at College Park	82.4	19	48	24	20	54	1,155	$7,000,000	1.82	40.9%
22. University of Michigan at Ann Arbor	81.8	9	7	13	81	60	291	$2,250,760	2.38	63.2%
23. University of Southern California	81.6	36	23	45	49	19	786	$3,127,814	3.79	46.8%
24. University of Colorado at Boulder	81.1	33	32	10	52	49	351	$3,300,000	2.31	56.8%
25. University of Minnesota at Twin Cities	80.6	9	29	115	7	20	1,965	$11,037,192	1.56	56.4%
25. Penn State University at University Park	80.6	15	22	65	42	36	1,037	$4,629,763	3.1	45.8%

(continued)

Louis-based James S. McDonnell Foundation, has laid out much of the history of the new research and its implications in *Schools for Thought,* a book much discussed at graduate schools of education. His study discredits teaching prac-tices based on the "mental calisthenics" theory of learning—drill and practice—and lays out three basic requirements before real learning can take place: The learners must have a base of knowledge about the subject upon which to draw; they must be able to monitor their own mental processes and make adjustments as they go about learning, and the ma-terial being learned has to be presented to them in a way that has personal meaning. Teachers can control all of

GRADUATE SCHOOLS OF EDUCATION
THE SECOND TIER

Rank/School	Overall score	Reputation rank by academics	Rep. rank by school super-intendents	'94 ed. school research	'94 doctoral student/faculty ratio	'94 acceptance rate
27. University of Texas at Austin	80.3	19	21	$1,178,995	5.67	40.6%
28. Syracuse University (N.Y.)	79.7	25	37	$5,607,000	1.70	74.3%
28. University of Oregon	79.7	64	53	$11,795,426	3.12	46.1%
30. Florida State University	77.9	36	38	$6,209,693	2.08	61.0%
31. Boston University	76.6	52	50	$3,585,094	2.19	78.9%
32. University of North Carolina at Chapel Hill	76.3	19	5	$1,388,400	1.16	34.3%
33. Temple University (Pa.)	76.1	52	40	$3,700,000	1.01	45.9%
34. University of Missouri at Columbia	75.6	36	53	$5,317,561	1.31	54.4%
35. University of Arizona	74.8	25	64	$3,979,005	2.32	70.6%
36. University of Florida	74.1	25	53	$2,859,371	1.11	65.0%
37. University of North Carolina at Greensboro	74.0	77	74	$11,816,539	1.80	39.2%
38. University of Connecticut	73.9	52	58	$7,847,241	2.08	62.9%
39. State University of N.Y. at Buffalo	73.6	47	89	$1,926,700	3.40	37.3%
40. New York University	72.9	52	49	$1,400,000	1.05	47.3%
40. Texas A&M University at College Station	72.9	33	40	$6,651,837	1.64	48.1%
42. Cornell University (N.Y.)	72.5	25	25	$928,246	1.94	51.8%
43. College of William and Mary (Va.)	71.3	52	24	$1,375,820	1.53	56.3%
44. Univ. of Pittsburgh-Main Campus	70.8	25	68	$3,776,000	2.58	77.5%
45. George Washington University (D.C.)	70.1	77	36	$4,625,141	1.92	64.5%
46. University of Massachusetts at Amherst	69.6	47	44	$1,375,074	2.35	43.3%
47. Arizona State University at Tempe	67.2	33	40	$3,332,000	1.05	41.8%
48. University of Nebraska at Lincoln	66.8	36	34	$2,361,788	.84	45.2%
49. Rutgers Univ. at New Brunswick (N.J.)	66.1	36	32	$710,693	.55	50.6%
50. University of Tennessee at Knoxville	65.9	36	50	$1,676,301	1.53	51.1%

Note: Schools with the same number rank are tied. Basic data: *U.S. News* and the schools. Reputational surveys conducted by Market Facts Inc. Response rate to reputational surveys: academics, 43 percent; school superintendents, 32 percent.

METHODOLOGY

Here's how U.S. News determined the rankings for the 223 graduate education programs that grant Ph.D.'s or Ed.D.'s:

■ Student selectivity was based on data for doctoral and master's candidates who enrolled in fall 1994: average scores on the verbal, quantitative and analytical parts of the Graduate Record Examination (each counted for 30 percent) and proportion of applicants accepted in the program (10 percent).

■ Faculty resources was based on the current ratio of both full-time doctoral (25 percent) and master's degree (20 percent) candidates to full-time faculty; the proportion of graduate students who were doctoral candidates (10 percent); the number of doctoral (15 percent) and master's (10 percent) degrees granted in 1994, and the percent of faculty given Spencer Foundation-Young Faculty, Fulbright, Guggenheim or Humboldt awards in the past two years (20 percent).

■ Research activity was based on the 1994 dollar total of the publicly and privately funded research administered by the education school (75 percent) and that total divided by the number of faculty members engaged in research (25 percent).

■ Reputation was determined by two U.S. News reputational surveys conducted in early 1995. In the first, education school deans and top faculty were asked to rate by quartiles the reputation of each graduate education program. In the second, a nationwide cross section of 1,000 school superintendents in school districts with more than 5,000 students were asked to select the 25 graduate education programs that offer the highest-quality training.

■ Overall rank was determined by converting into number ranks (from 1 to 223) the scores achieved by each school in the above categories. The highest score in each category—or subcategory—received a rank of 1. The scores for the other schools were then converted into number ranks by sorting them in descending order from the score achieved by the No. 1 school. The rankings for research activity, faculty resources and selectivity were determined by totaling the weighted number ranks of their subvariables. Next, the number ranks in the five indicators were weighted: The two reputational surveys, faculty, selectivity and research each accounted for 20 percent of the final score. The final rankings were then determined by totaling the five weighted number-ranked scores. The weighted score for the top school was given a value of 100 percent. The scores for all the others were then determined by figuring their totals as percentages of the score achieved by the No. 1 school.

these factors, Bruer says. But they cannot teach well when any one of the three is missing.

As they incorporate research advances in their own discipline, schools of education also are adopting proven techniques and modern technologies from their counterparts elsewhere on campus. From business schools, for instance, comes the case-study method; from law schools, the videotape review of student performance. At the University of Virginia's education school, a pioneer in high-tech pedagogy, faculty and students combine the case-study method and computerized technologies to create multimedia and online materials. Virginia offers teachers-to-be computerized simulation of real-life decision making in the classroom.

In the long run, however, the technology, the research and the best of faculty intentions will not satisfy the tough-minded critics who put together the stinging Holmes report. Such critics argue that to avoid a wholesale collapse,

American schools must quickly gain the adherence of a new breed of teacher for whom the classroom is not merely a workplace but the expression of a personal commitment. And there seems to be a new level of commitment among prospective teachers. Indeed, many educators say the atmosphere among young teacher candidates reminds them of that in the 1960s. Herbert Kohl, currently a visiting professor at Carleton College in Northfield, Minn., who wrote the beginning-teacher classic, *36 Children*, observes that "teaching has become exciting again."

Alternate routes. Many of the new teaching enthusiasts are graduates of schools of education. But others are entering the profession through alternate routes, including the Teach for America program, which enlists liberal arts graduates from elite schools. Other programs are attracting military retirees and recently unemployed defense workers to teaching. For example, Capt. William Miller, 48, an operations officer at the

Philadelphia Navy Yard, is preparing for a new career in the classroom by taking night courses at Temple University. He hopes to begin student teaching this summer.

When a group of nontraditional teacher candidates were asked why they had pursued teaching, a striking 80 percent said: "Because of the significance it holds for society." The same spirit seems to inspire the young. Arthur Levine, the new president of Teachers College and a former ranking official at Harvard's graduate education school, delights in retelling the story of the answer given by one young woman when she was asked why she had chosen a career in teaching: because, she replied, "it is my generation's Peace Corps."

BY SANDRA REEVES

For education school rankings in specialty disciplines, see the 1995 *U.S. News* guide to *America's Best Graduate Schools,* now on newsstands.

Recognizing Diversity within a Common Historical Narrative

The Challenge to Teaching History and Social Studies

By John Wills & Hugh Mehan

The current debate about the history and social studies curriculum has been concerned primarily with the appropriate course content in these areas of study. Essentially, the debate has turned on these questions: Should courses in United States schools present a common narrative, one that presumably unites all citizens by celebrating the achievements of Western Civilization and United States History and that emphasizes values and standards derived from Western Civilization? Or, should schools open up the historical narrative to include the contributions of people who have been omitted, most often women and minorities? And/or, should schools participate in the struggle for cultural justice and seek to advance civil rights and democratic public life?

It is our contention that the current debate about the curriculum masks deeper issues, the most fundamental of which are: How is a society constituted? What differences make a difference in constituting a society? Or, a little more specifically: Who are we as Americans? Who do we include in the narrative of the history of American society?

There is also a debate about epistemology lurking beneath the surface of this discussion. On the one hand, those educators who call for a common historical narrative often treat history (that is, knowledge) as natural, fixed, context-free, and

John Wills is a faculty member at the University of Rochester and Hugh Mehan is a faculty member at the University of California, San Diego.

timeless. On the other hand, multiculturalists who call for an expanded view of history introduce alternative and competing narratives, which in turn lead to a different conception of history—one that is perspectival, constructed, and relative to historical setting and context.

It is our understanding that school knowledge, including historical knowledge, is socially constructed. The teaching and learning process has often been informed by a cultural transmission model in which teachers transmit school knowledge, located in the curriculum, to passive students who consume this knowledge with varying degrees of accuracy. In opposition to this unidirectional understanding of teaching and learning, we argue that school knowledge emerges in the interaction between teachers, students, and a variety of school texts that are used in instruction. While the determination of what counts as school and historical knowledge is a social and cultural accomplishment, this negotiation is not an even or level process. Teachers and other state-sanctioned officials have more authority in defining what counts as legitimate or useful knowledge in classrooms than do students.

We provide some orienting details concerning the current debate about the curriculum, pointing out that precious few of the participants in the debate have been very helpful in guiding teachers about how to teach history and social studies. Despite this lack of guidance from the national debate concerning what to teach on Monday, teachers have been working hard to

inject previously missing groups into their social studies and history curricula. Unfortunately, teachers have fallen into a number of traps when they have attempted to diversify their curriculum.

After reviewing the consequences of those difficulties, we propose an alternative perspective on the teaching of history and social studies that maintains the continuity of a unifying historical narrative (albeit one that emphasizes the struggle for civil rights instead of a celebration of a democracy achieved, a possession that must be protected and revered) while including previously omitted voices as active participants in significant historical events.

The Current Debate about the Curriculum

A significant group of educators in the current curriculum debate assert that the fundamental purpose of education is to unify society. According to these educators, in order to unify the citizenry, a common core curriculum and a common historical narrative is needed, and should be taught to all United States students. In the current debate, Hirsch (1987) and Bloom (1987) were among the first to call for a common core curriculum. They lamented the loss of a shared set of cultural facts, images, and allusions that enabled U.S. citizens to communicate effectively and understand each other. Hirsch (1987) traced the decline in shared knowledge to the adoption of value neutral and value relative curriculum in the 1960s, while

From *Multicultural Education*, Fall 1996, pp. 4-11. © 1996 by Caddo Gap Press, Inc. Reprinted by permission of *Multicultural Education*, the magazine of the National Association for Multicultural Education.

Bloom blamed elite universities for setting the current generation of students adrift on a sea of superficial and naive moral relativism. Education, they said, is no longer used to teach moral values. The way to overcome this value relativism, they said, is to teach a core set of ideas and facts to all American elementary and secondary students.

The relevant texts in Hirsh's proposal to regain "cultural literacy" would be drawn from Western Civilization, the core political values from American democracy, the ethical values from a secularized version of the Judeo-Christian tradition, coupled with industriousness, honesty, tolerance of others. The legal concepts would be drawn from the English legal tradition. The language for instructing students in cultural literacy would be English only.

This call for a common core curriculum occurred when the economic condition of the country was worsening. It was supported by many members of the Reagan and Bush administrations, including former Secretary of Education William Bennett (1992), former Assistant Secretary of Education Diane Ravitch (1990), former Assistant Secretary of Education Chester Finn (1991), and Chairman of the National Endowment of the Humanities Lynne Cheney (1995)—all of whom cited the numerous national and international academic surveys which showed U.S. students not doing as well as their German and Japanese counterparts. U.S. society is threatened, these commentators reasoned, because students are not accumulating the necessary knowledge to enable the U.S. to compete against Japan and Germany in the global economy.

Members of the Republican party transformed the common core curriculum position in an intellectual debate into a concrete course of action. President Bush included suggestions from the National Governor's Conference in "America 2000," which called for national curriculum standards and a regimen of testing to see how well states, schools, and K-12 students were mastering skills in basic courses of study (Bush, 1991). At the same time, the National Center for History in the Schools (Crabtree & Nash, 1994a, 1994b) developed a preliminary proposal for national standards for the teaching of United States and World History. After considerable controversy over the content of the draft standards, a final recommendation that emphasizes student inquiry, research, and interpretation has been produced (Crabtree & Nash, 1996).

A group of educators and researchers who have come to be called "multiculturalists" have criticized the existing curricula in history and social studies and the call by Hirsh and Bloom for a common core curriculum because ethnic minorities, women, people with disabilities, and gays have been excluded from the historical narrative (Sleeter & Grant, 1988; Banks, 1989; Nieto, 1992; Banks & Banks, 1995). Multicultural educators favor a robust plu-

...we propose an alternative perspective on the teaching of history and social studies that maintains the continuity of a unifying historical narrative...while including previously omitted voices as active participants in significant historical events.

ralism—which in its most extreme form, may include cultural separatism—but in general, favors diversified, highly contextualized curricula, those which not only include the standards of western culture, but also the historical and cultural experiences unique to the backgrounds of students (Massaro, 1993).

Multicultural educators want the historical narrative to include the contributions of outgroups whose histories have been trivialized, misstated, or omitted. Doing so, they claim, would give a richer, fuller, less romantic and sanitized view of history. As a result, students would learn that life, liberty, and the pursuit of happiness may be foundational principles of American society, but racism, sexism, and other forms of prejudice make it harder for some groups to compete equally for these goals. Unless the facts of gender, ethnic, and racial discrimination are acknowledged, they argue, then their harmful effects cannot be ameliorated and goals of liberty and justice will not be achieved.

In the process of calling for a more inclusive historical narrative, multicultural educators tend to reject universal and foundational claims to truth, value, and beauty. Instead, they adopt a form of anthropological relativism that argues that morality is rooted in a particular culture's history, conventions, practices, and beliefs. Therefore, they reason, the moral standards of one society can not be subjected to criticism from the point of view of an other culture's standards or by appeal to one transcultural standard.

Multicultural educators have been joined by advocates of "critical pedagogy" in their criticism of the way in which history and social studies are taught (see especially Aronowitz & Giroux, 1985; Darder, 1991: McLaren, 1991; Giroux, 1992; Giroux & McLaren, 1989; 1994; Apple & Beane, 1995; Sleeter & McLaren, 1995). Convinced that equality, justice, and social responsibility are the baseline conditions for a just society, they criticize the unequal distribution of economic and educational resources among groups, and say schools should participate in the struggle for cultural justice and should seek to advance civil rights and democratic public life.

Advocates of critical pedagogy share with multiculturalists the view that systemic and pervasive discrimination plays an important part in American culture. Conflict, not merit, choice, or personal effort often explains the gap between white and non-white, rich and poor. They agree with multicultural educators that curricular innovations are necessary to achieve equity, but educational changes are hardly sufficient, critical theorists assert, because the underlying inequalities in the society at large must be addressed if a just society is to be realized.

The call for multicultural education has not been universally or calmly accepted, however. It has been challenged by educators and parents who think education should teach respect for authority and emphasize foundational skills. The multicultural movement has also been lambasted by religious fundamentalists who think schools should teach Bible values, the constitution, and patriotism (Delfatorre, 1992).

Basically, its critics contend that the multicultural approach to education is politically and culturally divisive. Because multiculturalism sees race, ethnicity, class (and other **group** categories) as determinative of social action, Ravitch (1990) and Schlesinger (1991) say multicultural education encourages separatist tendencies. They cite Afrocentric curriculum as a particularly threatening case in point. In their enthusiasm to include omitted groups and achieve social justice, D'Souza (1991) fears universities are becoming bastions of political correctness. Cheney (1995) says multicultural education's move to diversify the canon trivializes "the great works of Western Civilization" because some lesser texts are included under the guise of a quota system.

Furthermore, multicultural education has been criticized because it relativises beauty, reason, truth, and merit. Educators and parents who believe that there are a set of values derived from "Western Civilization" that persevere, that transcend, argue against the anthropological idea incorporated within multiculturalism that measures of human achievement are bound by history, culture, and context. Cheney (1995: 25) is particularly vitriolic in her condemnation of the relativism she sees contained in the National History Standards because they engage in the "systematic denigration of America's Western heritage." Aspects of Western Civilization, starting from Hellenic Greece and continuing through industrialization, are presented in negative light, while aspects of Chinese, African, and Aztec cultures are celebrated, she says. Cheney is particularly upset that the draft standards (Crabtree & Nash, 1994a, 1994b) would encourage students to consider the architecture, labor systems, and agriculture of the Aztecs, but not their practice of human sacrifice, and the gathering of wealth by an African king would be celebrated but denigrated when practiced by railroad barons. In lieu of this "post modern" "politically correct" dogma, Cheney (1995: 29) wants to install a "celebratory history" in the schools, one that reminds students of the "true glory" of Western Civilization and United States history.

Traps and Pitfalls When Recognizing Diversity in the Curriculum

The debate about the curriculum (and its more foundational issues concerning the constitution of society and historical knowledge) is not just an abstract and general argument among academics and policy wonks. Educators in elementary, high school, and college classrooms have been wrestling with the best way to recognize diversity in their history and social studies curricula.

We have examined middle school classrooms in which teachers have attempted to present multicultural histories of the United States (Wills, 1996, 1994; Mehan, Lintz, Okamoto & Wills, 1995) and we have made more casual observations of the efforts by elementary and secondary school teachers to construct more inclusive versions of United States and world history. As these educators have attempted to recognize diversity in the curriculum, they have fallen into a number of traps. After we describe some of the pitfalls, we pro-

pose an alternative approach which can help teachers avoid these traps.

The Culture Trap in Reforming the Curriculum

"Cultural tourism" is one trap that awaits teachers who attempt to construct a more inclusive history. Cultural tourism results when underrepresented groups are treated as "cultural representatives" and not as "social" or "historical" actors. Cultural tourism also occurs when students are invited to study the cultural attributes of specific groups as static and fixed, rather than establishing the presence of members of cultural groups as social actors in particular historical events in American history. Like tourists, students are invited to travel to "foreign lands" and learn about exotic people and places, and then return home to a place in which these people have no relevance in their daily lives. And yet, the cultures that students are studying are not foreign to American history, but a part of it. When the approaches to including diverse groups in American history situate these groups outside of history, then students' knowledge of these groups becomes that of a tourist—knowlege of an exotic people, an "other," who have no bearing on their own lives, or our history. As a consequence, students may conclude incorrectly that certain people, being members of cultural groups, have fixed cultural attributes, perhaps with a unique culture or way of life and a unique and "different" perspective on the world.

For example, one eighth grade United States history teacher had her students conduct research on a variety of Native American tribes located in the Eastern Woodlands during the Colonial period of American history. Students produced "Fact or Fiction" books based on this research which addressed the material culture, religion, family life, clothing, social and political organization, and artistic expressions of selected Native American tribes.

The results of this engaging activity were a success as far as generating cultural information about Native American tribes, but this work failed to locate these Native American tribes within American history, or portray them as social actors within any specific historical events. For example, the students studying the Mohawk Indians reported that Mohawk children wore no clothing whenever possible, that the Mohawk did not live in teepees, that the Mohawk were skillful and fierce warriors, and that Mohawk Indians built bridges and skyscrapers in the United States and Canada because they had no fear of heights. But Mohawk actions in particular historical events, such

as the French-American War, were never mentioned. As a result, the Mohawks seem to exist outside of any narrative structure, sometimes in an elusive past, sometimes in an elusive present (e. g., gangs of Mohawk Indians building skyscrapers and bridges), but never in the events and happenings that constitute American history.

Brief essays that these students wrote on the origins of the United States reinforce our conclusion that they did not see Native American tribes as part of American history. Seldom did the students mention Native Americans during the colonial period in their origin narratives, even though they spent a number of weeks studying and talking about Native American cultures during this historical period. The information they had learned about the **cultures** of Native American tribes was simply not relevant to the **history** of colonial America.

Because these Native Americans exist outside of history, students have no knowledge of them as social actors in colonial America. What they thought of the White settlers, their interactions with these settlers, and the effects this had on their way of life are dormant topics. Even though these Native Americans can serve as "cultural representatives" of the Mohawk, Delaware, or other tribes studied, they cannot serve as examples of Native Americans as social or historical actors. If they were assigned the role of historical actors, then students would have an opportunity to understand the history of Native American-White relations in the United States which, in turn, is potentially useful knowledge for thinking about these relations in the present.

Other activities carried out in this classroom also fall victim to "cultural tourism" because they focus on cultural attributes rather than history or social action. The students read a novel, *The Light in the Forest* (Richter, 1953), about True Son, a white child abducted in a raid and raised by the Delaware Indians. As a young man, True Son is forcibly returned to his white family but refuses to renounce his Delaware heritage and attempts to return to his tribe. In a class discussion, students were asked to decide, having learned about Native American cultures, whether they would want to live with the Whites or with the Native Americans if they found themselves in a similar situation as True Son. The class discussion is telling, because students explain that they would rather live with the Indians because they are "better people" with "better moral values," while Whites are "kind of jerks" who like to "take over the land" and "control it." While this discussion is an opportunity for the students to explore their stereotypes concerning Native Americans, the discussion is in fact about deciding what kind of people Native Americans are, and what kind of people Whites are. The students conclude that Native Americans and Whites are distinct kinds of people, because they have unique cultures, which determine their outlook on the world and actions in it.

This incipient cultural determinism is also evident in a number of "Point of View" exercises that this eighth grade teacher conducted with her students. The exercises, revolving around *The Light in the Forest*, emphasize how culture influences the different outlook of Native Americans and Whites to the world—whether to adapt to the land or adapt the land to your needs, how Fort Pitt would seem like an "ugly, treeless prison" to Native Americans but a "safe home" to Whites, and the like. These activities and exercises are useful in establishing the cultural differences between Native Americans and White settlers. But these activities are not useful in explaining the role these differences played in shaping the interactions between Native Americans and Whites in colonial history.

This multicultural approach to recognizing diversity in history can lead teachers away from history; none of the exercises or activities dealing with Native Americans were focused on historical events, and so they failed to place Native Americans into American history. To the extent that Native Americans are present they are present as cultural representatives. While this multicultural approach exemplifies a way of life and perspective on the world which is different from that of Whites, it tells students little to nothing about the role of Native Americans in American history, their actions in specific events, and their interactions with other groups present in the colonial period. While these Native Americans are virtually present in the classroom, they are not actually present in American history.

The Pitfalls of Including Diverse Groups in History

Critics of "traditional" American history have pointed to the absence of women and people of color as evidence of the politics behind what counts as good history. They have noted women and minorities appear and disappear from the narrative, appearing during historical periods or in events of concern to Whites. Chinese Americans work on the railroad, African Americans are enslaved during the Civil War, Native Americans are obstacles to be removed during Westward Expansion. But they remain virtually absent from the remainder of American history (cf. Banks,

1989; Sleeter & Grant, 1991; Sleeter & MacLaren, 1995).

Many teachers attempt to recognize women and people of color by highlighting their contributions and accomplishments and allowing their previously missing voices to be heard. But these efforts can be flawed, because they unintentionally situate or position women and people of color outside the historical narrative being constructed, or outside the specific historical events being examined. As a consequence, diverse groups (or more accurately their representatives) are rarely constituted as social actors in history, but instead exist outside of history as shining examples of their gender/race/ethnicity, or as gendered or racialized commentators who are supposed to speak for their "people."

The troubles that can develop when teachers attempt to animate history with women and people of color is evident in a 4th grade musical recounting the history of California. Beginning with Spanish exploration and ending in the present, this musical has all the children in unison narrating the history of California and singing portions of popular songs related to the historical periods covered, interspersed with brief skits in which small groups of students act out specific historical events.

The Native American presence in California is noted early in the musical. Specific attention is paid to the culture of Indians, with the Chumash being identified by name. The sequence includes the establishment of the mission system (it notes that the Padres, who were "well-intentioned," nevertheless "neglected and misunderstood the Indian ways of life"), the movement westward into California, the discovery of gold, statehood for California, the establishment of the transcontinental railroad, the San Francisco earthquake, the rise of the Hollywood film industry, and the agricultural wealth of California. This history of California is "traditional" in that women and people of color are virtually absent, except for the mention of being thankful for "Chinese hard labor" in finishing the railroad.

The students conclude the musical by noting the contributions great individuals have made to California. They begin by naming great (male) authors such as Mark Twain, Jack London, Robert Louis Stevenson, and others. Suddenly, students in the chorus loudly ask: "But what about the women?" and are rewarded with the names of three women authors: Helen Hunt Jackson, Mary Austin, and Ina Coolbirth. This challenge opens the door to include other women—Isadora Duncan, the mother of modern dance; Lillian Gilbreth, an engineer and mother of 12; Dorothea Lange, a

photographer; and Amelia Earhart—and a few men—Jackie Robinson, a baseball player; Luther Burbank, a naturalist and experimenter; and Cesar Chavez, whose claim to fame is not mentioned—in this conclusion to the musical.

What is significant about this inclusion of women and people of color is their location in this musical. The achievements and contributions of individual women and people of color are recognized **outside** and **after** the narrative of California history constructed by the musical. It is only at the end of the musical, after the story of California finally arrives in the present, that these individuals appear on the stage, are introduced, and their accomplishments are recognized. The students—and their parents and families in the audience—witness history being made by others in the brief skits, while these notable individuals gathered on the stage in the conclusion are mere "add-ons" after the fact, after the story has been told. While these representative individuals are present on stage, they are not present in American history.

Another common multicultural approach used by teachers is to include women and people of color in history by allowing them to present their points of view in discussions of historical events. In role playing activities, for example, small groups of students adopt the role of a notable figure in history, and then comment on historical events from their unique perspective. Unlike the example of the musical on California history, this approach goes beyond the mere display of notable individuals by allowing individual women and people of color to discuss historical events, thereby providing them a somewhat more active role in the history curriculum. It is also useful in providing students with an understanding of history that is multiperspectival, allowing them to see how specific historical events were interpreted differently by different people.

This approach appeared in a discussion of the Boston Tea Party in an eighth grade United States history classroom. Small groups of students were assigned the role of important historical figures— King George, Samuel Adams (a radical patriot), John Dickinson (a moderate colonist), Abigail Adams (a female colonist), Logan (an Iroquois Indian), Crispus Attucks (an African American). After reading some information on their figures and the group they represented, students were asked to comment on the Boston Tea Party from the perspective of these people. Specifically, they were to address how they felt about what happened in this event, and what they thought about the actions of the men in this significant historical event.

There are a number of problems which

made this activity difficult for the students. The information the students have to work with is primarily biographical, and yet these voices are supposed to represent the perspective of their respective communities, about which the students have little or no information. Students lack much of the historical information necessary to successfully reanimate these voices. Additionally, having one individual speak for an entire community masks or obscures the diversity within communities; if Crispus Attucks speaks for all African Americans, then why did some African Americans support the colonists while other African Americans supported the British?

The absence of historical knowledge can plague any such role playing activity. In terms of creating a more inclusive history, however, the most significant problem with this activity concerns the situation of these individuals as speakers. The selection of the events to be discussed are "traditionally" important events. Individuals such as Logan and Attucks must speak about events that they themselves did not participate in. Logan and Attucks, unlike Samuel Adams, are not speaking as participants in the Boston Tea Party. Rather, both Logan and Crispus Attucks are asked to comment as representatives of the Native American and African American communities on the actions of radical patriots, such as Samuel Adams. In contrast, Adams gets to respond that "I think we did the right thing," speaking as an active participant in the Boston Tea Party.

Perhaps more importantly, the focus of this activity is not on history—on explaining what happened, who was involved, who did what, and the different perspectives that help to understand and explain their actions—but rather on getting the responses of people of color or women to give opinions on events that have already happened. This activity is not about explaining and understanding historical events. Instead, it is a lesson about multiple perspectives. As a result, individuals such as Logan and Attucks are positioned **outside** of history and constituted as commentators on the actions of others, individuals like Samuel Adams who exist as actors **inside** important historical events. Finally, other activities in the classroom confirm the role of patriots, loyalists, and moderates as historical actors, as the students read the Declaration of Independence, Paine's "Common Sense," and other important documents. These are the people who are quoted, pictured, and talked about in the students' textbook and other curriculum during this period in American history. Again, while diverse individuals such as Logan and Attucks are present in the classroom, they are not present in history.

The Discontinuity Trap

The *National Standards for History* (Crabtree & Nash, 1996) and the *California Framework for History and Social Studies* (State Department of Education, 1990) recommend that history be taught in such a way that students can use history to interpret current events. But when history is taught as discontinuous events, diverse groups appear in and then disappear from the narrative in unexplained ways. Therefore, students have difficulty relating the relevance of the past to current events.

For example, one eighth grade class spent a total of eight weeks studying the Civil War period, which included a detailed study of the experiences of African Americans as slaves in the South. The students learned a considerable amount about the brutalities, indignities, and injustices suffered by enslaved African Americans during this period in American history, which presented them with clear lessons about the immorality of slavery. And yet, when this teacher asked her students to connect the injustices experienced by African Americans under slavery to possible injustices experienced by African Americans in Los Angeles in the Spring of 1992—her students could not see the relevance of history in contemporary race relations.

These students had difficulty using the past to understand the present because their knowledge of the injustices experienced by African Americans in American history was anchored in slavery. Other than their presence as slaves during the Civil War, African Americans were virtually absent from the United States history they studied. The only injustices these students thought African Americans experienced were associated with their enslavement. To these students, moreover, slavery was a problem that was "solved" many years ago. Therefore, these students did not see history to be relevant in thinking about the possible injustices suffered by African Americans in contemporary United States society. Slavery was an historically specific event and, therefore, the injustice was also historically specific. Without a continuous history of African American experiences in the United States, connections between past and present injustices remained elusive.

Recognizing Diversity within a Common Historical Narrative

As we've suggested above, efforts to include diverse groups in history have fallen into some unforeseen traps. Calls for cultural diversity have unintentionally led many teachers to focus their attention on cultural attributes and not on social action in history. While culture is certainly a resource or tool which mediates social action, the task of history is not to appreciate cultural diversity (although an appreciation of cultural diversity will be a natural byproduct of history that is well taught). **The purpose of history is to understand and explain the past so that we can better understand contemporary relations in our increasingly diverse society.**

The Need For a Sociological Perspective

Focusing on cultural attributes often leads to the study of groups ahistorically, statically, and in isolation, rather than the study of groups in interaction. History is made in interaction. If history is to provide any lessons for the present, then students need to examine and understand these relations in the past. In addition, teaching history involves constructing an historical narrative (Zinn, 1980).

With this conception of history in mind, the criteria for including diverse groups becomes more clear. Women and people of color must be visible in specific historical events to be visible in history. Furthermore, they must appear as active participants, that is, social actors who made sense of their circumstances and orient their actions to others around them.

In what follows, we revisit the examples we presented above in order to construct an approach to history that includes women and people of color as participants in specific historical events. Our sociological approach avoids the traps and pitfalls of previous efforts and is more likely to achieve the goals that both common-culturalists and multiculturalists espouse. On the one hand, it recognizes diversity in the curriculum. On the other hand, it treats history as a common unifying theme, the struggle for civil rights. An added benefit of this sociological approach is that it doesn't necessarily require new curricular materials, only a shift in perspective, one which would enable teachers to make better use of the materials already at hand.

Recall the research on Native American cultures during the colonial period and the teacher's emphasis on cultural difference and point of view. Shifting the focus to an examination of social relations between Native Americans and White settlers would allow this teacher to get the same points about culture across, as well as construct a more usable history of the colonial period. The novel the students read, *The Light in the Forest*, is ripe with information on the relations between the White settlers and the local Native American tribes. With more attention to this aspect of the novel, class discussions on point of view and cultural difference would look quite different. Students could use these differences in outlook and world view to explain the actions of Native Americans and White settlers in this period of American history. **In this revised approach, the question is no longer whether culture makes a difference, but what difference did cultural difference make in the interactions between Native Americans and White settlers.**

The students' "Fact or Fiction" books could be made a more useful activity with a shift toward our sociological perspective. Rather than studying the cultural attributes of Native American tribes in isolation, attention could be redirected to examining facts concerning Native American-White relations during the colonial period, as well as the changes Native American-white contact wrought in the way of life and outlook of these Native American tribes.

The focus on groups in interaction in specific historical events would also facilitate the meaningful integration of diverse groups into the history of California recounted in the fourth grade musical. Recall that women and people of color were only showcased at the conclusion of the musical. At a minimum, shifting to a sociological perspective would make obvious the need to always situate individuals or groups in history, and to portray what they were doing in concert with others. In this instance, the relations between Native Americans and the Spanish missionaries would not simply be mentioned but acted out. A similar change would occur with the Chinese labor used to build the railroads. Diverse groups would appear uniformly throughout the American historical narrative, such as Native Americans, Chinese, and Mexican Americans in California during the Gold Rush. Shifting attention away from cultural attributes and toward social life would help students understand how history is made as diverse peoples came together in specific times and places.

Finally, this shift to a sociological perspective would affect the approach to integrating or recognizing multiple perspectives in the discussion of historical events. When teachers recognize that history consists of social actors, then teachers would be encouraged to choose certain kinds of events rather than others for discussion. Teachers would want to be careful to include events in which women and people of color could authentically speak as active participants in them. In the case of the Boston Tea Party, for example, Crispus Attucks could debate Samuel Adams, a radical patriot, and Thomas Peters, an African American contemporary who allied himself with the British, about whether or not African Americans should support the colonists or the British in the Revolutionary War. Juxtaposing Attucks, Peters, and Adams would not only constitute African Americans as actors in history, but would also demonstrate to students the diversity of opinion within cultural/racial/ethnic groups. This approach does not mean that a representative of every cultural/racial/ethnic group would necessarily have to speak as a participant in every event; but, when representatives of groups do appear, they would appear in appropriate historical events, thus constituting them as participants in history, speakers inside rather than outside the narrative of American history.

Our sociological approach to teaching history adds a new dimension to what Banks (1989) has called the "transformative approach" to multicultural education. In Banks' approach, the curriculum is changed to enable students to view concepts, issues, events, and themes from the perspective of diverse ethnic and cultural groups. Central to his approach is the infusion of various frames of reference that provide students with a more complex understanding of United States society.

In fact, the "multiple perspective" activities implemented in the classrooms we studied could be seen as examples of Banks' transformative approach. In the "Point of View" exercises in particular, students were not simply exposed to the view of European colonists; they were asked to view issues and events from the cultural standpoint of different communities within colonial America.

As we've seen, however, a multiple perspective approach is not as transformative as one might imagine, because women, Native Americans, and African Americans are not situated as actors in American history. Students learned about the existence of diverse perspectives to be sure, but these were divorced from any examination of the specific actions taken by these groups in specific historical events. While students learned about distinct cultural points of view, they did not learn how the actions of distinct groups, informed by their unique perspectives, contributed to our common history. The lesson is that a transformative approach can be inclusive, but it is not necessarily inclusive in any meaningful way unless the people who hold diverse perspectives are rendered as active participants in history.

Studying Social Life In History

The emphasis in our sociological approach to history is on social life. We believe that history should prepare and enable students to think critically about contemporary society by providing them relevant lessons from the past. To do this, history must help students understand and explain the interactions between diverse groups in specific historical events and during particular historical periods because these events constitute our common history.

There are a number of features in our sociological approach that will enable teachers to successfully recognize diversity in their history curriculum. First, the focus is on society, which means students should not study groups in isolation, but rather groups in interaction. Society—whether equal or unequal, just or unjust—is constituted in this interactional space between groups. If students are going to learn lessons from history that are relevant to the present, then this is where the lessons are going to be found. Therefore, diverse groups must always be situated in society. They must always be constituted as social actors who are interacting with others. The focus of inquiry within history and social studies must be on explaining and understanding these actions.

A second recommendation that emerges from our approach is situating diverse groups in time and space. Commentators who disagree on other points (such as Crabtree, Nash, and Cheney) agree that history is, or should be, in the words of the *National Standards for History* and the *California History-Social Studies Framework*, a "story well told." History, as a well-told story, is a sequence of events about the struggle for civil rights that adds up to the story of America. Teachers need to recognize that along with their students, they are constructing a narrative of events about the struggle for rights which constitutes American history. This story about the struggle for rights tells us who we are as Americans (Gitlin, 1995). If diverse groups are to be meaningfully included in the curriculum, then they need to exist in this civil rights narrative. To do so means situating them as social actors, as active participants, in specific historical events and periods.

Third, our sociological approach to teaching history is necessarily conversational and, therefore, multiperspectival. The goal in learning about American history is to understand and explain historical events. Why did this event turn out this way and not some other way? Explaining historical events necessitates including all the participants in them. Consider, for example, the Revolutionary

War. Students will gain a deeper and richer understanding of this event if the views of women, African Americans, and Native Americans are included along with the views of those that are usually presented, White male colonists and the British. After all, Native Americans were a force to be reckoned with in the colonial period. It mattered to the British and the colonists who they decided to support. Similarly, African Americans did fight on both the British side and the colonists' side. Therefore, understanding their participation will enrich students' understanding of this crucial and significant event in American history. Studying history as social interaction then not only tells us about African Americans and Native Americans, but also the views of the White colonists as well. A conversational or multiperspectival approach provides us the opportunity to learn about all the parties involved (Zinn, 1980).

This sociological approach is evident in one sixth grade teacher's approach to studying Ancient Civilizations. Faced with the problem of meaningfully including the civilizations of India and China in the more traditional study of Egypt, Greece, and Rome (i.e., Western Civilization), this teacher developed a curriculum that focused on society and social life, rather than exploring the cultures of these groups. This teacher did not simply teach the food, clothing, music, and art of these groups, which is the approach so often taken by teachers attempting to include diversity in their curriculum (Cochran-Smith, 1995; Sleeter & Grant, 1987). Instead, she organized her students into small groups to research either the daily life, religion, political organization, economic organization, or science and technology of one of these civilizations. Students had to work on different civilizations throughout the year. Therefore, the group that reported on daily life in China would study the political organization in Egypt, science in China and India, etc.

In this way, the students became familiar with different aspects of all five civilizations and were able to recognize the contributions and accomplishments of each. For example, the Egypt and China research groups each declared that they were the first to make paper. This led to a comparison of dates to establish who was actually first, followed by a discussion of the nature of history, and how history gets written. Similar discoveries occurred throughout the year as students discovered equivalent scientific and technological accomplishments shared by these diverse civilizations. Because students continually studied all of these civilizations—

rather than studying Egypt, Greece, and Rome (Western Civilization), and then adding on the study of India and China if time permitted—India and China were recognized as equally significant civilizations in the ancient world.

Students discovered the social interactions that existed between these civilizations during their investigations. When entering this class, these students had perceived each civilization to be distinct, existing in isolation, with one civilization dying as another one rose to take its place. By the end of the school year, the students had gained the sense that these civilizations inhabited the same world over a period of many years and interacted with one another through trade, warfare, and cultural exchange. Instead of seeing these civilizations as distinct cultural groups, students came to realize, often on their own, the interconnectedness of these civilizations, and the mutual influences they had on one

References

Apple, Michael W. & J.A. Beane. 1995. *Democratic Schools.*

Aronowitz, Stanley & Henry A. Giroux. 1985. *Education Under Siege: The Conservative, Liberal and Radical Debate Over Schooling.* Hadley, MA: Bergin & Garvey.

Banks, James A. 1989. Multicultural Education: Characteristics and Goals. In: James A. Banks & Cherry A. McGee Banks (Eds.), *Multicultural Education: Issues and Perspectives* (pp. 2—26). Boston, MA: Allyn & Bacon.

Banks, James A. & Cherry A. McGee Banks (Eds.). 1995. *Handbook on Research on Multicultural Education.* New York: MacMillan.

Bennett, William J. 1992. *The De-Valuing of America: The Fight for our Culture and Our Children.* New York: Summit Books.

Bloom, Alan. 1987. *The Closing of the American Mind: How Higher Education Has Failed Democracy and Impoverished the Souls of Today's Students.* New York: Simon & Schuster.

Bush, George. 1991. *Goals 2000: An American Educational Strategy.* Washington. DC: U.S. Department of Education.

California State Department of Education. 1990. *Framework for History and Social Studies.* Sacramento, CA: Department of Education.

Cheney, Lynne V. 1995. *Telling the Truth: Why Our Culture and Our Country Have Stopped Making Sense—and What We Can Do About It.* New York: Simon & Schuster.

Cochran-Smith, Marilyn. 1995. Color Blindness and Basket Making Are Not the Answers: Confronting the Dilemmas of Race, Culture, and Language Diversity in Teacher Education. *American Educational Research Journal* 32 (3): 493—522.

Crabtree, Charlotte & Gary B. Nash. 1994a. *National Standards for United States History: Exploring the United States Experience, Grades 5—12.* Los Angeles, CA: National Center for History in the Schools.

Crabtree, Charlotte & Gary B. Nash. 1994b. *National Standards for World History: Exploring the Paths to the Present, Grades 5—12.* Los Angeles, CA: National Center for History in the Schools.

Crabtree, Charlotte & Gary B. Nash. 1996. *National Standards for Teaching History: Basic Edition.* Los Angeles, CA: National Center for History in the Schools.

Darder, Antonia. 1991. *Culture and Power in the Classroom: A Critical Foundation for Education.* New York: Bergin & Garvey.

Delfattore, Jean. 1992. *What Johnny Shouldn't Read.* New Haven: Yale University Press.

D'Souza, Dinish. 1991. *Illiberal Education: The Politics of Race and Sex on Campus.* New York: Free Press.

Finn, Chester. 1991. *We Must Take Charge.* New York: Basic Books.

Giroux, Henry A. & Peter L. McLaren (Eds.). 1989. *Critical Pedagogy, The State and Cultural Struggle.* Albany, NY: State University of New York Press.

Giroux, Henry A. & Peter McLaren (Eds.). 1994. *Between Borders: Pedagogy and the Politics of Cultural Studies.* New York: Routledge & Kegan Paul.

Gitlin, Todd. 1995. *The Twilight of Common Dreams: Why America Is Wracked by Culture Wars.* New York: Henry Holt.

Hirsch, E.D., Jr. 1987. *Cultural Literacy: What Every American Needs to Know.* Boston, MA: Houghton Mifflin..

MacLaren, Peter L. 1991. Critical Pedagogy, Multiculturalism and the Politics of Risk and Resistance. *Journal of Education* 173 (3): 109-139.

Massaro, Toni Marie. 1993. *Constitutional Literacy: A Core Curriculum for a Multicultural Nation.* Durham, NC: Duke University Press.

Mehan, Hugh, Angela Lintz, Dina Okamoto & John S. Wills. 1995. Ethnographic Studies of Multicultural Education in Classrooms and Schools. In: James A. Banks & Cherry A. McGee Banks (Eds.), *Handbook on Research on Multicultural Education.* New York: MacMillan.

Nieto, Sonia. 1992. *Affirming Diversity: The Sociopolitical Context of Multicultural Education.* White Plains, NY: Longman Publishers.

Ravitch, Diane. 1990. Multiculturalism: E Pluribus Plures. *The Key Reporter* 56 (1): 1-4.

Richter, Conrad. 1953. *The Light in the Forest.* New York: Knopf.

Schlesinger, Arthur, M. Jr. 1992. *The Disuniting of America.* New York: Norton.

Sleeter, Christine E. & Carl A. Grant. 1987. An Analysis of Multicultural Education in the United States. *Harvard Educational Review* 57 (4): 421—444.

Sleeter, Christine E. & Carl A. Grant. 1991. Mapping Terrains of Power: Student Knowledge vs. Classroom Knowledge. In: C. E. Sleeter (Ed.), *Empowerment Through Multicultural Education.* Albany, NY: State University of New York Press.

Sleeter, Christine E. & Peter L. McLaren. 1995. *Multicultural Education, Critical Pedagogy and the Politics of Difference.* Albany, NY: State University of New York Press.

Wills, John S. 1994. Popular Culture, Curriculum, and Historical Representation: The Situation of Native Americans in American History and the Perpetuation of Stereotypes. *Journal of Narrative and Life History* 4 (4): 277—294.

Wills, John S. 1996. Who Needs Multicultural Education? White Students, U.S. History, and the Construction of a Usable Past. *Anthropology and Education Quarterly* 27 (3): xx—yy.

Zinn, Howard. 1980. *A People's History of the United States.* New York: HarperCollins.

another. Locating these civilizations on a timeline and establishing their location in the world, students were surprised to discover that Egypt, Greece, and Rome shared the Mediterranean world, and that India and China shared the Himalayan Mountains on their borders. The end result of this teacher's sociological approach to the teaching of history was the construction of a narrative of the ancient world, a common story that united Egypt, Rome, and Greece without marginalizing the civilizations of India and China. **Perhaps more importantly, the students learned that history is about explaining and understanding social life, not on evaluating the "cultural worth" of civilizations.**

Conclusions

Critics have complained that the introduction of multiple perspectives in the curriculum makes history radically relativistic. Students will no longer be able to evaluate the merits of competing points of view about contentious historical events such as the Holocaust, the Vietnam War, or the Civil Rights movement. Or, if students study the social organization of the Upic, the Americans, and the Mexicans, and learn that one cultural system is as functional as another, then how do students judge the superiority of any one society? Our response to this criticism is that the purpose of history is to explain, not to evaluate. When a multi-perspectival history is taught well, it will provide students with the grounds upon which

they can make judgments and evaluations about significant historical events.

Another important result of our sociological approach to the teaching of history is it invites us to rethink the relationship between identity and society. Multicultural approaches—as they exist in practice in actual classrooms—begin with peoples' ethnic or racial identity, which relegates society to a residual status. We suggest beginning with society, which, of necessity, will turn our attention to how racial and ethnic identities are constituted in social life. Identity is not a fixed characteristic of individuals and groups. It is not always a relevant attribute that affects interactions in particular ways. Identity is instead a fluid process that emerges in interaction. Such features as race, ethnicity, and gender **may** be relevant in a variety of ways, **may** be relevant in some situations, but not in others. Furthermore, the "identity politics" that emerge from multiculturalism celebrates membership in a racial, ethnic, or gendered group, which deflects attention away from the civic identities that are needed to maintain a democratic, civil society (Gitlin, 1995).

The question to address, then, is not simply what difference does cultural difference make, because this approach can fall into the essentialist trap of assuming that race, ethnicity, and gender are ascribed, indeed permanent characteristics of people. The question to address is: What differences make a difference in specific historical events and periods?—an approach that assumes identities are fluid and ever-changing, something that is achieved, constructed, and constituted in

and through social interaction. This sociological view of identity in relationship to society necessitates a different kind of work in the history classroom, one which we have tried to outline above. In this approach the relevance of diversity in history is always an empirical question, and the focus of attention is always on society, out of which identity emerges.

We accept the premise that the teaching of history requires a common narrative, although we believe that the common core of this narrative is the struggle for civil rights, not the celebration of inevitable progress. We also accept the critique that the historical narrative often taught in schools is Eurocentric, has excluded the voices of minorities and women, and has neglected or suppressed issues of injustice. We also recognize that the task of teaching history is a complex one: how to construct and teach a narrative that tells us who we are as Americans while being inclusive and honest about institutional racism, exploitation, and discrimination.

If we begin the teaching of history with an inclusive narrative about the struggle for civil rights, then students will draw upon it unconsciously. The inclusive narrative will provide them "naturally" with a diverse view of what it means to be an American. **When an inclusive narrative is the taken-for-granted starting point, then issues concerning social justice, equality, and discrimination are more easily raised, because everyone is present, everyone is an active participant, and everyone is a speaker in the conversation about the constitution of American society.**

Multicultural Education as an Academic Discipline

A spirited dialogue is occurring among scholars in multicultural education on the future directions and philosophical foundations of this field of study. The essays in this unit reflect the results of some of this dialogue. How can multicultural education be integrated into professional educational studies so as to achieve its objectives?

Multicultural education developed out of the social upheavals of the 1960s and the concern of many scholars with the critical need for research-based knowledge of the cultural contexts of education. Much of our early knowledge came from important research in anthropology and sociology, as well as psychiatric studies of the impact of prejudice and victimization on targeted racial and cultural minorities, from the 1920s on. These studies examined intercultural relations in all sorts of urban, suburban, and rural settings in the United States. They used ethnographic field inquiry methods initially developed by anthropologists and later used by some sociologists and educators. Studies in the 1920s through the 1950s focused on such concerns as child-rearing practices, rites of passage into adulthood, perceptions of other cultural groups, and the social stratification systems of communities and neighborhoods. Studies in the 1930s and 1940s showed how victimized and involuntarily segregated racial and cultural groups responded to being targeted for discriminatory treatment. This body of social science knowledge became important documentation for the plaintiffs in *Brown v. Board of Education of Topeka* in 1954, the historic U.S. Supreme Court case that declared segregation on the basis of race to be unconstitutional.

As the civil rights movement begun in the 1950s in the United States grew in momentum throughout the 1960s, anthropological and sociological inquiry about the education of minority youth continued to develop. Out of the urban and other social crises of the 1960s emerged a belief among educators concerned with racial and cultural justice that there was a serious need for an area of educational study that would specifically focus on intercultural relations in the schools from a "multi-" cultural perspective. They envisioned studies that would challenge the by-then-traditional Eurocentric "melting pot" visions of how one became "American." The problem with the Eurocentric melting pot was that it was a very exclusionary pot; not everyone was welcome to jump into it. The philosophy of a culturally pluralist democracy in which all cultural heritages would be treasured and none rejected became attractive to those who witnessed the arbitrary and cruel effects of racial and cultural prejudice in schools as well as in other areas of life in "mainstream" society.

The belief that all teachers should respect the cultural heritages of their students and that all students have the right to know their cultural heritages as well as to develop self-esteem and pride in them began to spread among socially concerned educators. Studies conducted on intercultural relations among teachers and students by the early 1970s clearly demonstrated the need for an academic discipline that would specifically focus on building knowledge bases about our multicultural social reality as well as on how to teach about other cultural heritages and to improve the quality and the pedagogical effectiveness of instruction in multicultural school settings. Many of us realize today that all young Americans need to know about this nation from a perspective that rejects and transcends the old Anglo and Eurocentric presuppositions of melting pot theories of assimilation into American social life.

As part of the movement for civil rights, people from non-English-speaking backgrounds also sought to guarantee that their children would be given the opportunity to grow up both bilingual and bicultural. By the time the U.S. Supreme Court handed down its decision in *Lau v. Nichols* in 1974, there were dozens of federal court cases concerning the issues of bilingual education and English as a second language.

The academic leadership of the nation's cultural minorities and many other concerned scholars have forged a competent community dedicated to the task of setting standards of practice for multicultural education as a discipline. There is spirited dialogue in the field as to what these standards should be as well as about what academic qualifications people ought to have to conduct multicultural education. James A. Banks, professor at the University of Washington, and others are concerned about survival and development of multicultural education as

an academic discipline that must maintain its focus on classroom practice as well as on defensible theoretical constructs.

Multicultural education must develop an ongoing cadre of competent leaders to direct its development as well as to ensure that attempts to merely infuse multicultural content into existing teacher education course content does not dilute the academic quality of multicultural education or dilute the quality of standards of practice in the field. Banks argues that merely integrating multicultural education content into existing teacher education

course work must be resisted. He calls for a "Multicultural Education (MCE) + Integration" model for the practice of multicultural education. There should be qualified academic specialists in multicultural education on school faculties. Multicultural education is an interdiscipline that draws from anthropology, sociology, social history, and even psychiatry. Focused, adequately prepared specialists in this new interdiscipline are necessary if it is to maintain its academic integrity.

The essays in this unit reflect concerns regarding academic standards and goals for multicultural education as the field develops and enters a new period in its history. The authors of these essays raise important issues that must be addressed as the time approaches when a majority of Americans will be from "minority" cultural heritages and when traditional conceptions of "minority" and "majority" relations in the United States will have little meaning.

The essays in this unit are relevant to courses in curriculum theory and construction, educational policy studies, history and philosophy of education, cultural foundations of education, and multicultural education.

Looking Ahead: Challenge Questions

What should be some minimal standards of practice in the field of multicultural education?

What should be the qualifications for people who wish to become specialists in multicultural education?

It has been argued that all American students should learn the multicultural reality of our nation. Do you feel that this is true? How might it be accomplished?

What does it mean to speak of multicultural education as an interdiscipline?

What issues are raised by total "infusion" models of multicultural education in teacher education programs?

What should every American student know about racism and prejudice by the time they graduate from high school?

How do we help people learn to accept cultural diversity? What can teachers do to foster acceptance of cultural differences?

The Challenges of National Standards in a Multicultural Society

by Cherry A. McGee Banks

Ms. Banks argues that numerous considerations have not been addressed in the course of developing national standards.

Cherry A. McGee Banks is Associate Professor of Education, University of Washington, Bothell.

Since the late 1980s, national standards have been part of the discourse on school reform. An examination of that discourse reveals the extent to which the development and implementation of national standards have been shaped by forces that minimize the importance of diversity in U.S. society. Diversity is a salient characteristic of U.S. society. It is manifested in the racial and ethnic diversity of its citizens, their multiple identities, and the social-class positions they occupy. Developing and implementing national standards in a multicultural society should incorporate and give voice to diversity. When diversity is recognized as an important component of national standards questions such as "Whose Standards?" "Who benefits from the standards?" and "Whom will the standards harm?" will be raised by people outside the standards movement, but rarely by those within it.

When questions related to equity are raised by people inside the standards movement, they are addressed with a promise of high standards for all students. However, this promise will go unfulfilled if it is not accompanied by essential resources. In this article, I discuss the development of national standards and examine three types of standards: content, performance, and opportunity to learn. I then discuss multicultural literacy, a standard that is missing from the discourse on national standards.

 From *Educational Horizons*, Spring 1997, pp. 126-132.

The Development of National Standards

The development of national standards can be viewed as a case study in the way to develop educational policy without recognition of the complex characteristics of U.S. schools and students. The developers of national standards, who used a "top down" approach, did not realize the extent to which state governments and local school districts would oppose attempts to direct school reform from the federal level. Nor were they prepared to provide funding to address the tremendous inequalities in the facilities, resources, curricula, and teachers in schools.[1] Most important, the purpose of schooling has not been a significant topic in the discourse on national standards. The assumption that schooling was essentially preparation for the world of work was such a fundamental part of the thinking of those framing national standards that it was rarely questioned. The idea that schooling should also be a means for developing democratic values and commitments to social justice and equity was rarely considered or discussed.[2]

The standards movement was officially launched in 1989 when President George Bush held an education summit for the nation's governors in Charlottesville, Virginia. The summit took place at a time when the manufactured reality that our schools were in a dire condition and that drastic action was required was widely accepted without question.[3] The lack of discourse about the multiple interpretations of student performance and the realities of U.S. schools resulted in a national obsession about fixing the nation's schools. There was increasing concern about the ability of U.S. students to compete in a global economy. Business leaders pointed out that the U.S. economy had undergone significant changes, but the nation's schools had remained essentially the same as they had been for most of the twentieth century. The perceived mismatch between schools and the needs of the economy was the focus of media attention. Books describing how bad U.S. schools had become and listing what every educated person needed to know became best-sellers.[4] Proposed solutions for fixing the schools included returning to the basics, developing a national curriculum, and using standardized tests to assess student knowledge.

Within this atmosphere, President Bush and the state governors proposed six goals to guide educational reform and to raise the achievement levels of all students by the year 2000. The goals, known as America 2000, moved national standards to the center of school reform discourse. To support America 2000, Congress created the National Council on Education Standards and Testing (NCEST) in 1991 to advise it on matters related to standards and testing. "Raising Standards for American Education," a report

issued by NCEST in 1992, defined and affirmed the importance of content standards, performance standards, assessment, and opportunity to learn.

President Clinton, who attended Bush's education summit, began work on his own education program after he became president in 1993. His education program, which proposed voluntary goals for the states, was signed into law in 1994 as the Goals 2000: Educate America Act. Communities throughout the United States began using Goals 2000 to facilitate their own standards-based education improvements. In 1996, state governors joined with business leaders to issue a policy statement endorsing academic and performance standards. The policy statement, along with an appropriation bill that amended the Goals 2000: Educate America Act, was designed to strengthen the role of the states in the standards movement and to make standards more palatable to the conservatives who saw national standards as an expansion of the federal government's role in education. Language related to opportunity-to-learn and the National Education Standards and Improvement Council were eliminated from Goals 2000. Little, however, was done to assuage the concerns of educators who believe that standards can increase race and class stratification in U.S. society.

The Meaning and Possible Consequences of National Standards

National standards is a multifaceted idea. Three types of standards comprise national standards: content, performance, and opportunity to learn. Each type of standard provides different insights into the meaning and possible consequences of national standards. Some aspects of national standards focus on course content and teaching methods. Others focus on student performance; still others focus on factors that influence student achievement.

Content Standards

Content standards provide a structure to guide curriculum and instruction by framing core academic content areas in terms of what and how teachers should teach and what students should know and be able to do. Emphasis is put on students' developing an understanding of the key concepts and issues in the content area and being able to reason and communicate in ways that are characteristic of the discipline. Content standards have been developed in a number of disciplines, including history, science, and mathematics.

The National History Standards (NHS) are an example of content standards. The NHS, frequently misrepresented in the media as a school text, was a series of guide-

lines for teaching U.S. and world history. The first version of the history standards was published in November 1994. Those standards were revised in the spring of 1996 and reduced from three volumes to one. Both versions were directed by Charlotte Crabtree and Gary B. Nash at the National Center for History in the Schools at the University of California, Los Angeles, and funded by the National Endowment for the Humanities and the U.S. Department of Education. The development of the history standards purported to be an objective approach for reforming schools. However, the response they received upon their publication, which included political intervention and the privileging of conservative ideological perspectives, suggested otherwise.

The response to the NHS was immediate, bitter, and widespread. The NHS were perceived by conservatives as not focusing on what was most worth knowing in history.[5] Conservatives believed the NHS devoted too much space to women and people of color. Critics of the standards—many of whom are not historians—counted the number of times historical figures they admired were included in the standards. They concluded that major historical figures had been omitted or slighted in the NHS.[6] Conservatives called for the repeal of the NHS and the development of what they termed "true reliable national standards."

Even though the NHS were strongly supported by the two leading history professional associations, the American Historical Association and the Organization of American Historians, the attacks continued and eventually culminated in an official repudiation of the standards by the U.S. Congress. Sen. Slade Gordon of Washington state led the attack on the history standards on the floor of the U.S. Senate. He argued that the standards were not balanced or objective because they emphasized what was negative in America's past and celebrated "politically correct" culture and causes.

The attack on the original version of the history standards and their forced revision raises the specter of political power coupled with intimidation, public attack, and humiliation as a means to create "official" history.[7] The original history standards were neither as radical nor as irresponsible as they were described by their critics. They did, however, provide a framework for teachers and students to uncover unlearned lessons from the past and to study U.S. history from the perspective of the vanquished as well as the victors. The attacks on the history standards helped to maintain the established history curriculum and to halt efforts to legitimize the histories, voices, and experiences of groups who traditionally have been excluded from school history.[8]

Democracy requires citizens who understand that the development of the United States has not been a straight path to freedom, liberty, and justice.[9] Many groups of Americans have been victimized in the past and are still being victimized today. If we are to build a just society, we must give students opportunities to learn from our mistakes as well as to celebrate our victories. An authentic history of the U.S. must not only include the stories of people who are at the center of U.S. society; also it must include the historic struggles of people on the margins. Students need to understand how these struggles are reflected in quests for equality today. The discourse on the national history standards was shaped by

of the attained curriculum. Disaggregating the curriculum into three components reveals the extent to which education is a highly contextualized system and highlights the relationship between educational experiences and student achievement.

Opportunity to learn (OTL) is used by advocates of disenfranchised students to acknowledge the political and economic link between schools and society and to identify and demonstrate how factors such as income and access to knowledge, influence academic achievement. OTL is also used to identify how variables such as quality of

in general or vocational tracks have limited access to college preparatory courses.[10] Students of color and low-income students are disproportionately represented in general and vocational tracks. In 1985, 51.5 percent of white students and only 28.1 percent of black and Hispanic students were enrolled in academic math classes.[11] Students who are tracked into college-preparatory courses have greater access to more challenging and rewarding curricula than students in lower tracks. Students in college-preparation tracks are disproportionately from advantaged socioeconomic groups. Moreover, important gate-keeping courses such as calculus are not available in many schools with large numbers of low-income students and students of color.

OTL factors also call attention to the differences in the quality and credentials of teachers of students who teach in central city schools and those who teach in middle-class suburban schools. Students in the central city are more likely to be taught by teachers who have less experience and who are less qualified than suburban teachers. In 1983, more than 14 percent of the new teachers in central cities were uncertified in their primary fields of instruction. This was almost double the percentage of such teachers in suburban districts.[12]

Schools in central-city schools have fewer resources and less funding than suburban schools. In *Savage Inequalities,* Jonathan Kozol describes a school that offered a computer course but did not have computers for students.[13] Disparity in funding among districts is especially evident when school districts that are primarily populated by upper-middle-class students are compared to school districts in which most of the students are from low-income families. For example, in the 1990–91 school year New York City, which has a large percentage of low-income students and students of color, spent $7,300 per student, while Great Neck, a nearby suburban school district, spent $15,000 per student.[14]

Given the tremendous disparity in educational resources and opportunities of U.S. students, it is understandable why OTL factors are embraced by advocates of disenfranchised students. OTL standards are very meaningful for low-income students, students of color, students who do not speak English as their first language, and other disenfranchised students. Disparity in the educational resources affects the course offerings, facilities, books, computers, labs, the quality of teachers, and the quality of teaching in the schools they attend. School reform efforts that do not acknowledge these disparities will fail.

Are you saying, Senator, that after the thirty-seventh rewrite of this textbook, we should cut out some of the minor characters of American history to explain the importance of horses, pigs, and chickens?

forces that muted the importance of diversity in U.S. society. In arguing against the history standards, conservatives failed to recognize that U.S. history is the story of all its peoples, not just the powerful few who want school history to tell only their stories.

Opportunity to Learn Standards

Opportunity-to-learn (OTL) is a concept that was introduced in the 1960s by researchers who were trying to validate cross-national comparisons of mathematics achievement. These researchers recognized that achievement is complex and influenced by many factors. They identified three different levels of curricula that influence achievement: the intended curriculum, the implemented curriculum, and the attained curriculum. The intended curriculum is articulated by officials at the national level. The implemented curriculum is enacted by teachers in their classrooms. Student achievement on standardized tests provides evidence

school facilities, availability of teaching materials, and teacher expertise influence achievement. Language related to opportunity to learn was included in both America 2000 and Goals 2000. However, it was deleted from the 1996 budget bill for Goals 2000 and from the 1996 National Education Summit policy statement. Conservatives were able to argue successfully that OTL standards would take attention away from achievement and put the focus on resources or input variables. They took the position that OTL issues should be addressed at the state level, not directed by the federal government. As a result, addressing OTL factors will likely have a low priority as states and local school districts respond to the national standards. The money saved by deleting OTL standards from the national standards agenda will be paid for by sacrificing the futures of disenfranchised students.

OTL factors highlight the inequalities that exist in the educational experiences of many low-income students and students of color. For example, students who are placed

Performance Standards

Performance standards provide concrete examples and explicit definitions of what students need to know and be able to do in order to demonstrate proficiency in the skills and knowledge specified by content standards. Most advocates of national standards believe that performance standards are a logical consequence of content standards and that content standards would be meaningless without performance standards. Therefore, as new curriculum frameworks are being developed, new assessments are also being developed. The New Standards Project developed and piloted performance tasks that are designed to provide information on what students know and can do. These tasks, sometimes referred to as authentic assessment, are also intended to improve teaching and curriculum. They include videotapes of performances, debates, exhibitions, teacher observations and inventories of student work, as well as other examples of student behavior in real-world situations. Although these new approaches to assessment will be more closely aligned to the curriculum than in the past, they do not provide a means for educators and policymakers to differentiate levels of achievement in terms of OTL factors.

Proponents of performance standards claim that differentiating levels of achievement in terms of OTL factors is not necessary. They argue that performance standards are the best hope for low-income students and students of color because performance standards promote "high standards for all students." Without resources, that slogan will be an empty promise. Low-income students and students of color will be left to suffer the consequences of low performance on their own. Consequences such as grade retention, placement in remedial programs, and denial of diplomas can have a devastating impact on students. Moreover, these kinds of consequences are not only ineffective, they may serve as justifications for further exclusion.

Parents who are concerned about consequences that will likely be viewed as a confirmation of their students' low ability will have very few options available to them. They can talk to their children's teachers; have their children transferred to new schools; put their children in private or parochial schools; complain to the principal, superintendent, or school board; implement a tutorial program at home; or engage in some other form of action. All of these options assume that all students have informed active, and academically capable parents. Students whose parents face language, financial, or other barriers to active school involvement will not likely benefit from performance standards.

The lack of recognition and response to the connection between assessment and performance, perhaps more than any other aspect of the standards movement, raises historic and troubling concerns related to fairness, justice, and educational equality. Even though we know that unequal re-

To be effective, assessments must consider the adequacy of resources when identifying what a student knows and can do.

sources can affect quality of teachers, availability of advanced courses, the safety of the school environment, and other factors that can contribute to what students know and can do, performance assessments do not account for these factors. Without information on the factors that contribute to high and low performance, students from low-income families as well as many students of color may fall victim to historic beliefs about their genetic inferiority that are accepted by many educators. The success of *The Bell Curve* attests to the continuing saliency of beliefs about inherited ability and academic achievement.[15]

Highly motivated students who have high potential should not be penalized for factors in the school or community environment that are beyond their control. To be effective, assessments must consider the adequacy of resources when identifying what a student knows and can do. In that way assessment will not simply be a way to identify what students know and can do. They will identify what students know and can do as a result of their educational experiences.

National standards will not substitute for needed resources and programs such as bilingual education. The number of students who do not speak English is increasing as the funding for bilingual programs is decreasing. In 1990, 14 percent of school-age youths lived in homes in which English was not their first language.[16] Parents whose children speak English poorly will be more interested in what the school is doing to teach their children English than their children's scores on tests that they had trouble reading.

The Missing Standard: Multicultural Literacy

In a society that continues to be deeply divided along race, gender, and social-class lines, students need to recognize and understand the historic and contemporary role of diversity in U.S. society. Multicultural literacy will provide a framework for teachers to develop course content that will challenge students to recognize the multifaceted and complex ways in which structural inequality continues to exist in U.S. society.[17] For example, even though many African-Americans have historically viewed education as a means to upward mobility, many inner-city African-American students know that an education will not necessarily result in a better life.[18] They see many people in their communities who have a very difficult time securing gainful employment even when they have a high school diploma. In 1992, more than half of African-American high school graduates, compared to almost three-fourths of high school dropouts were unemployed. While less than twenty percent of white high school graduates, compared to mroe than one third of high school dropouts were unemployed.[19] White males and females are more likely to hire a white female over either an African-American male or female.[20] These data suggest that blacks have

Many of the advocates of national standards seem prepared to abandon these students if they are not able to succeed against great odds.

fewer economic incentives to stay in school than whites.

Racial incidents and gender discrimination are increasing in U.S. society and in the nation's schools. Prejudice and discrimination not only indicate the level of injustice in our society, they are also barriers to learning.[21] Multicultural literacy helps schools to resolve intergroup tensions in the schools and society and students to develop the knowledge, skills, and commitment needed to participate in personal, social, and civic action to make our society more democratic and just.[22] Teachers need support and further education to work effectively with students to reduce sexism, racism, and class inequality.

Multicultural literacy would provide a vehicle for schools to recognize the importance of educating the hearts as well as the minds of students. It would also provide a basis for students to think deeply about citizenship in a pluralistic democratic society and encourage students to engage in citizen action to extend the principles of freedom, equality, and justice. Multicultural literacy is needed to develop creative and reflective citizens who are prepared to compete in a global workforce, but who also have the skills, knowledge, and confidence to question the status quo and to work for social justice.[23]

Conclusion

The standards movement is our latest magic bullet in a long line of school-reform strategies. Standards provide a false sense of security by suggesting that we have found a way to cure our educational ills. However, the cure may prove to be more deleterious than the problems. The active involvement of politicians, commentators, and political appointees in what should have been a professional and academic endeavor raises questions about who constructs school knowledge and for what purposes. The almost exclusive focus on the relationship between schooling and the world of work potentially marginalizes subjects such as art, music, and foreign languages and raises the question of what knowledge will be privileged in the school curriculum. Most important, even though diversity is increasing in U.S. society, content that can help students

become effective citizens in a pluralistic democratic society has been jeopardized by the standards movement. Many of the responses to the history standards questioned whether the roles of women and people of color should be integral parts of U.S. history.

National standards obscure more than they reveal. They divert attention from the realities of schools in low-income, rural, and urban communities. Those realities include schools with leaky roofs, limited access to advanced curricula offerings, and teachers who are overworked and underpaid. In the next few decades, the nation's schools will enroll increasing numbers of low-income students, students of color, and students who do not speak English as their first language. These students will need more than content and performance standards to increase their academic achievement and social success in school. Many of the advocates of national standards seem prepared to abandon these students if they are not able to succeed against great odds. If educators ignore how opportunities to learn influence student performance, these students are likely to be blamed for their academic failure and doomed to second-class citizenship.

1. Michael W. Apple, "The Dangers of a National Curriculum," *In These Times* 17 (November 15, 1993): 26–27.
2. James A. Banks, *Educating Citizens in a Multicultural Society* (New York: Teachers College Press, 1997).
3. David C. Berliner, Bruce J. Biddle, and James Bell, *The Manufactured Crisis: Myths, Fraud, and the Attack on America's Public Schools* (Reading, Mass.: Addison Wesley, Longman, 1996).
4. Diane Ravitch and Chester E. Finn, Jr., *What Do Our 17-Year-Olds Know?* (New York: Harper & Row, 1987) and E. D. Hirsch, Jr., *Cultural Literacy: What Every American Needs to Know* (Boston: Houghton Mifflin, 1987).
5. Lynne V. Cheney, "The End of History," *Wall Street Journal,* 20 October 1994, 26, and David W. Sax, "The National History Standards: Time for Common Sense," *Social Education* 60 (January 1995): 44–48.
6. Robert Cohen, "Moving Beyond Name Games: The Conservative Attack on the U.S. History," *Social Education* 60 (January 1995): 49–54.
7. Gary B. Nash and Ross E. Dunn, "National History Standards: Controversy and Com-

mentary," *Social Studies Review* 34 (Winter 1995): 4–12.
8. Joyce Appleby, "Controversy Over the National History Standards," *OAH Magazine of History* 9 (Spring 1995), 4.
9. Arthur M. Schlesinger, Jr., *The Cycles of American History* (Boston: Houghton Mifflin, 1986).
10. Gretchen Guiton and Jeannie Oakes, "Opportunity to Learn and Conceptions of Educational Equality," *Educational Evaluation and Policy Analysis* 17 (Fall 1995): 323–336.
11. National Center for Education Statistics, *The Condition of Education* (Washington, D.C.: U.S. Department of Education, 1985).
12. Linda Darling-Hammond, "Inequality and Access to Knowledge," in *Handbook of Research on Multicultural Education,* ed. James A. Banks and Cherry A. McGee Banks (New York: Macmillan, 1995).
13. Jonathan Kozol, *Savage Inequalities* (New York: Crown Publishing, 1991).
14. Ibid.
15. Richard Hernstein and Charles Murray, *The Bell Curve* (New York: Free Press, 1994).
16. Committee on Developing a Research Agenda on the Education of Limited-English-Proficient and Bilingual Students Board on Children, Youth, and Families, *Improving Schooling for Language-Minority Children* (New York: National Academy Press, 1997).
17. James A. Banks and Cherry A. McGee Banks, *Handbook of Research on Multicultural Education* (New York: Macmillan, 1995).
18. William Julius Wilson, *When Work Disappears: The World of the Urban Poor* (New York: Knopf, 1996).
19. Antoine M. Garibaldi, "African-American Students as Dropouts," in *Encyclopedia of African-American Culture and History,* ed. Jack Salzman, David Lionel Smith, and Cornel West (New York: Macmillan, 1996), 181–184.
20. Luethel Tate Green, "Gender Differences and African-American Education" in *Encyclopedia of African-American Culture and History,* ed. Jack Salzman, David Lionel Smith, and Cornel West (New York: Macmillan, 1996), 181–184.
21. Claude M. Steele and Joshua Aronson, "Stereotype Threat and the Intellectual Test Performance of African Americans," *Journal of Personality and Social Psychology* 69, No. 5: 797–811.
22. Cherry A. McGee Banks and James A. Banks, "Teaching for Multicultural Literacy," *Louisiana Social Studies Journal* 16 (Fall 1989): 5–9.
23. Ibid.

Multicultural Education and Curriculum Transformation

James A. Banks

James A. Banks, Center for Multicultural Education, University of Washington-Seattle*

In this, the text of the 1995 Charles H. Thompson Lecture, the author describes five dimensions of multicultural education, focusing on the knowledge construction process. This dimension is emphasized to show how the cultural assumptions, frames of reference, and perspectives of mainstream scholars and researchers influence the ways in which they construct academic knowledge to legitimize institutionalized inequality. The process by which transformative scholars create oppositional knowledge and liberatory curricula that challenge the status quo and sanction action and reform is also described. This process is endorsed as a means of helping students become effective citizens in a pluralistic, democratic society.

The racial crisis in America, the large number of immigrants that are entering the nation each year, the widening gap between the rich and the poor, the changing characteristics of the nation's student population make it imperative that schools be reformed in ways that will help students and teachers to re-envision, rethink, and reconceptualize America. Fundamental changes in our educational system are essential so that we can, in the words of Rodney King, "all get along." The nation's student population is changing dramatically. By 2020, nearly half (about 48%) of the nation's students will be students of color. Today, about 31% of the youth in the United States under 18 are of color and about one out of every five students is living below the official poverty level (U.S. Bureau of the Census, 1993).

> *It is imperative that schools be reformed in ways that will help students and teachers to re-envision, rethink, and reconceptualize America.*

Multicultural education, a school reform movement that arose out of the civil rights movement of

From the *Journal of Negro Education*, pp. 390-400, Vol. 64, No. 4, Fall 1995. © 1996 by Howard University. Reprinted by permission.

Teachers play an important part in helping students understand how knowledge is created and how it can be influenced by race, ethnic, and social class. (Photo by Steve Takatsuno)

the 1960s and 1970s, if implemented in thoughtful, creative, and effective ways, has the potential to transform schools and other educational institutions in ways that will enable them to prepare students to live and function effectively in the coming century (Banks & Banks, 1995a). I will describe the major goals and dimensions of multicultural education, discuss knowledge construction and curriculum transformation, and describe how transformative academic knowledge can be used to re-invent and re-imagine the curriculum in the nation's schools, colleges, and universities.

Multicultural Education and School Reform

There is a great deal of confusion about multicultural education in both the popular mind and among teachers and other educational practitioners. Much of this confusion is created by critics of multicultural education such as Schlesinger (1991), D'Souza (1995), and Sacks and Theil (1995). The critics create confusion by stating and repeating claims about multiculturalism and diversity that are documented with isolated incidents, anecdotes, and examples of poorly conceptualized and implemented educational practices. The research and theory that have been developed by the leading theorists in multicultural education are rarely cited by the field's critics (Sleeter, 1995).

The critics of multicultural education often direct their criticism toward what they call multiculturalism. This term is rarely used by theorists and researchers in multicultural education. Consequently, it is important to distinguish what the critics call multiculturalism from what multicultural education theorists call multicultural education. Multiculturalism is a term often used by the critics of diversity to describe a set of educational practices they oppose. They use this term to describe educational practices they consider antithetical to the Western canon, to the democratic tradition, and to a universalized and free society.

Multicultural education is an educational reform movement that tries to reform schools in ways that will give all students an equal opportunity to learn.

Multiculturalism and multicultural education have different meanings. I have conceptualized multicultural education in a way that consists of three major components: an idea or concept, an educational reform movement, and a process (Banks, 1993a). As an idea or concept, multicultural education maintains that all students should have equal opportunities to learn regardless of racial, ethnic, social-class, or gender group to which they belong. Additionally, multicultural education describes ways in which some students are denied equal educational opportunities because of their racial, ethnic, social-class, or gender characteristics (Lee & Slaughter-Defoe, 1995; Nieto, 1995). Multicultural education is an educational reform movement that tries to reform schools in ways that will give all students an equal opportunity to learn. It describes teaching strategies that empower all students and give them voice.

Multicultural education is a continuing process. One of its major goals is to create within schools and society the democratic ideals that Myrdal (1944) called "American Creed" values—values such as justice, equality, and freedom. These ideals are stated in the nation's founding documents—in the Declaration of Independence, the Constitution, and the Bill of Rights. They can never be totally achieved, but citizens within a democratic society must constantly work toward attaining them. Yet, when we approach the realization of these ideals for particular groups, other groups become victimized by racism, sexism, and discrimination. Consequently, within a democratic, pluralistic society, multicultural education is a continuing process that never ends.

The Dimensions of Multicultural Education

To effectively conceptualize and implement multicultural education curricula, programs, and practices, it is necessary not only to define the concept in general terms but to describe it programmatically. To facilitate this process, I have developed a typology called the dimensions of multicultural education (Banks, 1993b, 1995a). This dimensions typology can help practitioners identify and formulate reforms that implement multicultural education in thoughtful, creative, and effective ways. It is also designed to help theorists and researchers delineate the scope of the field and identify related research and theories. The dimensions typology is an ideal-type construct in the Weberian sense. The dimensions are highly interrelated, and the boundaries between and within them overlap. However, they are conceptually distinct.

A description of the conceptual scope of each dimension facilitates conceptual clarity and the development of sound educational practices. As Gay (1995) has pointed out, there is a wide gap between theory, research, and practice in multicultural education. The practices within schools that violate sound principles in multicultural education theory and research are cannon fodder for the field's critics, who often cite questionable practices that masquerade as multicultural education to support the validity of their claims. Although there is a significant gap between theory and practice within all fields in education, the consequences of such a gap are especially serious within new fields that are marginal and trying to obtain legitimacy within schools, colleges, and universities. Thus, the dimensions of multicultural education can serve as benchmark criteria for conceptualizing, developing, and assessing theory, research, and practice.

In my research, I have identified five dimensions of multicultural education (Banks, 1995a). They are: (a) content integration, (b) the knowledge construction process, (c) prejudice reduction, (d) an equity pedagogy; and an (e) empowering school culture and social structure. I will briefly describe each of these dimensions.

Content integration describes the ways in which teachers use examples and content from a variety of cultures and groups to illustrate key concepts, principles, generalizations, and theories in their subject area or discipline. The knowledge construction process consists of the methods, activities, and questions used by teachers to help students understand, investigate, and determine how implicit cultural assumptions, frames of reference, perspectives, and biases within a discipline influence the ways in which knowledge is constructed. When the knowledge construction process is implemented, teachers help students understand how knowledge is created and how it is influenced by the racial, ethnic, and social-class positions of individuals and groups (Code, 1991; Collins, 1990).

The prejudice reduction dimension of multicultural education relates to the characteristics of students' racial attitudes and strategies that teachers can use to help them develop more democratic values and attitudes. Since the late 1930s, researchers have been studying racial awareness, racial identification, and racial preference in young children (Clark & Clark, 1939; Cross, 1991; Spencer, 1982). This research is too vast and complex to summarize here; however, studies indicate, for example, that both children of color and White children develop a "White bias" by the time they enter kindergarten (Phinney & Rotheram, 1987; Spencer, 1982). This research suggests that teachers in all subject areas need to take action to help students develop more democratic racial attitudes and values. It also suggests that interventions work best when children are young. As children grow older, it becomes increasingly difficult to modify their racial attitudes and beliefs (Banks, 1995b).

An empowering school culture and social structure conceptualizes the school as a complex social system.

An equity pedagogy exists when teachers modify their teaching in ways that will facilitate the academic achievement of students from diverse racial, ethnic, cultural, and gender groups (Banks &

Banks, 1995b). A number of researchers such as Au (1980), Boykin (1982), Depit (1995), Kleinfeld (1975), Ladson-Billings (1995), and Shade and New (1993) have described culturally sensitive (sometimes called culturally congruent) teaching strategies whose purpose is to enhance the academic achievement of students from diverse cultural and ethnic groups and the characteristics of effective teachers of these students. This research indicates that the academic achievement of students of color and low-income students can be increased when teaching strategies and activities build upon the cultural and linguistic strengths of students, and when teachers have cultural competency in the cultures of their students. Kleinfeld, for example, found that teachers who were "warm demanders" were the most effective teachers of Indian and Eskimo youths. Other researchers maintain that teachers also need to have high academic expectations for these students, to explicitly teach them the rules of power governing classroom interactions, and to create equal-status situations in the classroom (Cohen & Lotan, 1995).

An empowering school culture and social structure conceptualizes the school as a complex social system, whereas the other dimensions deal with particular aspects of a school or educational setting. This dimension conceptualizes the school as a social system that is larger than any of its constituent parts such as the curriculum, teaching materials, and teacher attitudes and perceptions. The systemic view of the schools requires that in order to effectively reform schools, the entire system must be restructured, not just some of its parts. Although reform may begin with any one of the parts of a system (such as with the curriculum or with staff development), the other parts of the system (such as textbooks and the assessment program) must also be restructured in order to effectively implement school reform related to diversity.

A systemic view of educational reform is especially important when reform is related to issues as complex and emotionally laden as race, class, and gender. Educational practitioners—because of the intractable challenges they face, their scarce resources, and the perceived limited time they have to solve problems due to the high expectations of an impatient public—often want quick fixes to complex educational problems. The search for quick solutions to problems related to race and ethnicity partially explains some of the practices, often called multicultural education, that violate theory and research. These include marginalizing content about ethnic groups by limiting them to specific days and holidays such as Black History month and Cinco de Mayo. A systemic view of educational reform is essential for the implementation of thoughtful, creative, and meaningful educational reform.

Knowledge Construction and Curriculum Transformation

I will focus on only one of the dimensions of multicultural education: knowledge construction. In my latest book, *Multicultural Education, Transformative Knowledge, and Action* (1996), I describe a typology of knowledge that consists of five types: (a) personal/cultural, (b) popular, (c) mainstream academic, (d) transformative academic, and (e) school knowledge. I will discuss only two of these knowledge types: mainstream academic and transformative academic.

Mainstream Academic Knowledge

Mainstream academic knowledge consists of the concepts, paradigms, theories, and explanations that constitute traditional and established knowledge in the behavioral and social sciences. An important tenet within mainstream academic knowledge is that there is a set of objective truths that can be verified through rigorous and objective research procedures that are uninfluenced by human interests, values, and perspectives. Most of the knowledge that constitutes the established canon in the nation's schools, colleges, and universities is mainstream academic knowledge.

Today, the West paradigm in American history and culture is powerful, cogent, and deeply entrenched in the curriculum of the nation's institutions of learning.

The traditional conceptualization of the settlement of the West is a powerful example of the way in which mainstream academic knowledge has shaped the paradigms, canons, and perspectives that become institutionalized within the college, university, and school curriculum. In an influential paper presented at a meeting of the American Historical Association in 1893, Frederick Jackson Turner (1894/1989) argued that the frontier, which he regarded as a sparsely populated wilderness and lacking in civilization, was the main source of American democracy and freedom. Although Turner's thesis is now being criticized by revisionist historians, his paper established a conception of the West that has been highly influential in American scholarship, popular culture, and school books. His ideas, however, are closely related to other European conceptions of the Americas, of "the other" (Todorov, 1982), and of the native peoples who lived in the land that the European conceptualized as "the West." Turner's paradigm, and the interpretations that derive from it, largely ignore the large number of indigenous peoples who were living in the Americas when the Europeans arrived (Thornton [1995] estimates seven million). It also fails to acknowledge the rich cultures and civilizations that existed in the Americas, and the fact that the freedom the Europeans found in the West meant destruction and genocide for the various groups of Native Americans. By the beginning of the 20th century, most American Indian groups had been defeated by U.S. military force (Hyatt & Nettleford, 1995). Their collective will, however, was not broken, as evidenced by the renewed quest for Indian rights that emerged during the civil rights movement of the 1960s and 1970s.

Today, the West paradigm in American history and culture is powerful, cogent, and deeply entrenched in the curriculum of the nation's institutions of learning. As such, it often prevents students at all levels of education from gaining a sophisticated, complex, and compassionate understanding of American history, society, and culture. The West paradigm must therefore be seriously examined and deconstructed in order for students to acquire such an understanding. Students must be taught, for example, that the concept of the West is a Eurocentric idea, and they must be helped to understand how different groups in American society conceptualized and viewed the West differently.

For example, the Mexicans who became a part of the United States after the Treaty of Guadalupe Hidalgo in 1848 did not view or conceptualize the Southwest as the West. Rather, they viewed the territory that Mexico lost to the United States after the war as Mexico's "North." The Indian groups living in the western territories did not view their homelands as the West but as the center of the universe. To the various immigrants to the U.S. from Asia such as those from Japan and China, the land to which they immigrated was "the East" or the "land of the Golden Mountain." By helping students view Eurocentric concepts such as the West, "the Discovery of America," and "the New World" from different perspectives and points of view, we can increase their ability to conceptualize, to determine the implicit perspectives embedded in curriculum materials, and to become more thoughtful and reflective citizens.

Transformative Academic Knowledge

Teachers can help students acquire new perspectives on the development of American history and society by reforming the curriculum with the use of paradigms, perspectives, and points of view from transformative academic knowledge. Transformative academic knowledge consists of the concepts, paradigms, themes, and explanations that challenge mainstream academic knowledge and that expand the historical and literary canon (Banks, 1996). It thus challenges some of the key assumptions that mainstream scholars make about the nature of knowledge as well as some of their major paradigms, findings, theories, and interpretations. While mainstream academic scholars claim that their findings and interpretations are universalistic and unrelated to human interests, transformative scholars view knowledge as related to the cultural experiences of individuals and groups (Collins, 1990). Transformative scholars also believe that a major goal of knowledge is to improve society (Clark, 1965).

Louie Psihoyos—Woodfin Camp

Transformative Scholarship and the Quest for Democracy

Within the last two decades, there has been a rich proliferation of transformative scholarship developed by scholars on the margins of society (Banks & Banks, 1995a). This scholarship challenges many of the paradigms, concepts, and interpretations that are institutionalized within the nation's schools, colleges, and universities. Much, but not all, of this scholarship has been developed by scholars of color and feminist scholars. For example, in this book, *Margins and Mainstreams: Asians in American History and Culture,* Gary Okhiro (1994) argues that groups on the margins of society have played significant roles in maintaining democratic values in American society by challenging practices that violated democracy and human rights. Okhiro notes that America's minorities were among the first to challenge institutionalized racist

practices such as slavery, the forced removal of the American Indians from native lands, segregation, and the internment of Japanese Americans during World War II. By so doing, they helped to keep democracy alive in the United States.

As I point out in my most recent book, transformative scholars and transformative scholarship have long histories in the United States (Banks, 1996). Transformative scholars and their work have helped to maintain democracy in the academic community by challenging racist scholarship and ideologies that provided the ideological and scholarly justification for institutionalized racist practices and policies. This lecture honors Charles H. Thompson, a transformative scholar and educator who was founding editor of the *Journal of Negro Education.* The *Journal* was established to provide a forum for transformative scholars and researchers to publish their findings and interpretations related to the education of Black people throughout the world. Much of their research challenged mainstream research and contributed to the education and liberation of African Americans.

Transformative scholars and their work have helped to maintain democracy in the academic community by challenging racist scholarship and ideologies.

In his editorial comment in the first issue of the *Journal,* entitled "Why a Journal of Negro Education?" Thompson (1932) advocated Black self-determination. He believed that the *Journal* would provide African Americans with a vehicle for assuming a greater role in their own education. As Thompson stated:

> . . . leadership in the investigation of the education of Negroes should be assumed to a greater extent by Negro educators . . . [yet there is] no ready and empathetic outlet for the publication of the results of [the Negro's] investigations. . . . Thus, it is believed that the launching of this project will stimulate Negroes to take a greater part in the solutions of the problems that arise in connection with their own education. (p. 2)

Black self-determination is as important today as when Thompson penned these words. The first issue of the *Journal of Negro Education* was published in April 1932. The *Journal* has continued its transformative tradition for 63 years. Other transformative journals founded by African American scholars include the *Journal of Negro History,* founded by Carter G. Woodson in 1916, and *Phylon,* founded by W. E. B. DuBois at Atlanta University in 1940. Prior to the founding of these journals, transformative scholars had few outlets for the publication of their works. The mainstream academic community and its journal editors had little interest in research and work on communities of color prior to the 19690s, especially work that presented positive descriptions of minority communities and that was oppositional to mainstream racist scholarship. When we examine the history of scholarship in the United States, it is striking how both racist scholarship and transformative scholarship have been consistent through time. Near the

turn of the century, research and theories that described innate distinctions among racial groups was institutionalized within American social science (Tucker, 1994). A group of transformative scholars including thinkers as DuBois, Kelly Miller, and Franz Boas seriously challenged these conceptions (Banks, 1996).

The relationship between transformative and mainstream social science is interactive; each influences the other. Over time, transformative knowledge influences mainstream knowledge, and elements of tranformative knowledge become incorporated into mainstream knowledge. For example, the conceptions about race that were constructed by transformative scholars near the turn of the century became the accepted concepts and theories in mainstream social science during the 1940s and 1950s. Nevertheless, a group of scholars continued to invent research and construct ideas about the inferiority of particular racial groups.

Prior to the civil rights movement of the 1960s and 1970s, the White mainstream academic community ignored most of the scholarship created by African American scholars.

The history of research about race in America indicates that theories about the racial inferiority of certain groups—and challenges to them from transformative scholars—never disappear (Tucker, 1994). What varies is the extent to which theories of racial inferiority and other theories that support inequality attain public legitimacy and respectability. Since the beginning of the 20th century, every decade has witnessed the development of such theories. The extent to which these theories, and the individuals who purported them, experienced public respectability, awards, and recognitions has varied considerably. The amount of recognition that transformative scholars who challenged these theories have received from the public and academic communities has also varied considerably through time.

Prior to the civil rights movement of the 1960s and 1970s, the White mainstream academic community ignored most of the scholarship created by

(Photo: AP/Wide World/Carlos Osorio)

Teachers can help their students learn new perspectives on American history and society development through curriculum reformation.

African American scholars. Most African American scholars had to take jobs in historically Black colleges. Most of these colleges were teaching institutions that had few resources with which to support and encourage research. Professors at these institutions had demanding teaching loads. Nevertheless, important research was done by African American and by a few White transformative scholars prior to the 1960s. Yet, because this research was largely ignored by the mainstream academic community, it had little influence on the knowledge about racial and ethnic groups that became institutionalized within the popular culture and the mainstream academic community. Consequently, it had little influence on the curriculum and the textbooks used in most of the nation's schools, colleges, and universities.

Although it was largely ignored by the mainstream community, a rich body of transformative scholarship was created in the years from the turn of the century to the 1950s. Much of this research was incorporated into popular textbooks that were used in Black schools and colleges. For example,

Carter G. Woodson's *The Negro in Our History*, first published in 1930, was published in a 10th edition in 1962. John Hope Franklin's *From Slavery to Freedom*, first published in 1947, is still a popular history textbook in its seventh edition. Scholarly works published during this period included *The Philadelphia Negro* by W. E. B. DuBois (1899/1975), *American Negro Slave Revolt* by Herbert Aptheker (1943), *The Negro in the Civil War* by Benjamin Quarles (1953), *The Free Negro in North Carolina, 1790–1860*, by John Hope Franklin (1943), and Woodson's *The Education of the Negro Prior to 1861* (1919/1968).

The Need for a Transformative, Liberatory Curriculum

Prior to the 1960s, African American scholars and their White colleagues who did research on the African American community remained primarily at the margins of the mainstream academic community. Most of the paradigms and explanations related to racial ethnic groups that became institutionalized within the mainstream academic community were created by scholars outside these groups. Most of the paradigms, concepts, and theories created by mainstream scholars reinforced the status quo and provided intellectual justifications for institutionalized stereotypes and misconceptions about groups of color. An important example of this kind of scholarship is *American Negro Slavery* by Ulrich B. Phillips, published in 1918. Phillips described slaves as happy, inferior, and as benefiting from Western civilization. His interpretation of slavery became the institutionalized one within American colleges and universities, and he became one of the nation's most respected historians.

Phillips's view of slavery was not seriously challenged within the mainstream scholarly community until historians such as Stanley M. Elkins (1959), Kenneth M. Stampp (1956), John Blassingame (1972), and Eugene D. Genovese (1972) published new interpretations of slavery during the 1950s, 1960s, and 1970s. Transformative scholarship that presented other interpretations of slavery had been published as early as 1943, when Aptheker published *American Negro Slave Revolts*. However, this work was largely ignored and marginalized by the mainstream community partly because it was inconsistent with established views of slaves and slavery.

More recent research on the cognitive and intellectual abilities of African Americans indicates the extent to which antiegalitarian research is still influential in the mainstream academic community. In 1969, for example, the prestigious *Harvard Educational Review* devoted 123 pages of its first issue that year to Arthur Jensen's article on the differential intellectual abilities of Whites and African Americans. Papers by transformative scholars who embraced paradigms different from Jensen's were not published in this influential issue, although comments on the article by other scholars were published in the next issue of the *Review* (Kagan et al., 1969). Even though Jensen's article occupied most of the pages in an issue of a well-known scholarly journal, he experienced much public scorn and rejection when he appeared in public lectures and forums on university campuses.

Published nearly a quarter century after Jensen's article, *The Bell Curve* by Herrnstein and Murray (1994) received an enthusiastic and warm reception in both the academic and public communities. It was widely discussed in the public media and remained on the *New York Times* bestseller list for many weeks. Although it evoked much discussion and controversy (Jacoby & Glauberman, 1995), it

attained a high degree of legitimacy within both the academic and public communities.

The publication of *The Bell Curve*, its warm and enthusiastic public reception, and the social and political context out of which it emerged provide an excellent case study for discussion and analysis by students who are studying knowledge construction. They can examine the arguments made by the authors, their major assumptions, and find out how these arguments and assumptions relate to the social and political context. Students can discuss these questions: Why, at this time in our history, was *The Bell Curve* written and published? Why was it so widely disseminated and well-received by the educated public? Who benefits from the arguments in *The Bell Curve*? Who loses? Why do arguments and theories about the genetic inferiority of African Americans keep re-emerging? How do such arguments relate to the social and political climate?

The work of transformative scholars indicates that the quest for human freedom is irrepressible.

Stephen Jay Gould (1994) responded to the last question in a *New Yorker* article by noting the following:

> *The Bell Curve*, with its claim and supposed documentation that race and class differences are largely caused by genetic factors and are therefore essentially immutable, contains no new arguments and presents no compelling data to support its anachronistic social Darwinism, so I can only conclude that its success in winning attention must reflect the depressing temper of our time—a historical moment of unprecedented ungenerosity, when a mood for slashing social programs can be powerfully abetted by an argument that beneficiaries cannot be helped, owing to inborn cognitive limits expressed as low IQ scores. (p. 139)

The publication and public reception of *The Bell Curve* is a cogent example of the extent to which much institutionalized knowledge within out society still supports inequality, dominant group hegemony, and the disempowerment of marginalized groups. *The Bell Curve*, its reception, and its legitimacy also underscore the need to educate students to become critical consumers of knowledge, to become knowledge producers themselves, and to be able to take thoughtful and decisive action that will help to create and maintain a democratic and just society. Works such as *The Bell Curve*, and the public response to them, remind us that democracies are fragile and that the threats to them are serious. Fortunately, the work of transformative scholars indicates that the quest for human freedom is irrepressible.

*Presented November 1, 1995, at Howard University. The speech has been slightly modified for publication.
James A. Banks is a professor of education at the University of Washington-Seattle and director of its Center for Multicultural Education. A past president of the National Council for the Social Studies, Banks has over 20 years of experience in the multicultural education field, serving as a professor and consultant to school districts, professional organizations, and universities throughout the United States and internationally. He has written over 100 articles and authored or edited 18 books, the most recent being *Multicultural Education, Transformative Knowledge, and Action* (1996), and the landmark *Handbook of Research on Multicultural Education* (1995). His other publications include *Curriculum Guidelines for Multicultural Education, Teaching Strategies for Ethnic Studies, Multicultural Education: Issues and Perspectives* (with Cherry A. McGee Banks), *Multiethnic Education: Theory and Practice, Teaching Strategies for the Social Studies,* and *An Introduction to Multicultural Education.* His achievements have earned him considerable recognition, including the 1986 Distinguished Scholar/Researcher on Minority Education and 1994 Research Review awards of the American Educational Research Association, and an honorary Doctorate of Humane Letters from the Bank Street College of Education in 1993.

References

Aptheker, H. (1943). *American Negro slave revolts.* New York: International Publishers.

Au, K. H. (1980). Participation structures in a reading lesson with Hawaiian children. *Anthropology and Education Quarterly, 11*(2), (91–115.

Banks, J. A. (1993a). Multicultural education: Characteristics and goals. In J. A. Banks & C. A. M. Banks (Eds.), *Multicultural education: Issues and perspectives* (2nd ed.) (pp. 3–28). Boston: Allyn & Bacon.

Banks, J. A. (1993b). *Multiethnic education: Theory and practice* (3rd ed.). Boston: Allyn & Bacon.

Banks, J. A. (1995a). Multicultural education: Historical development, dimensions, and practice. In J. A. Banks & C. A. M. Banks (Eds.), *Handbook of research on multicultural education* (pp. 3–24). New York: Macmillan.

Banks, J. A. (1995b). Multicultural education: Its effects on students' racial and gender role attitudes. In J. A. Banks & C. A. M. Banks (Eds.), *Handbook of research on multicultural education* (pp. 617–627). New York: Macmillan.

Banks, J. A. (1996). *Multicultural education, transformative knowledge, and action.* New York: Teachers College Press.

Banks, J. A., & Banks, C. A. M. (Eds.). (1995a). *Handbook of research on multicultural education.* New York: Macmillan.

Banks, J. A., & Banks, C. A. M. (1995b). Equity pedagogy. An essential component of multicultural education. *Theory into Practice, 34*(3), 152–168.

Blassingame, J. W. (1972). *The slave community: Plantation life in the antebellum south.* New York: Oxford University Press.

Boykin, A. W. (1982). Task variability and the performance of Black and White school children: Vervistic explorations. *Journal of Black Studies, 12,* 469–485.

Clark, K. B. (1965). *Dark ghetto: Dilemmas of social power.* New York: Harper & Row.

Clark, K. B., & Clark, M. P. (1939). The development of consciousness of self and the emergence of racial identification in Negro preschool children. *Journal of Social Psychology, 10,* 591–599.

Code, L. (1991). *What can she know? Feminist theory and the construction of knowledge.* Ithaca, NY: Cornell University Press.

Cohen, E. G., & Lotan, R. A. (1995). Producing equal-status interactions in the heterogeneous classroom. *American Educational Research Journal, 32*(1), 99–120.

Collins, P. H. (1990). *Black feminist thought: Feminist theory and the construction of knowledge.* New York: Routledge.

Cross, W. E., Jr. (1991). *Shades of Black: Diversity in African American identity.* Philadelphia: Temple University Press.

Delpit, L. (1995). *Other people's children: Cultural conflict in the classroom.* New York: The New Press.

D'Souza, D. (1995). *The end of racism: Principles for a multicultural society.* New York: The Free Press.

DuBois, W. E. B. (1940). Apology. *Phylon, 1*(1), 3–5.

DuBois, W. E. B. (19750. *The Philadelphia Negro: A social study.* Millwood, NY: Kraus-Thomson Organization Limited. (Original work published in 1899)

Elkins, S. M. (1959). *Slavery: A problem in American institutional and intellectual life.* Chicago: The University of Chicago Press.

Franklin, J. H. (1943). *The free Negro in North Carolina, 1790–1860.* New York: Russell & Russell.

Franklin, J. H. (1947). *From slavery to freedom: A history of Negro Americans.* New York: Knopf.

Gay, G. (1995). Curriculum theory and multicultural education. In J. A. Banks & C. A. M. Banks (Eds.), *Handbook of research on multicultural education* (pp. 25–43). New York: Macmillan.

Genovese, E. D. (1972). *Roll, Jordan, roll: The world the slaves made.* New York: Pantheon.

Gould, S. J. (1994, November 28). Curveball. *The New Yorker, 70*(38), 139–149.

Herrnstein, R. J., & Murray C. (1994). *The bell curve: Intelligence and class structure in American life.* New York: The Free Press.

Hyatt, V. L., & Nettleford, R. (Eds.). (1995). *Race, discourse, and the origin of the Americas: A new world view.* Washington, DC: Smithsonian Institution Press.

Jacoby, R., & Glauberman, N. (Eds.). (1995). *The Bell Curve debate: History, documents, opinions.* New York: Times Books/Random House.

Jensen, A. R. (1969). How much can we boost IQ and scholastic achievement? *Harvard Educational Review, 39*(1), 1–123.

Kagan, J. S., Hunt, J. M., Crow, J. F., Bereiter, C., Elkin, D., & Cronbach, L. (1969). Discussion: How much can we boost IQ and scholastic achievement? *Harvard Educational Review, 39*(2), 274–347.

Kleinfeld, J. (1975). Effective teachers of Eskimo and Indian students. *School Review, 83,* 301–344.

Ladson-Billings, G. (1995). Toward a theory of culturally relevant pedagogy. *American Educational Research Journal, 32*(3), 465–491.

Lee, C., & Slaughter-Defoe, D. T. (1995). Historical and sociocultural influences on African American education. In J. A. Banks & C. A. M. Banks (Eds.), *Handbook of research on multicultural education* (pp. 348–371). New York: Macmillan.

Nieto, S. (1995). A history of the education of Puerto Rican students in U.S. mainland schools: "Losers," "outsiders," or "leaders"? In J. A. Banks & C. A. M. Banks (Eds.), *Handbook of research on multicultural education* (pp. 388–411). New York: Macmillan.

Myrdal, D. (with R. Sterner & A. Rose). (1944). *An American dilemma: The Negro problem in modern democracy.* New York: Harper.

Okhiro, G. (1994). *Margins and mainstreams: Asians in American history and culture.* Seattle, WA: University of Washington Press.

Phillips, U. B. (1918). *American Negro slavery.* New York: Appleton.

Phinney, J. S., & Rotherman, M. J. (Eds.). (1987). *Children's ethnic socialization: Pluralism and development.* Beverly Hills, CA: Sage Publications.

Quarles, B. (1953). *The Negro in the Civil War.* Boston: Little, Brown.

Sacks, D. O., & Theil, P. A. (1995). *The diversity myth: "Multiculturalism" and the politics of intolerance at Stanford,* Oakland, CA: The Independent Institute.

Schlesinger, A., Jr. (1991). *The disuniting of America: Reflections on a multicultural society.* Knoxville, TN: Whittle Direct Books.

Shade, B. A., & New, C. A. (1993). Cultural influences on learning: Teaching implications. In J. A. Banks & C. A. M. Banks (Eds.), *Multicultural education: Issues and perspectives* (2nd ed.) (pp. 317–331). Boston: Allyn & Bacon.

Sleeter, C. A. (1995). An analysis of the critiques of multicultural education. In J. A. Banks and C. A. M. Banks (Eds.), *Handbook of research on multicultural education* (pp. 81–94). New York: Macmillan.

Spencer, M. B. (1982). Personal and group identity of Black children: An alternative synthesis. *Genetic Psychology Monographs, 106,* 59–84.

Stampp, K. M. (1956). *The peculiar institution: Slavery in the ante-bellum south.* New York: Vintage.

Thompson, C. H. (1932). Editorial comment: Why a journal of Negro education? *Journal of Negro Education, 1*(1), 1–4.

Thornton, R. (1995). North American Indians and the demography of contact. In V. L. Hyatt & R. Nettleford (Eds.), *Race, discourse, and the origin of the Americas: A new world view* (pp. 213–230). Washington, DC: Smithsonian Institution Press.

Todorov, T. (1982). *The conquest of America: The question of the other.* New York: Harper Collins.

Tucker, W. H. (1994). *The science and politics of racial research.* Urbana, IL: University of Illinois Press.

Turner, F. J. (1989). The significance of the frontier in American history. In C. A. Milner, II (Ed.), *Major problems in the history of the American West* (pp. 2–21). Lexington, MA: Heath. (Original work published in 1894)

U.S. Bureau of the Census. (1993). *We, the American children.* Washington, DC: U.S. Government Printing Office.

Woodson, C. G. (1930). *The Negro in our history.* Washington, DC: The Associated Publishers.

Woodson, C. G. (1968). *The education of the Negro prior to 1861.* New York: Arno Press. (Original work published in 1919)

Multiculturalism and Multicultural Education in an International Perspective

Lotty Eldering

Leiden University

In many countries with a population of mixed ethnicity and culture, some form of multicultural education is given. Comparisons between the various approaches to multicultural education in these countries are hampered by a lack of conceptual clarity and by differences in social context and views on cultural diversity. In this article the concept of multiculturalism is explored and several approaches to multicultural education are discussed, drawing examples from North America, Europe, and Australia. This conceptual framework is used to describe and analyze the current state of affairs in these fields in the Netherlands.

As a member of two committees advising the Dutch Minister of Education and Science on the state of multicultural education, I have visited several countries on the European and North American continents and have perceived that transnational comparisons are hampered at two levels, first, by differences in the kind of diversity in each society and, second, by differences in the connotation attached to the concepts of multiculturalism and multicultural education. In this article the dimensions of multiculturalism and multicultural education are explored and a contextual approach that enables transnational comparisons to be made is presented. In the second part of the article the current state of affairs regarding multiculturalism and multicultural education in the Netherlands will be analyzed, using the conceptual framework developed in the first section.

Multiculturalism

To analyze the nature of multiculturalism in a society, one must distinguish the following dimensions or levels:

- objective reality,
- ideology,
- official policy,
- process or practical implementation. [Fleras and Elliott 1992]

Multiculturalism as an objective reality concerns the coexistence of different ethnic or cultural groups in one country (state). These groups often differ in history, numbers, social position, power, culture, and ethnic/racial origins. Ethnic and cultural diversity in a society is usually the result of (colonial) expansion, slavery, or immigration. Each multicultural society has its own genesis and, consequently, its own diversity. Northwestern European countries, for instance, have experienced immigration from a variety of continents and countries, as a result of decolonization and economic expansion after the Second World War (Eldering and Kloprogge 1989). The immigrants in these countries comprise no more than ten percent of the total population, whereas the populations of traditional immigration countries like Canada, the United States, Israel, and Australia consist predominantly of immigrants and their descendants. Besides their numerical strength, the power relations between ethnic/cultural groups are an important factor. Ethnic groups that are a majority in the numerical sense may have no political weight in nondemocratic societies, as was formerly the case in South Africa.

A second dimension of multiculturalism concerns the ideology with regard to the identity of society and how cultural differences between groups are to be dealt with. The ideology may fluctuate between the extremes of assimilation and pluralism. Assimilation means the merging of ethnic/cultural groups into a dominant group, culturally as well as structurally. Pluralism in its extreme form implies that the society is comprised of groups whose distinctive cultures are maintained by structural pluralism. Cultural pluralism cannot exist without duplication of institutions and hence without structural pluralism, according to sociologist Van den Berghe (1967). Many varieties exist between the extremes of assimilation and pluralism. In the political debate between interest groups, the identity and culture of a society are always the object of discussion. Views on the identity of a society or the desirable degree of cultural diversity may change over the course of time. One of the relevant issues in the current political debate in Europe is the compatibility of two values: equality of opportunity and a person's right to maintain his or her cultural identity. In his book *Race and Ethnicity* (1986), Rex discusses how to resolve the conflict between these values. He concludes that a society with equality of opportunity in the public domain and multiculturalism in the private domain would appear to be the ideal situation. In a later publication, he distances himself from this point of view, mainly for sociological reasons (Rex 1991), arguing that according to the functionalist theory in sociology and anthropology, the various institutions constituting a sociocultural system are all necessarily interrelated and that in this theory there is no place for the idea of two separate sociocultural domains. The public and private do-

From *Anthropology & Education Quarterly,* Vol. 27, No. 3, September 1996, pp. 315-330. © 1996 by the American Anthropological Association. Reprinted by permission. Not for further reproduction.

mains are interacting subsystems. Schools, for instance, have a function in preparing children for their public role, but at the same time, by transmitting cultural values they have an impact on the private lives of the pupils and their families (Eldering 1993). For their values to be accepted in the public domain, ethnic and cultural minorities should organize themselves and negotiate with other interest groups in society. In addition to the official ideology, which is at best the result of a negotiation process between political parties and other interest groups, other ideologies may exist in society. A popular "man in the street" ideology or a teachers' ideology on cultural diversity may not coincide with official ideology; indeed, they may even contradict that ideology and hamper the implementation of official policy.

The terminology used in the description of a society's objective reality is often ideologically colored and is often influenced by history and policy. In the Netherlands, for instance, the terms *guest workers, immigrants, minorities,* and *allochthones* have been used successively in past decades. Guest workers refers to the predominantly male workers recruited in the 1950s and 1960s from Mediterranean countries to work in the mines and expanding industries. This term emphasizes the temporariness of the workers' stay in the host country. The right of their families to come to the Netherlands has long been an issue on the policy agenda. *Minorities,* a term introduced at the end of the 1970s and currently in general use, refers to immigrant groups that occupy a low socioeconomic position (Ministry of Internal Affairs 1983). Because of the negative connotations and stigmatizing effects of that term, the neutral *allochthones,* referring to immigrants from outside the Netherlands up to and including the third generation, was proposed by the Wetenschappelijke Rand voor het Regeringsbeleid, or Scientific Council for Governmental Policy (WRR 1989). *Immigrants* and *minorities* are currently used in many northwestern European countries, with the exception of Germany, a country that officially does not admit that the migrants have become immigrants and continues to call the foreign workers and their families *Gastarbeiter.*

Allochthon and *autochthon* are also applied in Canada. The Inuit (Eskimos) and Indians are autochthons, also re-

cently called *First Nations.* The allochthonous English- and French-speaking groups form the dominant majority. In the United States, a similar situation exists. Here, however, the Indian groups are called *natives* or *American Indians,* and *allochthon* and *autochthon* are rarely used. Autochthons form a numerical minority in Canada and the United States and the majority in countries such as the United Kingdom, France, Germany, Netherlands, and Belgium.

As in the Netherlands, *minorities* is used in Canada and the United States, but with different connotations. Whereas in the Netherlands the term refers to groups with a low socioeconomic position, Canadian and U.S. use of this term emphasizes mainly the cultural "deviation" from the majority (in terms of language, religion, art, music, behavior, etc.) or racial characteristics ("visible minorities" in Canadian policy documents). U.S. opinion is rather divided as to which groups should be rated as "mainstream." Some consider only Anglo-American groups to belong to the mainstream (see, for example, Banks 1988); others opine that all groups of European origin belong to it (Spindler and Spindler 1990). In Canada, only the "Charter Groups," the groups of English and French origin, are considered as such (Fleras and Elliott 1992). This results in immigrants of German origin being considered a minority in Canada, whereas in the United States they may or may not be called a minority, depending on personal opinion. Chinese groups are considered to be minorities in both Canada and the United States, but not in the Netherlands since they do not have a low socioeconomic position there.

Minorities is usually preceded by an adjective that indicates another distinguishing feature of the group concerned (e.g., "racial minorities"). The choice of this adjective reflects the ideological perspective from which the problems are examined. In the United States and the United Kingdom, the racial perspective dominates. Relationships between the majority and minorities are often described in terms of color and race. Troyna and Edwards (1993) state that the specific U.K. terminology can become a problem in European research since, on the European continent, differences in culture are emphasized (mostly in terms of language and religion), rather than differences in ethnicity or race.

As to the policy dimension of multiculturalism, a distinction must be made between immigration policy and minorities policy. Immigration policy primarily regulates the categories of immigrants which are accepted and the conditions of immigration. Canada and Australia, for instance, have populations of predominantly northwestern European origin (mainly British and French) because of their selective immigration policy. The immigrant population of many northwestern European countries largely consists of foreign workers from Mediterranean countries and their families and of immigrants from former colonies. If it reacts at all, a country often reacts slowly to demographic changes, for example, by formulating a minorities policy. A minorities policy in principle reflects a country's official ideology. In its elaboration and implementation, however, there may be discrepancies—for instance, when values and goals are incompatible or when one goal is given priority, as I will show regarding the Netherlands.

Approaches to Multicultural Education

The lack of clarity surrounding concepts and the controversy regarding the term multicultural education (also known as *intercultural education, multiethnic education, or antiracist education*) complicate comparative research. A number of researchers have tried to bring order to the multitude of views on and approaches to multicultural education (Baker 1983; Banks 1983, 1988; Cummins and Danesi 1990; Fleras and Elliott 1992; Gollnick and Chinn 1990; Ogbu 1987, 1992; Sleeter and Grant 1987; Troyna and Edwards 1993). Using this literature, I have developed the following scheme of multicultural education (see Table 1). Multicultural education is considered in a broad sense here and is defined as being education that takes into account in some way the ethnic/cultural differences between pupils. The scheme is based on two principles of order: the target groups at which multicultural education is aimed and the approach from which this occurs. Multicultural education can be limited solely to pupils from ethnic/cultural groups (a particularist approach) or can be directed at all pupils (a universalistic

Table 1
Approaches to Multicultural Education (Eldering 1994)

Approach	Target groups	
	Pupils from ethnic groups	All pupils
Disadvantage	– attunement of education to development level – second-language education – bilingual education – culturally responsive education	
Enrichment	monocultural courses aimed at – language – literature – geography – religion – history – art	multicultural courses aimed at – language – literature – geography – religion – history – art
Bicultural competence	bicultural education	bicultural education
Collective equality groups	private schools	multicultural curriculum

approach). Multicultural education can be approached from various perspectives according to the position of the minority cultures in the curriculum and the attention paid to individual or collective inequality.

The Disadvantage Approach

The assumption underlying multicultural education with a disadvantage approach is that pupils from ethnic/cultural groups have educational arrears that pupils from the majority group do not have. Multicultural education under this approach is aimed at removing these disadvantages. The educative activities in this framework are intended solely for pupils from ethnic/cultural groups of low socioeconomic position. Catching up on disadvantages occurs with an eye to gaining better school achievements and realizing equality of opportunity. The degree to which account is taken of the specific cultural characteristics of the pupils depends on the perception and appreciation of cultural differences. If one begins with a deficit approach, no account is taken of the cultural features of the pupil, but if one has a positive attitude toward the culture of the pupils concerned, then the cultural features of the pupils such as their home language, communication and learning style may serve as education's point of departure ("culturally responsive teaching") (Erickson 1987; McDermott and Goldman 1983; Ogbu 1987). Under the disadvantage approach, the removal of the disadvantage comes first, and the ethnic culture plays a sustaining and temporary role at most. Different forms of multicultural education can be placed under this heading, varying from the immersion model, in which education is exclusively in the second language, to bilingual education with a transitional character (Extra and Vallen 1989).

The Enrichment Approach

The assumption behind this approach is that cultural diversity implies an enrichment of society, which should be reflected in education (in Canadian terms, "celebrating diversity"). Multicultural education under this approach may be aimed at pupils from specific ethnic/cultural groups; it may also be for all pupils, irrespective of ethnic/cultural origin.

Monocultural courses are set up for a variety of reasons: as an acknowledgement of the language and culture of the ethnic communities ("heritage-language courses" in Canada), as a means for making pupils from ethnic/cultural groups aware of the contribution made by their group to the establishment of society ("black stud-

ies," followed later by "Mexican American studies" "American Indian studies," and "Asian studies" in the United States), or as a preparation for returning to the country of origin (the Netherlands and Germany) (Banks 1988; Eldering 1989; Seller 1992).

Multicultural courses are intended for all pupils, irrespective of ethnic/cultural background. The most important objective is for pupils from all groups to become acquainted with each other's cultures, learn to appreciate them, and learn how to relate to each other (the *human relations approach,* also known as the *intergroup approach* or *multicultural education*). The assumption of multicultural education is that knowledge of each other's cultures leads to mutual appreciation and respect and to a better understanding. The culture elements dealt with in the curriculum mostly concern language, literature, history, geography, and religion. It is evident that the culture of the various groups within the multicultural courses will receive only marginal attention if the pupils in a school come from a number of ethnic groups. Although recommended by several governments, multicultural courses have never become an integral part of the curriculum. (For the United Kingdom see Education for All 1985; Troyna and Edwards 1993; for the Netherlands see CEB 1994; Eldering 1989). This approach has some serious shortcomings. No theoretical connection has been sought in psychological theories on intergroup conflicts and prejudice, and the cultural content of these courses is usually not based on empirical research on the culture of the groups concerned (Ogbu 1992; Sleeter and Grant 1987; Vedder 1993).

The Bicultural Competence Approach

Multicultural education under this approach goes one step further than the previous approach and is mainly intended to make pupils from ethnic/cultural groups competent in two cultures through bicultural education. Education in the culture of the ethnic/cultural groups aims at the preservation of the cultures (including languages) concerned. According to Banks (1988), bicultural education should not be limited to pupils from ethnic/cultural groups, but all pupils and teachers should at least have bicultural competence and preferably be cross-culturally competent. Bicultural education for ethnic minority pupils rarely occurs in practice. It requires at least a sufficient number of pupils from one ethnic/cultural group, like the Finns in Sweden or the Mexican Americans in the U.S. Southwest (see, for example, Warren 1983).

The Collective Equality Approach

The approaches discussed so far are limited to mostly minor adaptations of the existing curriculum. The education system itself, the structure of society, and the mechanisms that support inequality are not questioned in these approaches. But this happens to be the case in multicultural education under the collective equality approach. This approach emphasizes the collective equality of groups or cultures rather than the equality of individuals. Two approaches can be distinguished. The first approach assumes the equal rights of the diverse ethnic/cultural groups in society. Supporters of this view strive for a society that is pluralistic in cultural and structural sense (Van den Berghe 1967). Canada with its French and English school system, Belgium with its French and Flemish school system, and the Netherlands with its denominational school system ("pillarization") are examples of this approach.

In the second approach, the objective is to make the existing school system more multicultural: not just the curriculum but also the teaching methods, the staff, and the representative bodies. Some supporters hold the view that the inequality of ethnic/cultural groups cannot be regarded separately from other inequalities in society. Within multicultural education, attention must also be paid to other social categories in an unequal position such as women, low socioeconomic groups, the handicapped (Banks 1988; Cummins and Danesi 1990; Gollnick and Chinn 1990; Troyna and Edwards 1993).

Summary of the Approaches

As we have seen, multicultural education has several approaches and many modalities. These do not occur equally often in practice. Multicultural education is usually aimed at pupils from ethnic/cultural groups. Multicultural education for all pupils still has not properly got off the ground in practice and is often limited to an ideological discourse. In most cases, multicultural education exists merely as an addition to or a minor adaptation of the regular curriculum. Multicultural education therefore tends to lean toward assimilation rather than toward cultural pluralism. This is hardly surprising, given the population ratio of the majority to the minorities, and the social position of both categories in many countries. Recurring points in the discussion on multicultural education are the questions of how far cultural diversity threatens the unity of a society, and to what degree cultural diversity hampers or encourages the realization of equality of opportunity for all pupils, as will be shown by the case of the Netherlands.

The Case of the Netherlands

In this section the state of affairs of multiculturalism and multicultural education in the Netherlands will be described and analyzed, using the conceptual framework presented in the previous sections. The first question is whether Dutch society is multicultural in an objective, ideological, and political sense. The second concerns the approaches to multicultural education in this country.

A Multicultural Society?

The Dutch government officially stated in 1983 that the Netherlands is a multicultural society and acknowledged that most migrants from former colonies (the Moluccans, Surinam, and the Dutch Antilles) and Mediterranean countries (predominantly Turkey and Morocco) had become immigrants. Today these immigrants compose about six percent of the total population of 14 million, and they live mainly concentrated in cities with more than 100,000 inhabitants. For the population in these cities, the multicultural nature of Dutch society is a daily reality, whereas people living in other parts of the country, particularly in rural areas, are only incidentally confronted with the changed character of Dutch society.

The ideological discourse concerning immigrants centers around two basic values of Dutch society: equality of opportunity and equivalence of cultures. Equivalence of cultures (religions), a value with a long tradition in the Netherlands, has been the basis of the compartmentalization manifest in many sectors of Dutch public life. The "school battle" in 1917 resulted in a state-supported school system compartmentalized along religious lines. About two-thirds of pupils currently attend private state-funded denominational schools. The religious segregation in other sectors of public life (health care, trades unions, broadcasting corporations) has slowly eroded in recent decades. With the arrival of large numbers of Muslims from Morocco, Turkey, and Surinam, the question arises whether a new Muslim "pillar" will be formed. It appears that Islam has become institutionalized in the Netherlands. There are currently about 380 mosques (separate ones for Moroccan, Turkish, Surinamese, and Pakistani Muslims) in the country. About one-quarter of the Muslim children attend Qur'an lessons at these mosques. Provisions have been made for ritual slaughter, and Muslim adults and children have the right to take days off to celebrate their religious festivals (Shadid and Van Koningsveld 1995). Although the constitutional right to establish schools is also given to immigrants, only four percent of pupils with an Islamic background currently attend schools based on Islamic principles. The low numbers of the Muslims and the national and religious differences among Muslims hamper the formation of a new religious compartment and the establishment of an Islamic school system (CEB 1994; Eldering 1993).

In 1979, the Netherlands Scientific Council for Government Policy (WRR) advised the government to create a minorities policy (WRR 1979). In its report, the council recommended that the idea of a temporary residence for all migrant groups be abandoned and that a policy aimed at integration should be outlined in order to prevent migrant groups from becoming ethnic minorities. Dutch government proposed a two-track ethnic minorities policy, aiming at "integration without loss of cultural identity." The WRR, evaluating the situation ten years later, concluded that, despite the minorities policy, the socioeconomic position of ethnic minorities had worsened and advised concentrating efforts on education and the labor-market position of minorities and to abandon the culture track of this policy (WRR 1989). Currently, target groups of Dutch minorities policy show unemployment rates four times as high as those for the Dutch majority.

The Dutch government has opted for a minorities policy that aims at integration of ethnic minorities as well as preservation of their cultural identity. How this two-track policy works out in the field of education will be explored in the next section.

Educational Minorities Policy

The Dutch Ministry of Education and Science launched a minorities policy plan in 1980. In consonance with the general minorities policy, this plan stipulated that educational practice should aim at equality of educational opportunity as well as equivalence of cultures. To realize equal opportunities for all pupils, the Educational Priority Policy came into effect in 1985. In this policy, priority (i.e., additional funds) is given to geographical areas and schools with a high percentage of disadvantaged children from ethnic-minority and Dutch backgrounds. Pupils are rated according to ethnicity and parents' educational level. Thus, pupils from ethnic-minority parents with a low educational level are given a weight of 1.9, and pupils from disadvantaged Dutch backgrounds, 1.25, compared to 1.0 for middle-class Dutch children. This weighting forms the basis for assessing the school score. High-scoring schools receive much more additional funding than low-scoring ones (Eldering 1989). About seventy percent of the primary schools received extra funds in 1993 (SCP 1994). The Educational Priority Policy is accompanied by a longitudinal evaluation. About 40,000 pupils are assessed every two years on school achievements (mainly reading and mathematics). Recent outcomes of this evaluation have shown that ethnic-minority pupils, in particular those of Moroccan and Turkish origin, still have serious arrears in secondary education and that more than eighty percent of these arrears originate in primary education (Kloprogge and Walraven 1994).

Policy (i.e., extra funding) is therefore concentrating on primary education and recently also on the preschool period, although the evaluation of preschool programs has not yet revealed that this is having any major effects (see Eldering and Vedder 1993).

Besides this policy aimed at eliminating educational arrears, there is a cultural policy, composed of monocultural courses (lessons in the language and culture of the country of origin) for minority pupils and multicultural education—called intercultural education in the Netherlands—for all pupils. Ethnic-minority children from Mediterranean countries are entitled to courses in the language and culture of their home country in primary education for $2\frac{1}{2}$ hours per week during school hours.

The range of financial aid for the activities indicates the relative weight of both approaches. Eliminating educational arrears (fostering equality of opportunity) has the highest priority in primary education. Although under the 1985 Primary Education Act schools must prepare children for life in a multicultural society, so far no financial aid has been made available for multicultural education. Strikingly, the budget available for the respective elements of the Educational Priority Policy is inversely proportional to the regulations concerning its spending. The lion's share of available monies is allocated for combating the educational arrears of disadvantaged children. The allocation of these funds, however, rarely corresponds to recommendations on how they should be spent. Schools are not even obliged to spend this money exclusively on the target groups. Most schools use it to reduce the number of pupils per class. In view of the disappointing effects of the Educational Priority Policy on school achievement, discussions are currently in progress on whether the system of input financing should be replaced by a system of output financing, thereby forcing schools to pay more attention to equality of outcomes than to equality of opportunity.

The situation regarding multicultural, or intercultural, education is the exact reverse. This education is surrounded by policy memoranda and documents containing indications of what schools should do, whereas no funds are given to realize its implementation.

Regarding education in the language and culture of the country of origin, the

Dutch government has pursued an ambiguous policy. Originally set up as education to prepare children from Mediterranean groups for return to their home country, its psychological functions (fostering the self-concept and the well-being of these children) were stressed in the 1980s (Eldering 1989). In the 1990s the Ministry of Education has stated that this education should primarily support the learning of Dutch. Despite these changes in official policy, however, the content of the lessons in the language and culture of the home country has changed only marginally over the past decades (CEB 1994).

Implementation

The number of pupils receiving education in the language and culture of their country of origin has increased considerably since 1982. About eighty percent of the Turkish and seventy percent of the Moroccan pupils participate in this education. Most pupils (85%) receive this education during school hours. The lessons are largely made up of language activities, followed by geography, history, and religion. Most teaching methods are oriented toward the home countries; only a few reflect the multicultural reality in the Netherlands. About ninety percent of the teachers have obtained their teaching qualification in their country of origin (CEB 1994). This situation reflects the original objective of this education (preparing children for return) rather than the current policy aim of supporting the learning of Dutch. Education in the language and culture of the country of origin has remained an isolated part of the curriculum. School staff are on average not interested in this education; they see these lessons as the sole responsibility of the ethnic-minority teachers. Many ethnic-minority teachers have a poor command of Dutch and have little contact with the Dutch teachers about the content of their lessons or the pupils. Changing the educational content toward current official goals would require a huge investment from both school staff and ethnic-minority teachers.

An issue currently being debated is whether it would not be better to hold these lessons outside school hours. The first reason might be that about half of the ethnic-minority pupils miss lessons in Dutch and other cognitive subjects because they clash with lessons in the language and culture of their home country. This poses the question of the compatibility of equality of opportunity and equality of cultures. Second, most ethnic-minority children are second- or even third-generation immigrants, and their home country is the Netherlands rather than Turkey, Morocco, Surinam, or the Moluccan Islands. Third, if given outside school hours, this education could retain its original function of preserving cultural heritage (cf. "heritage language courses" in Canada) rather than support the learning of Dutch (CEB 1994). Several political parties now argue for removing this education from the regular curriculum.

The 1985 Primary Education Act prescribes that schools prepare pupils for life in a multicultural society through multicultural, or intercultural, education. Multicultural education must be given to all pupils by all schools, regardless of the presence of ethnic minority children. At the end of the 1980s, policy makers at the Ministry of Education and at national educational organizations reached consensus on the objectives and content of multicultural education. According to them, multicultural education is neither a subject nor a separate part of the curriculum. The whole curriculum should reflect society's cultural diversity. Multicultural education should also have implications for school policy, staff ethnicity, and ethnic-minority parent representation on school boards. Its main objectives are that children acquire knowledge of each other's cultures, learn to live harmoniously together, and be free of prejudice, discrimination, and racism (Ministry of Education and Science 1987). To what degree does daily practice reflect this ambitious consensus?

The Committee for the Evaluation of Primary Education (CEB) recently analyzed the state of multicultural education (CEB 1994). This analysis showed that multicultural education has been integrated in the curriculum in only 20 percent of Dutch schools. This occurred proportionally more often in public (i.e., nondenominational) schools, in schools in large cities, and in schools with more than 20 percent ethnic-minority pupils. In 40 percent of the schools no steps have been undertaken since 1985 to make education more multicultural; 30 percent of the schools—again mostly schools in large cities with more than

20 percent ethnic-minority pupils—said that they were preparing to make the curriculum more multicultural. Multicultural education is almost nowhere the result of a well-thought-out school policy; rather, it depends on individual teachers' initiatives. In only one-third of Dutch schools has multicultural education been a topic on a staff meeting since 1985. Although school principals are of the opinion that the prevention of prejudice, discrimination, and racism is the most important objective of multicultural education, only a few schools have a formalized nondiscrimination code. This code concerns pupils only, not teachers or parents.

This short overview shows that there is a big gap between policy makers' ideological discourse and daily school practice. This is due to several factors. An important one is that multicultural education does not correspond to the daily life situation of many schools. More than 75 percent of Dutch schools have no or only a few pupils from ethnic minority backgrounds. They feel no need to make the curriculum more multicultural and tend to associate multicultural education more with educational problems than with educational enrichment. Multicultural education is more often reactive education, in the sense that teachers only react to interethnic or multicultural incidents or conflicts in their classroom. Although there are no indications that teachers have a negative attitude toward pupils from ethnic-minority backgrounds, teachers are not trained in coping with interethnic situations and conflicts. Research shows that the reactions of teachers who are not expert in this area may have the effect of encouraging rather than preventing prejudice (Troyna and Edwards 1993). As already mentioned, multicultural education has no solid theoretical basis. Nor has the concept of culture been defined and empirically tested. No research has been done so far in the Netherlands on interethnic and multicultural classroom situations and conflicts, and on the way in which teachers deal with these. This is a serious omission, as teachers in multiethnic classrooms are expected to teach pupils how to cope with ethnic and cultural differences.

Summary of Multiculturalism in the Netherlands

Ethnic minorities comprise only six percent of the population in the Netherlands. Despite this low percentage, the Dutch government officially stated in 1983 that the Netherlands is a multicultural society. To realize the ideological goal of "integration with preservation of their own culture," a "two-track" minorities policy was developed about fifteen years ago. In terms of government funding, however, equality of opportunity has been given a much higher priority in the policy's implementation than equality of cultures has been. Although the Dutch constitution permits the establishment of institutions based on religious principles, it is unlikely that Muslims will develop their own infrastructure and form an Islamic pillar.

The unequal priority of equality of opportunity and equality of cultures is also reflected in educational policy and practice. The elimination of educational disadvantages receives more funding and more attention from schools and teachers than cultural activities. Compared with many other countries, the Netherlands may be a front-runner in laying down statutory standards concerning the multicultural character of Dutch society and multicultural education, but in policy practice the emphasis lies more on integration of immigrants than on preservation of their original culture. Moreover, the gap between official policy and day-to-day practice remains great, particularly regarding the labor market and the educational system.

Conclusion and Discussion

The first part of this article discussed levels of multiculturalism and various approaches to multicultural education and then presented a contextual approach for international comparisons. The second part used this conceptual framework to describe and analyze multiculturalism and multicultural education in the Netherlands. The conceptual framework makes it possible to compare across societies and to generate issues for discussion. I conclude this article with some remarks on the relationship between the various dimensions of multiculturalism.

It will be clear that, although many societies consider themselves to be multicultural, multiculturalism has not permeated all the dimensions distinguished. Multiculturalism is often limited to the objective level of coexistence of ethnic-cultural groups in society and an ideological discourse about society's cultural identity. Monoculturalism prevails at the level of policy and its implementation.

The various dimensions of multiculturalism are only indirectly related. The presence of various ethnic-cultural groups in a society generally stimulates a public discussion on the society's cultural identity but does not necessarily lead to a multicultural policy and multicultural practice in its institutions, as is illustrated by the case of multicultural education in the Netherlands. The discrepancy between objective reality and ideology/policy may be caused by the imbalance of power between the ethnic-cultural interest groups in society, whereas the discrepancy between multicultural policy and practice may be due to several factors, such as the failure of policy to be geared toward implementation in practice. Only a minority of Dutch primary schools, for instance, has made multicultural education a structural part of its regular curriculum, although this education is prescribed in the 1985 Primary Education Act. Policy makers at the Dutch Ministry of Education and at national educational organizations have reached consensus about the principles and global content of multicultural education after many years of discussion about culture and the enrichment of contacts between cultures. They have, however, neglected to define the key concept of culture and to prepare guidelines for multicultural activities to teachers who have to deal with classes of pupils from various ethnic-cultural groups with different levels of acculturation or who teach monocultural classes. These questions arise in other countries too.

The concept of culture has been neglected not only by policy makers dealing with multicultural education but also by cultural anthropologists—for whom it is the raison d'etre of their discipline. Fortunately the discussion on this concept has recently been reopened (Borofsky 1994). I hope that educational anthropologists will follow this example and make this concept more workable for educational practice.

Lotty Eldering is a professor in intercultural pedagogics at Leiden University, in the Netherlands. She has published on immigrant families (particularly Moroccan families) and their children's education.

References Cited

Baker, Gwendolyn C. 1983. Planning and Organizing for Multicultural Instruction. Reading, MA: Addison-Wesley Publishing.

Banks, James A. 1983. Language, Ethnicity, Ideology and Education. *In* Multicultural Education: A Challenge for Teachers. Lotty van den Berg-Eldering, Ferry J. M. de Rijcke, and Louis V. Zuck, eds. Pp. 33–51. Dordrecht: Foris Publications.
    1988. Multiethnic Education. Theory and Practice. Boston: Allyn and Bacon.

Borofsky, R., ed. 1994. Assessing Cultural Anthropology. New York: McGraw-Hill.

CEB (Commissie Evaluatie Basisonderwijs). 1994. Onderwijs Gericht op een Multiculturele Samenleving. The Hague: SDU.

Cummins, James, and Marcel Danesi. 1990. Heritage Languages. The Development and Denial of Canada's Linguistic Resources. Toronto: Our Schools/Our Selves Education Foundation and Garamond Press.

Education for All. 1985. Education for All. The Report of the Committee of Inquiry into the Education of Children from Ethnic Minority Groups. London: Her Majesty's Stationery Office.

Eldering, Lotty. 1989. Ethnic Minority Children in Dutch Schools: Underachievement and its Explanations. *In* Different Cultures Same School. Ethnic Minority Children in Europe. Lotty Eldering and Jo Kloprogge, eds. Pp. 107–136. Amsterdam: Swets & Zeitlinger.
    1993. Cultuurverschillen in een Multiculturele Samenleving. Comenius 49:9–26.
    1994. Benaderingen van Multicultureel Onderwijs. *In* Christelijk Onderwijs in Ontwikkeling. S. Miedema and H. Klifman, eds. Pp. 30–44. Kampen, Netherlands: Kok.

Eldering, Lotty, and Jo Kloprogge, eds. 1989. Different Cultures Same School. Ethnic Minority Children in Europe. Amsterdam/Lisse: Swets & Zeitlinger.

Eldering, Lotty, and Paul Vedder. 1993. Culture Sensitive Home intervention. The Dutch HIPPY Experiment. *In* Early Intervention and Culture. Preparation for Literacy. Lotty Eldering and Paul Leseman, eds. Pp. 231–252. Paris: UNESCO Publishing, Netherlands National Commission for UNESCO.

Erickson, Frederick. 1987. Transformation and School Success: The Politics and Culture of Educational Achievement. Anthropology and Education Quarterly 18:335–357.

Extra, Guus, and Ton Vallen. 1989. Second Language Acquisition in Elementary School: A Crossnational Perspective on the Netherlands, Flanders and the Federal Republic of Germany. *In* Different Cultures Same School: Ethnic Minority Children in Europe. Lotty Eldering and Jo Kloprogge, eds. Pp. 153–188. Amsterdam: Swets & Zeitlinger.

Fleras, Augie, and Jean Leonard Elliott. 1992. Multiculturalism in Canada. The Challenge of Diversity. Ontario: Nelson Canada.

Gollnick, Donna M., and Philip C. Chinn. 1990. Multicultural Education in a Pluralistic Society. New York: Merrill, Macmillan Publishing.

Kloprogge, Jo, and Guido Walraven. 1994. Vernieuwde Kaders, Veranderende Structuren. Notitie over het Onderwijsvoor rangsbeleid 1993. The Hague: Stichting Onderzoek Onderwijs.

McDermott, Ray P., and Shelley V. Goldman. 1983. Teaching in Multicultural Settings. *In* Multicultural Education: A Challenge for Teachers. Lotty van den Berg-Eldering, Ferry J. M. de Rijcke, and Louis V. Zuck, eds. Pp. 145–165. Dordrecht: Foris Publications.

Ministry of Education and Science, Netherlands. 1987. Intercultureel Onderwijs Verder op Weg [Verslag miniconferentie]. Zoetermeer, Netherlands: Ministry of Education and Science.

Ministry of Internal Affairs, Netherlands. 1983. Minderhedennota. The Hague: Staatsuitgeverij.

Ogbu, John U. 1987. Variability in Minority School Performance: A Problem in Search of an Explanation. E. Jacob and C. Jordan, eds. Explaining the School Performance of Minority Students. Anthropology and Education Quarterly (theme issue) 18:312–334.
    1992. Understanding Cultural Diversity and Learning. Educational Researcher 21(8):5–14.

Rex, John. 1986. Race and Ethnicity. Milton Keynes: Open University Press.
    1991. The Political Sociology in a Multi-Cultural Society. European Journal of Intercultural Studies 2(1):7–19.

Seller, M. 1992. Historical Perspectives on Multicultural Education. What Kind? By Whom? For Whom? And Why? Paper presented at the American Educational Research Association Annual Meeting, San Francisco, April.

Shadid, W. A. R., and P. S. van Koningsveld. 1995. Religious Freedom and the Position of Islam in Western Europe: Opportunities and Obstacles in the Acquisition of Equal Rights. Kampen, Netherlands: Kok Pharos.

Sleeter, Christine E., and Carl A. Grant. 1987. An Analysis of Multicultural Education in the United States. Harvard Educational Review 57:421–444.

SCP (Sociaal Cultureel Planbureau). 1994. Sociaal en Cultureel Rapport. Rijswijk, Netherlands: Sociaal en Cultureel Planbureau.

Spindler, George, and Louise Spindler. 1990. The American Cultural Dialogue and Its Transmission. London: Falmer Press.

Troyna, Barry, and Viv Edwards. 1993. The Educational Needs of a Multiracial Society. Coventry, England: University of Warwick.

Van den Berghe, Pierre L. 1967. Race and Racism. A Comparative Perspective. New York: Wiley.

Vedder, Paul H. 1993. Intercultureel Onderwijs Vanuit Psychologisch Perspectief. Leiden: Rijksuniversiteit, Sectie Interculturele Pedagogiek.

Warren, Richard L. 1983. The Application of Ethnographic Research in Multicultural Education. *In* Multicultural Education: A Challenge for Teachers. Lotty van den Berg-Eldering, Ferry J. M. de Rijcke, and Louis V. Zuck, eds. Pp. 121–135. Dordrecht: Foris Publications.

WRR (Wetenschappelijke Raad voor het Regeringsbeleid). 1979. Etnische Minderheden. The Hague: SDU.
    1989. Allochtonenbeleid. The Hague: SDU.

Bridging Multicultural Theory and Practice

Geneva Gay

Geneva Gay is a professor of education and an associate with the Center of Multicultural Education at the University of Washington, Seattle, Washington.

The current state of multicultural education is at once exciting and troubling. A significant part of this dilemma—and the one of interest here—results from disparities in the developmental growth of its theory and practice. Ideally, educational theory and practice develop in tandem, and the relationship between them is complementary, reciprocal, and dialectic. This is not yet happening, in any systematic way, in multicultural education. Its theoretical development is far out-stripping its practical development, and its further refinement is stimulated more by proposals of what should be than by lessons learned from what is.

Multicultural theory is becoming more thorough, complex, and comprehensive, while its practice in K-12 and college classrooms continues to be rather questionable, simplistic, and fragmentary. This gap is growing exponentially; it fuels much of the current debate because critics fail to distinguish between the two in their critiques; and it limits the overall effectiveness of multi-cultural reform efforts.

These divergent growth patterns also make it difficult for multicultural advocates in different aspects of the educational enterprise to engage in constructive dialogue, and to work as collaboratively as they might for the achievement of common goals. As a result, multicultural classroom instruction is often not synchronized with curriculum development. Policy statements governing school practices may specify that multiculturalism must be included in instructional materials and program designs, but routinely fail to make similar requirements for hiring personnel and for assessing the performance of students and teachers. Yet, theorists consistently argue that for multicultural education to be maximally successful, all parts of the educational system must be responsive to and inclusive of cultural diversity.

The gaps between multicultural theory and practice present some serious challenges and opportunities for future directions in the field. In this discussion, I will offer some thoughts about why these gaps exist, and make some suggestions for how the challenges they present might be addressed.

INVERSE GROWTH PATTERNS

According to George Beauchamp (1968), an essential function of educational theorizing is to constantly search for new conceptual ideas, understandings, and principles to describe, explain, and predict issues of interest or study. He adds that the theorist "seeks out new relationships by combining sets of events into a new universal set and then [proceeds] with the search for new relationships and new laws in a new theory" (p. 19). This search has both internal and external dimensions. It analyzes the components of an existing paradigm to achieve greater depths and clarity of meanings, while simultaneously bringing ideas and insights from other sources to bear upon the phenomenon being studied.

For example, multicultural education was initially conceptualized as a discrete program of studies with heavy emphasis on teaching factual content about the histories, heritages, and contributions of groups of color. Over the last 25 years, this conceptualization has been re-examined, revised, and refined so that now multicultural education is conceived more as a particular ideological and methodological approach to the entire educational enterprise than a separate curriculum or program *per se.*

The relationships between culture, ethnicity, and learning, which are so central to multicultural education are continually analyzed and reinterpreted. Different ways to systematize the implementation of commonly-agreed-upon elements of multicultural education are constantly being proposed by various scholars. In the rhetoric of today's educational thinking, these processes might be coded as self-reflection, critical interrogation, knowledge reconstruction, meta-analysis or meta-cognition, and multiple perspectives. Thus, the evolvement of educational theory from inception to maturity is a self-renewing, regenerative process. One of its natural effects is the creation of subsidiary theories and conceptual models.

Even a quick and cursory look at the scholarship of leading multiculturalists (see, for example, Banks & Banks, 1993, 1995; Hollins, King, & Hayman, 1994; Bennett, 1995; Sleeter, 1992; Sleeter & Grant, 1995; Foster, 1991) provides persuasive evidence of these processes taking place. Senior scholars are revisioning and elaborating on some of their earlier thinking, as well as using knowledge and interpretive filters from other disciplines to enrich, elaborate, and extend the conceptual contours, attributes, and principles of multicultural education.

Several specific examples illustrate this trend. In a recent publication, Gay (1994) explained the relationship between canonical principles of general education commonly endorsed by United States schools and those of multicultural education. She argued that these are fundamentally the same, with the only differences being in context and constituency. Multicultural education merely translates general educational principles to fit the specific contexts of ethnic and cultural diversity. James Banks (1995) is now exploring intersections between feminist theory, knowledge reconstruction, and multicultural education, as well as ideological antecedents to it found in the thinking of early 20th century African American educators. Christine Bennett (1995) and Sonia Nieto (1992), along with Banks and many others, evoke democratic principles and ethics to support their claims about the multicultural imperative in education. Carl Grant, Christine Sleeter, Joyce King, Gloria Ladson-Billings, and Antonia Darder (1992) incorporate ideas from critical theory, post-modernism, social reconstructionism, and political empowerment into their explanations of the essential goals, purposes, and anticipated outcomes of multicultural education. Other theorists are beginning to establish direct linkages between economic development, international diplomacy, and being responsive to cultural diversity in the educational process.

This "conceptual webbing" is producing both encouraging and disturbing results for multicultural education. It is stimulating and enriching discussions among theorists about the necessities, contours, and potentialities of multicultural education. The thoughts and ideas which result from these discussions are at increasingly higher levels of sophistication, abstraction, and complexity. In this sense, the field is developing the way it should, from the perspective of theory development. As any kind of educational theory matures, its ideological contours become more complex and abstract, and thus moves further and further away from direct and immediate translation to classroom application.

Ironically, its theoretical strengths are also the nemesis of multicultural education practice. Rather than enlightening practitioners and stimulating them to higher levels of instructional action, complex theoretical explanations often have the reverse effects. They can intimidate, confuse, overwhelm, and incapacitate classroom teachers. The language used to expressed key ideas and concepts become more esoteric, thereby making them less clear to everyone except other theorists with similar developmental status and understanding. More attention is devoted to conceptualizing than to actualizing multicultural components and characteristics. That is, as theorists pre-scribe and visualize what **should be done,** they speak increasingly in terms of ideals without clearly articulating directions for how these are to be operationalized in practice.

This situation is complicated even further by differences in the ideological ideas disciplinary emphases, and maturational levels of theorists themselves. Some multiculturalists are influenced heavily by history and sociology, while others speak through the conceptual and linguistic filters of politics, psychology, anthropology, and pedagogy. Consequently, classroom teachers and school administrators are left to their own devices to translate theory to practice. Frequently what they do in practice is inconsistent with or even violates what is meant by the theory.

Thus, while multicultural theorists argue that cultural diversity should be infused into the learning experiences of all students regardless of the ethnic demographics of specific school and classroom sites, practitioners still tend to make its implementation contingent upon the presence of specific ethnic groups of color. If there are no African-American, Latino, Native-American, or certain Asian-American students enrolled in their schools, they find it difficult to see the relevance of doing multicultural education. When theorists propose that the K-12 educational process be **transformed** by cultural diversity, they mean the most fundamental and deeply ingrained values, beliefs, and assumptions which determine all educational policies, content, procedures, and structures schooling will be **revolutionalized** by being culturally pluralized.

However, their college and university counterparts do not necessarily conceive of transformation in the same way. They, as well as many K-12 practitioners, use a more restricted notion of transformation as simply "change." They assume that multicultural transformation is accomplished by merely including information about ethnically diverse individuals and achievements into the content of instruction, or disciplinary canons. In this sense, the curriculum of a United States literature course is thought to have been transformed when writings by authors of color and females are routinely included for study. These conceptions and practices fail to realize that curriculum involves more than content, that the educational enterprise is not analogous to curriculum, and that the mere presence of ethnic information is not enough to constitute transformation.

These kinds of discrepancies in meanings between theorists and practitioners, are understandable, given their differential levels of mastery of and maturity in the field. But they also are confusing and can have negative effects on the overall advancement of multiculturalism in all levels of the educational enterprise. They place both the practitioners and the theorists in reactive, rather than pro-active positions. The practitioners are faced with having to explain away their unintended misinterpretations and possible accusations that theorists are too esoteric in their explanations of key multicultural ideas. The theorists feel the need to re-examine and re-explain their intended original meanings to avoid future misinterpretations. This "back-stepping" slows down the forward thrust and continuous development of multicultural education in both theory and practice.

A strongly endorsed theoretical idea that is often misunderstood and is another powerful illustration of the lack of **operational bridging** between multicultural educational theory and practice is **infusion.** Virtually every multicultural theorist supports the idea that cultural diversity should be an integral part of the total educational experiences of all students in all school settings. This means it should impact the contexts and structures of teaching and learning as well as their content and text. Stated somewhat differently, all policies, programs, and procedures in school curriculum, instruction, administration, guidance, assessment, and governance should be responsive to cultural diversity. This responsiveness is multidimensional, too, including recognition, knowledge, acceptance, respect, praise, and promotion. But, very few theorists explain how to actually do these all-encompassing mandates in the various dimensions of the educational enterprise.

What do school principals do to multiculturalize the different tasks which comprise their administrative and leadership functions? What are the operational steps and decision-making points involved in multiculturalizing the curriculum creation process? How can these general principles be specified to different domains of learning such as math, science, reading, and social studies? How does one make the content as well as the administrative styles of student assessment culturally pluralistic? These are the kinds of questions that remain after most theoretical pronouncements are made regarding multicultural education infusion. They must be answered more precisely in order to establish better connections between theory and practice.

The few attempts that are made to create these bridges often are unsuccessful because they tend be "finished or product examples" of what infusion looks like, instead of clearly articulated and functional explanations of the **processes** of infusion itself. For example, theorists may present illustrations of multiculturally-infused reading units, but fail to explain how decisions about their specific components were made, or why they embody and personify different principles of multicultural education.

Consequently, these samples are of limited value in empowering other educators to create similar ones, and thereby continuing to advance the development of multicultural education practice. This places practitioners in a situation of trying to imitate or replicate the sample lessons without being sufficiently informed about how the original decisions were made. The results are not very successful which can cause instructional program designers to become frustrated and discouraged. This frustration then becomes a convenient excuse for them to abandon future efforts to implement multicultural education in their classrooms.

Another tension between multicultural theory and practice is the fact that many application models suggested for classroom use are **decontextualized.** They are not connected in any systematic way to what teachers routinely do in the day-to-day operations of their curricula and classrooms. Excellent books which present authentic and accurate portrayals of different ethnic groups' cultures, contributions, and experiences are now available. A wide variety of richly textured and significant learning activities have been developed for teaching various aspects of multicultural education, such as prejudice reduction, ethnic identity development, intergroup relations, and self-esteem.

Despite their inherent worth, decontextualized multicultural activities are of limited use in classrooms because the authors do not explain where and how they fit into typical instructional tasks and responsibilities. If, for example, designers were to demonstrate how learning non-pejorative terms for ethnic groups can be incorporated into standard vocabulary lessons in reading instruction, how ethnic population statistics can be used in teaching math skills such as proportions, ratios, and graphing, and how participating in

inter-ethnic group social exchanges approximate some of the skills social studies teach about international diplomacy classroom teachers may be more willing and capable of using them.

Without this **functional contextualization,** teachers are likely to continue to perceive multicultural education as an intrusive addition to an already over-burdened workload, or something that requires extra efforts and special skills. It then becomes very easy for them to dismiss the idea of cultural diversity without due consideration because they "don't have time to teach anything else," or because "it jeopardizes other important things that must be taught, such as basic literacy skills."

Another occurrence common to a profession which causes a split between theory and practice is variability in the positional responsibilities of the membership. Educational theorists tend to be more highly specialized in selected aspects of a discipline than school practitioners. They have the luxury of concentrating their professional activities on fewer things, and becoming more thoroughly involved in exploring even deeper conceptual parameters and possibilities of their areas of expertise.

By comparison, school practitioners tend to be more generalists than specialists, and are more engaged in applying than creating new knowledge. The more deeply involved they are in a pedagogical field, the more devoted they become to improving its practical applications. It seems only natural that these positional emphases would produce more divergent than convergent developments. As the field of study advances, both groups grow in clarity and coherency, but in opposite directions—practice seeks increasing conciseness, while theory searches for greater complexity. These kinds of developments support the need for specialists who can translate theory to practice.

These **patterns of professional participation** are evident in the field of multicultural education. Most nationally-known multiculturalists are scholars and specialists whose units of study and analysis are precollegiate educational programs, processes, and practices. Their suggestions and proposals are **ideal prescriptions** about what cultural education should be.

By comparison, most school practitioners are specialists in something other than multicultural education, such as reading, history, math, or science instruction. They are concerned more with **real-**

istic and functional descriptions of what to do, and how—about cultural diversity in relation to their other pedagogical responsibilities.

When these different professionals appeal to each other to satisfy their respective needs, they are often disappointed, and may even doubt the value of each other's contributions because their quality may not be readily apparent in other domains of operations. Thus, when multicultural practitioners appeal to theorists for suggestions on how cultural diversity should be taught, they expect procedural specificities, but get conceptual guidelines instead. They are advised to be integrative, authentic, and transformative. These are great principles, but they do not have any action directives.

Conversely, when theorists look to practitioners for evidence of the application of conceptual ideas in classroom actions they expect composites and systems of varieties of methods, materials, and tools, since concepts embed a multitude of action possibilities. Instead, they frequently see isolated activities and fragmented events.

These situations are understandable from the perspective of both the theorist and the practitioner. Multicultural theorists should be pursuing deeper conceptual understandings and explanations of the field, and practitioners should be looking for more pragmatic ways to implement cultural diversity in the classroom. It does little toward advancing both theory and practice for either to indict the other for not being maximally accountable for quality performance. Theorists should not be expected to perform as practitioners do; nor should practitioners be held accountable for being theorists. Both should be valued for their respective skills and functions. Yet, the need to establish better linkages between multicultural education theory and practice is imperative. Therefore, individuals who can translate theoretical ideas to the functional operations of actual classroom instruction can contribute significantly to the overall development of the field.

BUILDING BETTER BRIDGES BETWEEN THEORY AND PRACTICE

Two ideas are discussed here to illustrate how multicultural education theory and practice can be linked closer together. One involves approaches to multicultural education implementation, and the other has to do with the personal and professional empowerment of teachers in cultural diversity. Hopefully, they are instructive of the kinds of opportunities this challenge offers for enriching current developments in the field, as well as adding new dimensions of growth in the future.

All major multicultural scholars have developed models of different approaches to implementing cultural diversity in classroom curriculum and instruction. In some form or another, they include variations of **inclusion, infusion, deconstruction,** and **transformation.** The progression of these is from teaching information about ethnic groups in rather fragmentary, haphazard, and additive ways; to incorporating cultural pluralism throughout the educational process systemically and systematically; to using culturally pluralistic knowledge, perspectives, and experiences as criteria for re-examining the basic premises and assumptions on which the United States educational system is grounded; to creating new educational and social systems that are based upon the ethics, morality, and legalities of cultural diversity.

Embedded in all of these models are ideas of historical context, developmental growth, and increasing referential and conceptual complexity. Each model also conveys the message that some approaches to dealing with cultural diversity are inherently better than others, and everyone should aim to adopt these. It will help to establish closer and more functional linkages between multicultural theory and practice if these conceptualizations were reconsidered to be more developmental than hierarchical.

Rather than continuing to argue that there is **a single best** way to do multicultural education to which everyone should adhere, it is more feasible, pragmatic, inclusive, and empowering to legitimize multiple levels appropriateness in participation. Currently the theoretical message is that efforts to do multicultural education are inadequate if they are not at least at the infusion and preferably the transformation level. To impose these expectations on everyone is unrealistic. Educators just entering the field of multiculturalism simply do not have the background information, the pedagogical skills, or the personal confidence needed to fully understand what infusion and transformation are, least of all how to translate these ideals to practice. When they try to do so, the results are disastrous for everyone concerned—the professionals, the students, and the field.

The theoretical ideas of **developmental progression and appropriateness** have far greater potential for improving the quality of participation of educators at various stages of personal growth and professional positions in the promotion of multicultural education, as well as closer synchronizing its theory and practice. Developmental progression means that people's understanding of and capabilities in multicultural education move through different stages of conceptualization and practice; that each stage has inherent worth and legitimacy; and that the emergence of more advanced stages are contingent upon the development of earlier, more basic stages. It also means that there is growth potential within each stage.

While the inclusion of ethnic content into selective curriculum lessons or units of instruction is a more rudimentary and basic approach to multicultural education than transforming the entire schooling enterprise, it has conceptual value and practical utility. Educators have to master this approach before they move on to more advanced levels of implementation. They have to learn how to do good multicultural lessons before they can design effective units on cultural diversity, or redesign topics in other subjects so that they include multicultural perspectives. Teachers most certainly cannot deconstruct the cultural hegemony ingrained in their instructional styles, or make them multiculturally responsive until they have learned a great deal about how cultural elements of different ethnic groups are embedded in the rituals and routines of teaching and learning.

Viewing multicultural education theory and practice as developmental and progressional enfranchises more people to be active advocates. Relatively few educators are ready now to actually transform the educational system so that it reflects cultural diversity in all of its content, values, and structures even though they may believe this is necessary. Therefore, if its practice were solely dependent upon them, very little would be accomplished. As others engage in practical actions at other levels of conceptualization the numbers of advocates who promote diversity increases significantly. The field needs these numbers to create a critical mass of change agents who can impact the educational system at multiple levels and in diverse ways. Diversified personnel with differentiated abilities and skills are imperative to operationalize the multicultural mandate of **systemic reform.**

This idea of individuals involved at various levels of complexity, and using a variety of techniques to incorporate cultural diversity in the educational enterprise, is highly consistent with the nature of the field. The heart of multicultural education is diversity and plurality. Just as advocates demand that these principles be applied in teaching students about cultural differences, the field should apply similar criteria to itself. If it does, then both multicultural theory and practice must provide opportunities for educators in various stages of professional development to be involved in a variety of ways in promoting cultural diversity that are legitimized and compatible with their capabilities. They also should have the chance to improve the quality of their present state of being before they are expected to move to new planes of performance. These ideas evoke the learning principles of readiness and prerequisites. Just as classroom teachers use them to help guide their students' learning, similar applications should be made to the professional growth of teachers in cultural diversity.

More systematic ways to **empower practice** are needed within each of the developmental stages of multicultural education theory. These can be accomplished by carefully analyzing essential components of teaching functions endemic to each stage, and then demonstrating how these can be modified to illustrate stage related principles of multicultural education. Four brief examples will suffice to illustrate this point. A powerful feature of the **inclusion** stage of multicultural education theory and practice is the concept of heroism. Students are introduced to a host of ethnic individuals who have made major contributions to their own cultural groups, as well as to United States society and humankind. The theoretical idea of selecting authentic ethnic individuals and artifacts to be taught can be applied in practice by teachers understanding what is a cultural hero or heroine according to the standards of different ethnic groups. Using these as criteria to select candidates for this distinction will help educators to avoid using their own cultural standards to select heroes and then imposing them upon students from other ethnic groups. Understanding cultural standards of heroism and how different candidates manifest them thus empowers teachers and curriculum designers to select better examples of ethnic heroes and contributions to teach to students.

At the **infusion** level of multicultural education, implementation educators can be empowered in practice by demonstrating how the typical components of curriculum development can be culturally diversified. For example, how can sensitivity to cultural diversity be embedded in a curriculum rationale, statement of goals and objectives, content and learning objectives, and students' performance assessment? Other natural infusion opportunities can be identified by analyzing the teaching act to determine things that teachers routinely do, and then changing them to be responsive to cultural diversity. The notions of impacting that which is habitual, routine, and fundamental in the educational process are central to the multicultural education infusion. Because teacher talk is a major component of instruction, and it affects culturally diverse students differently, it should be a primary target for multicultural infusion. But, in order to do this well, how teachers talk needs to be carefully analyzed, and then changed accordingly. This analysis might include the kinds of questions asked of which students, turn-taking rules, wait time for responses, and mechanisms used to convey praise and criticism to students.

At the essence of **deconstruction** approaches to multicultural education is what is often referred to as critique, interrogation, and knowledge reconstruction. In practice this means that students are groomed to be healthy skeptics who are constantly questioning existing claims to social and academic truths and accuracy in search of new explanations, and to determine if the perspectives of different ethnic and cultural groups are represented. Nothing is considered sacrosanct, infallible, perfect, totally finished, or purely objective. Students are taught how to discern authors' biases, determine whose story is being told and vali-

dated from which vantage point, how to engage in perspective taking, as well as how to be self-monitoring, self-reflective, and self-renewing, especially in relation to issues of cultural diversity. These are the behavioral or practical manifestations of such deconstructive principles as multiple perspectives, giving voice, and the positionality of knowledge.

In practice, **transformative** approaches to multicultural education focus on constructing new realities, new systems, and new possibilities. They are the **action response** to deconstructive processes. Whereas deconstruction focuses on thinking and imagining new explanations of culturally pluralistic social situations, transformation takes the revisioning processes to its ultimate conclusion by acting upon the mental constructions. This building of new systems that are fully culturally pluralistic may include models, facsimiles, simulations, and actual creations. In creating them students are engaged in various forms of social and political actions, both within and outside of schools, which symbolize their moral and ethical commitments to freedom, equality, and justice for culturally diverse peoples.

CONCLUSION

The challenges posed by the need to bridge multicultural education theory and practice require that one is able to think analytically about current developments to explicate their most salient intersecting possibilities. With some careful thinking from individuals with the necessary expertise, it is possible to generate a whole new body of research and scholarship in multicultural education which demonstrates, with operational clarity, how theoretical principles can be translated into actual practices in schools and classrooms.

However, the act of creating these strategies will prompt yet another generation of multicultural theorizing. But, this evolving vitality and potential should not be seen as a problem to the field. As long as multicultural education has the regenerative power to create new thoughts, critiques, possibilities, and proposals for its own refinement, it is alive and well both as a theoretical endeavor and a practical necessity.

REFERENCES

Banks, J. A. (1995). The historical reconstruction of knowledge about race: Implications for transformative teaching. *Educational Researcher,* 24 (20), 15–25.

Banks, J. A., & Banks, C. A. M. (Eds.). (1993). *Multicultural education: Issues and perspectives.* Boston, MA: Allyn & Bacon.

Banks, J. A., & Banks, C. A. M. (Eds.). (1995). *Handbook of research on multicultural education.* New York: Macmillan.

Beauchamp, G. A. (1968). *Curriculum theory* (2d. ed.). Wilmette, IL: Kagg Press.

Bennett, C. I. (1995). *Comprehensive multicultural education: Theory and practice* (3rd ed.). Boston, MA: Allyn & Bacon.

Darder, A., (1991). *Culture and power in the classroom: A critical foundation for bicultural education.* New York: Bergin & Garvey.

Foster, M. (Ed.). (1991). *Readings on equal education. Volume 11: Qualitative investigations into schools and schooling.* New York: AMS Press.

Gay, G. (1994). *At the essence of learning: Multicultural education.* West Lafayette, IN: Kappa Delta Pi.

Hollins, E. R., King, J. E., & Hayman, W. C. (Eds.). (1994). *Teaching diverse populations: Formulating a knowledge base.* Albany, NY: State University of New York Press.

Nieto, S. (1992). *Affirming diversity: The sociopolitical context of multicultural education.* New York: Longman.

Sleeter, C. E. (Ed.). (1991). *Empowerment through multicultural education.* Albany, NY: State University of New York Press.

Sleeter, C. E., & Grant, C. A. (1995). *Making choices for multicultural education: Five approaches to race, class, and gender* (2d ed.). Columbus, OH: Merrill.

Identity and Personal Development: A Multicultural Focus

We have known for several decades that all human affective behavior (emotional response, values assessment, and so on) is learned behavior. Anything that can be learned can be unlearned or modified. There is no more important task for human beings than learning how to define themselves as people within a cultural as well as a global societal context. People are influenced by many social forces as they interact with others in the process of forming themselves as individuals. Multicultural education can help students as well as teachers to identify those social forces that affect their personal development.

The development of each person's unique concept of self (the development of one's identity as a person) is the most important developmental learning task that any of us undertakes. Multicultural education seeks to help people develop intellectual and emotional responses that will be accepting and empathic toward other people. Educators have the opportunity as they work with students to provide good examples of tolerant behavior and to help students develop positive, affirmative views of themselves and others. Gordon A. Allport, in his classic book *The Nature of Prejudice*, commented that early instruction and practice in accepting diversity is very important in directing a child toward becoming a tolerant person. Thus, we take up the topic of personal identity development in this unit.

As teachers, we must be aware of the interconnections among such factors as gender, social class position in society, racial or ethnic heritage, and the primary cultural values that inform the way people see the world and

themselves. We need to be sensitive to their visions of who they are and of how things are in the world. We need to "see our clients whole." It is important for teachers to set positive examples of empathy, compassion, and concern for the well-being of each student.

Self-definition can be integrated and effectively achieved within the intellectual mission of the school. One way to do this is by encouraging students to critically interpret and evaluate the texts they read and to discuss issues in class openly and actively. Identity development is an ongoing process. Each student needs to be able to explore the boundaries of his or her intellectual strengths and weaknesses and explore the social boundaries encountered in and out of school.

Cultural values are of primary importance in the process of a person's conceptualization of him- or herself. This unit's articles explore various models of human interaction and the psychosocial foundations for the formation of students' knowledge.

Students live in a hierarchy of social contexts in which their racial, cultural, gender, and social class backgrounds, and the degree of their personal identification with each of these factors, influence their choices and individual decisions. Research on how teachers can achieve more effective intercultural socialization is also considered. Under what circumstances may higher rates of intercultural friendship develop is one of the questions being studied in desegregated school settings. How to get all cultural group members willing to learn each others' cultural heritages is one of the challenges being studied. Helping stu-

dents to learn from the cultural perspectives of other groups is one of the tasks of multicultural education. Another purpose is to teach tolerant, accepting attitudes toward others of differing cultural backgrounds. Educators are *not* powerless in the face of the prejudiced views that many students bring to school from their homes.

The essays in this unit are relevant to courses in educational policy studies and leadership, cultural foundations of education, sociology or anthropology of education, history and philosophy of education, and curriculum theory and construction, among others.

Looking Ahead: Challenge Questions

What are the primary gender issues in multicultural school settings?

What should children learn about the cultural heritages and values of other children in their schools?

How do class differences relate to misunderstandings among students from different social positions in a community?

What can educators learn from developing close communications linkages with the families of their students?

What challenges do minority students encounter that majority students in a desegregated school do not encounter?

How does community structure affect adolescent identity development?

What can teachers do to foster positive personal identity development in their students?

Acquisition and Manifestation of Prejudice in Children

Clifford Carter
C. Lynne Rice

Three major categories of prejudice have been identified in this article: Conscious/Intentional, Conscious/Unintentional, and Unconscious/Unintentional. Prejudice plays a large role in the development of our children, and through exposure to and understanding of the development of prejudice, the strength that it holds can be understood and diminished.

Prejudice is both a rational and an irrational attitude. It is rational in the sense that it allows the person manifesting it to cover inadequacies by calling attention to another person or group. The targeted group is usually one that deviates from the criteria of appearance and behavior that the dominant group ranks as ideal. With these criteria, all other groups can be ranked by comparison with the dominant group. When the dominant group incorporates the devaluation of the lower ranking groups into religion, mass media, and the law, then that belief is viewed as morally correct. Therefore, anyone who deviates from the reference group is considered deserving of maltreatment. In some cases, the proponent of prejudice even seems brave when reinforced by other groups who display similar behavior. Prejudice is also irrational because it is a conclusion about an entire group or race based only on observations of individuals within that group. The result of this generalization is an attitude of hostility for an individual, a group, sex, or race that results in different treatment based on other than individual merit.

Allport (1979) defined prejudice as the following:

An antipathy based upon a faulty and inflexible generalization. It may be felt or expressed. It may be directed toward a group as a whole, or toward

Clifford Carter *is an associate professor and* ***C. Lynne Rice*** *is a graduate student, both in the Department of Counseling and Psychological Services in the College of Education at Georgia State University, Atlanta. Correspondence regarding this article should be sent to Clifford Carter, Georgia State University, Department of Counseling and Psychological Services, College of Education, CPS Dept., University Plaza, Atlanta, GA 30303-3083.*

From *Journal of Multicultural Counselling and Development,* July 1997, pp. 185-194. © 1997 by the American Counselling Association. Reprinted by permission. Not for further reproduction.

an individual because he is a member of that group. The net effect of prejudice is to place the object of prejudice at some disadvantage not merited by his own misconduct. (p. 9)

Prejudice plays a role in developing children's self-concept or esteem, their socialization with peers, and ultimately their confidence to perform and succeed in the classroom.

Children learn in their homes about animosity toward another group. Richard Rogers and Oscar Hammerstein's (1949) poignant lyric summarizes this learning concept:

> You've got to be taught to hate and fear
> You've got to be taught from year to year
> It's got to be drummed in your dear little ear
> You've got to be carefully taught
> You've got to be taught to be afraid
> Of people whose eyes are oddly made
> And people whose skin is a different shade
> You've got to be carefully taught
> You've got to be taught before it's too late
> Before you are six or seven or eight
> To hate all the people your relatives hate
> You've got to be carefully taught.

Young children assimilate the behaviors and attitudes of their environment. They mimic what they hear and see without understanding the implications to please the parent, guardian, or teacher whom they view as the provider of security and nourishment.

Prejudice has its origins in the individual's group identity. As early as 5 years of age, a child begins to understand that he or she belongs to a particular group and by the age of 10 can distinguish differences between groups (Allport, 1979). The in-group's (group setting the criteria the culture ranks as ideal) views serve as a reference by which the out-group (group that deviates from the norm established by the in-group) is judged. Deaux and Wrightsman (1988) defined ethnocentrism as the rating of all others by comparison with their own group. Prejudice occurs when the in-group excludes others from the group process (Sherman, 1990).

We have identified three major categories of prejudice (1995): *Conscious/Intentional, Conscious/Unintentional,* and *Unconscious/Unintentional.* The first type, Conscious/Intentional prejudice, is manifested as a blatant antipathy for a group of individuals. Persons with this type of prejudice are aware of the hatred they have for a particular group and express these beliefs to perpetuate the hate, feel superior, find a scapegoat, or humiliate others they have targeted as inferior. By drawing attention to another person or group they can cover up their own inadequacies.

Conscious/Intentional prejudice is rooted in feelings or affect. Fear, hatred, and feelings of inadequacy serve as motivators. The affect that exacerbates the expression of Conscious/Intentional prejudice can only be sustained by playing on the fears of others. This occurs by exaggerating the negative qualities or the generalizability of those qualities to evoke fear of the unknown.

Conscious/Unintentional prejudice, on the other hand, is likely to be expressed only in socially acceptable venues. Those in this group are in an unresolved state with their belief system and are confused. These individuals have distanced themselves from reacting predominantly on affect and realize cognitively that prejudice is harmful and unjustified. However, they resort to expressions of prejudice when the targeted group is too close for comfort. The reason this occurs is because on a cognitive level the individual gives some validity to the stereotypes that reinforce prejudice.

Unconscious/Unintentional prejudice is the proverbial "slip-up." Persons in this category are unaware of their prejudiced beliefs and deny these feelings if questioned. They do not intend to hurt or to label with their comments but may, without being aware of it, express a concept or statement that perpetuates prejudicial beliefs. The slip-ups may be more deeply rooted in repressed prejudicial statements or beliefs. Without consciously intending to say these things, an individual may let them surface in his or her speech when least expected.

Children who are exposed to Conscious/Intentional prejudice will continue to repeat the negative verbal expressions and behaviors as long as they are positively reinforced with either attention or praise. Perhaps more important than words are the actions of the role models toward individuals outside of their familial group. To be accepted, a child will imitate the behaviors that he or she sees accepted. By acting as the adults act, children receive a positive reaction from adults for the perceived compliment of imitation of conduct. Without understanding the results of their derogatory actions toward others, children will do that which follows the path of least resistance and brings maximal praise. From this perspective, prejudice is reinforced in the child's environment.

Even in politically correct families in which adults, who practice Conscious/Unintentional prejudice, would never say anything negative or stereotypical of a person of another ethnicity, sex, sexual preference, religion, or capability, a child will pick up on any hidden messages. The parents who tell their child that all people are created equal is verbalizing a positive belief promoting harmony. However, when that same child asks his parents if a friend, who is of a darker shade, can spend the night at his or her house, he or she receives a very different nonverbal message. The mixed message received is that "those people" are all right to socialize with outside the home, but they should not be brought home. This message is confusing to the child, but trust has been placed in the perception and experience of the adults in his or her life. A child reasons that the parents must know what they are talking about, even if he or she cannot understand, because parents are "older and wiser." This reasoning is compounded by the ambiguity of the expression of racial prejudice in American society. Overt prejudice has become more subtle than in the past (Sherman, 1990). Conscious/Unintentional prejudice is particularly damaging to a young child who receives a reward–punishment message from parents. The child is rewarded for making friends with others from outside of the group but is punished through rejection when he or she wants to bring this new friend home. So, the child learns not to embrace others fully because this acceptance brings punishment and unhappiness from the adults.

The confusion felt by the child and the mixed messages he or she receives are reflected in interactions with the outside world. There, one must decide to accept the message and continue to be reinforced at home or break from the prejudicial notions and develop a perception of others based on personal interactions and experiences. The child who has a base of beliefs from a prejudiced family life will act in accordance with these beliefs as he or she deals with others. If the majority of the people in the outside world feel and act as his or her family did, with prejudice toward those who are different, the child will do the same. If one has little contact during early childhood with outside groups, then erroneous beliefs will not be challenged.

A defining moment in the development of prejudice is in the child's first encounters with the targeted groups. Prejudice is often a feeling toward a person or group that may not be based on actual experience. Therefore, if the first experience reinforces the stereotype in the child's mind and he or she continues to have limited contact with the group, it is very likely that he or she will maintain these negative generalizations on the basis of interactions with only a few individuals. The child may actually be mentally prepared to view this initial encounter in a way that will fit with the negative stereotype regardless of the actual encounter. This stagnant thought process allows the child to eliminate contradictory information that will challenge his or her perception.

Prejudice affects both the bearer of the hostility and those it is directed toward. Allport (1954) defined five stages in acting out prejudice. Assessing the expression of the following five forms of prejudice can help school personnel understand the severity of racial conflict they observe.

1. *Antilocution* refers to racist literature or verbal assaults and may be the first overt symptom of prejudice.
2. *Avoidance* occurs when prejudice intensifies and individuals actively avoid contact with the disliked group. Esteem based on pride in the homogeny of the dominant group is strengthened through group support when challenged.
3. *Discrimination* is the power held by the majority group. This person will exclude members of the targeted group from social privilege.
4. *Physical attacks* may occur.
5. *Extermination* is uncommon.

Physical attack and extermination are the ultimate expressions of prejudice. In today's society many prefer to believe these extreme forms of prejudice are foreign and predominantly historical. Most individuals will never move past antilocution and thus believe that they are distanced from discrimination, physical attack, and extermination. However, as Allport (1954) would point out, participation in any stage makes escalation to the next stage easier. By condoning or ignoring antilocution as a benign expression, one plants the seeds for further prejudice. By contributing on even the lowest level of acting out prejudice, one is supporting the highest levels. If the child's first encounters with the targeted group are positive or do not fit with preconceived notions, that individual child is confused. When one's prejudiced beliefs are confronted with contrary religious teaching or education, an internal conflict arises. Allport (1954) acknowledged four ways people deal with such conflict:

1. Repression: One refuses to believe there is a contradiction in the way he or she thinks versus the out-group's perspective.
2. Defense: One who uses defense will alter his or her experiences to justify faulty thinking.
3. Compromise: One compromises and uses the belief system that is the best option for his or her purposes.
4. Integration: One may decide to open thought patterns and experiences to true integration and practice respect for all groups.

School is a time for learning and socialization. However, for the child who is the target of prejudice, it can be a time filled with feelings of worthlessness and confusion. Children are vulnerable to criticism and are especially sensitive to the views of their peers. For many children, school is the first environment in which they can explore the world with others their own age. One seeks to be included as part of the new group and is easily influenced by any suggestion that he or she is different or does not belong. For the targeted child, esteem can be greatly affected. Characteristics that seemed normal before are now seen in a devastating manner when exaggerated by the cruel teasing that one may experience as a result of being different. When the child is focusing on those qualities that he or she has come to feel are different or inferior, he or she is unable to focus on learning. In the child's mind, he or she is struggling with characteristics that have been singled out. The child reasons that if one or two children have pointed out this negative component he or she possesses, then everyone must be aware of the deficit. When bombarded with self-consciousness, it is not surprising that many children cannot focus on the concept of learning. The impact of learning is minimal compared with the current rejection and pain. Children that feel different or rejected will want to fade into the background in the hope that they do not stand out and make themselves a target for attack. By withdrawing from being the focus of attention, the child chooses not to excel in a manner that will make others notice. Therefore, the child will fail to achieve full potential academically in an attempt to blend into the background. Teachers have a tremendous role in determining the outcome. Instructors must be familiar with what prejudice means and how it is manifested in the classroom.

Semons (1991) found that in one high school, "Negative comments about Asians were overheard in the presence of teachers, who did nothing to interrupt them. Students could therefore infer that prejudice against Asians was acceptable" (p. 147). The teacher who ignores or denies the problem will only serve to give quiet approval to the prejudiced behavior. The teachers may serve to preserve prejudice in the classroom by practicing Unconscious/ Unintentional prejudice. Benign comments that serve to reinforce stereotypes are frequently made. Most of the time, these comments are not intended to single out an individual or group but are said out of frustration or from ignorance of what constitutes prejudiced comments or behavior. The teacher who tells the energetic students to "stop acting like a bunch of wild Indians" may not intend to further a negative stereotype, however many children will absorb such comments as literal.

Although negative stereotypes have some obvious implications, teachers also need to be aware of the effect that positive stereotypes have on a child's development. Positive stereotypes are also a form of prejudice, because they are based on a faulty and inflexible generalization of a particular group. "All boys can excel at sports." "All Asians are good at math; it is easy for them." These blanket statements serve to reinforce a child who does exhibit these qualities. However, a child who does not have these attributes will inevitably feel that he or she is not adequate. These expectations create unfair pressure on the developing child.

Teachers serve as role models to students by manifesting acceptance through interactions with the children. The child that is taught all persons of the majority race are bigots or are "out to get them" experiences a break in the prejudice chain when he or she encounters a teacher of this race who embraces all children equally. Instructional programs can be implemented to include multicultural education, which fosters the appreciation and understanding of others. Many of these programs have their focus on (a) teaching multicultural understanding and (b) assisting minority students in maximizing academic potential. These goals are ideal, but one must be careful not to simply accelerate acculturation rather than teach respect and appreciation for cultural differences. Semons (1991) stated the following:

> When culture is understood to mean one's system for perceiving, evaluating, believing, and acting, the impact of ethnicity on school performance becomes more evident. Research has indicated that the kind of interaction that a learner has with a school varies significantly by ethnic and cultural background. (p. 145)

Masking ethnic identity restricts learning opportunity through culturally linked learning styles and can result in negative self-esteem, which negatively affects learning (Semons, 1991). Sensitivity training for teachers and administrators is also effective in minimizing misinterpretation of comments. Research shows that minorities will interpret ambiguous behaviors as prejudice and that minorities and women show strong negative reactions to ethnic jokes and demeaning language (Triandis, Kurowski, Tecktiel, & Chan 1993) Training that promotes awareness of these behaviors can reduce negative reactions.

Cooperative teaching methods also have shown a positive effect on interethnic behavior and academic learning in school children (Rooney-Rebeck & Jason, 1986). Members of a cooperative learning group work toward a common goal and are more motivated to help all group members. Cooperative learning increases cross-race friendships equally for students of different sexes, races, and achievement levels (Singh, 1991).

If teachers and administrators are trained to demonstrate sensitivity to the different ways other groups communicate and behave, they can convey that understanding to their pupils. How the teacher introduces the concept of acceptance and respect for others is important. When a teacher recognizes a prejudiced comment from a child, it should be second nature to demand that the child stop and apologize for such an insensitive remark. Many children, however, view rules as those things to be broken. Thus, the child who made the comment learns simply not to make the prejudiced comment in front of the teacher. One who enjoys the feeling of superiority associated with making comments that reflect Conscious/Intentional prejudice will also enjoy the power that is associated with breaking rules behind the teacher's back. Now the targeted child is confronted out of the reach of disapproving adults. A long-term approach to reducing prejudice in the classroom is through modeling. In one example, classmates were teasing a child who spoke English as a second language. A caring teacher acknowledged how lucky this child was to speak not only one language, but two. The little boy was asked to teach the class a few words in his native language. This demonstration of respect for the child for being "positively different," was emulated by his classmates. This is an important concept to remember in implementing change in our society—a concept that can be used positively or negatively (as in the case of Conscious/Intentional prejudice).

One of the most important components in reducing prejudice is contact with other groups. Prejudice is rooted in generalization of experiences with individuals to the entire group. It makes sense that the more exposure one has with members of that group, the less strength the stereotypes will hold. Allport (1954) described two types of interaction in his contact theory. Casual contact is superficial (e.g., briefly interacting). These contacts seem to increase prejudice. On the other hand, acquaintance lessens prejudice. When members of different groups are well acquainted with each other, attitudes improve. Contacts that result in knowledge and acquaintance are likely to produce more sound beliefs about the out-group and thus reduce prejudice. In addition, recent research shows that prejudice is present in children as young as 5 years old, but that it declines as a function of social-cognitive development by age 8 or 9. Decreases in prejudice were associated with the developmental perception that different races are more similar, that people of the same race are more different, and that racially different perspectives are acceptable (Doyle & Aboud, 1995).

In the schools, programs can be developed that include contact resulting in positive relationships. Ponterotto (1991) believed it was important to have four precursors to promote these meaningful positive relationships: (a) all individuals must be given equal status, (b) contact should not be just superficial, (c) relationships revolve around a group goal, and (d) there should be some form of social norms associated with positive relationship development.

If generational prejudice is not stopped, it will continue to prosper with each generation. Prejudice does not originate with an individual, but rather through society and the family. Therefore, prejudice needs to be addressed in these settings. By intervening in the school system, school personnel can combat prejudice. Exposure to other groups of individuals challenges the prejudicial concepts by which many children are conditioned in their home environments. When a schoolmate who is of a different color, ethnicity, religion, sex, or ability does not fit the preconceived notions in the young child's mind, he or she is forced to process this information. If the school is simultaneously promoting acceptance and understanding of other groups, the confusion is more easily explained. Education and positive role models can reduce prejudice. Prejudicial thoughts will not disappear quickly; however, interventions can weaken the strength they have. Children who are reinforced and accepted for their lack of prejudicial thought at school will be better able to deal with prejudicial thoughts at home.

Perhaps children can turn the tables and teach their parents how abhorrent prejudice is and what effect it has on others. Influencing parents to accept others is an ideal goal that is infrequently fulfilled. A scenario that can occur more often, however, is sibling influence on other siblings. If the acceptance of others can be taught through words and actions to siblings, then the chain of prejudice can be weakened in the place it started.

Allport (1954) reported that although prejudice may seem hereditary, "the course of transmission is one of teaching and learning, not heredity" (p. 291). Therefore, one reasons, the very same tools used to transmit prejudice can be used just as effectively to block its transmission. The difference is merely on the focus of the teaching and learning. Prejudice is learned and taught at home and in society at large, but the acceptance of these thoughts and behaviors is what reinforces the behavior. Lack of exposure to other groups and fixed stereotypes allow prejudice to thrive, but teaching acceptance and understanding of differences can weaken its strength. The same child that learns through erroneous beliefs at home can bring enlightened beliefs back into the very environment that fostered the growth of prejudice. Finally, a clay link in the chain of prejudice!

REFERENCES

Allport, G. W. (1954). *The nature of prejudice.* Cambridge: Addison-Wesley.

Allport, G. W. (1979). *The nature of prejudice* (25th anniversary ed.). Reading, MA: Addison-Wesley.

Carter, C., & Rice, C. L. (1995, March). *Acquisition of prejudice* (Unpublished paper presented in race relations class at Georgia State University). Atlanta, Georgia.

Deaux, K., & Wrightsman, L. (1988). *Social psychology* (5th ed.) Monterey, CA: Brooks/ Cole.

Doyle, A., & Aboud, F. (1995). A longitudinal study of White children's racial prejudice as a social-cognitive development. *Merrill-Palmer Quarterly, 41*(2), 209–228.

McElroy-Johnson, B. (1993). Teaching and practice: Giving voice to the voiceless. *Harvard Educational Review, 63*(1), 85–104.

Ponterotto, J. (1991). The nature of prejudice revisited: Implications for counseling intervention. *Journal of Counseling & Development, 70,* 216–224.

Rogers, R., & Hammerstein, O. (1949). You've got to be carefully taught. From *South Pacific.* New York: Chappell.

Rooney-Rebeck, P., & Jason, L. (1986). Prevention of prejudice in elementary school students. *Journal of Primary Prevention, 7*(2), 63–73.

Semons, M. (1991). Ethnicity in the urban high school: a naturalistic study of student experiences. *The Urban Review, 23*(3), 137–157.

Sherman, R. L. (1990). Intergroup conflict on high school campuses. *Journal of Multicultural Counseling and Development, 18,* 11–18.

Singh, B. R. (1991). Teaching methods for reducing prejudice and enhancing achievement for all children. *Educational Studies, 17*(2), 157–171.

Triandis, H., Kurowski, L., Tecktiel, A., & Chan, D. (1993). Extracting the emics of diversity. *International Journal of Intercultural Relations, 17*(2), 217–234.

RACE AND CLASS CONSCIOUSNESS AMONG LOWER- AND MIDDLE-CLASS BLACKS

THOMAS J. DURANT, JR.
Louisiana State University

KATHLEEN H. SPARROW
University of Southwestern Louisiana

Past studies have revealed that to a great extent, America is a racially stratified society. Early studies revealed that race was a significant factor influencing the life chances and social status of Blacks in America (Cox, 1948; Davis, Gardner, & Gardner, 1941; Drake & Cayton, 1945; DuBois, 1899; Frazier, 1957; Johnson, 1943; Myrdal, 1964). During the 1960s, the U.S. Riot Commission report (1967) concluded that "Our nation is moving toward two societies, one Black, one White—separate and unequal; discrimination and segregation have long permeated much of American life; they now threaten the future of every American." More recent studies have also found that race continues to be a primary factor influencing Black life chances in America (Clark, 1978, 1980; Pettigrew, 1980; West, 1993; Willie, 1989). Past studies have concluded that racial stratification gives rise to race consciousness, which emerges from members of both the dominant and subordinate racial groups (Allen, 1970; Brown, 1931; Ferguson, 1936; Park, 1913, 1923; Pitts, 1974; Rose, 1964).

On the other hand, America is also stratified by social class, which gives rise to class consciousness among members of both the dominant and subordinate classes. As such, both race consciousness and class consciousness are two forms of group consciousness that result from social structured inequality, based on race and class. The theoretical value in studying these concepts lies in their capacity to enhance our understanding of the nature, patterns, and variations in race and class consciousness among subgroups of the Black population. For example, many believe that increased social mobility among Blacks and the reduction of racial prejudice and discrimination have led to an increase in class consciousness and a decrease in race consciousness (Handy, 1984).

Whereas some attention has been given to structural determinants of race and class consciousness among Blacks, little attention has been given to the attributes of race and class consciousness based on the perceptions of lower-class Blacks, compared to middle-class Blacks. Although an earlier study (Handy, 1984) compared the level of race and class consciousness among Blacks and their social correlates, a content analysis of the qualities, patterns, and variations in race and class consciousness respectively, was not conducted. In other words, what are the elements that comprise race and class consciousness? And what are the attitudinal patterns of race and class consciousness, as perceived by lower-class

 From *Journal of Black Studies*, January 1997, pp. 334-351. © 1997 by Sage Publications, Inc. Reprinted by permission.

Blacks, compared to middle-class Blacks? This study will explore these questions.

The specific objectives of this study are (1) to lay the background for the current study by briefly reviewing the broader issue on the significance of race versus class in determining the life chances of Blacks, (2) to discuss the sociological meaning and derivation of the concepts of race consciousness and class consciousness, and (3) to discuss and summarize the results of a study on differences in attitudinal patterns of race consciousness and class consciousness among lower-class Blacks, compared with middle-class Blacks of a large southern city.

THE CLASS PERSPECTIVE

Wilson (1978), the chief proponent of the class perspective, contends that the life chances of Blacks have more to do with their economic class position than with their race. In other words, race can no longer be considered as important as class in determining the life chances of Blacks. Wilson states that access to higher paying jobs is increasingly based on education and that relations between racial groups are shaped largely by the character of the economic system of production. According to Wilson, American society has undergone three stages in Black-White relations—preindustrial, industrial, and modern; each period has brought a distinct pattern of race relations.

In the preindustrial period, largely characterized as a slave-based plantation economy of the South, the social order was such that the slaveholding elite relegated Blacks to indefinite servitude and promoted its own class interests. In stage two, the industrial period, a new pattern of race relations evolved. This period was characterized by a growing industrial system that put Whites and Blacks into competition for jobs in the North, which produced racial tension and even riots, and a system of Jim Crow segregation laws was imposed by Whites in the South. In stage three, the modern period, class replaces race as the most important factor influencing Black life chances. This development contributed to internal class differentiation within the Black communities.

In summary, Wilson (1978) argues that race is less determinative of fortunes and destinies than it once was, and that Blacks with the requisite skills can now advance economically whereas the Black underclass without the

skills cannot advance. Proponents of the class perspective would probably argue that increased social mobility among Blacks has increased their class consciousness and decreased their race consciousness.

THE RACE PERSPECTIVE

Willie (1989), a chief critic of Wilson's (1978) class perspective, argues that race, not class, is the primary factor underlying the plight of Blacks in America. Willie states that there is a "unified Black experience" within the United States that transcends class. He makes the point that race is the most pervasive factor in the Black experience. Willie cites the large gaps that still exist between Blacks and Whites in employment, education, housing, and other similar socioeconomic characteristics that are not treated equal in the marketplace. In identifying race as an explanation, Willie stresses the role that institutional racism plays in American life. He contends that White elites have structured institutional life so that valued items such as wealth, status, and power flow to the advantaged White group.

Willie's (1989) perspective has been supported by Pettigrew (1980), who argues that race remains as important as ever in determining the life chances of Blacks. According to Pettigrew, the Black poor are far worse off than the White poor and the Black middle class still has a long way to go before it catches up with the White middle class in economic security, status, and wealth. Clark (1978, 1980), also notes that Whites continue to control corporate, educational, and governmental life and hence Blacks always remain vulnerable to White racism. Proponents of the race perspective would probably argue that the persistence of racial discrimination and subordination of Blacks has made Blacks more race conscious than class conscious.

EVOLUTION OF THE CONCEPTS OF RACE CONSCIOUSNESS AND CLASS CONSCIOUSNESS

Our perspective is that race consciousness and class consciousness involve interaction between two components: (1) status, based on race and class; and (2) attitudinal perceptions of race and class. The basic assumption of this perspective is that both race (ascribed status) and class (achieved status) are determinants of social inequality, which in turn lead to attitudinal formations that are conceptualized here as race consciousness and class consciousness. In other words, race consciousness and class consciousness are manifestations of one's racial and class status, as determined by the system of social stratification (Frazier, 1957; Hewitt, 1970; Noel, 1968). Noel (1968) uses the term ethnic stratification to refer to a system wherein some relatively fixed group membership, such as race, religion, or nationality, is used as a major criterion for assigning social positions and their attendant rewards. Achieved status factors, such as education, income, and occupation, may act in concert with ethnic or ascribed factors, such as race, in determining one's position in the stratification system (Noel, 1968). Both Frazier (1957) and Noel (1968) assumed that racial and class inequality may give rise to different types of social and psychological attitudes, such as racial or class identity and class consciousness.

To gain an understanding of the theoretical meaning and usage of the concepts of race consciousness and class consciousness, it is essential to provide some background on the sociological evolution of these concepts. For Karl Marx (1969), class consciousness involved an awareness of common interests and common membership in a distinct community of economic interests that lead to social action on the part of group members. For Marx, social action was viewed as the prerequisite for the transformation of society into a new social order. Marx implied that class consciousness will inevitably arise in response to conflict and oppression that are inherent in the class system (Abrahamson, Mizruchi, & Hornung, 1976). When the proletariat develops consciousness of its distinct interests, it becomes a "class in itself" rather than a class "for itself" (Heller, 1969, p. 9). Marx postulated the relationship between social structure and class consciousness was that social existence determines one's class consciousness.

A critical issue concerning Marx's definition of class consciousness that has been raised by contemporary scholars, who have sought to define the concept, is whether both attitudinal and behavioral (class actions) elements must be included in the definition of class consciousness. Morris and Murphy (1966) address this issue by asserting that it is theoretically useful to view class consciousness with or without class action on the part of individual members. However, others argue that it is essential to the very idea of class consciousness that some sort of commitment to class interest or ideology be present together with participation in a program of action in the name of the class (Glantz, 1958; Leggett, 1968; Manis & Meltzer, 1963). However, Lewis (1965) states that class consciousness involves a common predisposition to class action held by people of a particular class and an awareness of common class interests. Moreover, Landecker (1963) distinguished three types of class consciousness, namely class status consciousness, class structure consciousness, and class interest consciousness. This suggests that class consciousness is a multifaceted concept that can take a number of interrelated attitudinal forms that derive from different dimensions of group structure.

Our view is that it is theoretically useful to study class consciousness as an attitudinal predisposition toward class status, position in the class structure, and class interests, which are predisposed indicators of social action. In other words, we believe there is value in treating attitudes about class consciousness as predisposed social actions, while recognizing that attitudes and behavior may not always coincide. In other words, subjective attitudes toward class do not necessarily coincide with objective class status. Also, it is important to note that class consciousness among Blacks is not static but changes with the dynamic transformations of racial and class status in society. And all of the above factors influence variation in class consciousness among Blacks.

Early attempts to define the concept of race consciousness have been made by a number of scholars (Brown, 1931; Ferguson, 1936; Park, 1913, 1923). These scholars assumed that race consciousness, as a major form of group consciousness, emerges among both domin[ant] and subordin[ant] racial groups. They viewed race consciousness as a tendency toward sentimental and ideological identification with a racial group (Woldemikael, 1989). Accordingly, the individual who is race conscious considers race as an object of loyalty, devotion, and pride, exalting its virtues, taking pride in achievements, and possessing a feeling of solidarity among group members (Brown, 1931; Ferguson, 1936; Hraba, 1979). Awareness of Black subordination and inequality relative to Whites has also been viewed as an element of race consciousness (DuBois, 1953).

A more recent definition of race consciousness emphasizes affective commitment to Blacks in their relations to Whites (Pitts, 1974). Two components have been viewed as essential to the definition of race consciousness, namely (1) accepting the racial identity and groupings of others on the basis of race; and (2) acting to redefine the inequality in status, privilege, and power between the two racial groups (Woldemikael, 1989). In addition to these definitions, recent studies have focused on a wide range of concepts that imply the existence of race consciousness, such as racial group identity, black nationalism, and racial subordination (Broman, Neighbors, & Jackson, 1988; Gurin & Epps, 1975; Woldemikael, 1989).

The common assumption of most of the above conceptualizations of race consciousness is that race consciousness emerges when members of a particular racial group become aware of their position and status vis-à-vis other racial groups and develop a sense of collective identity that may be expressed in different social and psychological forms, such as loyalty, devotion, pride, commitment, and identity. For example, the common thread of historical experience, referred to by Thompson (1974) as the "Black experience," created a strong Black group identity and an awareness of the bond of unity and strength that lies in the group (Erikson, 1966).

THEORETICAL PERSPECTIVE

For the purpose of this study, class consciousness is defined as one's perception of the meaning of social class in terms of awareness of factors that influence social class position. This awareness could be expressed in terms of one's perception of appropriate behavior, lifestyle, social action, and status inequality.

For the purpose of this study, race consciousness is defined as one's awareness of his racial identity and group membership, as reflected by attitudinal expressions of identity, devotion, unity, pride, culture, status, behavior, and iniquities. As such, race consciousness may be expressed in different forms, and is not static, due to social changes, differentiation, transformations, and stratification occurring within the group as well as within the larger society. Thus the type and degree of race consciousness of members of a particular racial group may vary over time.

Two dimensions of race consciousness are included in this study—individual and collective. Individual race consciousness is an orientation that one's racial identity, status, and actions are a function of individual efforts and attitudes about race. Collective race con-

sciousness is defined as an awareness of common racial group identity, and the need for collective group actions to further the collective group interests (Gurin & Epps, 1975; Lopreato & Hazelrigg, 1972).

It should also be noted that racial and class groups overlap, which may sometimes lead to competing and conflicting behavior and attitudes of group members. For example, a Black physician may view himself as a member of the middle class, but due to racial prejudice and discrimination against him, may hold the perception that his racial status takes preceden[ce] over his class status in terms of prestige and attendant rewards. On the other hand, many middle-class Blacks may identify more with other Blacks in their own class rather than with Blacks of the lower class (Rose, 1964). However, many lower-class Blacks may expect middle-class Blacks to identify with their race because of the prevalence of the common foe of racial discrimination and the commonality of the Black experience. Thus this discrepancy may place many Blacks in a race and class dilemma and may influence their level of consciousness about membership in their race and in their class. This suggests that both race and class consciousness evolve from social structured inequality based on membership in different groups—race and class—that can lead to both conflict and consensus.

One of the assumptions of this study is that Black attitudes toward race and class are shaped by their experiences and their status within the race and class hierarchy. As mentioned earlier, attitudes and perceptions toward race and class do not necessarily coincide with the objective reality. For example, it is possible that middle-class Blacks may perceive their race as being relatively more important than their class because they have experienced rejection and discrimination by Whites regardless of their class. For example, a nationwide poll revealed that 61% of all Blacks sampled believed that Whites either do not care whether Blacks get a break or were actively trying to keep Blacks down (Herbers, 1978).

Based on the above theoretical assumptions, in this study we expect race consciousness and class consciousness to differ between lower-class and middle-class Blacks. Also, due to the past Black experience that has been a part of the current and historical experiences of Blacks in America, both lower-class and middle-class Black[s] are expected to have

119

higher race consciousness than class consciousness. The significance of race and class by Blacks will be determined on the basis of perceptions pertaining to subjective attitudes that reflect the meaning attached to race and class.

METHODOLOGY

The location of the study was a southern city with a total population of approximately 200,000 in which Blacks comprised 30% of the total population. A representative sample of 205 subjects was selected by an area-stratified random-block-sampling method. First, the entire study area was divided into blocks based on the stratifying criteria of race and socioeconomic status. Using the U.S. Bureau of the Census *Block Statistics* (1970) publication, which lists the percentage Black population by block, any block with 25% or more Blacks was considered. New additions of blocks with 25% or more Blacks that developed since the 1970 census were determined by knowledgeable informants, mainly real estate agents.

A group frequency distribution of the mean house value for each eligible block was obtained from the U.S. Bureau of the Census *Block Statistics* (1970). From this distribution, house values were divided into four quartiles. Each quartile was representative of the percentage of Blacks in the total population of the city. Each block quartile was fully enumerated on a listing, and the number of dwellings per block was obtained from U.S. *Block Statistics*. Each intersection and midblock was numbered, and a random number was chosen as the starting point. Individuals aged 18 and older were randomly selected in each household and interviewed, using the personal interview technique.

Social class was defined on the basis of education and income. Those individuals with at least some college education and with an income of $16,000 or more were defined as

middle class. Those with no college education and earning less than $16,000 were defined as lower class. Class consciousness was operationalized by a 6-item Likert-type scale derived by a factor-analysis procedure that was used to measure the extent of attitudes, awareness, and commitment to one's class as a group. Both individual race consciousness and collective race consciousness were respectively operationalized by Likert-type scales that were used to measure the extent of attitudes, awareness, and commitment to one's race. Each scale was also constructed with the use of factor analysis. In all of the scales, each item had five response levels: (1) *strongly disagree*, (2) *disagree*, (3) *undecided*, (4) *agree*, and (5) *strongly agree*.

DISCUSSION OF FINDINGS

Table 1 shows the mean scores for each of the three types of class and race consciousness for lower-class and middle-class Blacks. The data clearly show that lower-class Blacks express more class consciousness than middle-class Blacks. The data also show that there is more compatibility of race consciousness than class consciousness between lower- and middle-class Blacks. These results are also supported by the data in Table 2, which show the mean response level for each item for each of the three types of consciousness for lower-class Blacks compared to middle-class Blacks. In other words, our data reveal that there is more consensus among Blacks of the study about the meaning of their race than the meaning of their class. This finding suggests that increased social mobility and social differentiation occurring within the Black population have resulted in differential perceptions of the meaning of social class. This finding also reflects an increasing awareness of class differences between middle-class and lower-class Blacks, whereas at the same time, both groups express a similar degree of race con-

TABLE 1

Class Consciousness and Race Consciousness By Social Class: Mean Scores

	Lower Class			Middle Class		
	M	*SD*	*Range*	*M*	*SD*	*Range*
Class consciousness	10.0	2.4	4.7 to 16.9	7.9	1.7	4.3 to 11.7
Race consciousness individual	4.5	1.9	1.9 to 8.5	3.3	2.2	1.6 to 7.8
Race consciousness collective	13.4	2.5	5.8 to 18.2	12.8	2.5	6.2 to 18.2

TABLE 2

Class Consciousness and Race Consciousness By Social Class: Mean Response Level[a]

	Item	Lower Class	Middle Class
CC1	It is more important to have a career with prestige than a skilled job making lots more money.	2.74	2.08
CC2	Immediate success is more important than long range planning.	2.68	2.30
CC3	If people would just work hard, they would get ahead in life.	3.47	2.20
CC4	Community decisions should be made by those individuals who are financially well off.	1.87	1.50
CC5	The wealth of our country should be divided up equally so that people would have an equal chance to get ahead.	3.61	2.75
CC6	One should choose friends and associates from his own social class.	2.64	2.10
RC1	Schools with mostly Black children should have mostly Black teachers and principals.	3.18	3.25
RC2	Only if Blacks pull together in civil rights groups and activities can anything be done about discrimination.	4.01	4.07
RC3	The only way Blacks will gain their civil rights is by constant protest and pressure.	3.40	2.83
RC4	The attempt to "fit in" and do what's proper has not paid off for Blacks. It does not matter how "proper" you are, you will still meet serious discrimination.	3.97	4.03
RC5	Educated Blacks who have good jobs should try to use their talents and leadership abilities to help other Blacks.	4.56	4.50
RC6	The best way to overcome discrimination is through pressure and social action.	3.30	3.02
RI1	The Black Panther Party and other similar militant organizations have not done a lot for Blacks.	2.81	3.45
RI2	Blacks should not identify with Africa by wearing African-styled clothing, jewelry, and hairstyles.	3.16	3.55
RI3	The best way to overcome discrimination is for each individual Black to be even better trained and more qualified than the most qualified White person.	4.11	3.65
RI4	Many Blacks have only themselves to blame for not doing better in life; if they tried harder, they would do better.	4.56	4.50
RI5	Blacks may not have the same opportunities as Whites, but many Blacks have not prepared themselves enough to make use of the opportunities that come their way.	4.16	3.92

NOTE: CC = Class Consciousness; RC = Race Consciousness: Collective Orientation; RI = Race Consciousness: Individual Orientation.
a. 1 = Low, 5 = High.

sciousness. Thus we can conclude that both lower-class Blacks and middle-class Blacks believe that they are victimized by their race. Consequently, Blacks tend to have a more similar awareness of the meaning of their race than the meaning of their class.

The fact that there are differences and similarities in race consciousness and class consciousness between lower-class and middle-class Blacks does not identify differences in specific attitudinal dispositions toward race and class. To assess the substantive differences in specific attitudes, a content analysis of the responses to the items that comprise race consciousness and class consciousness was conducted. Table 3 shows the responses to the

TABLE 3

**Class Consciousness Among Lower- and Middle-Class Blacks:
Percentage of Agreement and Difference**

Class Consciousness Item	LC	MC	D
The wealth of our country should be divided up equally so that people would have an equal chance to get ahead.	73	36	37
If people would just work hard, they would get ahead in life.	68	35	33
Immediate success is more important than long range planning.	39	12	33
One should choose friends and associates from his own social class.	35	10	25
It is more important to have a career with prestige than a skilled job making lots more money.	35	13	22
Community decisions should be made by those individuals who are financially well off.	11	00	11

NOTE: LC = Lower Class, MC = Middle Class, D = Difference.

class consciousness items for lower-class and middle-class Blacks. The data reveal that much larger proportions of lower-class Blacks, compared to middle-class Blacks, agreed with the class consciousness items. In essence, lower-class Blacks were much more likely to feel that the inequality gap in wealth in America should be reduced or eliminated. Almost three fourths of lower-class Blacks, compared to only 36% of middle-class Blacks, reported that the wealth of our country should be divided up equally so that people would have an equal chance to get ahead. A larger proportion of lower-class Blacks than middle-class Blacks felt that people could get ahead in life if they worked hard.

Although less than half of the lower-class Blacks agreed with the remainder of the four class consciousness items, in all cases these proportions were much higher than those for middle-class Blacks. One observation of particular interest is that 35% of lower-class Blacks and only 10% of middle-class Blacks agreed that "one should choose his friends and associates from his own social class." Surprisingly, this suggests a greater orientation toward interclass integration among middle-class Blacks than lower-class Blacks.

Table 4 shows the responses to items pertaining to individual race consciousness for lower-class and middle-class Blacks. A much larger percentage of middle-class Blacks (67%) than lower-class Blacks (31%) believed that

militant organizations, such as the Black Panther Party, have not done a lot for Blacks. This indicates that middle-class Blacks were more strongly opposed to militant strategies as the best means for the advancement of Blacks. However, both lower-class and middle-class Blacks overwhelmingly disagreed that many Blacks have not prepared themselves enough to take advantage of the opportunities that come their way. Thus regardless of social class, Blacks of the study felt that their status and opportunities were limited because of their race.

There was a high degree of consensus among both groups that the best way to overcome racial discrimination is for each Black person to be better trained and more qualified than the most qualified White person when competing for the same job. Neither lower-class Blacks nor middle-class Blacks tended to blame themselves for not doing better in life or for lack of hard work, although the percentage of middle-class Blacks who expressed this attitude was almost twice as large as that for lower-class Blacks. This finding suggests that Blacks who blame themselves for racial discrimination would be tantamount to blaming the victim. Slightly more than one third of lower-class Blacks compared to one fourth of middle-class Blacks agreed with the statement that Blacks should not attempt to express their identity by wearing African attire. This suggests that middle-class Blacks tend to approve of such "Afrocentric" expressions of

TABLE 4

Individual Race Consciousness Among Lower- and Middle-Class Blacks: Percentage of Agreement and Difference

Individual Race Consciousness Item	LC	MC	D
The Black Panther Party and other similar militant organizations have not done a lot for Blacks.	31	67	36
Blacks may not have the same opportunities as Whites, but many Blacks have not prepared themselves enough to make use of the opportunities that come their way.	06	15	09
The best way to overcome discrimination is for each individual Black to be even better trained and more qualified than the most qualified White person.	76	68	08
Many Blacks have only themselves to blame for not doing better in life; if they tried harder, they would do better.	12	23	11
Blacks should not identify with Africa by wearing African-styled clothing, jewelry and hairstyles.	37	25	12

NOTE: LC = Lower Class, MC = Middle Class, D = Difference.

culture slightly more than Blacks from the lower class.

Table 5 shows the responses to the items pertaining to collective race consciousness. The data reveal several patterns of race consciousness that are highly prevalent among both lower-class and middle-class Blacks, namely: (1) the need for unity among Blacks, (2) the consensus that race/color is a basis for discrimination, and (3) the expectation that Blacks with educational and economic means and resources should help elevate less fortunate Blacks (items 4, 5, and 6). These responses suggest that both lower-class and middle-class Blacks feel that Blacks must pool their resources, unite, and take action on behalf of their own interests to combat racial discrimination if they are to make substantial progress. These responses reveal that regardless of social class, Blacks feel that race is still a dominant factor that influences life chances and opportunities. These responses also reveal that racial discrimination is expected by most Blacks, over which they have little control.

Strong but somewhat less prevalent among both lower-class and middle-class Blacks was the attitude that Blacks must engage in constructive actions to overcome racial discrimination and gain full socioeconomic equality. However, lower-class Blacks tended to be more oriented toward protests and social pressure than did middle-class Blacks. As shown in Table 5, at least 60% of lower-class Blacks agreed with items 1 and 2 that "the only way to gain civil rights and overcome discrimination is through constant protest, pressure, or social action," compared to less than half of the middle-class Blacks. However, middle-class Blacks, being in a better position to take advantage of available opportunities, were more likely to agree that "schools with mostly Black children should have Black teachers and principals." This is not only an expression of racial unity but also an awareness of the importance of power and control over their own social institutions.

SUMMARY

It was found in this study that both race and class are perceived as important factors influencing social stratification—that is, who gets what, how much, and why. As an alternative to exploring this question with the use of socioeconomic status or structural variables, our study focuses on attitudinal perceptions of Blacks about the meaning of their race and class. In this way, our study captures the perceptions of the reality of race and class of both lower-class and middle-class Blacks based on their beliefs, observations, experiences, and socialization.

Increasing social status differentiation and socioeconomic opportunities have apparently

TABLE 5

Collective Race Consciousness Among Lower-Class and Middle-Class Blacks: Percentage of Agreement and Difference

Collective Race Consciousness Item	LC	MC	D
The only way Blacks will gain their civil rights is by constant protest and pressure.	65	43	21
The best way to overcome discrimination is through pressure and social action.	60	43	17
Schools with mostly Black children should have mostly Black teachers and principals.	47	52	05
Only if Blacks pull together in civil rights groups and activities can anything be done about discrimination.	85	80	05
The attempt to "fit in" and do what's proper has not paid off for Blacks. It does not matter how "proper" you are, you will still meet serious discrimination.	87	83	04
Educated Blacks who have good jobs should try to use their talents and leadership abilities to help other Blacks.	98	100	02

NOTE: LC = Lower Class, MC = Middle Class, D = Difference.

led to differential perceptions about social class among Blacks. Our study reveals that lower-class Blacks have much more class consciousness than middle-class Blacks. Specifically, lower-class Blacks express much more consciousness about the inequality gap between them and the middle class, especially in terms of the distribution of wealth, power, and prestige.

Our study reveals that both lower-class and middle-class Blacks are more race conscious than class conscious, but middle-class Blacks are slightly more race conscious than class conscious. The implication here is that regardless of social class, most Blacks feel that race is still a very significant factor in determining their life chances and opportunities. Black middle-class individuals, in spite of their socioeconomic achievements, are often confronted with racial discrimination, racial barriers, and blocked opportunities due to their race. Our study found that lower-class Blacks tend to place greater emphasis on protests, social pressures, and social actions to eliminate racial discrimination. However, three attitudinal patterns were found among both lower-class and middle-class Blacks: (1) the belief that racial discrimination imposes real and serious obstacles to socioeconomic progress for Blacks, (2) the need for Blacks to unite to combat racial discrimination, and (3)

the expectation that Blacks with the most education and economic means should help elevate less fortunate Blacks.

On the basis of the findings of our study, we can conclude that, indeed, race is still seen by Blacks as a very important factor that can inhibit their progress. Yet the interaction between race and class, accompanied by increasing social diversity and differentiation within the Black population and in the larger society, makes the assessment of the influences of race and class a much more complex matter than heretofore. However, race is likely to continue to be a real issue in the future, whereas increasing status differentiation will likely lead to greater differences in perceptions about class.

REFERENCES

Abrahamson, M., Mizruchi, E., & Hornung, C. (1976). *Stratification and mobility*. New York: Macmillan.

Allen, R. L. (1970). *Black awakening in capitalist America*. New York: Anchor Doubleday.

Broman, C. L., Neighbors, H. W., & Jackson, J. S. (1988). Racial group identification among Black adults. *Social Forces, 67*, 146–158.

Brown, W. (1931). The nature of race consciousness. *Social Forces, 10*, 90–97.

Clark, K. B. (1978, October 5). The role of race. *New York Times Magazine*, p. 24.

Clark, K. B. (1980, March 22). Race, not class is still at the wheel. *New York Times*, p. 22.

Cox, O. (1948). *Caste, class and race*. New York: Doubleday.

Davis, A., Gardner, B., & Gardner, M. (1941). *Deep south: A social anthropological study of caste and class*. Chicago: University of Chicago Press.

Drake, S. C., & Cayton, H. R. (1945). *Black metropolis: A study of negro life in a northern city* (Vol. 2). New York: Harcourt, Brace & World.

DuBois, W.E.B. (1899). *The Philadelphia negro*. New York: Schocken.

DuBois, W.E.B. (1953). *The souls of Black folk*. New York: Fawcett. (Originally published in 1903).

Erikson, E. (1966). The concept of identity in race relations: Notes and queries. In T. Parsons & K. Clark (Eds.), *The negro American* (pp. 227–253). Boston: Beacon.

Ferguson, E. (1936). Race consciousness among American negroes. *Journal of Negro Education, 7*, 32–40.

Frazier, E. F. (1957). *Black bourgeoisie*. New York: Macmillan.

Glantz, O. (1958). Class consciousness and political solidarity. *American Sociological Review, 23*, 375–382.

Gurin, P., & Epps, E. (1975). *Black consciousness, identity and achievement*. New York: John Wiley.

Handy, K. (1984). Race and class consciousness among southern Blacks. *Sociological Spectrum, 4*, 383–403.

Heller, C. (1969). *Structured social inequality: A reader in comparative social stratification*. New York: Macmillan.

Herbers, J. (1978, February 26). Decade after Kerner report: Division of races persists. *New York Times*, p. A1.

Hewitt, J. (1970). *Social stratification and deviant behavior*. New York: Random House.

Hraba, J. (1979). *American ethnicity*. Itasca, IL: Peacock.

Johnson, C. (1943). *Patterns of negro segregation*. New York: Harper.

Landecker, W. (1963). Class crystallization and class consciousness. *American Sociological Review, 28*, 219–229.

Leggett, J. (1968). *Class, race and labor: Working class consciousness in Detroit*. New York: Oxford University Press.

Lewis, L. (1965). Class consciousness and inter-class sentiments. *The Sociological Quarterly, 6*, 325–338.

Lopreato, J., & Hazelrigg, L. (1972). *Class conflict and mobility: Theories and studies of class structure*. San Francisco: Chandler.

Manis, J., & Meltzer, B. (1963). Some correlates of class consciousness among textile workers. *American Sociological Review, 69*, 177–184.

Marx, K. (1969). *The communist manifesto*. Chicago: Regnery.

Morris, R., & Murphy, R. (1966). A paradigm for the study of class consciousness. *Sociology and Social Research, 50*, 314–324.

Myrdal, G. (1964). *An American dilemma*. New York: McGraw-Hill.

Noel, D. (1968). A theory of the origin of ethnic stratification. In N. Yetman & H. Steele (Eds.), *Majority and minority* (pp. 32–44). Boston: Allyn & Bacon.

Park, R. E. (1913). Racial assimilation in secondary groups with particular reference to the negro. *American Sociological Society, 8*, 66–83.

Park, R. E. (1923). Negro race consciousness as reflected in race literature. *American Sociological Review, 1*, 505–516.

Pettigrew, T. (1980). The changing—not declining—significance of race. *Contemporary Sociology, 9*, 19–21.

Pitts, J. (1974). The study of race consciousness: Comments on new directions. *American Journal of Sociology, 80*, 665–687.

Rose, P. I. (1964). *They and we: Racial and ethnic relations in the United States*. New York: Random House.

Thompson, D. (1974). *Sociology of the Black experience*. Westport, CT: Greenwood.

U.S. Bureau of the Census. (1970). *Block statistics*. Washington, DC: Author.

U.S. Riot Commission. (1968). *Report of the National Advisory Commission on Civil Disorders*. New York: Bantam.

West, C. (1993). *Race matters*. Boston: Beacon Press.

Willie, C. (1989). *Caste and class controversy on race and poverty*. Dix Hills, NY: General Hall.

Wilson, W. J. (1978). *The declining significance of race*. Chicago: University of Chicago Press.

Woldemikael, T. (1989). A case study of race consciousness among Haitian immigrants. *Journal of Black Studies, 20*, 224–239.

Thomas J. Durant, Jr. is a full professor of sociology at Louisiana State University—Baton Rouge. He received his Ph.D. degree in sociology from the University of Wisconsin—Madison. His research interests include ethnic minorities, social stratification, and global development.

Kathleen H. Sparrow is director of minority affairs and professor of sociology at the University of Southwestern Louisiana. She received her Ph.D. in sociology from Louisiana State University—Baton Rouge. Her interests are ethnic minorities, race relations, and social stratification.

Decentering Whiteness

In Search of a Revolutionary Multiculturalism

By Peter McLaren

I wish to make two claims in this article. One is that multicultural education has largely refused to acknowledge how imperialism, colonialism, and the transnational circulation of capitalism influences the ways in which many oppressed minority groups cognitively map their paradigm of democracy in the United States. The other claim is that the present focus on diversity in multicultural education is often misguided because the struggle for ethnic diversity makes progressive political sense only if it can be accompanied by a sustained analysis of the cultural logics of white supremacy. While these two claims mutually inform each other, it is the latter claim that will occupy most of the space in this article.

Shifts in the Global Economy

Sustaining a meager existence is becoming frighteningly more difficult with the passage of time for millions of Third World peoples as well as First World urban dwellers, including millions of inhabitants of the United States.

Labor markets are growing more segmented as full-time workers are replaced with part-time workers who are unable to secure even meager health or dental benefits. The days of high-wage, high-benefit mass production manufacturing are receding into the horizon. Yet manufacturing has

Peter McLaren is a professor of education with the Graduate School of Education and Information Studies, University of California, Los Angeles.

not completely disappeared from the United States. Of Los Angeles County's labor force now, 36 percent is in manufacturing (the nation's largest manufacturing base). The exploitation of these workers continues to increase. The information revolution that has accompanied the global shift to post-Fordism and flexible accumulation has increased social inequality rather than diminished it.

The greed and avarice of the United States ruling class is seemingly unparalleled in history. Yet its goals remain decidedly the same. Michael Parenti writes:

> Throughout history there has been only one thing that ruling interests have ever wanted—and that is everything: all the choice lands, forest, game, herds, harvests, mineral deposits, and precious metals of the earth; all the wealth, riches, and profitable returns; all the productive facilities, gainful inventiveness and technologies; all the control positions of the state and other major institutions; all public supports and subsidies, privileges and immunities; all the protections of the law with none of its constraints; all the services, comforts, luxuries, and advantages of civil society with none of the taxes and costs. Every ruling class has wanted only this: all the rewards and none of the burdens. The operational code is: we have a lot; we can get more; we want it all. (1996, p. 46)

The application of market principles to higher education, the vulgar mercantilism that undergirds public educational

reform, the bureaucratic centralism, new class managerialism, hyperprofessionalism, evisceration of public protection programs, shamefully absent enforcement of environmental standards, rising health insurance premiums, and drastic declines in salaries for working people have catapulted the United States onto a tragic course towards social decay and human misery— a course that is far from inevitable.

The kindling of fascism lies in the furnace of United States democracy, waiting for a spark to ignite a firestorm of state repression. Previous firestorms have occurred in the Watts rebellion of August, 1965, the civil rights movement, and the anti-war movement of the 1960s, but also in more current forms such as the Los Angeles uprising of April 29, 1992, and the East L. A. high school walk-outs of 1994 over Proposition 187. We don't get many firestorms because, as Parenti (1996) has so presciently noted, fascism is already here on low-flame, camouflaged by codes of commerce and corporate correctness, a fascism that burns steadily with an occasional stoking from reactionary governors such as Pete Wilson and other sunbelt political leviathans.

As long as global economic advancement and the integration of U.S. workers into the international economy is synonymous with educational success, and as long as development discourse increasingly drives school reform efforts, then an emphasis on diversity makes little sense when it comes to developing a view of multiculturalism linked to the struggle for social justice.

No task is more urgent for multicultural education today than to re-understand its

From *Multicultural Education,* Fall 1997, pp. 12-15. © 1997 by Caddo Gap Press, Inc. Reprinted by permission of *Multicultural Education,* the magazine of the National Association for Multicultural Education.

project as that of accounting for the exploitation of people of color in materialist, historical, and global terms. Multicultural education, for the most part, is little more than the interminable deferral of this urgent historical and class accounting. Capitalism not only structures opportunities for dislocated and disenfranchised groups, it also structures the way such groups **think about** their choices, values, and opportunities within a global market economy.

With shifts in the global economy placing increased pressure not only on economically disenfranchised groups but also upon increasing numbers of the white middle class, we are witnessing increasing assaults on affirmative action, political correctness, and practices and policies established to lessen discrimination and increase the opportunities of historically disenfranchised groups.

While on the one hand this current historical juncture is witnessing an unprecedented growth of immigrant populations within the United States and elsewhere, on the other hand white supremacist organizations living on the fringes of social life are also expanding exponentially. Establishment conservatives and liberals stridently assert nativistic and populist sentiments that barely distinguish them ideologically from their counterparts in racialist far right groups and citizen militias. The Ku Klux Klan, Posse Comitatus, The Order, White Aryan Resistance, Christian Identity, National Alliance, Aryan Nations, American Front, Gun Owners of America, United Citizens of Justice, and militia groups have organizations in most, if not all, of the fifty states.

Latinophobia, Affirmative Action, and White Supremacy

Young white males and females who may find these racist groups unappealing can still find solace in politicians such as Wilson and Bob Dole, whose anti-immigrant and Latinophobic policies and practices deflect their racializing sentiments through flag waving, jingoism, and triumphalist acts of self-aggrandizement—such as the disguising of Proposition 209 as a civil rights initiative—designed to appeal to frightened white voters who feel that growing numbers of Spanish-speaking immigrants will soon outnumber them. Politicians have become white warriors in blue suits and red ties dedicated to taking back the country from the infidel.

On the day of General Colin L. Powell's address to the 1996 Republican Convention in San Diego, former Education Secretary and current director of Empower America, William J. Bennett, published a commentary in the *Los Angeles Times* entitled "Civil Rights is the GOP's mission" (Monday, August 12, 1996, B5). Evoking the figure of Dr. Martin Luther King Jr. (in a manner similar to his neoconservative counterpart, Dinesh D'Souza), Bennett called for the end of racial discrimination through the abolition of affirmative action. He putatively wants African Americans, Latino/as, and other ethnic minority groups to be judged by the "content of their character." He cites African Americans such as Ward Connerly, chairman of the Civil Rights Initiative, and Powell as continuing "the great civil rights tradition of Dr. King."

However, Bennett's vision is shortsighted, maleficent, and effectively domesticates King's place in the Civil Rights struggle. His logic is as flawed as that of the conservative school board that abolishes school breakfast programs for hungry children because such programs are "anti-family." Supposedly, it is better to go hungry with your family than to be fed at school.

First, Bennett appears to work under an assumption that U.S. society has reached a point of relative economic justice and affirmative action is no longer necessary. Yet it is clear that while there has been increased representation by African Americans in some trade and blue-collar jobs, African Americans have not made significant advances in certain fields (Feinberg, 1996). Walter Feinberg elaborates:

> Take, for example, a number of important professional fields: Whereas blacks represent over 12 percent of the population in the United States, they comprise only 4.2 percent of the doctors, 3.3. percent of the lawyers, 5 percent of the university teachers, 3.7 percent of the engineers. The percentage of black lawyers and judges has risen from 1983 to 1993 by but one-tenth of 1 percent and the number of black college teachers rose by just four-tenths of 1 percent during the same period. Moreover, salary equity continues to be an elusive goal. The average salary of white women is 70.8 percent of the salary of white men; for black women the figure is 63.7 percent and for Hispanic women it is 53.9 percent. And the salaries of black and Hispanic men relative to those of white men actually dropped between 1975 and 1993. Moreover, while a smaller percentage of white men are in the active labor force now than in 1970, there has been a larger percentage drop for black males. However, the percentage for both black and white women has increased. (1996, pp. 366-367)

Second, Bennett appears either to be unable or unwilling to fathom the nearly intractable reality of white privilege and uncontested hegemony in the arena of the economy. For instance, Feinberg notes that were affirmative action to be reorganized according to need-based policies without attending to the present racial distribution of position, this would have severe consequences for African Americans and "would clearly be to redirect some of the resources presently being spent on African Americans" to white males.

Third, Bennett fails to realize that racist white people are going to be suspicious of African Americans and Latinos whether they are assisted by affirmative action initiatives or not. And fourth, his vision is propelled by a nostalgic view of the United States as a middle-class suburban neighborhood in which people of color don't have so much "attitude" and where whites are the uncontested caretakers of this prelapsarian nation of consensus and harmony. To be colorblind in Bennett's restricted use of the term is to be naive at best and ignorant at worst. Because not to see color in Bennett's view really amounts in ideological terms to be blind to the disproportionate advantage enjoyed by white people in nearly all sectors of society. Bennett has turned the logic of Martin Luther King upside down. He has replaced social analysis with homilies about "character."

Politicians of Bennett's ilk want to increase the role of charitable institutions in this country. If economically disenfranchised people of color are to be helped, then it should be done by private individuals or organizations and not the government—or so these conservatives maintain. But wealthy private organizations have benefited from the hegemony of white privilege in the government and the marketplace for centuries. Nevertheless, transferring the challenge of economic justice from the government into the hands of philanthropists who feel "pity" for the poor is not the solution. Bennett misses the crucial point: that not to have affirmative action for people of color in the present social structure amounts to a hidden affirmative action for white people.

Bennett's position tacitly seeks the incorporation of racialized groups into the corporate ethics of consumption where white privilege increasingly holds sway. His ethics of racial tolerance can therefore work as a means of social control of populations of color. There is a false assumption at work in Bennett's logic that views culture as essentially self-equilibrating, as providing similar sets of shared experiences to all social groups. The culture of diversity heralded by Bennett is a decidedly homogenized one, cut off from the contingencies of state power and economic practices. Bennett betrays a stubborn unwillingness to recognize the asymmetrical allocation of resources and power that overwhelmingly favor white people as much now as during King's era.

A Special Kind of Disadvantage

Bennett fails to understand how, in the case of African Americans especially, race presents a very special kind of disadvantage in the United States. Whereas some politicians of Bennett's ilk have argued that affirmative action stigmatizes all those women and minorities who would have been successful even without affirmative action, this position "actually begs the question and assumes what it sets out to prove" according to Feinberg. Feinberg also notes that this is an effective position "only if it assumed that most remnants of discrimination have been eliminated and that few, if any, **truly deserving** candidates are now admitted under affirmative action standards" (p. 375).

For those who, like Bennett, would argue that affirmative action balkanizes the United States by providing certain groups with rights over others, Feinberg argues that affirmative action is not a group right but rather a **group-based** right. The distinction is worth noting. A group-based right "results when some people are wrongly denied the treatment that should be afforded to individual, rights-bearing citizens because of characteristics that they all share" (p. 377). Affirmative action does not try to advance the coherence or the status of one group over another.

The moral force behind affirmative action is that African Americans are less well served by professional talent than other Americans due to profound historical reasons. A debt is owed to African Americans as a result of unprecedented violation of human rights and liberties during slavery. To accept such a debt is not to accept a group right. Such a debt "results from a forced, involuntary act that brings about serious and long-standing intergenerational disadvantages." Immigrants to the United States, despite how cruelly they were or in some cases continue to be treated, "were not forced by anyone in this country to come **here**" (Feinberg, p. 384).

While we do not owe a debt to present individuals as compensation because of the injury done to their ancestors by slavery, we still owe a debt to the slave which cannot be canceled because slavery has ended. Compensating the descendants of slaves in general is, Feinberg argues, the best we can do under present circumstances to compensate any particular slave. Slaves were not recognized as human beings, and this lack of recognition and public denial of intentionality and of their right to have rights has cultural and intergenerational significance. Present-day descendants of slaves deserve compensation "because the institution of slavery violated essential elements of collective and individual development and that this institution and those that followed it must be seen as accountable for many of the problems confronting the African-American community today" (p. 393).

Rather than stressing the importance of diversity and inclusion, as do many multiculturalists, more emphasis should be placed on the social and political construction of white supremacy and the dispensation of white hegemony. The reality-distortion field know as "Whiteness" needs to be identified as a cultural disposition and ideology linked to specific political, social, and historical arrangements. This is a theme to which I shall shortly return.

A related theme that I wish to emphasize is the need to affirm with caution, yet move beyond the politics of diversity and inclusion when developing programs and policies related to multicultural education. What is often not recognized is the fact that positions on diversity and inclusion are often predicated on hidden assumptions of assimilation and consensus that serve as supports for liberal democratic models of identity. Further, identity politics are often predicated on modernist conceptions of negatively defined difference.

In the pluralizing move to become a society of diverse voices, liberal democracy has often succumbed to a recolonization of multiculturalism by failing to challenge ideological assumptions surrounding difference that are installed in its current anti-affirmative action and anti-welfare "reform" initiatives. In this sense people of color are still placed under the threshold of candidacy for inclusion into the universal right to self-determination, and interpolated as exiles from United States citizenship. After all, as a shrinking minority, whites are running scared, conscious of their own vulnerability, and erecting fortresses of social regulation while they still have the power to do so.

Today, immigrants from Latin America—primarily Mexican—have become the new scapegoats for the strain that the global economy has put on white constituencies. When immigrants speak out against injustice and racism in the United States, this greatly disturbs many white peop[le] who accuse the new immigrants for n[ot] being "grateful" enough to their new ho[me] country for giving them a better standard [of] living. Yet the imperatives of global cap[i]talism have challenged many of the co[re] values of immigrant communities. Berto[n] (1992) speaks to the process of social disorga[ni]zation that the discourse of developmen[t] creates among what Western research[ers] call "underdeveloped people" when he write[s]:

economic development of an underdeveloped people by themselves [premodern Europeans included] is not compatible with the maintenance of their traditional customs and mores. A break with the latter is prerequisite to economic progress. What is needed is a revolution in the totality of social, cultural, and religious institutions and habits, and thus in their psychological attitude, their philosophy and way of life. What is, therefore, required amounts in reality to social dis-organization. (pp. 72-73)

No task is more urgent for multicultura[l] education today than to re-understand it[s] project as that of accounting for the exploi[?] tation and oppression of people of color i[n] historical and materialist terms. The his[?] torical present demands a return to th[e] issues of people's fundamental material need[s] as distinct from what they have been told b[y] custodians of consumer culture that the[y] should want. This will not be easy in an era[?] in which the promotion of commerce is now[?] a cultural event, while simultaneously culture is used to valorize capitalist social relations, the international division of labor, and[?] the individualization of cultural practices.

In the last analysis, what conservative and liberal multiculturalists espouse is a cultural politics of diversity. True, within a cultural politics of diversity the individual is seen as socially constructed rather than metaphysical or autonomous. But the construction of the individual is accounted for ultimately in terms of how it is constructed within an economy of signs or a regime of representation (read "a discourse community"). Representation, however, deals mainly with the level of culture as it is implicated in the production of desire or in economies of pleasure that are discursively fashioned by the media, the culture industries, etc.

This approach to multicultural education, while important, ignores the concept of individual **need** which is linked to the material mode of production of individuals within capitalism. The difference between desire and need cannot be emphasized nough. Multicultural education needs a stronger conceptual analysis of the social totality and how individuals are constructed within it. This means understanding how individuals are positioned within economic determinations and social relations of production. Social conditions determine production and consumption, and thus social needs are not a **natural** development of productive forces. What must be analyzed is the role of social relations and class struggle in the formation of needs. Needs, or social demand, cannot pre-exist or be placed outside of social relations. Needs cannot be linked solely to the requirements of value realization, but must be understood as linked to conditions of production and reproduction.

Models of Global Culture

Jan Nederveen Pieterse (1996) has offered three models of understanding global culture. Pieterse defines what he calls *cultural differentiation*, which views culture as lasting and immutable, *cultural convergence* or growing sameness, which views culture as erasable and being erased, and *cultural hybridization* or ongoing mixing which views culture as mixing and in the process of generating new, translocal forms of difference. Each of these positions represents a particular politics of difference and speaks to a distinct form of subjectivity.

Conservatives often adopt a cultural differentiation model in which the West is viewed as a universal civilization. From this perspective, culture is politicized and bound in civilizational packages linked to geopolitical entities. Culture becomes an ideological battleground or clash of civilizations. Culture becomes a set of characteristics which distinguish "us" from "them." The world, in other words, is divided into civilizational spheres. Ignored in this model is the way in which the United States has historically controlled important geopolitical security games. Intergroup or transnational cultures cannot, within this model, exist. This model can only work within the binary opposition of sameness-difference. Intergroup diversity would therefore be outside the domain of culture. Fields of cultural tension which flow from this model include the east-west polarity of communism-capitalism and the north-south polarity of imperialism and the colonising and colonized world. This is the model of global culture that reflects the ideas of Bennett and other conservative educationists.

For some multiculturalists, culture is often conceived along the "McDonaldzation" model of cultural standarization and worldwide homogenization brought about through multinational corporations. According to this model, the world is going through a process of modernization and universal progress. It is important in this model for individuals to adapt to local cultures and markets in order to succeed—something known as "insiderization" or "glocalization." This is a model of global culture that many conservative educationists feel will benefit underdeveloped nations as they become more Americanized (*i.e.*, civilized).

Pieterse refers to the third model of culture as hybridization. Hybridization offers an antidote to essentialist forms of cultural identity that occur in the cultural differentialism of racial and nationalist doctrines. It achieves this since it takes as its central premise the primacy and legitimacy of subjugated voices and knowledges of marginalized peoples. In this way it is able to contest those who would valorize ethnic or racial "purity." It foregrounds the fundamental processes of syncretization, creolization, metissage, mestizaje, and border-crossing.

Culture hybridization is a paradigm of culture that is generally supported by progressive left-liberal multiculturalists. While preferable to the other two models that suggest either a lasting conflict and rivalry leading to a policy of closure and cultural apartheid among cultures, or a triumphalist Americanism leading to assimilation, hybridization contains some serious limitations. Hybridization does offer a model of assimilation without the need to sacrifice identity and the development of cross-cultural patterns of difference.

Yet too often progressive multiculturalists will argue for the construction of a border identity or border-crossing without paying sufficient attention to the asymmetry of power relations that occur in the process of cultural mixing. For some, border-crossing is easier than others, especially when the reality of institutionalized racism is taken into account. Some groups, such as whites, have more options in the mix than others. Border-crossing is evaluated differently depending upon the cultural context in which it occurs. As my Chicano/a students are quick to remind me: "We didn't cross the border, the border crossed us."

Democratic Citizenry: A White Thing

In addition to emphasizing the relationship among global economic restructuring, growing anti-immigrant sentiment, and current efforts to abolish affirmative action, multicultural education should place an increasing emphasis on understanding the social construction of whiteness. Such an effort will help put a different and important focus on the problems surrounding identity formation at this particular juncture in our particular and global history.

When North Americans talk about race, they inevitably refer to African Americans, Asians, Latino/as, Native Americans, to the consistent exclusion of Euro-Americans. I want to challenge the prevailing assumption that in order to defeat racism we need to put our initiatives behind the inclusions of minoritarian populations—in other words, of non-whites. I want to argue instead that in addition to calling for diversity and inclusion we need to put our emphasis on the analysis of white ethnicity, and the necessary destabilization of white identity, specifically white supremacist ideology and practice.

I would ask you to consider Pat Buchanan's remarks in light of United States history. First, I offer some comments made by Abraham Lincoln during a speech made in southern Illinois in 1858:

> I am not, nor ever have been, in favor of bringing about in any way the social or political equality of the white and black races.... I will say in addition that there is a physical difference between the white and black races which, I suppose, will forever forbid the two races living together upon terms of social and political equality; and in as much as they cannot so live, that while they do remain together there must be a position of the superiors and the inferiors; and that I, as much as any other man, am in favor of the superior being assigned to the white man." (Zinn, 1970, p. 148)

Another United States hero, Benjamin Franklin, wrote:

> Why increase the Sons of **Africa**, by planting them in **America**, where we have so fair an Opportunity, by excluding all Blacks and Tawneys, of increasing the lovely White and Red?" (Cited in Perea, 1995, p. 973)

The educational left has failed to address the issue of whiteness and the insecurities that young whites harbor regarding their future during times of diminishing economic expectations. With their "racially coded and divisive rhetoric," neoconservatives may be able to enjoy tremendous success in helping insecure young white populations develop white identity along racist lines.

Cornel West has identified three white supremacist logics: the Judeo-Christian racist logic, the scientific racist logic, and the psycho-sexual racist logic. The Judeo-Christian racist logic is reflected in the Biblical story of Ham, Son of Noah, who, in failing to cover Noah's nakedness had his progeny blackened by God. In this logic, unruly behavior and chaotic rebellion are linked to racist practices. The scientific racist logic is identified with the evaluation of physical bodies in light of Greco-Roman standards. Within this logic, racist practices are identified with physical ugliness, cultural deficiency, and intellectual inferiority. The psycho-sexual racist logic identifies black people with Western sexual discourses associated with sexual prowess, lust, dirt, and subordination.

A serious question is raised by West's typology in relation to the construction of whiteness: What are the historically concrete and sociologically specific ways that white supremacist discourses are guided by Western philosophies of identity and universality and capitalist relations of production and consumption? West has located racist practices in the commentaries by the Church Fathers on the Song of Solomon and the Ywain narratives in medieval Brittany, to name just a few historical sources. West has also observed that human bodies were classified according to skin color as early as 1684 (before the rise of modern capitalism) by a French physician, Francois Bernier. The famous 18th century naturalist, Carolus Linnaeus, produced the first major written account of racial division in *Natural System* (1735). White supremacy is linked to the way culture is problematized and defined. As we have seen, theories of culture are themselves by-products of—and symptoms of—the theorists's relation to an ongoing global struggle over issues of social class.

When I refer to whiteness or to the cultural logics of whiteness, I need to qualify what I mean. Here I adopt Ruth Frankenberg's injunction that cultural practices considered to be white need to be seen as contingent, historically produced, and transformable. White culture is not monolithic and its borders must be understood as malleable and porous. According to Alastair Bonnett (1996), whiteness is neither a discrete entity nor a fixed, asocial category. Rather, it is an "immutable social construction" (1996, p. 98). White identity is an ensemble of discourses, contrapuntal and contradictory. Whiteness—and the meanings attributed to it—is always in a state of flux and fibrillation. Bonnett notes that "even if one ignores the transgressive youth or ethnic borderlands of Western identities, and focuses on the "center" or "heartlands" of "whiteness," one will discover racialized subjectivities, that, far from being settled and confidant, exhibit a constantly reformulated panic over the meaning of 'whiteness' and the defining presence of 'non-whiteness' within it" (1996, p. 106). According to Frankenberg, white culture is a material and discursive space that:

> is inflected by nationhood, such that whiteness and Americanness, though by no means coterminous, are profoundly shaped by one another... ...Similarly, whiteness, masculinity, and femininity are coproducers of one another, in ways that are, in their turn, crosscut by class and by the histories of racism and colonialism (1993, p. 233).

Whiteness needs to be seen as **cultural**, as **processual**, and not ontologically different from processes that are non-white. It works, as Frankenberg notes, as "an unmarked marker of others' differentness—whiteness not so much void or formlessness as norm" (p. 198). Whiteness functions through social practices of assimilation and cultural homogenization; whiteness is linked to the expansion of capitalism in the sense that "whiteness signifies the production and consumption of commodities under capitalism" (p. 203).

Whiteness is a sociohistorical form of consciousness, given birth at the nexus of capitalism, colonial rule, and the emergent relationships among dominant and subordinate groups. Whiteness constitutes and demarcates ideas, feelings, knowledge, social practices, cultural formations, and systems of intelligibility that are identified with or attributed to white people and that are invested in by white people as "white." Whiteness is also a refusal to acknowledge how white people are implicated in certain social relations of privilege and relations of domination and subordination.

Whiteness, then, can be considered as a form of social amnesia associated with certain modes of subjectivity within particular social sites considered to be normative. As a lived domain of meaning, whiteness represents particular social and historical formations that are reproduced through specific discursive and material processes and circuits of desire and power. Whiteness can be considered to be a conflictual sociocultural, sociopolitical, and geopolitical process that animates commonsensical practical action in relationship to dominant social practices and normative ideological productions. As an ideological formation transformed into a principle of life, into an ensemble of social relations and practices, whiteness needs to be understood as conjunctural, as a composite term that shifts in denotative and connotative emphasis depending upon how its elements are combined and upon the contexts in which it operates.

Whiteness in the United States can be understood largely through the social consequences it provides for those who are considered to be non-white. Such consequences can be seen in the criminal justice system, in prisons, in schools, and in the board rooms of corporations such as Texaco. It can be defined in relation to immigration practices and social policies and practices of sexism, racism, and nationalism. It can be seen historically in widespread acts of imperialism and genocide and linked to an erotic economy of "excess." Eric Lott writes that white people organize their own enjoyment through the other (1993). For instance, Zizek (1992, p. 196) writes that we always impute to the "other" an excessive enjoyment. The "other" is "either a workaholic stealing our jobs or an idler living on our labor; and it is quite amusing to note the ease with which one passes from reproaching the other with a refusal to work, to reproaching him for the theft of work."

Whiteness is a type of articulatory practice that can be located in the convergence of colonialism, capitalism, and subject formation. It both fixes and sustains discursive regimes that represent self and "other"; that is, whiteness represents a regime of differences that produces and racializes an abject other. In other words, whiteness is a discursive regime that enables real effects to take place. Whiteness displaces blackness and brownness—specific forms of non-whiteness—into signifiers of deviance and criminality within social, cultural, cognitive, and political contexts. White subjects discursively construct identity through producing, naming, "bounding," and marginalizing a range of others (Frankenberg, 1993, p. 193).

Whiteness constitutes unmarked patriarchal, heterosexist, Euro-American practices that have negative effects on and consequences for those who do not participate in them. Inflected by nationhood, whiteness can be considered an ensemble of discursive practices constantly in the process of being constructed, negotiated, and changed. Yet it functions to instantiate a structured exclusion of certain groups from social arenas of normativity (Giroux, 1997).

Whiteness is not only mythopoetical in the sense that it constructs a totality of illusions formed around the ontological superiority of the Euro-American subject, it is also metastructural in that it connects whiteness across specific differences; it solders fugitive, breakaway discourses and re-hegemonizes them. Consumer utopias and global capital flows rearticulate whiteness by means of relational differences.

Whiteness is dialectically reinitiated across epistemological fissures, contradictions, and oppositions through new regimes of desire that connects the consumption of goods to the everyday logic of Western democracy. The cultural encoding of the typography of whiteness is achieved by remapping Western European identity onto economic transactions, by recementing desire to capitalist flows, by concretizing personal history into collective memory linked to place, to a myth of origin. Whiteness offers a safe "home" for those imperiled by the flux of change.

Whiteness can be considered as a conscription of the process of positive self-identification into the service of domination through inscribing identity into an onto-epistemological framework of "us" against "them." For those who are non-white, the seduction of whiteness can produce a self-definition that disconnects the subject from his or her history of oppression and struggle, exiling identity into the unmoored, chaotic realm of abject otherness (and tacitly accepting the positioned superiority of the Western subject). Whiteness provides the subject with a known boundary that places nothing "off limits," yet which provides a fantasy of belongingness. It's not that whiteness signifies preferentially one pole of the white-non-white binarism. Rather, whiteness seduces the subject to accept the idea of polarity as the limit-text of identity, as the constitutive foundation of subjectivity.

Whiteness offers coherency and stability in a world in which capital produces regimes of desire linked to commodity utopias where fantasies of omnipotence must find a stable home. Of course, the "them" is always located within the "us." The marginalized are always foundational to the stability of the central actors. The excluded in this case establish the condition of existence of the included. So we find that it is impossible to separate the identities of both oppressor and oppressed. They depend upon each other. To resist whiteness means developing a politics of difference. Since we lack the full semantic availability to understand whiteness and to resist it, we need to rethink difference and identity outside of sets of binary oppositions. We need to view them as coalitional, as collective, as processual, as grounded in the struggle for social justice.

Ian F. Haney López argues that one is not born white but becomes white "by virtue of the social context in which one finds

oneself, to be sure, but also by virtue of the choices one makes" (1996, p. 190). But how can one born into the culture of whiteness, who is defined as white, undo that whiteness? Lopez addresses this question in his formulation of whiteness. López locates whiteness in the overlapping of **chance** (e.g., features and ancestry that we have no control over, morphology); **context** (context-specific meanings that are attached to race, the social setting in which races are recognized, constructed, and contested); and **choice** (conscious choices with regard to the morphology and ancestries of social actors in order to "alter the readability of their identity" (1996, p. 191).

Lopez's perspective offers potential, it would seem, for abolishing racism since it refuses to locate whiteness only as anti-racism's "other." I agree with Bonnett when he remarks that "to continue to cast 'whites' as anti-racism's 'other,' as the eternally guilty and/or altruistic observers of 'race' equality work, is to maintain 'white' privilege and undermine the movement's intellectual and practical reach and utility" (1996, p. 107). In other words, Whites need to ask themselves to what extent their identity is a function of their whiteness in the process of their ongoing daily lives and what choices they might make to escape whiteness. López outlines—productively in my view—three steps in dismantling whiteness. They are worth quoting in full:

> First, Whites must overcome the omnipresent effects of transparency and of the naturalization of race in order to recognize the many racial aspects of their identity, paying particular attention to the daily acts that draw upon and in turn confirm their whiteness. Second, they must recognize and accept the personal and social consequences of breaking out of a White identity. Third, they must embark on a daily process of choosing against Whiteness. (López, 1996, p. 193)

Of course, the difficulty of taking such steps is partly due to the fact that, as López notes, the unconscious acceptance of a racialized identity is predicated upon a circular definition of the self. It's hard to step outside of whiteness if you are white because of all the social, cultural and economic privilege that accompany whiteness. Yet, whiteness must be dismantled if the United States is to overcome racism. Lipsitz remarks:

> Those of us who are "white" can only become part of the solution if we recognize the degree to which we are

already part of the problem—not because of our race, but because of our possessive investment in it." (1995, p. 384).

I am acutely aware that people of color might find troubling the idea that whites populations can simply reinvent themselves by making the simple choice of not being white. Of course, this is not what López and others appear to be saying. The choices one makes and the reinvention one aspires to as a race traitor are not "simple" nor are they easy choices for groups of whites to make. Yet it is possible that when viewed from the perspective of some people of color, offering the choice to white people of opting out of their whiteness could seem to set up an easy path for those whites who don't want to assume responsibility for their privilege as white people. Indeed, there is certainly cause for concern. Choosing not to be white is not an easy option for white people, like deciding to make a change in one's wardrobe. To understand the processes involved in the racialization of identity and to consistently choose nonwhiteness is a difficult act of apostasy, for it implies a heightened sense of social criticism and an unwavering commitment to social justice (Roediger, 1994). Of course, the question needs to be asked: If we can choose to be nonwhite, then can we choose to be black or brown? Insofar as blackness is a social construction (often "parasitic" on whiteness) then I would answer yes. Theologian James H. Cone, author of A Black Theology of Liberation, urges white folks to free themselves from the shackles of their whiteness and become "created anew in black being" (1986, p. 97).

I would stress that choosing against whiteness is not a "mere" choice but a self-consciously political choice, a spiritual choice, and a critical choice. To choose blackness or brownness merely as a way to escape the stigma of whiteness and to avoid responsibility for owning whiteness, is still very much an act of whiteness. To choose blackness or brownness as a way of politically disidentifying with white privilege is, on the other hand, an act of transgression, a traitorous act that reveals a fidelity to the struggle for justice. Of course, in a very real sense choosing against whiteness, while necessary, can be only partial since white people will often be privileged even against their own wishes given the dominant cultural currency that trades in phenotype and skin color.

Towards a Revolutionary Multiculturalism

The work of revolutionary multiculturalists attempts to unsettle both conservative assaults on multiculturalism and liberal paradigms of multiculturalism, the latter of which in my view simply repackage conservative and neo-liberal ideologies under a discursive mantle of diversity without sufficiently addressing the questions: Diversity for what purpose? Diversity standing for what vision of the future? Diversity for the benefit of whom?

Multicultural education as a politics of praxis and a field of inquiry has to navigate through and then move beyond the Scylla of a liberal humanism which in its stress on hybridization all too easily sidesteps the social division of labor and the global circuits of white, patriarchal capitalist production as these are implicated—along with race, class, and gender—in the construction of subjectivity, and the Charybdis of an ethnic essentialism that articulates ethnicity as a monolithic and homogeneous range of discursive practices linked to biology and nature.

Revolutionary multiculturalism as an alternative considers not just the ways in which difference is represented at the level of language and culture, but the ways in which subjectivities are constructed within material relations of power and privilege linked to the globalisation of capitalism.

Sections of this essay (with some revisions) will appear in the following: Enrique Trueba & Yali Zou (Editors), Ethnic Identity and Power, Albany, NY: State University of New York Press, in press;

Peter McLaren, Revolutionar Multiculturalism: Pedagogies of Dissent fo the New Millennium, Boulder, CO: Westvie Press, in press; Jim O'Donnell & Christin Clark (Editors), Becoming White: Owning Racial Identity, Albany, NY: Stat University of New York Press, in press (with Patricia Duenas) in Razateca; and Jo Kincheloe & Shirley Steinberg, editors White Reign: Learning and Deployin Whiteness in America, New York: St Martin's Press, forthcoming. This materia was initially presented as the R. Freeman Butts Lecture at the 1996 meetings of the American Educational Studies Association and appeared in that form in the Spring 1997 issue of Educational Foundations. The author thanks Priscilla H. Walton and Alan H. Jones for their excellent editorial suggestions on the article as it appears here.

References

Bennett, William J. (1996). "Civil Rights is the GOP Mission." *Los Angeles Times*, Monday, August 13, 1996. B5.

Bertoud, G. (1992). Market. In W. Sachs (Ed.), *The Development Dictionary: A Guide to Knowledge as Power*. Atlantic Highlands, NJ: Zed Books.

Bonnett, Alastair. (1996). *Anti-Racism and the Critique of White Identities. New Community*, 22(1): 97-110.

Cone, James H. (1986). *A Black Theology of Liberation*. New York: Orbis Books.

Feinberg, Walter. (1996). Affirmative Action and Beyond: A Case for a Backward-Looking Gender- and Race-Based Policy. *Teachers College Record*. Vol 97, Number 3, Spring, pp. 363-399.

Frankenberg, Ruth. (1993). *The Social Construction of Whiteness: White Women, Race Matters*. Minneapolis, MN: The University of Minnesota Press.

Giroux, Henry. (1997). Channel Surfing: Race Talk and the Destruction of Today's Youth. New York: St. Martin's Press.

Lipsitz, George. (1995). "The Possessive Investment in Whiteness: Racialized Social Democracy and the 'White' Problem in American Studies." *American Quarterly*, Vol. 47, No. 3, pp. 369-387.

López, Ian F. Haney. (1996). *White by Law*. New York: New York University Press.

Lott, Eric. (1993) "White Like Me: Racial Cross-Dressing and the Construction of American Whiteness." In Amy Kaplan & Donald E. Pease (eds.) *Cultures of United States Imperialism*. Durham, NC: Duke University Press, pp. 474-498.

Parenti, Michael (1996). *Dirty Truths*. San Francisco, CA: City Lights Books.

Perea, Juan, F. (1995). Los Olvidados: On the Making of Invisible People. *New York University Law Review*, Vol. 70, No. 4, pp. 965-991.

Roediger, David (1993). *The Wages of Whiteness*. London, United Kingdom: Verso.

West, Cornel. (1993). *Keeping Faith: Philosophy and Race in America*. New York: Routledge.

Zinn, Howard. (1970). *The Politics of History*. Boston, MA: Beacon Press.

Zizek, Slavoj. (1992). Eastern Europe's Republics of Gilead. In Chantal Mouffe, editor, *Dimesions of Radical Democracy*. London, United Kingdom: Verso, pp. 193-207.

Additional Bibliography

Balibar, Etienne & Wallerstein, Immanuel (1993). Race, Nation, Class: Ambiguous Identities. London and New York: Verso.

Balibar, Etienne. (1996). "Is European Citizenship Possible?" *Public Culture*, No. 19, pp. 355-376.

Bannerji, Himani (1995). *Thinking Through*. Toronto, Canada: Women's Press.

Barrs, Rick (1996). "The Real Story about How the Use of Crack Cocaine Exploded in South-Central." *New Times*, Sept. 12-18, Vol. 1, No. 4, p. 9.

Bauman, Zygmunt. (1992). *Mortality, Immortality & and Other Life Strategies*. Stanford, CA: Stanford University Press.

Bauman, Zygmunt. (1996, May). "On Communitarians and Human Freedom, or, How to Square the Circle." *Theory, Culture and Society*, Vol. 13, No. 2, pp. 79-90.

Bernstein, Sharon. (1996). "Storm Rises Over Ex-Klansman in Debate." *Los Angeles Times*, Wednesday, September 11, A3, A14.

Bhachu, Parminder. (1996). "The Multiple Landscapes of Transnational Asian Women in the Diaspora." In Vered Amit-Talai & Caroline Knowles, eds., *Re-Situating Identities: The Politics of Race, Ethnicity, and Culture*. Peterborough, Canada and Essex, London: Broadview Press, pp. 283-303.

Boggs, C. (1995, Dec. 22-28). *The God Reborn: Pondering the Revival of Russian Communism*. Los Angeles View, 10(20), 8.

Bradlee Jr., B. (1996). "The Buchanan Role: GOP Protagonist." *Boston Sunday Globe*, March 3, 1996, Vol. 249, No. 63, pp. 1 and 12.

Cashmore, Ellis. (1996). *Dictionary of Race and Ethnic Relations* (fourth edition). London and New York: Routledge.

Chomsky, Noam. (1996). *Class Warfare: Interviews with David Barsamian*. Monroe, ME: Common Courage Press.

Connell, Rich (1996). "2,000 Protest Alleged U.S. Role in Crack Influx." *Los Angeles Times*, Sept. 29, p. B1, B4.

Connolly, William (1995). *The Ethos of Pluralization*. Minneapolis, MN: University of Minnesota Press.

Cruz, Jon. (1996). "From Farce to Tragedy: Reflections on the Reification of Race at Century's End." In Avery Gordon and Christopher Newfield, eds., *Mapping Multiculturalism*. Minneapolis and London: University of Minnesota Press, pp. 19-39.

Dussel, Enrique. (1993). "Eurocentrism and Modernity." *Boundary 2*, Vol. 20, No. 3, pp. 65-77.

Fanon, Frantz. (1967). *Black Skin, White Masks*. New

York: Grove Press.

Feagin, Joe R., Vera, Hernan (1995). *White Racism.* London and New York: Routledge.

Fraser, Nancy. (1993). "Clintonism, Welfare, and the Antisocial Wage: The Emergence of a Neoliberal Political Imaginary." *Rethinking Marxism*, Vol. 6, No. 1, pp. 9-23.

Gallagher, Charles A. (1994). "White Construction in the University." *Socialist Review*, Vol. 1 & 2, pp. 165-187.

Gardiner, Michael. (1996, May). "Alterity and Ethics: A Dialogical Perspective." *Theory, Culture and Society,* Vol 13, No. 2, pp. 121-144.

Gatens, Moria (1996). *Imaginary Bodies.* London and New York: Routledge.

Giroux, Henry (1993). *Border Crossings.* London and New York: Routledge.

Giroux, Henry (1996). "Race and the Debate on Public Intellectuals." *International Journal of Educational Reform*, Vol. 5, No. 3, pp. 345-350.

Goldberg, David Theo. (1993). *Racist Culture: Philosophy and the Politics of Meaning.* Cambridge, MA: Blackwell Publishers.

Gómez-Peña, Guillermo (1996). *The New World Border.* San Francisco: City Lights Bookstore.

Gutierrez, Ramón. (1996). "The Erotic Zone Sexual Transgression on the U.S.-Mexican Border." In Avery Gordon & Christopher Newfield, eds., *Mapping Multiculturalism.* Minneapolis, MN: University of Minnesota Press.

Hicks, Emily (1991). *Border Writing.* Minneapolis, MN: University of Minnesota Press.

Holston, James & Appadurai, Arjun. (1996). *Cities and Citizenship. Public Culture,* No. 19, pp. 187-204.

Ignatiev, Noel (1995). *How the Irish Became White.* London and New York: Routledge.

Ignatiev, Noel, & Garvey, John. (1996). *Race Traitor.* New York and London: Routledge.

Kahn, Joel S. (1995). *Culture, Multiculture, Postculture.* Thousand Oaks: Sage Publications.

Laclau, Ernesto. (1992). "Universalism, Particularism, and the Question of Identity." *October*, Vol. 61 (Summer), pp. 83-90.

Lash, Scott. (1996, May). "Postmodern Ethics: The Missing Ground." *Theory, Culture and Society,* Vol. 13, No. 2, pp. 91-104.

Lipsitz, George. (1994). *Dangerous Crossroads: Popular Music, Postmodernism and the Poetics of Place.* London and New York: Verso.

Lipsitz, George. (1996). "It's All Wrong, but its All Right: Creative Misunderstandings in Intercultural Communication." In Avery Gordon & Christopher Newfield, eds., *Mapping Multiculturalism.* Minneapolis, MN: University of Minnesota Press, pp. 403-412.

Loewen, James W. (1995). *Lies my Teacher Told Me: Everything Your American History Textbook Got Wrong.* New York: Touchstone.

Luhrmann, T.M. (1996). *The Good Parsi.* Cambridge, MA: Harvard University Press.

Macedo, Donald & Bartolome, Lilia. (forthcoming). "Dancing with Bigotry: The Poisoning of Racial and Ethnic Identities." In Enrique Torres Trueba & Yali Zou, eds., *Ethnic Identity and Power.* Albany, NY: State University of New York Press.

Martin-Barbero, Jesus (1993). *Communication, Culture and Hegemony.* New Park, CA: Sage Publications.

McLaren, Peter (1995). *Critical Pedagogy and Predatory Culture.* London and New York: Routledge.

McLaren, Peter (in press). *Revolutionary Multiculturalism: Pedagogies of Dissent for the New Millennium,* Boulder, CO: Westview Press.

Miles, Robert (1982). *Racism and Migrant Labour: A Critical Text.* London: Routledge.

Miles, Robert (1993). *Racism After "Race Relations"* London: Routledge.

Miles, Robert (1994). "Explaining Racism in Contemporary Europe" in Ali Rattansi & Sallie Westwood (eds.), *Racism, Modernity and Identity.* Cambridge, MA and Cambridge, UK: Polity Press.

Miles, Robert and Torres, Rudy (1996). "Does 'Race' Matter? Transatlantic Perspectives on Racism after "Race Relations" in Vered Amit-Talai & Caroline Knowles (eds.), *Re-Situating Identities.* Toronto, Canada: Broadview Press.

Moore, Joan, & Pachon, Harry (1985). *Hispanics in the United States.* Englewood Cliffs, NJ: Prentice-Hall, Inc.

Morales, Marcia. (1996). *Bilingual Education: A Dialogue with the Bakhtin Circle.* Albany, NY: The State University of New York Press.

Nederveen Pieterse. J. (1996). Globalisation and Culture: Three Paradigms. *Economic and Political Weekly.* June 8, 1996, pp. 1389-1393.

Novik, Michael. (1995). *White Lies, White Power: The Fight Against White Supremacy and Reactionary Violence.* Monroe, ME: Common Courage Press.

O'Brien, Conor Cruise. (1996). "Thomas Jefferson: Radical and Racist." *The Atlantic Monthly*, October, pp. 53-74.

Omi, Michael & Winant, Howard (1993). "The Los Angeles 'Race Riot' and Contemporary U.S. Politics" in Robert Goding-Williams (ed.), *Reading Rodney King.* London: Routledge.

Radhakrishnan. R. (1996). *Diasporic Mediations.* Minneapolis, MN: University of Minnesota Press.

Rattansi, Ali. (1994). "'Western' Racisms, Ethnicities and Identities in a 'Postmodern' Frame." In Ali Rattansi & Sallie Westwood, eds., *Racism, Modernity, and Identity on the Western Front.* Cambridge, MA: Polity Press, pp. 403-412.

Ridgeway, James (1995). *Blood in the Face.* New York: Thunder's Mouth Press.

Roediger, David (1994). *Towards the Abolition of Whiteness.* London: Verso.

Rugoff, Ralph (1995). *Circus Americanus.* London: Verso.

Said, Edward. (1985). *Orientalism.* London: Penguin.

San Juan, Jr., E. (1995). *Hegemony and Strategies of Transgression.* Albany, NY: State of New York University Press.

Sarup, Madan ((1996). *Identity, Culture and the Postmodern World.* Athens, GA: The University of Georgia Press.

Shohat, Ella & Stam, Robert (1994). *Unthinking Eurocentrism.* London: Routledge.

Shohat, Ella. (1995). "The Struggle Over Representation: Casting, Coalitions, and the Politics of Indentification." In Román de la Campa, E. Ann Kaplan & Michael Sprinker, eds., *Late Imperial Culture* (pp. 166-178). London: Verso.

Simon, S. (1996, January 2). "Job Hunt's Wild Side in Russia." *Los Angeles Times*, pp. 1, 9.

Sleeter, Christine E. (1996). "White Silence, White Solidarity" in Noel Ignatiev & John Gavey (eds.), *Race Traitor.* London: Routledge.

Southern Poverty Law Center. (1996). *False Patriots: The Threat of Antigovernment Extremists.* Montgomery, AL.

Stowe, David W. "Uncolored People: The Rise of Whiteness Studies." *Lingua Franca*, Vol. 6, No. 6, 1996, pp. 68-77.

The Boston Globe, January 26, 1990.

Time. Banker to Mexico: "Go get 'em." February 20, 1995, Vol. 145, No. 7, p. 9.

Trembath, Paul. (1996). "Aesthetics without Art or Culture: Toward an Alternative Sense of Materialist Agency." *Strategies*, Vol. 9/10, pp. 122-151.

Tsing, Anna Lowenhaupt (1993). *In the Realm of the Diamond Queen.* Princeton, NJ: Princeton University Press.

Visweswaran, Kamala. (1994). *Fictions of Feminist Ethnography.* Minneapolis, MN: University of Minnesota Press.

Wallace, Amy. (1996). "Less Diversity Seen as UC Preferences End." *Los Angeles Times*, Wednesday, October 2, A1, 18.

Webb, Gary (1996). "Unholy Connection." *New Times*, Sept. 12-18, vol.1, no. 4, pp. 10-24.

Welsch, Wolfgang. (1996). "Aestheticization Processes: Phenomena, Distinctions and Prospects." *Theory, Culture and Society*, Vol. 13, No. 2, pp. 1-24.

Williams, Raymond (1974). *Politics and Letters.* London: Verso.

Winant, Howard. (1994). *Racial Conditions: Politics, Theory, Comparisons.* Minneapolis, MN: University of Minnesota Press.

Wolin, Sheldon. (1992). "What Revolutionary Action Means Today". In Chantal Mouffe, editor, *Dimesions of Radical Democracy.* London: Verso, pp. 240-253.

Yudice, George (1995). "Neither Impugning nor Disavowing Whiteness Does a Viable Politics Make: The Limits of Identity Politics" in Christopher Newfield & Ronald Strickland (eds.), *After Political Correctness. The Humanities and Society in the 1990s*, pp. 255-285.

Zamichow, N. (1996, January 23). "Captains Courageous Enough Not to Fight." *Los Angeles Times*, pp. 1, 9-10.

Opening the Closet

Multiculturalism That is Fully Inclusive

By Cathy A. Pohan and Norma J. Bailey

I have learned that oppression and the intolerance of difference come in all shapes and sexes and colors and sexualities; and that among those of us who share the goals of liberation and a workable future for our children, there is no hierarchy of oppression.
——Audre Lorde (Lorde, 1983, 9)

Recognizing that too many children in this country were not receiving an equal educational opportunity, many voices rose up demanding that schools address the needs of those groups who had traditionally been denied access and representation in the educational process. Yet, "with few exceptions, most school districts still fail to acknowledge or serve the needs of gay, lesbian, bisexual students, parents, and staff" (Goodman, 1996, 10). Coupled with the homophobia[1] and heterosexism[2] in society, the lack of recognition, resources, and support for gay and lesbian[3] youth makes these youngsters perhaps one of the most at-risk of all student populations.

It is encouraging to see The National

Cathy A. Pohan is an assistant professor of educational psychology in the College of Education at San Diego State University, San Diego, California; Norma J. Bailey is an assistant professor of middle level education in the Department of Teacher Education and Professional Development at the University of Northern Colorado, Greeley, Colorado

Association for Multicultural Education (NAME) add its name to a growing list of professional organizations that are addressing the needs of gay and lesbian youth today. Yet, while several scholars leading the field of multicultural education (*e.g.*, executive committee of NAME; Nieto, 1996; Sleeter & Grant, 1993) have broadened the umbrella of multiculturalism to be inclusive of sexual orientation, many educators may still feel unable to articulate why such inclusion is imperative. In this article, we seek to build a rationale for inclusion by reviewing: (a) the experiences of gay and lesbian youth that place them at-risk in society and school; (b) how homophobia and heterosexism hurts both gay and non-gay individuals; and (c) the goals and role of multicultural education in helping to create a more just and equitable society.

Gay and Lesbian Youth: An At-Risk Population

Adolescence can be a difficult, if not tumultuous, developmental period for youngsters to navigate. In addition to the challenge of integrating increasing biological, psychological, and social demands, adolescents are also becoming aware of their sexuality. The reluctance of parents and "educators to deal candidly with teenage sexual orientation issues, particularly if that orientation is homosexual, places a significant number of adolescents at risk, not only of school failure, but of personal and social crises—even death" (Walling, 1993,

7). The following words illustrate the intense struggles faced by many adolescents in our schools today:

> I hear homophobic comments all the time in my classes. Sometimes I think teachers don't hear what goes on in their classrooms. I want teachers to remember that I can't block out the homophobia. I hear it even when I don't want to listen. I hear it every day that I am in this school. And it hurts a lot. (A 16-year-old lesbian, Jennings, 1996, 258)

> I was very different from other students and they picked up on it. Immediately the words "faggot" and "queer" were used to describe me. Freshman year of high school was hard enough; but with the big seniors pushing you around because the rumor is you're a faggot, it's ten times worse. I knew I was gay. But who could I talk to? I was spit upon, pushed, and ridiculed. My school life was hell. I decided to leave school because I couldn't handle it. (An 18-year-old gay male, Jennings, 1996, 259)

> I felt as though I was the only gay person my age in the world. I felt as though I had nowhere to go to talk to anybody. Throughout eighth grade, I went to bed every night praying that I would not be able to wake up in the morning, and every morning waking up and being disappointed. And so finally I decided that if I was going to die, it would have to be at my own

hands. (An 18-year-old gay male, The Governor's Commission on Gay and Lesbian Youth, 1993, 12)

In addition to such testimonies, there is mounting evidence suggesting that gay and lesbian youth are believed to be at greater risk than their heterosexual counterparts for substance abuse, poor mental health, running away, dropping out of school, suicide, risky sexual behavior, and hate violence (Denver Area Alliance for Hate Free Schools, 1995; The Governor's Commission on Gay and Lesbian Youth, 1993). Indeed, the most disturbing fact is that young lives are being needlessly lost. It is estimated that 30 percent of the completed teen suicides are committed by gay or lesbian youth or those struggling with their sexual identity. Further, gay and lesbian youth are two to three times more likely to attempt suicide than their heterosexual counterparts (The Governor's Commission on Gay and Lesbian Youth, 1993; Remafedi, 1994).

Even if suicide is not chosen as an avenue of escape, gay and lesbian youth face many other problems which put them at high risk. Because of the negative self-images they buy into as a result of living in a homophobic society and the pain of the internal conflicts, gay and lesbian youth are three times more likely than their heterosexual peers to abuse substances (Gibson, 1989). Twenty-six percent of those who "come out" to their families are "thrown out" of their homes because of conflicts with moral and religious values (Gibson, 1989). Further, it is estimated that between 30 percent and 40 percent of the homeless youth in large cities are gay and lesbian youth. Tragically, many often engage in prostitution to survive (Denver Area Alliance for Hate Free Schools, 1995).

In addition to the previously mentioned risk behaviors, it is not uncommon for youth who are struggling with their sexual identity to increase their sexual experimentation. Some increase sexual activity with heterosexuals just to "prove" that they are not gay or lesbian. Still others may experiment with the same gender to determine if they really are gay or lesbian. Unfortunately, participation in risky and unprotected sexual activity increases the likelihood of contracting sexually transmitted diseases or HIV (Gibson, 1989; Remafedi, 1994).

Still further, while members of many minority groups are the victims of hate violence, gays and lesbians are increasingly the most frequent victims, particularly of brutal crimes. According to the *Klanwatch Intelligence Report* of the Southern Poverty Law Center, gays and lesbians bore the brunt of hate violence in 1994. Among the assault victims documented in their re-

port, over 25 percent were gay or lesbian, and of the 18 murders Klanwatch verified, 11 were motivated by anti-gay bias (*Klanwatch Intelligence Report*, 1995).

It is tragic that adolescents struggling with their sexual orientation find themselves in an often hostile society with little (if any) support even at home. It is even more tragic that while school is the other primary social institution where all young people

> It is tragic that adolescents struggling with their sexual orientation find themselves in an often hostile society with little (if any) support even at home. It is even more tragic that while school... [is] ...where all young people should be able to feel safe, this is often not the case.

should be able to feel safe, this is often not the case. Harassment, threats, and/or violence against gay and lesbian youth (and those perceived to be gay or lesbian) continues to increase on high school, middle school, and junior high school campuses across our nation (The Governor's Commission on Gay and Lesbian Youth, 1993).

The School Experiences of Gay and Lesbian Youth

Of 289 secondary school counselors surveyed nationally, 54 percent strongly agreed that "students are very degrading toward fellow students whom they discover are homosexual," and 67 percent strongly agreed that "homosexual students are more likely to feel isolated and rejected" (Price & Telljohann, 1991). As well, "45 percent of the males and 20 percent of the females [surveyed] reported having experienced verbal or physical assaults in secondary school because they were perceived to be gay or lesbian" (The Governor's Commission on Gay and Lesbian Youth, 1993, 9).

While some teachers and administrators harass, ridicule, and unfairly punish gay students, or those "suspected" or "ac-

cused" of being gay, the predominant feature of the discriminatory school environment for gay youth is the failure of school officials to provide protection from peer harassment and violence (Dennis & Harlow, 1986; Governor's Commission on Gay and Lesbian Youth, 1993). Counselors, who should provide confidential and supportive counseling to gay and lesbian youth, often do not do so for a number of reasons: too busy; themselves uncomfortable with the issue of homosexuality; not trained to deal with the issue; afraid of controversy; or, worse yet, strongly homophobic themselves (Gibson, 1989).

Another school practice that needs to be addressed in order to provide a more equitable education for gay and lesbian youth is the "conspiracy of silence" that envelops most schools (Sears, 1991). In the majority of schools, neither curriculum—including sex education classes—nor library resources provide students, gay or non-gay, with accurate and positive information about homosexuality. As with people of color or women 30 to 40 years ago, this leaves gay and lesbian youth with no sense of history and historical role models with whom to identify. Nor do these students have role models in their schools because the majority of gay and lesbian teachers are not "out" because of fears for their job security, etc.

In addition, the vast majority of schools do not have anti-slur or anti-discrimination policies in place which include sexual orientation. This means that gay and lesbian students have no recourse when harassed, nor have teachers been trained to ensure their safety. As well, there are virtually no support groups for gay and lesbian students, at the very time when they are desperate for support and someone to talk to in order to alleviate their feelings of difference and aloneness and when acceptance from a peer group is so important (Woog, 1995). What makes this void so devastating is that while students of different ethnicities, races, and religions can go home for emotional support from the family, students who are gay or lesbian often have no place to go for the much needed support.

Much of the school situation for gay and lesbian youth today is similar to the situation for students of color, the poor, women, and students with disabilities, before the efforts of multicultural educators began to create environments which were more supportive and inclusive of the lives and needs of these individuals. Thirty to 40 years ago (and still sometimes today), individuals from these groups experienced verbal and physical harassment, lack of protection, counselors untrained regarding their needs, curriculum which did not include their history and role models, libraries/media centers which did not have adequate holdings reflecting their existence, no teachers as role models, and school policies that did not offer protections. Much progress has been made for many of these minority groups, but the situation for gay and lesbian youth is still shamefully bleak.

Homophobia and Heterosexism Hurt Everyone

Homophobia, and these often unspoken, and/or unrecognized, practices of ignorance, denial, repression and discrimination toward homosexuality on the part of the educational community, have an enormous effect on all the youth in the American public school system—both gay and non-gay. In elementary school, children quickly learn that one of the worst insults is to call someone a **queer** or a **sissy**. By the time students are in middle schools and high schools, this name-calling becomes a powerful weapon when directed against gay and lesbian youth and also has an enormous power to keep all others from expressing any emotions or actions that deviate from the accepted gender-role expectations. In its 1993 report on sexual harassment in America's schools, the American Association of University Women (AAUW) Educational Foundation found that when students were asked to what degree they would be upset if they were the targets of the 14 different types of sexual harassment outlined in the survey, 85 percent of the boys and 87 percent of the girls surveyed said they would be "very upset" if they were called gay or lesbian. No other type of harassment—including actual physical abuse—provoked a reaction this strong among boys (Louis Harris & Associates, 1993).

Thus, it is clear that homophobic attitudes are powerful and pervasive, also limiting the potential of heterosexual youth. Fearing being called gay or lesbian, many heterosexual adolescents change their behaviors in order to accommodate this fear. For example, heterosexual youth may: become sexually active earlier than they might normally in order to prove their heterosexuality; choose classes, activities, and/or career goals which are not expressions of what they really want to be doing; engage in anti-gay harassment which diminishes their humanity; or limit themselves from the development of emotional intimacy between same-sex friends. As Elze (1992) summarizes:

> Homophobia serves to squeeze young men and women into rigid gender roles, limiting their aspirations, squelching their dreams of what they

can be, isolating those youths whose behaviors defy traditional ideals of "masculine" and "feminine," and fostering violence against gay and lesbian youths and those perceived to be gay or lesbian. (p. 101)

Another group of young people who are also the victims of homophobia are those students whose parents are gay or lesbian or who have other family members who are homosexual. "Schools are often the first place children from gay and lesbian families learn the insults that describe their mothers and fathers. They learn that one of the worst accusations someone can make about you is to say you are gay" (Walling, 1996, 12). Thus, children are torn between positive and negative images about their family and soon realize that it may be unsafe to defend those whom they love. Even the more benign heterosexism (the presumption of heterosexuality as the norm in society) plays a part with these children in that children of gays and lesbians receive a mixed message about family. At home, these children learn that their family is "natural, acceptable, and loving, but at school, only heterosexual families are validated in the stories/books/movies children are exposed to or in the assumptions made by their teachers/peers" (Walling, 1996, 12).

In light of the data outlining the unique challenges facing gays and lesbians and the impact of homophobia and heterosexism on society at large, it is imperative that we, as multicultural educators, take seriously our obligation to understand the role multicultural education can (and should) play in making schools and society a safer, more accepting place for all individuals. Therefore, it is important that we review the goals of multicultural education in continuing to build a rationale for making multicultural education fully inclusive.

The Goals of Multicultural Education

Growing out of the civil rights movement which was grounded in the democratic ideals of freedom, justice, and equality, multicultural education seeks to extend to all people the ideals and rights that were originally meant for only an elite few (Banks, 1993b). In *Affirming Diversity: The Sociopolitical Context for Multicultural Education*, Sonia Nieto (1996) poignantly reminds us that "multicultural education is for everyone, regardless of ethnicity, race, language, social class, religion, gender, sexual orientation, ability, and any differences." Few would disagree that multicultural education aims to create a more just society and schools that are more inclusive and repre-

sentative of the diversity in our nation (Banks, 1993a; Nieto, 1996; Sleeter & Grant, 1993). Though programs implementing a multicultural approach come in many shapes and sizes (Banks, 1993a; Sleeter & Grant, 1993), some common purposes and goals which would clearly apply to gays and lesbians can be readily identified. These include:

1. Combating a narrow and/or mono-dimensional curriculum; affirming and legitimizing the presence and contributions of diverse groups;
2. Creating a climate that promotes an appreciation of diverse peoples, values, perspectives, and ways of life;
3. Reducing prejudice and working toward the elimination of discrimination in teaching and in society;
4. Working toward equality and justice for all;
5. Respecting the rights and dignity of all individuals;
6. Supporting pluralism within the educational system;
7. Broadening and/or diversifying the values schools promote. (Cushner, McClelland, & Safford, 1992; Miller-Lachmann & Taylor, 1995)

In essence, teachers who align themselves with multicultural education believe that schools and classrooms are to be "places of hope, where students and teachers gain glimpses of the kind of society we could live in and where students learn the academic and critical skills needed to make it a reality" (Bigelow, Christensen, Karp, Miner, & Peterson, 1994, 4). Certainly, these goals and hope should be inclusive of gays and lesbians.

Multicultural Education's Role and Responsibility

Schools are often reluctant to support the implementation of policies and practices that prohibit discrimination on the basis of sexual orientation and to make the curriculum and social structure more inclusive and representative of gays and lesbians. This reluctance is usually a result of inaccurate or misguided assumptions about homosexuality and/or pressure from special interest groups (*e.g.*, the Religious Right). For example, many educators feel that since we have made "great strides" in dealing with racism and sexism, that is enough. But the reality is that schools will not be safe for all students until we eliminate all forms of discrimination. Further, the notion that this commitment is "too controversial" fails to acknowledge the fact that human rights issues are always controversial. Still further, many want educators to steer clear of gay and lesbian issues because they believe that this is a moral issue. However, what these individuals fail to recognize is that it is a moral issue when any student population is systematically denied support, representation, and/or resources within the educational system (Walling, 1996).

If those of us who adhere to the tenets of multicultural education are committed to creating more inclusive and democratic schools, then we must confront even the most controversial social justice issues. Clearly, the most recent challenges facing gays and lesbians (e.g., recognition/acknowledgment as contributing individuals; discrimination policies in housing and employment; domestic partnership benefits; etc.) are directly related to civil rights and social justice in a democratic society. In *Democratic Schools,* Beane and Apple (1995) propose several conditions on which a democracy depends. Four of these conditions are relevant to making multicultural education inclusive of sexual orientation:

1. Concern for the welfare of others and for "the common good";
2. Concern for the dignity and rights of individuals and minorities [those not belonging to the dominant group];
3. The open flow of ideas, regardless of their popularity, that enables people to be as fully informed as possible; and
4. The organization of social institutions to promote and extend the democratic way of life. (Beane & Apple, 1995, 6-7)

"Xenophobia, discrimination, ethnocentrism, racism, classism, sexism, and homophobia are societal phenomena that are inconsistent with the principles of democracy and lead to the counterproductive reasoning that differences are deficiencies" (NAME brochure, 1996). As educators, we have an obligation to confront such counterproductive thinking. Further, since we must work toward the elimination of all forms of oppression, it is impossible to ignore gays and lesbians as a group that continues to experience oppression and discrimination (Gordon, 1995). To do so would be shortsighted. In the words of Audre Lorde (1983), a Black, lesbian, feminist, and member of an interracial couple, we are reminded that what affects one group affects all other groups:

I cannot afford the luxury of fighting one form of oppression only. I cannot afford to believe that freedom from intolerance is the right of only one particular group. And I cannot afford to choose between the fronts upon which I must battle these forces of discrimination, wherever they appear to destroy me. And when they appear to destroy me, it will not be long before

they appear to destroy you. (Lorde, 1983, 9)

Indeed, issues facing individuals who are gay or lesbian will eventually affect all who have historically been oppressed. As educators who believe so passionately in the promise and practice of multicultural education, may we challenge ourselves once again to come to a fuller understanding of Lorde's words "there is no hierarchy of oppression" and strengthen our commitment to fight for the dignity and rights of all individuals, including our sisters and brothers who are gay.

Notes

1. Homophobia: The irrational fear, dislike, anger, or intolerance of homosexuality, bisexuality, gay men, lesbians, or bisexuals which can be both personal or institutional prejudice and often results in acts of discrimination. (A composite of several popular definitions. See Bailey, 1996).
2. Heterosexism: The institutional and societal reinforcement of the belief that heterosexuality is better and more natural than homosexuality or bisexuality. The presumption that everyone is heterosexual. (A composite of several popular definitions. See Bailey, 1996).
3. Gay and Lesbian: In order not to be too cumbersome, the authors will use the phrase "gay and lesbian" to describe all people who are homosexual, bisexual, or transgendered.

References

Bailey, N.J. (1996). Attitudes/Feelings, knowledge, and anticipated professional behaviors of middle level teachers regarding homosexuality and gay and lesbian issues as they relate to middle level students. Greeley, CO: Unpublished dissertation, The University of Northern Colorado.

Banks, J. (1993a). Multicultural education: Characteristics and goals. In J. Banks & C.A.M. Banks (Eds.), *Multicultural education: Issues and perspectives* (2nd ed.) (pp. 3-28). Boston, MA: Allyn & Bacon.

Banks, J. (1993b). Multicultural education: Development, dimensions, and challenges. *Phi Delta Kappan,* 75(1), 22-28.

Beane, J. & Apple, M. (1995). The case for democratic schools. In J. Beane & M. Apple, *Democratic Schools* (pp. 1-25). Alexandria, VA: Association for Supervision and Curriculum Development.

Bigelow, B., Christensen, L., Karp, S., Miner, B., & Peterson, B. (Eds.). (1994). *Rethinking our classrooms: Teaching for equity and justice.* Milwaukee, WI: Rethinking Schools.

Cushner, K., McClelland, A., & Safford, P. (1992). *Human diversity in education: An integrated study.* New York: McGraw-Hill.

Dennis, D.I. & Harlow, R.E. (1986). Gay youth and the right to education. *Yale Law and Policy Review,* 4, 445-455.

Denver Area Alliance for Hate Free Schools. (1995). *Youth at risk.* Denver, CO: Denver Area Alliance for Hate Free Schools.

Elze, D. (1992). It has nothing to do with me. In W. J. Blumenfeld (Ed.), *Homophobia: How we all pay the price* (pp. 95-113). Boston, MA: Beacon Press.

Gibson, P. (1989). Gay male and lesbian youth suicide. In *Report of the Secretary's Task Force on Youth Suicide. Volume 3: Prevention and interventions in youth suicide.* Washington, DC: U.S. Department of Health and Human Services.

Goodman, J.M. (1996). Lesbian, gay, and bisexual issues in education: A personal view. In D.R. Walling (Ed.), *Open lives, safe schools* (pp. 9-27). Bloomington, IN: Phi Delta Kappa Educational Foundation.

Gordon, L. (1994). What do we say when we hear 'faggot'? In D. Levine, R. Lowe, B. Peterson, & R. Tenorio (Eds.), *Rethinking schools: An agenda for change* (pp. 40-44). New York: The New Press.

The Governor's Commission on Gay and Lesbian Youth. (1993). *Making schools safe for gay and lesbian youth: Breaking the silence in schools and in families.* (Publication No. 17296-60-500-2/93-C.R.). Boston, MA: The Governor's Commission on Gay and Lesbian Youth.

Jennings, K. (1996). Together, for a change: Lessons from organizing the Gay, Lesbian, and Straight Teachers Network (GLSTN). In D.R. Walling (Ed.), *Open lives, safe schools* (pp. 251-260). Bloomington, IN: Phi Delta Kappa Educational Foundation.

Klanwatch Intelligence Report. (1995, March). 1994 hate crime recap: A year of close calls. (Special Year-End Edition: 1994). Montgomery, AL: Southern Poverty Law Center.

Lorde, A. (1983). There is no hierarchy of oppressions. *Council on Interracial Books for Children,* 14 (3/4), 9.

Louis Harris & Associates (1993, June). *Hostile hallways: The AAUW survey on sexual harassment in America's schools* [Study number 923012]. Washington, D.C: American Association of University Women Educational Foundation.

Miller-Lachmann, L. & Taylor, L. (1995). *Schools for all: Educating children in a diverse society.* Albany, NY: Delmar.

Nieto, S. (1996). *Affirming diversity: The sociopolitical context for multicultural education* (2nd ed.). New York: Longman.

Price, J.H. & Telljohann, S.K. (1991). School counselors' perceptions of adolescent homosexuals. *Journal of School Health,* 61(10), 433-438.

Remafedi, G. (1994). *Death by denial: Studies of suicide in gay and lesbian teenagers.* Boston, MA: Alyson.

Sears, J.T. (1991). Helping students understand and accept sexual diversity. *Educational Leadership,* 49 (11), 54-56.

Sleeter, C. & Grant, C. (1993). *Making choices for multicultural education: Five approaches to race, class, and gender* (2nd Ed.). New York: Macmillan.

Snowder, F. (1996). Preventing gay teen suicide. In D.R. Walling (Ed.), *Open lives, safe schools* (pp. 261-268). Bloomington, IN: Phi Delta Kappa Educational Foundation.

Walling, D.R. (Ed.) (1996). *Open lives, safe schools.* Bloomington, IN: Phi Delta Kappa Educational Foundation.

Walling, D.R. (1993). *Gay teens at risk* (Fastback 357). Bloomington, IL: Phi Delta Kappa Educational Foundation.

Woog, D. (1995). *School's out: The impact of gay and lesbian issues on America's schools.* Boston, MA: Alyson.

CULTURE & IDEAS

The making of a hip-hop intellectual

Deconstructing the puzzle of race and identity

The best way to comprehend Michael Eric Dyson's many voices is to hear him lecture. He starts off quietly professorial, talking learnedly about the historical and economic roots of rap music and hip-hop culture. Students are still drifting into the basement amphitheater in Swain Hall, on the University of North Carolina's Chapel Hill campus. Before long he's up and pacing the dais, his speech a bit more pressurized as he describes the rhythms and sonic wizardry of black oral traditions. Now he's preaching, like the Baptist minister he is, gesticulating as he inveighs against society's relentless policing of black youth. All the time, he moves effortlessly from French critical theory to gangsta culture to politics, alternately quoting Foucault and Farrakhan and Ice Cube, Derrida and Tupac and Malcolm, occasionally breaking into an extended and flawless rap groove as he bangs out the background rhythms on the lectern. Seamless, and completely self-assured.

But is he a "real nigga"?

Real nigga. It's a vulgar formulation from the world of gangsta rap and could easily be dismissed as just another unsavory example of that musical genre's ghetto talk. But Dyson doesn't want to dismiss the question, or the culture that insists on it. Indeed, Dyson considers obsession with "the real" (or with "racial authenticity," in the more polite vocabulary of intellectual discourse) one of the most significant and troubling cultural issues facing African-Americans today. It is a political and deeply philosophical issue—one that runs through this Princeton-trained theorist's scholarship and teaching, his many public lectures and his writing, including the last of his four books, the newly published *Race Rules.* For Dyson, grasping the complexity of racial identity is the key to understanding everything from our fascination with O.J. and deep ambivalence about black nationalism to our uneasiness about gangsta culture and—most important—the apparent self-destructiveness of many young black men living in American cities today.

Dyson's intellectual starting point is the rather arcane world of critical theory, from which he borrows a couple of core concepts to illuminate race in the 1990s. He starts with a critique of the traditional definition of "identity" as a fixed collection of traits and experiences. The world, viewed from a postmodern perspective, is simply too chaotic to allow for such stability, he says; rather, identity is something fluid, amorphous and evolving. Dyson also takes from the so-called deconstructionist philosophers the idea that all cultural "texts"—whether the Million Man March, rap lyrics or the O.J. trial—can and should be examined for cultural significance. If you accept these premises, he argues, it's crucial to

take gangsta and other societal subcurrents seriously, but indefensible to pick one racial "essence" as *more* authentic than another.

More insular. The problem, Dyson says, is that such rarefied philosophical lessons have not reached the streets, where blacks are involved in a sometimes deadly tug of war over "the real." Where once ghetto culture vied with black bourgeois experience in claiming authenticity, today ghetto culture is itself fragmented: Is the West Coast world of Compton more real than New York gangsta culture? The fragments of African-American reality are increasingly exclusive and insular, a trend that's also detectable in the Nation of Islam, the Million Man March and other nationalistic impulses.

Dyson is not an opponent of racial solidarity movements, and he supports some policies based on race, because of the persistence of white racism in American society. Indeed, he argues that the fragmentation of racial identity can only be understood against the historical background of slavery and racist stereotyping. Plantation stereotypes—the good "house Negro," the bad "field nigger"—persisted long after the abolition of slavery, Dyson notes, and are still potent today. White America's distorted sense of betrayal over O.J., he suggests, has a lot to do with the safe, raceless "house

Negro" violating white society's "race rules."

Dyson's interest in these issues is not entirely academic. Born in a working-class neighborhood of Detroit, his rise has been bumpy and fraught with identity crises. A gifted student, he won a scholarship to a tony white suburban prep school as a teenager, but was paralyzed by the racism he encountered. He failed his classes and returned home to become a welfare father at age 19. At one point he was homeless, living in his car, his self-esteem shattered.

Dyson eventually got himself back on track, attended a small black college in the South and joined the Baptist ministry. But his personal life was a wreck. His first marriage ended in divorce, as did his second, and he lost custody of his son, Michael, for years. All the while he struggled with the very issues he now writes about—what it means to be a black man in America when you can't find a job, provide for a family or make a loving relationship work.

Dyson's story has a happy ending. He regained custody of his son, who is now in college. He's remarried, solidly this time. He got his Ivy League doctorate, a tenured professorship and considerable acclaim as a writer and public intellectual. But he has one constant reminder of how it might have gone otherwise:

His brother, Everett, is now seven years into a life sentence for a brutal murder, a crime Dyson is convinced he didn't commit.

Nagging questions. Given this history, Dyson says, it's difficult to imagine losing touch with his less privileged past. It's part of what compels him to respect gangsta culture even as he criticizes its violence and misogynistic bent. But questions of authenticity still nag at him. How is it possible, he wonders, to make a lot of money, appear on *Oprah* and the op-ed page of the *New York Times* and still claim a connection to the ghetto?

Dyson's latest career move is in part an attempt to answer that question. He has decided to take an appointment at Columbia University's Institute for Research in African-American Studies. The institute's mission is to link the best of African-American scholarship with social responsibility and on-the-ground political solutions in local communities, including nearby Harlem. He believes his ideas have a powerful street-level resonance. "Postmodern theory of identity does help us appreciate the danger of fragmentation," he says, "but it also suggests the possibility of change. It says, think of yourself as a project, an experiment in the making. What you used to be you don't always have to be. That's a powerful and hopeful message we can teach to real black men."

BY WRAY HERBERT

Curriculum and Instruction in Multicultural Perspective

Curriculum and instruction includes all concerns relative to subject matter to be taught and pedagogical theory. All pedagogical theory is based on philosophical ideas regarding what is worth knowing and what actions are good. Every school curriculum is the product of specific choices among all those available. Since classroom teachers are the "delivery systems" for a curriculum, along with whatever texts are used, they have the opportunity to interpret and add their own insights regarding what they teach.

It is in the area of curriculum and instruction in the elementary and secondary schools, as well as in teacher education curricula, that a fundamental transformation must occur to sensitize all young people, including those living in isolated communities, to the multicultural reality of our national civilization. There are several different approaches to multicultural education in use today. Some school systems merely include the study of minority groups living in their area in elective or required courses. This is not the approach to multicultural education favored by current leaders in the field. Today, most experienced multicultural educators prefer a more holistic, inclusive approach to the subject—the infusion of multicultural themes into the entire life of the school and all possible course content. Such an inclusive approach to multicultural education seeks to help students and teachers to develop a sense of social consciousness, which, coupled with a more global and integrated conception of our social reality, will empower them to make more critical assessments than have been made in the past about such distinctions as the disparity between public democratic rhetoric and the reality of some social groups, which still are not accepted into society's mainstream.

An important focus of multicultural education is that a democratic nation has a moral responsibility to see that minority ethnic, cultural, or religious groups are not isolated or marginalized. What students learn informally in their communities about groups different from themselves can be misleading or incorrect. This is how our past sad heritage of racism and negative stereotypes evolved. There has been much progress in the area of civil rights in the past 40 years, but there has also been resurgent racism and intercultural misunderstanding. School is the one place where children and adolescents can daily learn an objective view of their culturally pluralistic national heritage—their present and future social reality. When students leave high school to go into military service, attend college, or begin careers in the corporate sector, government, or the arts, they may encounter a multicultural world very different from that of their local community or cultural group.

Teachers can help their students to recognize and respect ethnic and cultural diversity and to value the ways in which it enhances and enriches the quality of our civilization. Children and adolescents should also be made aware that each of them has the right to choose how fully to identify with his or her own ethnic or cultural group.

The essays in this unit provide a wide variety of perspectives on how to broaden the multicultural effort in

our schools. The authors seek to incorporate more inter-cultural and global content and experiences into the main body of curriculum and instruction. Educators will find that, taken together, these essays provide a sound basis for understanding what multicultural curriculum and instruction should be about. They are relevant to course work in curriculum and instruction, curriculum theory and construction, educational policy studies and leadership, history and philosophy of education, and cultural foundations of education.

Looking Ahead: Challenge Questions

How can teachers best teach about human ethnicity and culture?

How should teachers and students deal with xenophobic reactions when they occur?

What are the similarities and distinctions between a "culture" and an "ethnic group"?

Why might it be effective to integrate multicultural content into all aspects of a school curriculum?

What are the varying ways in which multicultural education is defined? Which model of multicultural education do you prefer?

What is the rationale for multicultural education in elementary and secondary schools? Should all students be exposed to it?

How can inservice teachers be better prepared to engage in multicultural instruction and learning experiences?

Becoming Multicultural
Focusing on the Process

By Hee-Won Kang
and Bonnie Dutton

Among the broad range of concerns that multicultural education encompasses, an important concern is helping students develop knowledge and understanding about different cultures and ethnic groups. Sometimes in multicultural education for that purpose, the focus is on teaching facts and information about different cultures and peoples directly through social studies, cultural capsules, and lessons.

But a significant portion of students' acquisition of knowledge about other cultures comes through experience, either direct through contact with members of different cultural and ethnic groups or vicariously through exposure to other cultures in literature and other media. In fact, multicultural literature has been recommended for illuminating experiences of the lives of members of different cultural groups and of portraying culture through information that is present in such aspects of stories as the setting, events, actions and words of characters, overall theme, etc. (Yokota, 1993).

Though valuable, sometimes the emphasis may be too much on providing such knowledge or exposure and not enough on the process of interpreting and acquiring such knowledge. An equally important concern in multicultural education is helping students develop what C.I. Bennett (1990) refers to as intercultural competence. Developing such competence means developing "the ability to interpret intentional communications…some unconscious cues… and customs in cultural styles different from one's own," as well as "building an understanding of how one is shaped by the values, priorities, language, and norms of one's culture" (Bennett, 1990, p. 293).

We need to focus as much on students' processes of interpreting and learning information about other cultures as we do on the information we provide or expose them to. Though exposure to direct and indirect experiences in other cultures is necessary, we also have to be concerned with how students interpret these experiences. Sometimes such exposure can result in misunderstandings and reinforcement of stereotypes.

The importance of helping students develop intercultural competence and the integration of such instruction within the range of instructional activities for multicultural education is the focus here. Discussions of how problems and misunderstandings can arise in interaction with different cultures will be followed by discussions of the kinds of activities that can be used to help students overcome problems, use effective strategies, and develop intercultural competence.

Hee-Won Kang is an associate professor in the School of Education at Sonoma State University, Rohnert Park, California; Bonnie Dutton is a professor in the School of Education and Human Development at California State University, Fresno.

From *Multicultural Education,* Summer 1997, pp. 19-22. © 1997 by Caddo Gap Press, Inc. Reprinted by permission of *Multicultural Education,* the magazine of the National Association for Multicultural Education.

Interpreting Oral and Written Text

In comprehending and interpreting communication, the knowledge, beliefs, values, and attitudes that we develop over our lifetimes through our experiences and interactions within our culture and society influence our perceptions and interpretations of events, situations, and the linguistic or non-linguistic actions of people. In interaction between this background knowledge and oral or written discourse, listeners and readers make inferences concerning interpretations of verbal and nonverbal acts (and the intentions underlying them) and interpretations of written text.

Particularly when communicators or authors and readers are from different cultural backgrounds, the potential for varying interpretations exist. That is why the process of adapting, changing, and refining interpretations is so important. In an excellent article on teaching multicultural literature, Reed Way Dasenbrock (1992) argues that too much emphasis may be placed on the knowledge that readers possess and not enough on the learning of knowledge, particularly in the context of reading cross-cultural texts.

In a discussion of Donald Davidson's theories, Dasenbrock outlines a process of communication and interpretation that acknowledges the importance of the background knowledge people use to initially create a set of expectations about the meanings of words another person will use in a communicative event. But Dasenbrock places the main emphasis on the adaptations and changes people make in their interpretations as they encounter differences between prior interpretations and information in the communicative context that does not fit these prior expectations and interpretations.

Collins, Brown, and Larkin (1980) describe a similar process of adaptation and change in interpretations of written text. Using background knowledge and accumulating amounts of information they encounter in text, readers continually construct and refine models of the text. Readers make inferences and interpretations and evaluate these in terms of their consistency with other information in the text and their own knowledge of the world as they refine their models of the text. When readers encounter conflicts between inferences or interpretations and information from the text, they may use certain strategies such as confirming, disconfirming, or refining previous inferences or interpretations. In short, they modify and refine their interpretations of the text as they encounter conflicts.

The process is similar in communicative events. Listeners make inferences and interpretations about what people say and mean. They also check whether their inferences and interpretations are valid in a number of ways. They can evaluate whether the inference or interpretation of an utterance fits in with information from various sources in the communicative context, such as what was said before or after the utterance, nonverbal signals such as facial expressions, known purposes of the speaker, the speaker's mental state or feelings as inferred from nonverbal or other information, accompanying contextual cues to meaning and intention, or with their expectations of what one might hear in particular situations or at particular points in the conversation (Sanders, 1987).

These are greatly simplified descriptions of the process as outlined by Dasenbrock, Collins *et al.*, and Sanders, but, ideally, this is generally what happens when individuals interpret oral or written text. But people are not always ideal interpreters. In evaluating the match between interpretations and other information in the communicative or written context, people do not always detect failures to infer meanings and intentions of others. As the degree of difference in the knowledge of communicators from other cultures increases, it gets more difficult and requires progressively more vigilance and cognitive effort to adjust and readjust interpretations of utterances against each other and information from other sources in order to detect and remedy errors (Sanders, 1987).

Also, even when students are able to recognize contradictions or inconsistencies between interpretations and other information in the written or oral text or context, they may not always use appropriate strategies to deal with the problem. Instead of disconfirming present or prior interpretations or raising alternative inferences when faced with a contradiction, readers may sometimes ignore the conflict or dismiss it as unimportant, or they may distort the new information to make it fit a previous inference or interpretation (Phillips, 1987; Kang, 1992).

Instead of adjusting the interpretation of a specific utterance to make it fit in with or cohere with interpretations of prior utterances or adjusting interpretations of prior or following utterances, students in communicative situations may make first impressions of others and then interpret new information selectively to fit in with these impressions, discounting or distorting new information that does not fit these impressions (Robinson, 1985, p. 71). Sometimes inaccurate inferences or interpretations made by students may be due not only to differences in the background knowledge upon which they are based, but also to too much focus on the behavior of the person being observed and not enough on external factors related to the context of the situation in which the behavior occurs (Robinson, 1985).

The attempts to infer what is being said and meant, to evaluate inferences, and detect and solve problems with inferences may be paralleled with the effort to infer rules and conventions of other cultures, infer background knowledge members of those cultures may rely upon, evaluate such inferences, and solve potential problems or contradictions with such inferences. People learn from encountering anomalies or inconsistencies between their inferences or interpretations and other information and incorporate what they learn not only in their refined models or interpretations of what is written or said but also in theories and hypotheses about the culture they are interacting with.

Repeated interactions with people from other cultures, observation of regularities and patterns of verbal and nonverbal actions that cohere, and detection and remedy of misunderstandings provide support for making inferences concerning some rules and conventions of expression in other cultures (Sanders, 1987). As we make and test hypotheses about other cultures through interaction with people or texts, we may continually revise and update the knowledge we are relying upon in the interaction itself.

The background knowledge that we use in understanding communication or written text is not necessarily static, but may be continually changing as we comprehend written and oral text. Inferences and interpretations that we make both to comprehend written and oral text as well as to understand and learn aspects of the culture may be continually added to the knowledge that we are using as we communicate or read. The same type of evaluation and problem-solving strategies discussed earlier may be utilized in the process of making and testing hypotheses that eventually may lessen the degree of differences in the knowledge that people bring to the communicative situation.

Helping Students Develop Intercultural Competence

We can see that the process of interpreting direct and indirect experiences in other cultures that the ability to deal with inconsistencies and to refine interpretations when necessary is important for not only comprehending oral and written discourse but also learning about other cultures. In order for our students to develop intercultural competence (the ability to interpret and learn from other cultures), we need to find approaches, techniques, and activities to help students develop:

♦ Awareness that things may not always be as they first seem, and that our own background knowledge and experience filters our perceptions.
♦ Awareness of the potential for different interpretations based on different cultural perspectives and tolerance for different perspectives.
♦ The ability to critically evaluate interpretations and perceptions of nonverbal and verbal behavior, both in terms of what is known and the immediate and/or extended context.
♦ The ability to recognize when previously made inferences or interpretations are inconsistent with other information.
♦ Effective strategies to deal with inconsistencies and contradictions.

There are a number of techniques and activities that have been designed to increase knowledge and awareness of similarities and differences in cultural perspectives. For example, H.N. Seelye (1976) introduces activities such as culture assimilators, in which descriptions of incidents of cross cultural interaction that produce miscommunications are followed by questions and feedback on answers, and culture capsules, in which explanations of cross-cultural differences are followed by questions and multi-media activities, to teach cultural concepts and increase awareness of different cultural perspectives. Robinson (1985) discusses how to help students learn to cope with potentially threatening cultural situations through a social learning approach that emphasizes mastery through modeling, observation of positive consequences, and graduated participation in modeled tasks. In reading, teachers may introduce activities that assess what knowledge students have before reading and then help students activate or construct knowledge that is considered useful or necessary for understanding a particular text. Teachers may use different activities to help students obtain sociocultural knowledge through which a more effective understanding of verbal and nonverbal actions and behaviors of people from other cultures can be developed.

There are plenty of other exercises, simulations, and activities for giving students exposure to different cultures and helping them develop cultural knowledge and awareness. Such practices are good, but there is not always someone around, particularly someone knowledgeable with different cultures, that can help students with problems in understanding. Though we can give students knowledge either before, during, or after such exposure to help them interpret and learn from these experiences, we also need to help students develop abilities to learn through such experiences on their own.

To help students develop the abilities to understand and learn about different cultures on their own as they interact with people or literature from other cultures, activities are needed that give students chances to reflect on their own and others' processes and strategies of comprehending and understanding verbal and nonverbal behavior as they try to interpret such interaction. In other words, activities that give students chances to reflect on and report inferences or interpretations of verbal and nonverbal behavior, listen to reports of other students, evaluate those inferences and interpretations, recognize inconsistencies or confirm interpretations, and effectively deal with inconsistencies are needed to help students develop the competence and strategies to understand and learn from experience in different cultural situations on their own.

One such activity that could be utilized is the Directed Reading Thinking Activity (DRTA) (Stauffer, 1975). The DRTA is an instructional format for teaching reading that focuses not only on the active comprehension of text, but also on the process of understanding (Walker, 1988). It encourages students to make inferences about what is happening and what is going to happen and then read the text to confirm or disconfirm them.

In the activity, groups of students silently read a story together and stop at points to make hypotheses and predictions, discuss why they made them, and also discuss justifications or support found in the story for making previous inferences. In the prereading stage of the activity, the group looks over the title and initial illustrations, then predicts what will happen in the story. In the active reading stage, the students read the portion of the story, then stop at predetermined points to discuss questions such as the following:

◆ What do you think is happening now?
◆ What makes you think so?
◆ What do you think will happen next?
◆ What makes you think so?

The activity can be adapted to explicitly include questions that elicit inferences about motivations, intentions, mental states, emotions, etc., underlying characters' verbal and physical behavior, if such inferences are not elicited by the above questions. After discussing these questions, students then silently read to the next stopping point in the text, seeking to find information that may either confirm or disconfirm their previous inferences or predictions. Individual interpretations, inferences, or predictions may be justified by information in the text or the students' background knowledge.

The emphasis in such an activity is upon students to evaluate their interpretations and gain exposure to other interpretations, not to conform or agree to a particular interpretation. The internal criteria for evaluating their own interpretations should be whether or not readers can justify to themselves their own interpretations, inferences, or predictions through evaluation of their consistency with other information in the context. During monitoring or consultations with different groups or in a final whole group or whole class discussion, the teacher should always be on the lookout for evidence that the students are ignoring contradictions, transforming information in the text to fit previous interpretations or inferences, or that they are unable to consider the context in which the action or event took place.

The teacher should take every opportunity to reinforce the use of appropriate problem-solving strategies, point out information in the text that may have been ignored or distortions that the students have made, and encourage students to evaluate their interpretations and inferences in light of information from text. If the teacher feels that students need more direction in developing the abilities to recognize inconsistencies and to employ appropriate strategies when encountering inconsistencies, he or she may, through joining the reading group or through incorporation of other instructional activities, help students to find supporting clues, show them how to move from the clues to the answer, and model appropriate problem-solving strategies, moving gradually from modeling this process to guided practice to independent practice (Pearson, 1985)

Such an activity can be adapted to take advantage of cross-cultural literature in helping students not only learn but also learn how to interpret and learn about other cultures. One of the main values of the DRTA is the sharing of diverse experiences and perceptions of students from a variety of cultural backgrounds from which everyone in the class can gain (Ruddell, 1993). Grouping students from different cultural or ethnic backgrounds and using stories written from various cultural perspectives that reflect different values and sociolinguistic conventions may elicit more of a variety of inferences and interpretations.

Through this type of activity, students may recognize that there can be different ways of interpreting a particular event or behavior and begin to develop an awareness of the relationship between culture and behavior, both linguistic and non-linguistic. The discussion among students need not focus only on the differences in the interpretations or inferences made at any part of the story, but also on the similarities between interpretations and inferences that may help lead to the realization that there are similarities as well as differences between different cultures and between individuals. It will also help students develop the skills to monitor their comprehension of the text and use the context and other information to confirm or disconfirm inferences about the intentions, knowledge, and social customs underlying verbal and nonverbal behavior.

This is only one example of the type of activity that can be used to help students develop the monitoring and problem-solving strategies to help them in their generation of inferences and interpretations of verbal and nonverbal behavior. For example, video can be used in activities similar to the DRTA. Open-ended role-plays or semiscripted dramas, if extended enough, can also utilize pauses in the activities for students to reflect on and discuss inferences, interpretations, and justifications for such. The main point is to use activities that encourage students to introspectively or retrospectively reflect on the processes of their interpretation of written and oral text as they comprehend such text.

Concluding Remarks

The concerns and activities discussed here are only one aspect of a range of concerns in helping student become multicultural, and the activities mentioned above are only a fraction of the different types of approaches, activities, techniques, and exercises to increase intercultural awareness and competence.

For example, affective factors can and do influence interpretations, and students may need help in coping with these factors, particularly in cultural situations perceived as potentially threatening. But the concerns and activities above should be integrated into programs whose objectives include student development of intercultural competence. The main thing is to provide opportunities for students to reflect on inferences or interpretations they have made and how they may be different or similar to those of people from different as well as similar backgrounds.

Students need encouragement and practice in justifying their interpretations of verbal and nonverbal actions, recognizing inconsistencies when they arise, and employing appropriate strategies to deal with such inconsistencies. In short, they need opportunities to develop intercultural competence.

References

Bennett, C.I. (1990). *Comprehensive multicultural education: Theory and practice (2nd. ed.).* Boston, MA: Allyn and Bacon.

Collins, A., Brown, J.S., & Larkin, K.M. (1980). Inference in text understanding. In Spiro, R.J., Bruce, B.V., & Brewer, W.F. (Eds.), *Theoretical issues in reading comprehension.* Hillsdale, NJ: Lawrence Erlbaum Associates, pp. 385–407.

Dasenbrock, R.W. (1992). Teaching multicultural literature. In Trimmer, J. and Warnock, T. (Eds.), *Understanding others.* Urbana, IL: National Council of Teachers of English, pp. 35-46.

Kang, H.W. (1992). Cultural interference in second language reading. *International Journal of Applied Linguistics,* 2(1), pp. 95-119.

Pearson, P. D. (1985). Changing the face of reading comprehension instruction. *The Reading Teacher,* 38, pp. 724-738.

Phillips, L. M. (1987). *Inference strategies in reading comprehension.* (Tech. Rep. No. 410). Urbana–Champaign, IL: University of Illinois, Center for the Study of Reading.

Robinson, G.L. (1985). *Crosscultural understanding.* New York: Pergamon Press.

Ruddell, M.L. (1993). *Teaching content reading and writing.* Boston, MA: Allyn & Bacon.

Sanders, R.E. (1987). *Cognitive foundations of calculated speech: Controlling understandings in conversation and persuasion.* New York, NY: State University of New York Press.

Seelye, H.N. (1976). *Teaching culture.* Skokie, IL: National Textbook Company.

Stauffer, R.G. (1975). *Directing the reading-thinking process.* New York, NY: Harper & Row.

Walker, B.J. (1988). *Diagnostic teaching of reading.* Columbus, OH: Merrill Publishing Company.

Yokota, J. (1993). Issues in selecting multicultural children's literature. *Language Arts,* 70(3), pp. 156-167.

Linda Jean Holman

Meeting the Needs of Hispanic Immigrants

Lessening the intimidation factor and removing the language barrier are two prescriptions for helping newly arrived immigrant families feel at home in your school.

*T*he exact proportion of the Hispanic population that is composed of new immigrants (both legal and illegal) is not easily determined, but the growing number of students enrolled in bilingual education programs indicates that the number is substantial. (See " 'Hispanic' Families.")

As an elementary school administrator in El Paso, Texas, for the past eight years, I have worked with many newly arrived families. In my present school, 43 percent of the 700 students have limited English proficiency; 85 percent of these families have recently moved to the United States. On the whole, children from newly arrived Hispanic families are highly motivated and hard-working students. Their parents have sacrificed a familiar way of life and moved to the United States in search of opportunities that are not available at home, including access to a system of free public education.

Students at Hillside Elementary School display their Reading Fair Projects.

Photo courtesy of Linda Jean Holman

Consider my first experience working with a newly arrived family: The son came to us at age 7 knowing very little English. By the time he left our school at the end of 5th grade, he was an outstanding student. With great pride, the school presented him with the Presidential Academic Fitness Award. His younger sister Erica was also an outstanding student. In 6th grade she qualified to enter the gifted and talented program. Their mother, Socorro, spoke only some English when we first met. At the end of four years, I observed her reading *Wuthering Heights* before a PTA meeting.

Recognize the Challenges

Motivation notwithstanding, recent immigrants may face special challenges that can affect their children's ability to succeed in school. Educators must recognize these challenges and understand how they may translate into special needs. Following are some of the proactive steps teachers can take to help Hispanic immigrant families make a successful transition to school.

■ *Lessen the intimidation factor.* Particularly if they do not speak English well, newly arrived Hispanic parents may feel intimidated by highly educated school personnel. Provide a warm, welcoming, and nonjudgmental reception. They may have questions and concerns; taking the time to listen and respond respectfully can open important avenues of communication. Personal outreach in the form of home visits, phone calls, and personal greetings at school events also will send a strong message of welcome.

During the first week of school last year, for example, our prekindergarten and kindergarten teachers held individual parent-teacher-child conferences. They held some meetings at the school and others in the students' homes. They scheduled evening conferences to accommodate working parents. Parent involvement increased as a result of the improved communication.

Always give parents your full attention in conferences and during conversations. If you are pressed for time when a parent approaches you, set a time when you can give his or her concerns your full attention. You may not have multiple opportunities to work with newly arrived parents, so make the most of each opportunity.

■ *Remove the language barrier.* Provide second-language instruction to teachers and staff members. Ensure that someone on your staff can speak Spanish. If there are multiple second languages in your school, develop a core of bilingual parent volunteers to help staff members communicate with the recent arrivals.

Educate your staff about bilingual education. Frequently, immigrant parents view total immersion as the quickest way for their children to learn English and, in turn, to succeed in school. However, a young child whose oral language testing indicates that he or she is dominant in a language other than English should probably participate in a bilingual or English-as-a-second-language educational program. Such programs build both native language and English proficiency.

■ *Realize that some parents will lack formal education.* Parents who have had limited schooling themselves will generally have difficulty helping their children with homework. Adjust homework assignments accordingly. Avoid using educational jargon and acronyms; they will have little meaning for these parents. And, keep in mind that some parents may not be literate in their native language. Arrange to assist them by providing information verbally, rather than in writing.

Recent immigrants may face special challenges that can affect their children's ability to succeed in school.

■ *Recognize that economic survival is a primary concern for many immigrant families.* Economic and time constraints may limit their ability to attend school conferences and parent meetings. Failure to appear for a conference may reflect financial concerns rather than a lack of interest in their child's progress. And if the family breadwinner is unemployed, a newly arrived family may have even greater problems.

One such family in our school was unable to pay the monthly utility bills. As a result, the family was living in a place that did not have electricity or running water. When the problem came to our attention, we helped the family arrange payment plans with the utility companies. As is frequently the case, this family did not know that help was available to them through various social service agencies.

■ *Validate parents' strengths.* Encourage Hispanic parents to work with their children in their native language. By reading to them and reinforcing verbal skills, parents will help their children build a strong foundation for second-language learning.

■ *Recognize that Hispanic families bring with them a rich social context.* Rather than trying to "acculturate" them, validate and encourage them to share their own cultures and backgrounds. Search for areas of expertise that parents can demonstrate at meetings, in class lessons, and at assemblies.

■ *Familiarize families with your school's procedures and organization.* Provide a video or tour of the school in their language to assist them in this effort. At the beginning of the year, you might want to hold parent meetings by grade level for this purpose. Your school may be very different from schools in the home country of new immigrants' parents. Provide an opportunity for parents to ask questions, express concerns, and obtain answers.

Working with immigrant families has provided me with some of the most rewarding experiences I've had as an educator. By familiarizing yourself and your staff with the circumstances, needs, and strengths of the children and providing families with a friendly, welcoming environment, you will be taking action to ensure a positive partnership. Your school will be a richer, more exciting and fulfilling place in which to work and learn.

References

"Hispanic Gains Lag Behind Rest of U.S., Census Says." (June 23, 1994). *El Paso Times*, p. 5A.

Natriello, G., E. McDill, and A. Pallas. (1990). *Schooling Disadvantaged Children.* New York: Teacher's College Press.

Ramírez, C. (November 25, 1995). "Poverty Cuts Children on the Border." *El Paso Times*, p. 1A.

Rueda R., and J. Mercer. (1985). "A Predictive Analysis of Decision-Making Practices with Limited English Proficient Handicapped" (Report No. 300-83-0273). Washington, D.C.: U.S. Department of Education (ERIC Document Reproduction Service No. ED 266 590).

Linda Jean Holman is Principal at Hillside Elementary School, 4500 Clifton Ave., El Paso, TX 79903.

"Hispanic" Families

The category "Hispanic," as established by the U.S. Bureau of the Census, encompasses a broad range of persons of Latin American and Spanish origin. Although sometimes viewed by policymakers as a homogeneous group sharing many similarities, the Hispanic community is actually composed of several groups. These include recent immigrants to this country, as well as individuals whose families settled in what is now the United States as early as the 1600s.

Almost 74 percent of the entire Hispanic population is concentrated in California, Texas, New York, and Florida (Natriello et al. 1994). In many urban school districts, Hispanic youngsters now make up most of the student population (Rueda and Mercer 1985).

Many Hispanic children come from lower socioeconomic backgrounds. According to 1990 U.S. Census Bureau data, approximately 40 percent of Hispanic children live in poverty, compared to 13 percent of Caucasian children ("Hispanic Gains" 1994). As many as 45.7 percent of Hispanic children in communities along the U.S.-Mexico border, which traditionally have a high proportion of new immigrant families, live in poverty (Ramírez 1995).   —*Linda Jean Holman*

Is English in Trouble?

By Stephen Krashen

The impression we get from the media is that immigrants today are not acquiring English; in fact it is sometimes claimed that they resist it.

Beard-Williams (1994), in an Op-Ed article in the *Los Angeles Times*, asserts, "At what point do we hold non-English-speaking persons accountable for their disinterest (sic) in learning the language of this country...." Turbak (1994), in *Reader's Digest*, writes about "the erosion of English" (p. 178) and claims that "LEP children often remain in native-language classes for several years, and some never learn English" (p. 178).

Reports such as these motivate proposals to protect the English language in the United States, including the proposal to make English our official language. In reality, immigrants, both children and adults, are not at all reluctant to use English, and are doing an incredible job of acquiring it. In fact, it is the home languages that are eroding.

I present here a brief survey of a very consistent body of research that shows that non-native speakers of English who live in the United States use English a great deal and have acquired it remarkably well. Acquisition of conversational English, however, does not necessarily entail the acquisition of academic English

Studies of Language Use

Many studies have confirmed the presence of intergenerational shift, the finding

—Stephen Krashen is a professor in the School of Education, University of Southern California Los Angeles, California

(Cummins, 1989), and schools can do a great deal to ensure the development of academic English.

that English language use is much more common among children than among parents, and that first language use is much more common among parents than children. Table 1 presents a series of studies documenting this shift. Among the significant results of the studies are these:

◆ Hispanics who are members of the younger generation report far more use of English, and less use of Spanish, than their parents (Laosa, 1975; Skrabanek, 1970), and those born in the U.S. use English more than they use Spanish (Lopez, 1978; Veltman, 1983).

◆ Analyses of data from the U.S. Census shows that about 500 of those with Spanish as a first language report more use of English as their language of communication (Veltman, 1983; Grenier, 1984).

◆ English is very strong among high school students (Sole, 1982; Veltman, 1983; Garcia & Diaz, 1992; Hakuta & d'Andrea, 1992), and is evident even among very young children (Laosa, 1984).

Studies of Language Proficiency

Language use may or may not be an accurate reflection of proficiency. As Pedraza and Pousada (1992) point out, a speaker "may be forced out of circumstances to use a language other than the one he manipulates best" (p. 257). In their study, the relationship between language use and proficiency was positive, but not perfect (see also Veltman, 1983).

In several studies, actual proficiency was examined. Despite differences in methodology, year the study was published, and location, the results are similar and con-

verge with the results of language use studies. The results (Table 2) include the following:

◆ A surprising number of Mexican-American children appear to be English dominant for conversational language at a young age (Carrow, 1971).

◆ More members of the younger generation report higher proficiency in English than in Spanish; for the older generation, more report higher proficiency in Spanish (Hudson-Edwards & Bills, 1980).

◆ As children grow up, they become more English dominant (Merino, 1983; Veltman, 1983), even in heavily Spanish-speaking areas (McConnell, 1985).

◆ Spanish ability remains fairly high in high school seniors in Florida, but their English ability is also high, and students rank themselves more highly in English writing than Spanish writing (Garcia & Diaz, 1992).

◆ For those born in the United States, the shift to English is typically complete by high school, and even for those who immigrate, English is often strong at this age (Veltman, 1983; Tse (1995, in press (a)).[1]

◆ The number of English-only speakers among Navajos increased significantly over a ten year period; the increase was most marked in the age 5 to 17 group, with English-only speakers increasing from 12 to 28 percent (Crawford, 1995).

◆ Fewer young people of Hispanic origin report Spanish to be their home language (Bills, Hernandez-Chavez, & Hudson, 1995).[2]

Misreporting the Facts

Misreporting the facts has contributed to the impression that immigrants are not acquiring English. McArthur (1993) reports statistics from the U.S. Census on English language development of people ages five and older in 1979 and 1989. According to her analysis of the data, "Almost half of the Spanish speakers...reported speaking English with difficulty in 1989..." (p. iii), a conclusion that certainly supports public opinion.

Krashen and McQuillan (1995) reanalyzed McArthur's data and came to very different conclusions. In the census, respondents were asked to rate their English on a four-point scale: "very well," "well," "not well," and "not at all." Strangely, McArthur, in summarizing the data, categorized all those who reported that they spoke English "well," "not well," and "not at all" as having difficulty with English. In other words, those who said they spoke English well were classified as having difficulty! Consider the 1989 results for native speakers of Spanish:

I speak English:

Very well	50.5%
Well	21.0%
Not well	19.7%
Not at all	8.8%

According to McArthur's categorization, it is indeed true that almost half have difficulty with English. But if we include those who say they speak English "well" as not having difficulty, we can conclude that over 70 percent do not have difficulty with English, and fewer than 9 percent don't speak English at all. This is very impressive, considering that the figures undoubtedly include new arrivals.

Hispanics are usually portrayed as the most reluctant to acquire English. McArthur's report says otherwise. There was no difference at all between Spanish speakers and speakers of Asian/Pacific Island languages in self-report of English competence:

first language	"very well or well"	"not at all"
Spanish	71.5%	8.8%
Asian/Pacific Isl.	72.3%	7.6%

The impression some people have that Spanish speakers are not acquiring English is due to the presence of new immigrants and visitors. But even they have done remarkably well in acquiring English. McCarthy and Valdez (1985) reported that among Mexican-Americans born in the United States, more than 90 percent said they were proficient in English (see also Veltman, 1983). Among the foreign born who are permanent residents of the U.S., over 75 percent said they spoke some English and nearly half said they spoke English well. About 25 percent of short-term and cyclical visitors said they spoke English well and over half reported some competence in English. McCarthy and

Table 1—Studies of Language Use

Mexican-Americans —Rural Texas
Language Used Socially

Generation	Mostly Spanish	Equal	Mostly English
Adults	68%	26%	6%
Ages 18-24	44%	42%	14%
Ages 10-17	31%	45%	24%

(adults: 268 households; 18-24: 80 households; 10-17: 145 households) (Skrabanek, 1970)

Mexican-Americans—San Antonio
Language Used Socially

Generation	Mostly Spanish	Equal	Mostly English
Adults	58%	33%	9%
Ages 18-24	25%	39%	36%
Ages 10-17	17%	37%	46%

(adults: 276 households; 18-24: 43 households; 10-17: 128 households) (Skrabanek, 1970)

Mexican-Americans (Austin), most born in U.S., 100 families
Language Used Informally

Generation	English	Spanish
Adults	26%	23%
Children (grades 1-3)	89%	1%

(does not include subjects who used both or mixture) (Laosa, 1975)

Cuban-Americans, most born in Cuba, 100 families
Language Used Informally

Generation	English	Spanish
Adults	9%	84%
Children (grades 1-3)	26%	40%

(does not include subjects who used both or mixture) (Laosa, 1975)

Married Chicano women in Los Angeles
Current Use of Spanish

Generation	n	Spanish	Both	English
first	493	84%	14%	2%
second	158	15%	19%	66%
third	239	4%	12%	84%

(first: born and raised in Mexico; second: born and raised in U.S., parents born and raised in Mexico; third: parents born in U.S.). (Lopez, 1978)

268 Cuban-American high school students, ages 14-18, 80% born in Cuba, most came to the U.S. before age 10
Language Preference

English	25%
Both	42%

"The entire sample claimed to have acquired English" (p. 260). (Sole 1982)

1976 Survey of Income and Education, 18,000 households, ages 4-17

Parental language	Percent English usual language
Navajo	17.3%
Spanish	52.4%
Other	53.4%

(Veltman 1983)

1976 Survey of Income and Education, ages 14 and older
English Usual Language

Home language	Foreign Born	U.S. Born
Spanish	29%	65%
Other	64%	94%

(Veltman 1983)

High school students

Home language	n	Home language used with friends
Spanish	3594	1.63
Other	1154	.89

(0=never; 1=sometimes; 2=about half the time; 3=mostly; 4=always) (Veltman 1983)

"People of Spanish mother tongue"
Use of Spanish as Main Language of Communication

Mexican American	48%
Puerto-Rican	57%
Cuban-American	68%
All groups	50%

(N=7,366) (Grenier, 1984)

84 Chicano families (San Antonio), most born in U.S.A.

Mother speaks to child in English	64.4%
Child speaks to mother in English	74.4%
Father speaks to child in English	62.7%
Child speaks to father in English	74.2%

(Mean age of children=2 years, 6 months) (Laosa, 1984)

Children in all English or bilingual programs, 690 families
Using English Only or Mostly English

	with adults	with siblings
older children	31%	40%
middle	30.5%	41%
young	27%	34%

(Wong-Fillmore, 1981)

59 Sixth graders in bilingual programs (El Paso)

Which language do you feel most comfortable speaking in? "Almost a third...felt more comfortable speaking Spanish" (p. 26). (Two-thirds prefer English or have no preference.) (Gersten, Woodward, & Schneider, 1992)

394 Cuban-American high school seniors (Florida)
Language Used: Spanish or Spanish with Some English

preschool	85%
junior high school	37%
senior high school	18%

(Garcia & Diaz, 1992)

308 Mexican-American high school students
Language Used with Peers

Arrived in U.S.	
after age 10	2.1
between 6-10	2.8
age 5 or younger	3.2
Born in U.S.	
both parents born in Mexico	3.7
one parent born in U.S.	4.3
one parent, grandparent born in U.S.	4.2

(1=Spanish; 5=English) (Hakuta & d'Andrea, 1992)

3 fourth graders in bilingual education; teacher speaks English, some Spanish
English Use in School Year

	Beginning of year	End of year
Sebastian	90%	100%
Raul	80%	92%
Christina	30%	40%

(Pease-Alvarez and Winsler, 1994)

Valdez concluded that "the transition to English begins almost immediately and proceeds very rapidly" (p. 28).

Do We Need Special Programs?

If English is acquired by immigrants, do we need special programs? To see how special programs can help, we first need to consider the conversational-academic language distinction.

Conversational versus Academic Language

Cummins (1989) makes the important distinction between "conversational" and "academic" language. Conversational language is the language of everyday interaction. It is heavily "contextualized," that is, aspects of the situation help make input comprehensible and reduce the necessity of adding information for the speaker. "Academic" language is the language of school, politics, science, and business, and is more "decontextualized," that is, it must be comprehended with less contextual help.

Studies showing acquisition of English and intergenerational shift typically deal with conversational language, not academic language. Children rapidly pick up conversational language, but this does not automatically mean the acquisition of academic language. In their study of 100 Latino high school students designated as being "at risk" of dropping out of school, Romo and Falbo (1996) reported that "almost all the students in our sample were comfortable speaking in English...yet, almost all students in our sample experienced a skills deficit in reading" (p. 9); although the students were in the seventh to eleventh grades, their average reading score was sixth-grade. In other words, they had conversational English, but not academic English.

Why ESL

It is true that given enough exposure to language in the informal environment, acquisition of conversational language will take place. ESL classes can make the pro-

cess easier, quicker, and less painful. According to current theory (Krashen, 1994), we acquire language when we get comprehensible input, messages we understand. The "outside world" will not always provide comprehensible input; for the beginner, it may be weeks until even simple messages are comprehensible. In a well-taught language class, however, a beginner can get 40 minutes of comprehensible input the first day. ESL classes can be very efficient for beginners.

Beyond ESL

ESL is very helpful, but it is limited to conversational language. For most people, however, conversational language is not enough. There are several ways of developing academic language, and all of them can be used at the same time.

The first is free voluntary reading (Krashen, 1993). It has been established that free reading—reading we do because we want to—is the major source of our reading ability, our vocabulary knowledge,

---

Table 2——Proficiency

Tested Proficiency

99 Mexican-American children ages 3 to 9, low SES (Houston)
Scores on Test of Aural Comprehension

Age	English	Spanish
3-10 to 4-3	65	56
4-4 to 4-9	72	46
4-10 to 5-3	79	62
5-4 to 5-9	78	68
5-10 to 6-9	95	67

(Similar items tested in English and Spanish versions, weaker language tested first.)(Carrow, 1971)

32 children, K-4, all "balanced bilinguals" at age 5

Category	Time 1	Time 2*
Spanish production		
past tense	87%	74%
relatives	100%	44%
subjunctive	70%	55%
English production		
word order	42%	93%
relatives	66%	85%
conditionals	53%	84%

(*two years later) (Merino, 1983)

Children ages 5-8, Texas (Heavy Spanish-speaking area)
Percentage Of Children Dominant* in English

Years in bilingual program	Percent
1	2%
2	7%
3	28%

Children ages 5-8, Washington State (Heavy English-speaking area)

Years in bilingual program	Percent
1	33%
2	60%
3	70%

*Higher English scores than Spanish scores on Peabody vocabulary test. (N (both studies)=approx. 700) (McConnell, 1985)

Self-Report of Proficiency

Mexican-Americans in Albuquerque (Martineztown, Spanish-speaking community)
Number Claiming "Good" or "Very Good" Ability

Generation	Spanish ability	English ability
Junior	33% (26/80)	81% (69/81)
Senior	85% (74/87)	47% (41/88)

(Senior=heads of households, spouses, siblings; Junior=children) (Hudson-Edwards & Bills, 1980)

High school students' self-rating of reading and writing of Home Language (L₁) and English (L₂)

L₁	n	reading L₁	reading L₂	writing L₁	writing L₂
Spanish	3594	1.94	2.57	1.71	2.51
Other	1154	1.56	2.62	1.37	2.55

(0=not at all; 1=not very well; 2=pretty well; 3=very well) (Veltman, 1983)

Mexican-Americans
Percent Describing Themselves as Monolingual English

Second generation	50%
First generation	over 25%

(McCarthy & Valdez, 1985)

Cuban-American high school seniors, Dade County, Florida

	Spanish	English
Understand	90%	85%
Speak	87%	78%
Read	79%	75%
Write	66%	80%

(Garcia & Diaz, 1992)

High school students' self-rating of reading and writing home language (L₁) and English (L₂)

L₁	reading L₁	reading L₂	writing L₁	writing L₂
Asian	3.1	3.0	2.8	2.8
Spanish (born in U.S.A.)	3.6	3.8	3.2	3.8
Spanish (foreign born)	3.9	3.1	3.8	3.1

(1=not at all; 4=very well) Sample sizes: Asian, L₁=62, L₂ = 59; Spanish (born in U.S.A.)=16; Spanish (foreign born)=19 (Tse, 1995, in press (a))

Navajo speakers
Percent Who Speak Only English

1980	7%
1990	15%

(Crawford, 1995)

1980 Census for 22 cites (samples presented here)
Percent Of "Spanish Origin" Claiming Spanish as Home Language

City	Adults	Youth (ages 5-17)
El Paso	97	93
Los Angeles	92	83
Sacramento	80	69
Denver	56	31

(Bills, Hernandez-Chavez, & Hudson, 1995)

Parent Evaluation

Children in all-English or bilingual programs, 639 families
Speaks First Language Poorly or Inadequately for Age

Older children	35%
Middle	42%
Young	43%

(Wong-Fillmore, 1991)

our spelling ability, vocabulary size, and ability to deal with complex grammatical constructions. Richard Rodriquez developed conversational language from interaction, but developed academic language by becoming a voracious reader. In *Hunger of Memory*, he reports, "I entered high school having read hundreds of books. My habit of reading made me confident speaker and writer of English." (Rodriquez, 1982, p. 63).

Suggesting free reading is easy, but limited English proficient children may have a hard time doing it, because of lack of access to books (Pucci, 1994). Developing and giving children access to high quality school libraries, doing sustained silent reading, and developing a taste for reading through literature classes are means of overcoming this problem.

A second way is to participate in "sheltered" subject matter classes, academic classes taught in English that are made comprehensible for the second language acquirer. Participants in these classes acquire a great deal of academic language as well as subject matter knowledge (Krashen, 1991).

A third way is the proper use of the child's first language. Instruction delivered in the primary language can have a profound effect on the development of academic English. First, the primary language can be used to teach subject matter—if children know subject matter, they will understand much more of what goes on in classes taught in English, resulting in more language acquisition as well as knowledge. Second, the primary language can be used to develop literacy, which transfers to the second language. There is evidence that programs that utilize the first language in this way are effective in promoting academic English language development (Krashen & Biber, 1988).

Summary and Conclusion

English is clearly not in trouble. Studies consistently show that immigrants are acquiring English quite rapidly and are using it a great deal. The fact that immigrants typically do acquire conversational English does not mean, however, that educational efforts are useless (see also Waggoner, 1989). ESL classes can facilitate the development of conversational language, while efforts to promote free reading, sheltered subject matter teaching, and properly designed bilingual programs can help in the development of academic language.

Notes & References

1. Note that in Tse's studies, foreign born Spanish speakers reported very high competence in their primary language. These students were, however, enrolled in classes in Spanish for native speakers of Spanish.
2. Additional evidence confirming that children become quite competent in English at a surprisingly fast rate is their reported ability to act as interpreters for parents and others in a short time. Tse (in press) studied 64 high school students who acquired English as a second language, and who spoke either Chinese or Vietnamese as a first language. Nearly 90 percent said they had "brokered"; 52 percent said they began brokering within one year after their arrival in the United States, and 62 percent began within two years (ten subjects did not indicate the age at which they started brokering and two were born in the United States).

Tse (1995) did a similar study of Spanish speakers currently in high school. 56 percent of her United States-born subjects began brokering by age ten, and all brokered by age 14. Among those born abroad, 13 percent brokered within two years, 38 percent within four years and 88 percent within five years.

Finally, McQuillan and Tse (1995), in their study of nine subjects, ages 18 to 29, reported that brokering began soon after arrival in the U.S.

Beard-Williams, D. 1994. We speak English in L.A.; Don't apologize. *Los Angeles Times*, December 1. 1994.
Bills, G., Hernandez Chavez, E., & Hudson, A. 1995. The geography of language shift: Distance from the Mexican border and Spanish language claiming in the Southwestern U.S. *International Journal of the Sociology of Language*, 114: 9-27.
Carrow, E. 1971. Comprehension of English and Spanish by preschool Mexican-American children. *Modern Language Journal* 55: 299-306.
Crawford, J. 1995. Endangered Native American languages: What is to be done, and why? *Bilingual Research Journal* 19: 17-38.
Cummins, J. 1989. *Empowering Minority Students*. Ontario, CA: California Association for Bilingual Education.
Garcia, R. & Diaz, C. 1992. The status and use of Spanish and English among Hispanic youth in Dade County (Miami) Florida: A sociolinguistic study. *Language and Education* 6: 13-32.
Gersten, R., Woodward, J, & Schneider, S. 1992. Bilingual Immersion: A Longitudinal Evaluation of the El Paso Program. Washington, DC: The Read Institute.
Grenier, G. 1984. Shifts to English as usual language by Americans of Spanish mother tongue. *Social Science Quarterly* 65: 537-550.
Hakuta, R. & D'Andrea, D. 1992. Some properties of bilingual maintenance and 1088 in Mexican background high-school students. *Applied Linguistics* 13: 72-99.
Hudson-Edwards, A. & Bills, G. 1980. International language shift in an Albuquerque barrio. In E. Blansitt and R. Teschner (Eds.) *A Festschrift for Jacob Ornstein*. New York: Newbury House. pp. 139-158.
Krashen, S. 1991. Sheltered subject matter teaching. Cross Currents 18: 183-189.
Krashen, S. 1994. The input hypothesis and its rivals. In N. Ellis (Ed.) *Implicit and Explicit Learning of Languages*. London: Academic Press. pp. 45-77.
Krashen, S. & Biber, D. 1988. *On Course: Bilingual Education's Success in California*. Ontario, CA: California Association for Bilingual Education.
Krashen, S. & McQuillan, J. 1995. Contrary to popular opinion: English language proficiency and school performance on speakers of other languages in the United States. *NABE News*, 18,6: 17-19.
Laosa, L. 1975. Bilingualism in three United States Hispanic groups: Contextual use of language by children and adults in their families. *Journal of Educational Psychology* 67: 617-627.
Laosa, L. 1984. Ethnic, socioeconomic, and home language influence upon early performance on measures of abilities. *Journal of Educational Psychology* 76: 1178-1198.
Lopez, D. 1978. Chicano language loyalty in an urban setting. *Sociology and Social Research* 62: 267-78.
McCarthy, R. & Valdez, R.B. 1985. *Current and Future Effects of Mexican Immigration in California*. Santa Monica, CA: The Rand Corporation.
McConnell, B. 1985. Bilingual education and language shift. In Elias-Olivares, L., Leone, E., Cisneros, R., & Gutierrez, J.(Eds.) *Spanish Language Use and Public Life in the United States*. New York: Mouton. pp. 201-215.
McQuillan, J. & Tse, L. 1995. Child language brokering in linguistic minority communities. *Language and Education* 9: 195-215.
Merino, B. 1983. Language 1088 in bilingual Chicano children. *Journal of Applied Developmental Psychology* 4: 277-294.
Pease-Alvarez, L. & Winsler, A. 1994. Cuando el maestro no habla Espanol: Children's bilingual practices in the classroom. *TESOL Quarterly* 28: 507-535.
Perdraza, P. & Pousada, A. 1992. Bilingualism in and out of school: Ethnographic perspectives on the determination of language "dominance." In M. Saravia-Shore & S. Arvizu (Eds.) *Cross-Cultural Literacy*. New York: Garland, pp. 253-272.
Pucci, S. 1994. Supporting Spanish language literacy: Latino children and free reading resources in schools. *Bilingual Research Journal* 18: 67-82.
Rodriquez, R. 1982. *Hunger of Memory: The Education of Richard Rodriquez*. New York: Bantam Books.
Romo, H. & Falbo, T. 1996. *Latino High School Graduation: Defying the Odds*. Austin, TX: University of Texas Press.
Skrabanek, R. 1970. Language maintenance among Mexican-Americans. *International Journal of Comparative Sociology* 11: 272-282.
Sole, C. 1982. Language loyalty and language attitudes among Cuban-Americans. In J. Fishman & G. Reller, (Eds.) *Bilingual Education for Hispanic Students in the United States*. New York: Teachers College Press. pp. 254-268.
Tse, L. 1995. Language brokering among Latino adolescents: Prevalence, attitudes, and school performance. *Hispanic Journal of Behavioral Sciences* 17: 180-193.
Tse, L. Prevalence of language brokering among linguistic minority students: The case of Chinese and Vietnamese students. *Bilingual Research Journal*. In press.
Turbak, G. 1994. Let's hear it in English. *Reader's Digest* 145, number 869, September, 1994: 177-180.
Veltman, C. 1983. *Language Shift in the United States*. Berlin: Mouton.
Waggoner, D. 1989. Spanish language futures in the US: A methodological critique. *NABE Journal* 13: 253-261.
Wong Fillmore, L. 1991. When learning a second language means losing the first. *Early Childhood Research Quarterly* 6: 323-346.

"Let Me Take You Home in My One-Eyed Ford"

Popular Imagery in Contemporary Native American Fiction

CONTEMPORARY NATIVE AMERICAN FICTION is replete with imagery of both traditional tribal and mainstream American cultures. While maintaining the sovereignty of individual tribes and their representative material cultures, American Indian authors nevertheless utilize popular imagery of the dominant culture to represent and reinscribe minority worldview. Placing familiar images in new and unfamiliar contexts engages the reader with specific Native American tribes while allowing indigenous people to preserve their individual, yet transforming, cultures. This imagery demonstrates the capacity of minority literature to be, paradoxically, both particular and universal. An examination of *Love Medicine* and *The Bingo Palace* by Louise Erdrich, *The Lone Ranger and Tonto Fistfight in Heaven* by Sherman Alexie, *Black Eagle Child* by Ray Young Bear, and *The Grass Dancer* by Susan Power reveals this paradox. Each novel is set within a traditional American Indian culture—Chippewa, Spokane, Mesquakie, and Dakota, respectively—and shows contemporary reservation life. Common images of tomahawks, automobiles, rock and roll, movies, and additional popular images unite artistically and humorously to portray modern American Indian life. These images critique modern American popular culture and reinterpret tribal traditions to represent the dynamics of American Indian cultural survival.

From *MultiCultural Review,* June 1997, pp. 38-44. © 1997 by Greenwood Publishing Group, Inc. (Greenwood Subscription Publications), Westport, CT. Reprinted by permission.

Robert Berkhofer, Jr.'s 1979 seminal study of the construction of Indian images in *The White Man's Indian* and the recently published collection of essays, edited by S. Elizabeth Bird, *Dressing in Feathers: The Construction of the Indian in American Popular Culture*, both address the objectification of indigenous peoples by dominant cultural forces. Objectification and stereotyping are disempowering because they preclude the voices and visions of Native peoples who can and should represent themselves. However, Native peoples are not immune to the imposition of culturally constructed interpretations and objects. When American Indians participate in these cultural images, the effect can be multilayered. [See Rayna Green, "The Tribe Called Wannabee: Playing Indian in America and Europe," *Folklore* 99/1 (1988): 30-35 and Philip J. Deloria, *Playing Indian: Otherness and Authenticity in the Assumption of American Indian Identity*, forthcoming, Yale Univ. Press.] On one hand, a young Navajo girl who wears a Pocahontas T-shirt can be colluding with Disney's cartooning of Native history and peoples. On the other hand, she can be buffooning racial ignorance, subverting the stereotype, and openly proclaiming her own awareness of the absurdity; she could be saying, "Look, I know the real scoop about this Pocahontas stuff" or "The world finally recognized the power of Indian women." Thus, a singular gesture, object, or stereotype is subject to multiple and cultural interpretations. When Native peoples reclaim the images that have been imposed on them, they not only assert and reappropriate power, but they also demonstrate the skills of cultural mediation that have enabled five hundred years of survival.

The contemporary reservation novels of Louise Erdrich, Turtle Mountain Chippewa, exemplify this reinterpretation and reinscribing of cultural stereotypes. While the Chippewa elements of *Love Medicine* (1984, new and expanded version, 1993) and *The Bingo Palace* (1994) emphasize the uniqueness of that particular Native American culture, less obvious are iconic images of mainstream America woven throughout the novels: pickled eggs, pies, fishing hats, kitschy Indian art, Polar Bear refrigeration trucks, avocado green Sears appliances, learning enrichments, Sesame Street, and cars. Placed in a Native American context, these signs are given new meanings, disclosing the many dimensions of the novels. The reappropriated imagery brings home to a tribal center the characters who mediate the emblems of many cultures, yet maintain their individuality.

In *Love Medicine* Nector Kashpaw embraces the emblems of popular culture but survives their tempta-

> ## Contemporary Native American fiction is replete with imagery of both traditional tribal and mainstream American cultures

tions of assimilation and makes those images his own. As a youth he leaves the reservation for the celluloid promises of Hollywood. His language of survival refutes the tragic stereotype of the Vanishing American. He says:

I got hired on for the biggest Indian part. . . . right off I had to die.

"Clutch your chest. Fall off that horse," they directed. That was it. Death was the extent of Indian acting in the movie theater.

So I thought it was quite enough to be killed the once you have to die in this life, and I quit. (123)

Nector's short-lived acting career occurs on the screen, where many mainstream Americans encounter some of the most outdated and racist stereotypes of Native peoples. His refusal to fulfill the role allows not only his personal survival but inspires his search for meaning beyond celluloid images.

Nector's next career pursuit is to become the nude noble savage model for a painter. He says:

I could not believe it, later, when she showed me the picture. *Plunge of the Brave* was the title of it. Later on, that picture would become famous. It would hang in the Bismarck state capitol. There I was, jumping off a cliff, naked of course, down into a rocky river. Certain death. Remember Custer's saying? The only good Indian is a dead Indian? Well from my dealings with whites I would add to that quote: "The only interesting Indian is dead, or dying by falling backwards off a horse." (124)

Who cannot envision Nector's portrait? Erdrich's description is overlaid with images of Cyrus Dallin, Frederic Remington, The End of the Trail, and K-Mart faux Indian blue light special imitations. Nector exposes the stereotyped fallacies of this popular visual image and rejects its fatalism. Even though he participates, he imagines he would "fool that pitiful white woman and survive the raging water" (124). He returns home to tribal place and community. Erdrich turns the image into a metaphor of survival.

Nector misattributes the aphorism of the good and dead Indian from Phillip Sheridan to George Armstrong Custer. This identifies the intersection of popular culture with real history on the plane of the Plains battlefields where America has fixated its attention to Indians. Nector inverts the "all Indians are alike" stereotype by failing to distinguish the genocidal Army officers.

Another reappropriation of popular imagery occurs with the numerous cars that careen through Erdrich's novels. In a twist on the historic warrior pony, the automobile, sign of "advanced" technology, becomes a mode of mediation. In *Love Medicine*, Henry Lamartine, Sr., stalls his car on the railroad tracks, ending his life. Lyman Lamartine drives his red convertible into the river after witnessing Henry, Jr., drown. Lynette seeks refuge in the car that her husband, King, violently attacks. Lulu Nanapush Lamartine seduces Nector Kashpaw in a car, but Marie Lazarre, whom he marries, entices him in the wilderness. Gordie Kashpaw's reconciliation to the memory of his wife June is mediated by the transforming deer he hits with his car while driving drunk. Gerry Nanapush and his son, Lipsha Morrissey, reunite in June's blue Firebird, and again, in a stolen vehicle in *The Bingo Palace*.

In an early critical article about *Love Medicine*, Marvin Magalaner suggests a perilous assimilation:

[The] movement of the young Chippewas from fishing and swimming to reckless driving in automobiles signals the encroachment of a mechanical and impersonal civilization upon the natural environment of the families.

Magalaner's assessment assumes an unnatural historicism, a preservation of tradition in circumstances marked by dynamism and change. Indeed, he fails to see that the "res rod" (reservation hot rod) has become an emblem of reappropriation. Rather than a simple symbol of encroaching mechanism and modernism, the car is an adaptive mode, translating and modulating the lives of the characters as they establish Chippewa identity in the contemporary world. Erdrich, emphasizing the varied resonance of her symbol, says:

The cars really become sort of repositories for the souls of the dead in this book, and they're also shelter, they're many things. We've lived with cars that are alter-egos through the years. (Bonetti, 90)

Erdrich expands the automotive image in *The Bingo Palace* with a chapter titled "The Bingo Van." Taking advice from his mother's ghost and hoping to impress powwow dancer Shawnee Ray, Lipsha Morrissey is obsessed with winning the bingo grand prize, a converted van, a representation of the American dream:

> **When Native peoples reclaim the images that have been imposed on them, they not only assert and reappropriate power, but they also demonstrate the skills of cultural mediation that have enabled five hundred years of survival**

It has every option you can believe—blue plush on the steering wheel, diamond side windows, and complete carpeting interior. The seats are easy chairs, with little built-in headphones, and it is wired all through the walls. You can walk up close during intermission and touch the sides. The paint is cream, except for the design picked out in blue, which is a Sioux Drum border. In the back there is a small refrigerator and a padded platform for sleeping. It is a starter home, a portable den with front-wheel drive. . . . A four wheeled version of North Dakota. (63, 80)

Lipsha plays bingo nightly in his ritualized quest for the van. Though he finally wins the van, his triumph is short-lived. He has an encounter with some Montana rednecks he previously insulted. He describes the result:

My bingo van is dented on the sides, kicked and scratched, and the insides are scattered. Ripped pieces of carpet, stereo wires, glass, are spread here and there. . . . I force open a door that is bent inward. I wedge myself behind the wheel, tipped over at a crazy angle, and I look out. The windshield is shattered in a sunlight burst, a web through which the world is more complicated than I thought, and more peaceful. (83)

Lipsha's ideal material object has become a res rod, an indication that he cannot escape the reservation or his tribal heritage. Yet this image, along with the car images from *Love Medicine*, become mediators in the rites of passage. One reason Lipsha is in the wrong place at the wrong time is because he abandons his tribal and communal responsibilities by refusing to help Shawnee Ray and her sick baby. The wrecked van is a reminder of this failure. Erdrich uses the automobile imagery to demonstrate the power and desire for mobility and economic good fortune. At the same time the cars become spaces where characters encounter specific self-revelations. Ironically, Lipsha will make his final appearance in the novel in a stolen car, snow falling, and headed for apparent disaster. Erdrich writes about survival, though, and her most recent novel, *Tales of Burning Love*, confirms that Lipsha survives.

In the chapter from *Love Medicine* entitled "The Tomahawk Factory," Erdrich satirizes the mass marketing of stereotypical Indian goods. Entrepreneur Lyman Lamartine, son of Nector Kashpaw, plans a "tribal souvenir factory, a facility that would produce fake arrows and plastic bows, dyed-chicken feather headdresses for children, dress-up stuff" (303). However, by the time the tribal elders—including Lyman's mother, Lulu Lamartine, and Nector's widow, Marie Kashpaw—have their say, the factory has evolved into an upscale producer of "museum-quality" pieces run by a clan-organized work force. Personal rivalry between the two women elders, Lulu and Marie, erupts. Lyman describes the demise of Anishinabe Enterprises:

> The factory blew up. Order popped like a bubble. Kyle Morrissey whacked a friend of the Pillagers, Billy Nanapush, with an authentic reproduction of a Plains coup stick and, worse yet to a Chippewa, called him a puppy eating Sioux. Billy responded by pushing his press over on Kyle's girlfriend, Mary Fred, who threw her feathers aside, rolled out from under the machine, and came up swinging one of the light bone war clubs Felix Pukwan had put together. The head flew off, and Mary Fred gouged, whacked, and thrust at all in her path with the bared stick. . . . Rubber hatchets, dowels, leather pouches, flew through the air. (319)

Against the backdrop of personal conflict and intertribal antagonisms, the commercialization of Indian goods subverts stereotypes. Erdrich's characters take the cheapest clichés, the desires of the American public to possess objects that represent Indian otherness, and comically turn them into emblems of power and reappropriation. Although the enterprise fails, the tribe survives. Its members' economic situation may not be as secure, but they have reclaimed their culture through clan and family relationships instead of constructed material objects.

Erdrich's use of visual stereotypes, cars, and Indian crafts demonstrates the tensions between indigenous and mainstream cultures. Her characters survive by reappropriating images with humor and grace. Likewise, Spokane/Coeur D'Alene author Sherman Alexie uses American mainstream images, particularly rock and roll, to reveal his characters in *The Lone Ranger and Tonto Fistfight in Heaven* (1993), a collection of stories with recurring characters and themes.

As the title of his book indicates, Alexie condenses popular imagery with unexpected twists. A prime example is the chapter "Because My Father Always Said He Was the Only Indian Who Saw Jimi Hendrix Play 'The Star-Spangled Banner' at Woodstock." The title itself introduces a story of deconstructive images: Jimi bending, twisting, and screeching the National Anthem, playing notes not on the staff and rhythms outside the meter, rock-and-roll icon colliding with national icon, a gathering of indistinguishable nonconformists in the chaos of

the 1960s, all set against the backdrop of a lone Indian and the indeterminate narrative voice attributing the incident to the narration of the father.

In the first sentence of the story, the narrator identifies the unique role of Indians at the time: "During the sixties, my father was the perfect hippie, since all the hippies were trying to be Indians" (24). In a multilayered inversion, hippies represent the mainstream culture that appropriates images, not realities, of Indians. By joining the hippie community at Woodstock, the father reinterprets the image. He connects with the anti-image of Jimi, who also grew up in Washington state. Not only does the father capture this Woodstock moment but he ritually relives it by the playing and replaying of a cassette tape. As the narrator describes:

> Jimi Hendrix and my father became drinking buddies. Jimi Hendrix waited for my father to come home after a long night of drinking. Here's how the ceremony worked:
> 1. I would lie awake all night and listen for the sounds of my father's pickup.
> 2. When I heard my father's pickup, I would run upstairs and throw Jimi's tape into the stereo.
> 3. Jimi would bend his guitar into the first note of "The Star-Spangled Banner" just as my father walked inside.
> 4. My father would weep, attempt to hum along with Jimi, and then pass out with his head on the kitchen table.
> 5. I would fall asleep under the table with my head near my father's feet.
> 6. We'd dream together until the sun came up. The days after, my father would feel so guilty that he would tell me stories as a means of apology. (26)

The ritual initiates stories of reconciliation. Even though the ritual is orderly and numerically linear, it initiates the randomness of connecting lives through storytelling. The ritualized storytelling and music enable the child, Victor, to connect with his alcoholic parents and confront his feelings of alienation.

> "You know," I said to my father after the song was over, "my generation of Indian boys ain't ever had no real war to fight. The first Indians had Custer to fight. My great-grandfather had World War I, my grandfather had World War II, you had Vietnam. All I have is video games." (28)

Victor cannot connect to real history or his family except through pop culture, and Jimi becomes the mediating figure. Victor and his father make a pilgrimage to Seattle to visit Jimi's grave, where Victor observes that

Jimi died at a younger age than Jesus Christ. Through Victor and his father, we hear Jimi in a way we have never heard him before; we see, through these Spokane Indians, a side of American life and contemporary history we have not seen. This leads us to question history and cultural realities generally.

Alexie uses additional images of popular culture, from 7-11 stores to Creamsicles to basketball to Detectives Clayton and Moore, and back again, and always to rock and roll. He develops the music metaphor in his more recent novel, *Reservation Blues*, in which the same character, Victor, returns to seek the lost chord of Jimi Hendrix.

Ray Young Bear also employs rock-and-roll imagery in his novel *Black Eagle Child: The Facepaint Narratives*. In a semi-autobiographical story that integrates Mesquakie language with English as a second language narrative, Young Bear traces the life and experiences of Edgar Bearchild. Young Bear begins the book with popular imagery by discussing the multi-leveled meaning of national holidays.

> The Thanksgiving party at the Weeping Willow Elementary School had just concluded with the same lethargic atmosphere it started with. . . . tribal members were keenly aware affairs such as Christmas, Halloween, and Easter were meaningless. More so when wrapped gifts and fine grotesque masks were unnecessary expenditures. (1)

Young Bear is especially ironic by beginning with a Thanksgiving celebration at an elementary school. November is the month when tired stereotypes are trotted out. Children learn about Massasoit and Squanto, make tipis or paper garbage bag vests. Little attention is given to tribal distinctions, the rest of the Wampanoag story, or contemporary Indians. Misinformation is rarely corrected, and many people carry noble savage stereotypes into adult perceptions of Native peoples. The same holiday has varied implications depending on one's cultural point of view. For mainstream American culture, it represents affluence and historical tradition. Of course most Americans are not aware that many Native peoples celebrated an annual harvest feast while the Puritans eschewed such ritual celebration. Thanksgiving did not become a regular national holiday until Abraham Lincoln was president. To stimulate the national economy, Franklin Roosevelt designated the holiday as the fourth Thursday of November.

Nevertheless, Young Bear notes that national holidays celebrate prosperity and materialism. He contrasts material comforts with the poverty of reservation life, Christianity with Native experience: "even [the son of God] was far away from our despair, like the turkeys, stuffing, and cranberries that were absent from most tables" (2). The emblems of Thanksgiving are not shared but are markers of cultural divisions.

Young Bear's observations are accurate, but to polarize images through cultural interpretations may be misleading. Despite the divergent readings of Thanksgiving, it is a touchstone for common hopes. The Mesquakie do not boycott the Thanksgiving festivities, but use them as an opportunity to reappropriate their own concerns, as in this invocation:

> The elder['s] opening prayer touched all aspects of tribal life. He mentioned the need for people of all faiths to cooperate, and he asked for God to care for the ill whether they were present or elsewhere. He also asked for the safe return of sons in the armed forces overseas. He concluded Indians basically had little to be thankful for on this national holiday, but what was crucial was continuation of our culture. (18)

The chapter "Alfred E. Neuman Was an Arsonist" details Bearchild's eighth-grade adventures with high school senior Dolores Fox-King, her love notes, his uncle's diary, and a *MAD* magazine collection. These diverse writings lead to his appreciation of written language. Again, the personal discovery is mediated through rock and roll:

> In spite of the pleasure derived from my uncle's bizarre diary passages, I still regretted setting the artistically folded Fox-King notes ablaze, not because of what they once meant but how well they were written. They would begin with the opening lyrics of popular rock-and-roll songs, and there was always a connecting theme to our own turmoil. The most memorable was "Baby Love" by the Supremes. Listening to Diana Ross would forever remind me of the room given and lost in the dresser for Alfred E. Neuman. . . . (53-54)

Edgar Bearchild's trickster-like adventures exceed the impishness of the *MAD* magazine character. Edgar places himself in the role of madman and anarchist as he questions why historical narratives taught at Luther College do not include traditional stories. He then retells a Mesquakie sacred story of Boy Chief. He recollects his being the youngest member of the tribe to be treated for alcoholism and the stir this caused in the community. Juxtaposed against Bearchild's antics are Uncle Severt's diaries, which suggest the invasion of "extraterrestrials in the guise of Scandinavians" (51). These seemingly unconnected and bizarre sets of events and images are bound by the tribal cohesiveness of the Black Eagle

Child people. The disruptiveness of American pop culture mainstream bad boy, Alfred E. Neuman, is surpassed by Edgar Bearchild, who rebelliously reacts to his environment and tribe, as do many young Indians. Yet Edgar recovers and finds a voice to tell the stories by embarking on his writing career in the *Black Eagle Child Quarterly*.

Alfred E. Neuman and Diana Ross become touchstones connecting mainstream culture to Indian communities. They also become inverted as Young Bear presents these images again in the Black Eagle Child tribal experience. "The Introduction of Grape Jell-O" reveals tensions between Native beliefs and Christianity as the sweet dessert becomes a bribe for Edgar to attend Sunday School and to portray Joseph in the Christmas pageant.

Like Sherman Alexie, Young Bear utilizes images of rock and roll. The chapter that describes Bearchild's experience at college in California is titled "The Year of Jefferson Airplane." Although there are no specific references to the rock group in the chapter, its epigraph is from a Jefferson Airplane lyric (which also alludes to Alice in Wonderland) and telescopes transformational events in Bearchild's coming of age. Later in the chapter, Bearchild alludes to popular music by listening to the "refreshing" blues of John Lee Hooker. He also associates a girl he meets with Rita Hayworth and the Marty Robbins lyric: "Out in the West Texas town of El Paso/ I fell in love with a Mexican girl."

Ray Young Bear tells his story in English, and through popular imagery he shows how Mesquakie interact in the modern world. He presents Mesquakie tradition through his Native language and by reinterpreting symbols of mainstream culture.

Susan Power employs images from powwow culture to show how her Dakota characters mediate modernity in *The Grass Dancer*. The contemporary grass dancer is one whose fringed yarn costume has replaced traditional grass. The grass dancer metaphor bridges current reservation life with historical and mythic characters who all converge in the closing pages as Harley Wind Soldier and his mother, Lydia, find voices to sing their songs and tell their stories. Lydia reappropriates her heritage by reconstructing her great-grandmother's buckskin dress from a display in the Chicago Field Museum in order to participate in the powwow.

The powwow itself is also a space where historical rituals have transformed themselves into modern social structures. Participants symbolically alter their appearance when they change from Nikes and Levis to traditional feathered, boned, and yarned clothing. Ancestral songs are electronically amplified; lyrics (like the powwow song in the title of this article) infuse the contemporary into traditional vocals; the modern arena is furnished with tipis and arbors; make-up sticks have replaced organic face paints. As Power relates, the formal structure of the powwow begins with an invocation, often Christianized. The audience watches from their lawn chairs. In the modern powwow, grass dancing is no longer gender specific, and a woman can participate.

In addition to Power's detailed description of the powwow and how it mediates past and present for the characters, specific allusions incorporate contemporary popular imagery. The novel begins with the absurd irony of two Dakota characters listening to Patsy Cline's "Crazy" and speculating on a revival of Buffalo Bill's Wild West Show. The perceptive reader recalls that Buffalo Bill employed Sitting Bull and other survivors of the Battle of Greasy Grass to recreate ritually Custer's Last Stand for a popular audience. Powers inverts the image by suggesting the Dakota Indians claim the right to exploit popular imagination in the Wild West show.

Popular media become the means by which Charlene Thunder can connect to her grandmother's mystical powers:

> Charlene identified with Darrin from the television show *Bewitched*. He tried so hard to keep witchcraft out of his house, but his witch wife, Samantha, pulled him into the magic and rattled his mortal brain. Charlene sometimes talked to the TV set, addressing herself to the pretty blond wife with the twitching nose. "You'll give him an ulcer if you keep it up." (33)

What was an icon of situation comedy suddenly becomes more real when associated with the mystical powers of Charlene's grandmother. As the events of the novel unfold and characters tap into spiritual powers, commonly known characters of fantasy television programs become reinscribed into the mythic realities of tribal and material culture.

Like Louise Erdrich, Sherman Alexie, and Ray Young Bear, Susan Power presents the particularity of her own Dakota people and recognizes tribal sovereignty. At the same time each author shows the influence of and interaction with popular culture. Yet by presenting these images in tribal experiences, these authors take a commonality and make it particular. In her essay "Where I Ought to Be: A Writer's Sense of Place," Erdrich suggests:

> Whether we like it or not, we are bound together by that which may be cheapest and ugliest in our culture but which may also have an austere and resonant beauty in its economy of meaning. (23)

That economy of meaning is found in automobiles, in rock and roll, and especially in images of stereotypical Indians. When these authors take popular images of

Indians and present them from a Native viewpoint, the racism of stereotyping is disempowered. This reappropriation of Indian stereotypes and reclaiming of mainstream images are tools of survival.

WORKS CITED

Alexie, Sherman. *The Lone Ranger and Tonto Fistfight in Heaven*. New York: The Atlantic Monthly Press, 1993.

———. *Reservation Blues*. New York: The Atlantic Monthly Press, 1995.

Berkhofer, Robert, Jr. *The White Man's Indian: Images of the American Indian from Columbus to the Present*. New York: Vintage, 1979.

Bird, S. Elizabeth, ed. *Dressing in Feathers: The Construction of the Indian in American Popular Culture*. Boulder, Colorado: Westview Press, 1996.

Bonetti, Kay. "An Interview with Louise Erdrich and Michael Dorris." *The Missouri Review* 11 (1988): 19-99.

Erdrich, Louise. *The Bingo Palace*. New York: HarperCollins, 1994.

———. *Love Medicine*. New York: Holt, Rinehart & Winston, 1984. New and Expanded Version. New York: HarperCollins, 1993.

———. *Tales of Burning Love*. New York: HarperCollins, 1996.

——— "Where I Ought to Be: A Writer's Sense of Place." *New York Times Book Review*: July 28, 1985, 1, 23-24.

Magalaner, Marvin. "Louise Erdrich: Of Cars, Time, and the River," in *American Women Writing Fiction*. Mickey Pearlman, ed. Lexington: The Univ. Press of Kentucky, 1989.

Power, Susan. *The Grass Dancer*. New York: Putnam, 1994.

Young Bear, Ray. *Black Eagle Child: The Facepaint Narratives*. Iowa City: Univ. of Iowa Press, 1992.

P. Jane Hafen (Taos Pueblo) is Assistant Professor of English, University of Nevada–Las Vegas and Frances C. Allen Fellow, D'Arcy McNickle Center for History of the American Indian, Newberry Library.

Success for Hispanic Students

A 14-year veteran of teaching them describes his experiences.

By Ted Oviatt
From *The Hispanic Outlook in Higher Education*

DON'T all of our prejudices emanate from the people we happen to know, or don't know? Knowing even one person who has been held back or kept out by discrimination can evoke both sympathy and indignation. Knowing no one who is still an outsider too often leads to ignorance, apathy, and senseless hostility.

After 40 years of teaching, the last 14 in downtown Los Angeles, California, I have come to know many Hispanic and Asian students and their families, and I have been impressed by the values we share—honesty, hard work, and a genuine concern for others.

I have been saddened by the growing tension in this country, based on a melange of sincere desire to do the right thing by everyone (let's have a law that says there will be no discrimination, period), American materialism, and, especially, a deep-rooted ignorance of what the newest U.S. arrivals, legal or illegal, can offer this society.

My suburban friends are always surprised to hear that 65 percent of the graduates of my high school go on to college, that so many of our college graduates are making real contributions, and that I like my teaching and my students so much. I rave about their achievements because I, too, am amazed by what they accomplish.

As with wealthier, suburban kids I have taught, success comes in different ways, built on different strengths; but the successes have been extraordinary given the economic, linguistic, and environmental obstacles for the teenager who attends school in Los Angeles' Rampart district, famous for its crime rate and gang activity.

Ted Oviatt has been a teacher for 40 years, the last 14 in downtown Los Angeles, California, public schools.

As in any school, our parents run the gamut from supportive to destructive, and we see the customary aberrations of kids who succeed in spite of parents who, knowingly or not, do everything possible to undermine their chances. Some families provide such strong support that you can tell their kids will never fail. Others, sadly, don't know how to help their children achieve their goals.

With or without parents, our second-language, immigrant students have made us proud. Several of our finest teachers are graduates of our school who returned specifically in order to give back to the community.

Alex Carmona, a graduate of the University of California at Los Angeles, came from Mexico in junior high with one piece of advice from his father, who had only a second-grade education but a big heart and a knack for parenting: "Always go to school and learn. It is the way to success." Alex listened, studied, and graduated with good grades and excellent times as a distance runner. Undocumented at the time, he attended a small college in San Diego for two years, did well, became legal, and transferred to UCLA. Today he is a proud husband and father, an effective and creative teacher, and one of the most hardworking members of our staff, an excellent role model.

Patty Pacheco, a 1992 graduate from El Salvador who was documented, enjoyed few special advantages, worked hard, went all the way to fourth-year French, and was accepted to Wellesley College. She graduated with a double major in French and Spanish and got a Mellon Minority Undergraduate Fellowship that will help her fulfill her dream of teaching French and Spanish literature at the university level.

Another future teacher, **Lidia Lopez** of Sonoma State University, is spending the 1996-1997 school year studying in Spain, having raised $10,000 by working and soliciting contributions. No stranger to hard work on top of her school commitments, Lidia has been active in extracurricular activities in high school and college, maintained a better than 3.0 average, and worked since age 16 in jobs ranging from housecleaning to clerical work. Her mother is a single parent with six other children. How many full-time students will work two jobs and actively go out fund-raising to meet what must have seemed an impossible dollar total so she might expand her perspective and become a better-informed, more interesting teacher?

Stanley, a tough little guy who came to us with the right talent but the wrong attitude, found some help at school, but could always count on a firm, loving mother as his rock foundation. He was obviously bright but not very interested in studying. Later I found that he was one of our more active graffiti artists. I was fortunate to have him in both English and history. He found out how bright he was and became a very good student.

At barely 120 pounds, he went out for football, adding to his developing sense of discipline. As a senior, he was a starting defensive safety, with 10 tackles in one game. He became the school's pole-vault record-holder, also adding points in the hurdles. The

Reprinted with permission from *The Education Digest*, April 1997, pp. 48-51. Condensed from *The Hispanic Outlook in Higher Education*, January 3, 1997, pp. 7-9. © 1997 by Prakken Publications, Inc., Ann Arbor, MI.

road was open to an Educational Opportunity Program (EOP) scholarship at California State Polytechnic University at Pomona. He is now a junior doing well in the classroom and on the track.

Elizabeth was a gang kid when I first knew her, and she hated me because I made her be quiet. I nagged her as I found out how smart she was, and—probably worst of all—I took her makeup away. In spite of the chance to work on her two hours a day, I made little progress until spring, when two of her girlfriends were killed. They were wearing the wrong jackets in the wrong place.

Elizabeth, whose parents never worried about her performance in school and undermined her recovery by taking her out of school whimsically, took a step back, at age 14, and looked at the situation. "I don't think I want this for my life," her voice said. She started to study; her enemies, like me, became friends almost overnight.

By twelfth grade she was an excellent student and a class leader. When she was turned down for an EOP scholarship, I had a fit. Our college counselor joined the fight, and after three reviews of her application (and three rejections), Elizabeth was finally accepted at University of California at Riverside.

Her parents did not want her to go to college: "It went better than I expected. Nobody said anything. It was just as if someone died in the family." She took the Riverside summer bridge program, excelled, and was one of their cover students for the next year's brochure. Elizabeth did well for four years, incorporating marriage and a baby into the experience, still graduating with a degree in business.

Teferi Gebre, son of an anti-Communist in Ethiopia, escaped with a relative when the Communists took over, walking over 1,500 miles, mostly at night. Aged 15, he went through our school with little adult supervision at home. He largely supported himself, working in an all-night liquor store in downtown Los Angeles.

After a brief period of adjustment, Teferi maintained excellent grades, won the city cross-country championship, and was a mainstay of our distance running corps in track season. He also ran well and excelled academically at Cal Poly Pomona,

touring Europe with a traveling American track team. He is now employed by the state auditor's office and is working on his master's degree in business administration at the University of Southern California.

I recommend to all my English classes the "Rico method of education," named for **Gilberto Rico**, a Cuban student I taught for two months in an orientation class before his freshman year. All the students were new to the country, and their level of English was elementary. Gilberto's thoroughness was awesome.

My "Rico method" reflects what he did: "Come every day. Pay close attention. Take notes on everything. Star the things you don't understand. Ask about the stars before you leave school each day. Write it all down. Then go home and learn it."

Gilberto shot through all our levels of English as a Second Language, entered the mainstream by his second year, and graduated in four years with straight A's. He works with our school as a teacher's aide while finishing his math degree at UCLA. An achiever to be sure, Gilberto is a kind, humble, appreciative human being who will make a superb contribution to his community and his school. He is another beneficiary of a warm, supportive family.

Maria was never encouraged for her school endeavors at home; but she has an inner drive to succeed. She did her job academically and athletically, graduated eighteenth in a class of nearly 800, and holds the school record in high hurdles. She is 5 ft. 3 in. tall. With four years of an excellent French program, she wants to teach language, attending La Verne University with substantial scholarship aid.

I found the opposite in parental attitudes with **Mai**, a Vietnamese student whose mother took her few privileges away if she got a B! Fortunately, that didn't happen very often. Mai frequently stayed after school to assist another of our English teachers. One day, I witnessed an argument over whether Mai would accept pay for her time spent. Mai finally won when I interceded, explaining that Mai's mother would probably kill her if she found out she had accepted money for helping a teacher.

Although Mai, now a graduate of Brandeis University, is Asian, these

attributes—respect for teachers, eagerness to help, rigorous honesty, willingness to share—are not limited to any particular ethnic group. Most of our students who come from families that are relatively new to the country have a habit of sharing what they have. They have sympathy for anyone who is down, and they have great appreciation for any kindness shown to them. These traits are typical of our Hispanics, Ethiopians, Indians, Filipinos, and other Asians.

It is inconceivable to me that these wonderful young people—each honest and proud of being in a country that is the envy of the world for its acceptance and utilization of our multiethnic population—are in some quarters not welcome and that we as a society do not seek more of them, rather than fewer.

My examples are not rare successes. I have omitted hundreds like them, and there are hundreds more, in a school of nearly 5,000, whom I have never known. Our school functions well in the difficult world of secondary education because our students— in large majority—are well mannered, respectful, and appreciative. Their parents usually have little formal schooling but gave their children an old-world set of values, taught at home and in church, and modeled by the adults.

Not all our 5,000 students achieve the same heights. They are neither superhuman nor perfect, but the overwhelming number of triumphs, especially if you know the obstacles they overcame, has made my 14 years of teaching in Los Angeles exciting and rewarding. I love going to school, almost every day. Even the students who will never set the world on fire will make loyal mates, kindly neighbors, crusaders for peace, and lawful, contributing citizens.

These are positive virtues valued in my family, which first arrived in Boston in 1630. If my neighbors could know these newest arrivals to our country, could appreciate the pain they felt leaving home to seek survival for their families, and the kind and decent instincts the majority have, perhaps the approach of California and other parts of the country that have somehow found immigrants in general guilty without a trial might be very different.

Gerry D. Haukoos and
Archie B. Beauvais

Creating Positive Cultural Images:

Thoughts for Teaching About American Indians

Gerry D. Haukoos is Professor of Education, Department of Curriculum and Instruction, Illinois State University, Normal. Archie B. Beauvais is Dean of Education and Tribal Studies, Sinte Gleska University, Rosebud, South Dakota.

Most children enjoy stories and school lessons about American Indians. They often find something inspirational about the lives of Chief Joseph, Crazy Horse, Geronimo and other great American Indian leaders. Although it is important to learn about these great American leaders, it is even more important for children to construct positive images of present-day Native people to prevent racial or cultural stereotypes from becoming part of their beliefs.

American Indian people are among the many different peoples and cultures that live on the American continent. While we all are much more alike than different, it is the differences that too often compel us to erect barriers of misunderstanding. Consequently, we must learn more about each other. Educators especially require knowledge of other cultures, races and ethnicities. Otherwise, they may unknowingly spread their misunderstandings as stereotypes to students.

Two decades ago, Heinrich (1977) addressed Native and non-Native interracial issues when she published a list of "what not to teach about American Indians." Its purpose was to help elementary school teachers correct common errors. Although the Indian Nations at Risk Task Force (1994) found significant change in Native education since the mid-1970s, many of Heinrich's recommendations are as relevant today as when she first proposed them. This paper will revisit those suggestions, and then encourage teachers to rethink how they portray American Indian people. The authors hope to advance classroom teachers' understanding by providing current explanations and viewpoints from the Native community.

Restructuring the Knowledge Base
■ *Teach children that American Indian people prefer to be identified by their nation name.*

The name "Indian" was a white man's invention and still remains largely a white image, if not a stereotype. It was first used by members of Christopher Columbus's party when, upon landing in the Americas, they erroneously believed they had landed in India. Most Europeans, however, called Indian peoples "Americans" until immigrants from Europe appropriated that name (Sando, 1972). The term "Native American" also was derived from non-Natives, originally used by the United States Government to designate all Native peoples of the continent. Today, by most accounts, it includes American Indians, Alaska Natives and all Native peoples from the United States's territories and possessions— American Samoa, Baker Island, Howland Island, Guam, Jarvis Island, Kingman Reef, Palmyra Atoll, Johnston Atoll, Midway Islands, Navassa Island, Northern Mariana Islands, Trust Territory of the Pacific Islands, Puerto Rico, the Virgin Islands and Wake Island.

These appellations, however, do not distinguish Apache from Inuit or Samoans from Mohawks. As a result, federal dollars typically budgeted for American

Indians and Alaska Natives have now been reallocated to all peoples who declare themselves to be Native American. This interpretation increased competition for federal dollars and, in some cases, reduced treatied funds for those peoples originally identified as Native Americans.

Most American Indian and Alaska Native groups have therefore moved away from calling themselves Native Americans, and instead use the names of their original nations (e.g., Navajo Nation, Menominee Nation, Seneca Nation). Most electronic databases and publications edited by Native scholars now use the term American Indian (e.g., *Journal of American Indian Education, American Indian Quarterly, American Indian Culture and Research Journal*) when referring to Native peoples as a collective group. Although use of "American Indian" may suggest a return to the old image, those who choose American Indian terminology believe it more clearly identifies Native people of America as uniquely indigenous to the continent.

■ *Teach children that American Indian people do not live in tribes.*

Although the United States Government has used the term "tribe" as an official designation for identifying different populations of American Indian people, most Native people prefer to be recognized as belonging to a particular *nation* of people rather than a tribe. While "tribe" or "tribal society" may be acceptable to some Native people, others believe the words suggest primitive or nomadic peoples—a classification most modern populations would find offensive. When the term "tribe" is used in anthropology, it generally refers to a kin-based society (Winthrop, 1991). Seymour-Smith (1986) defined it as ". . . a group which possesses social institutions but not political ones" (p. 281).

A nation, on the other hand, is defined as having political organization and a differentiated administrative structure (Berndt, 1959; Winthrop, 1991). Although kin-based social units are common in most Native communities, American Indian societies today are nations that have been organized around democratic authority and political institutions: council government, chief executive officer and judiciary. Even today there are over 500 federally recognized American Indian and Alaska Native nations (U.S. Department of Commerce, Bureau of the Census, 1992). To-

ent Native nations. The culture of the Oneida nation in the forested eastern United States was quite different, for example, from that of the Cheyenne nation on the Great Plains. Furthermore, today's Northern Cheyenne culture in Montana differs from the Southern Cheyenne culture in Oklahoma. Such differences in Native culture compel teachers to consider both time and place when teaching about American Indians. All Native peoples cannot and should not be lumped together.

. . . most Native people prefer to be recognized as belonging to a particular *nation* **of people rather than a tribe.**

gether, they share the commonality of representing the original peoples of the modern continent.

■ *Teach children that American Indian culture differs by nation and in time.*

Banks (1981) described culture as a society's behavioral patterns, symbols, institutions, values and other human-related elements. While these qualities may display themselves differently among the American Indian peoples, they also change over time. If one is speaking about the Native Lakota culture, for example, a particular time period must be referenced. Before 1700, many reports placed Lakota people in Minnesota's lake and semiforested regions. By 1870, however, that same nation had relocated to the central and western Great Plains several hundred miles away. The relocation undoubtedly changed everyday life and influenced cultural elements. Furthermore, Lakota culture today reflects further variations of the same customs.

Such cultural variations can also be recognized when comparing differ-

■ *Teach children that the Pilgrim-Indian image may be false.*

Although an officially declared American Indian History Month does not exist, many teachers use October or November to study American Indians as they celebrate the traditions of Thanksgiving. While these studies may be well-intentioned, too often they perpetuate stereotypes, especially when they inappropriately portray American Indians with feathers in their hair standing alongside the Pilgrims. Many Native people, in fact, think such portrayals depict them frozen in time; that is, wearing costumes from an earlier century, complete with headdress, buckskin or loincloth, war paint, and bow and arrow. These Pilgrim-Indian images not only advance a stereotype (one the American public seems most comfortable with), but also communicate a traditional message that is primarily mythical. Deloria (1988), for example, described the Pilgrim-Indian relationship this way:

One day at a conference we were singing "My Country 'Tis of Thee" and we came across the part that goes: "Land where our fathers died, Land of the Pilgrims' pride." Some of us broke out laughing when we realized that our fathers undoubtedly died trying to keep those Pilgrims from stealing our land. In fact, many of our fathers died because the Pilgrims killed them as witches. We didn't feel much kinship with those Pilgrims, regardless of who they did in. (p. 2)[1]

Therefore, we need to examine the images we present to children in classrooms. Are the images fictional or do they represent reality?

■ *Teach children that certain symbols are derogatory to American Indian people.*

American Indians are often used as icons on commercial products, ranging from foods and automobiles to athletic teams. These symbols are thought, by some, to honor Native people. In a recent interview, however, one American Indian leader[2] responded to that belief in this way: ". . . thank you, but what if we don't feel honored?" (Wideman, 1995). Children must understand that representations of the bow and arrow, tomahawks, headbands, feathers, tipis and profiles in headdress and war paint are depictions of a mythical Indian from long gone eras. Native people have changed over the centuries, as have the many American immigrants who came later. It is just as demeaning to portray Native people as frozen in the past as it would be to treat America's immigrants that way. Moreover, activities associated with those images (e.g., the war dancing, tomahawk chop and appearances by "Chief Noc-a-Homa" at baseball games and other events) also denigrate the sacred rituals and social ceremonies of Native peoples. American Indians live in the present, and they ask for the same respect that other cultures, races and ethnicities desire (Beauvais, 1992). Children should be taught that it is not acceptable to use symbols or names that dishonor Native people.

■ *Teach children about the early Native model for democracy.*

Before Europeans first arrived in North America, many Native nations had already developed systems of government that were uniquely democratic. Most scholars believe those systems provided the model for the United States's own form of democracy. The European explorers who first arrived on the North American continent were seeking freedom from divine rights of kings, centralized governments and societies that were stratified into rigid classes (Gibson, 1980). Their discovery of successful Native governments that were decentralized, self-ruling and loosely confederated provided a stimulus for establishing democratic governments across North America. Europeans paid most attention to the Iroquoian Confederacy of Nations. This unique league included the nations of Cayuga, Mohawk, Seneca, Oneida and Onondaga; each provided a representative at the village, nation and league levels. Although the nations remained independent with their own internal council governments, they also elected peace chiefs to sit on a central council for the confederacy (LaBonty, 1995).

Considering the current debate over the role and responsibilities of government in the United States, it only seems appropriate that school children should learn more about democracy's origins in America and its influence over the centuries on Americans. In class discussions, for example, children could contrast the electoral caucus system used by the 17th century Iroquoian Confederacy with similar caucus procedures used today to nominate candidates for the American presidency. Another class discussion might examine examples of democracy's shameful times (e.g., the Chinese Exclusion Act of 1882, the Indian Allotment Act of 1887), as well as its tendency to self-correct over time (e.g., the Civil Rights Act of 1964, the Indian Civil Rights Act of 1968).

■ *Teach children about the Native legacy of world commerce.*

Only recently have economists and historians begun to fairly assess American Indians' commercial contributions. Although Native peoples benefited little from their relationship with early Europeans, their contributions to commerce have been immense. Early French explorers, for example, traded with Native people for furs, which altered clothing fashion and design around the world (Gibson, 1980). American Indian peoples' greatest commercial legacy will likely be the plants they domesticated for food, drugs and building supplies. Europeans quickly learned to use these plants in everyday living, and infused them into their global commerce. Among the more common food crops were corn, tomatoes, potatoes, squash, beans, pumpkins, melons and peanuts. These crops are used widely today and some, such as corn, rank among the most important staples of all populations. Native peoples have also contributed more than 200 drug-yielding plants that are listed in the American pharmacopoeia (U.S. Pharmacopeial Convention, 1995).

The commercial products listed here represent only a fraction of Native contributions to world commerce. By including these examples in lessons, children will begin to understand how the components of world trade are established, and how Native peoples have contributed to its development over many centuries. Children should understand how all nations must work together to produce a successful global community.

■ *Teach children about the American Indian peoples' rich cultural heritage.*

Most American Indian cultures regard the earth as their mother or grandmother. They believe all life began with the earth. As Means (Wideman, 1995) pointed out:

Because she is the mother of all living beings, you are related to everything that lives—every blade of grass, every pine needle, every grain of sand. Even the rocks have life. Since you rely on all this life for your sustenance, you have to be respectful. (p. 76)

This world view arose out of a need to live in harmony with nature, not in domination over it. Such a philosophy helped temper humans' excesses against the environment. This perspective has shaped not only American Indians' cultures, but also the cultures of all indigenous peoples—the Lapps in Scandinavia, the mountain people of Switzerland, the Berbers of North Africa, the Bedouins of the Middle East, the mountain people of Taiwan, the Ainu of northern Japan and the Inuit of the Arctic (Wideman, 1995).

As natural and social environments decline, Native peoples and philosophies may provide a model for physical and spiritual healing. Children can learn respect for the self and others if classroom lessons emulate Means's definition of respect as respect for *all* things.

Recommendations for Children's Studies

Teachers should remember that people learn by constructing knowledge from images and models. Teachers can avoid creating stereotypes from these images if they

Study Native people by using children's literature rather than social studies textbooks.

consider how they select and present symbols in the classroom (Haukoos, Bordeaux, LeBeau & Gunhammer, 1995). Rather than choosing one all-encompassing study of American Indians and Alaska Natives, select topics that can be studied in greater depth. Not only do these studies provide children with proper and lasting information, they also dispel myths. A short list of recommended strategies or topics for in-depth study includes:

■ Select one nation for in-depth study. Begin with the history of its leaders and people, but also look at the nation today. Where do the people live? How do they make a living? How is the nation's government structured? Where do children go to school? What colleges serve the people of the nation? What family or national traditions are practiced today?

■ Study the commonalities of Native people from a particular region in greater depth. Why were the Native nations of the Great Plains so mobile in past centuries? How has that mobility influenced those nations today? What factors have strongly influenced the cultures, nations and peoples of the Southwest, the Eastern Woodlands or the Great Lakes area?

■ Study Native people by using children's literature rather than social studies textbooks.[3] Native peoples used stories to teach each other and their children, and now many of those stories have been published for all to enjoy. In particular, look for stories about Spider, Coyote, Deer or Badger. These animals are tricksters in most Native cultures, and these stories always provide strong social messages for children. They also offer greater understanding of cultural development among Native peoples. Do not limit your stories to these characters alone. Instead, use a wide variety of books such as *Keepers of the Earth* (Caduto & Bruchac, 1989), which includes stories from many Native nations, and *Lakota Star Knowledge* (Goodman, 1992), which includes stories from only one nation.

■ Study one event from American history that had a major impact on Native people. Topical areas of interest may include: the forced removal of 125,000 men, women and children from five Native nations along the mid-Atlantic and Southeast, and their march to semi-arid reservations in the Oklahoma Territory (the Trail of Tears); the Black Hawk Wars, during which Chief Black Hawk dared to resist the Indian Removal Act of 1830; President Andrew Jackson's administration, when 75 different treaties were signed and broken between 1829-1837 (Caselli, 1972); and the reduction of American Indian populations from 1,500,000 in 1769 to 250,000 by 1890 (Gibson, 1980).

■ Develop an understanding of modern Native peoples by visiting a Native nation. Native nations or communities are widely dispersed throughout North America, even in large cities. Encourage families and children to visit a Native community. Select a cultural center for an initial visit. Then, select a school or community event to attend. Report on how children and parents in these communities are similar to those in your own community.

Conclusion

Popular culture's conceptions of American Indian people are not always correct or positive. Some of these views may be an unfortunate outgrowth of misguided education. Native educators are optimistic, however, that positive cultural images are possible through appropriate education. In fact, the Indian Nations at Risk Task Force has recommended that "a massive education and public relations effort . . . be launched to dispel stereotypic images of American Indian and Alaska Native students" (Cahape & Howley, 1992, pp. 83-84). The authors hope that by examining commonly held perceptions of Native people, teachers will be encouraged to rethink how they have portrayed American Indians in their classrooms. The Native community's own views and teaching strategies described here can help teachers develop a more authentic knowledge base. By working together, Native and non-Native teachers can help children construct positive cultural images of the American Indian peoples in today's society.

◆

References

Banks, J. A. (1981). *Multiethnic education: Theory and practice.* Boston: Allyn and Bacon.

Beauvais, A. (1992, May/June). 'Indians' are not icons of the past. *The Bulletin of the American Society of Newspaper Editors,* p. 21.

Berndt, R. M. (1959). The concept of 'the tribe' in the western desert of Australia. *Oceania, 30,* 81-107.

Caduto, M. J., & Bruchac, J. (1989). *Keepers of the earth.* Golden, CO: Fulcrum.

Cahape, P., & Howley, C. B. (Eds.). (1992). *Indian nations at risk: Listening to the people* (Contract No. RI-88-062016). Charleston, WV: ERIC Clearinghouse on Rural Education and Small Schools.

Caselli, R. (1972). Historic repression and Native Americans. In J. Henry (Ed.), *The American Indian reader* (pp. 61-65). San Francisco: American Indian Educational Publishers.

Deloria, V., Jr. (1988). *Custer died for your sins: An Indian manifesto.* Norman, OK: University of Oklahoma Press.

Gibson, A. M. (1980). *The American Indian: Prehistory to the present.* Lexington, MA: D. C. Heath.

Goodman, R. (1992). *Lakota star knowledge.* Rosebud, SD: Sinte Gleska University Printing.

Haukoos, G. D., Bordeaux, L., LeBeau, D., & Gunhammer, S. (1995). Importance of American Indian culture in teaching school science: A follow-up study. *Journal of American Indian Education, 34*(2), 18-26.

Heinrich, J. S. (1977). Native Americans: What not to teach. *Interracial Books for Children Bulletin, 8*(4-5), 26-27.

Indian Nations at Risk Task Force. (1994). Toward true Native education: A treaty of 1992. *Journal of American Indian Education, 32*(2), 7-56.

LaBonty, J. (1995). A demand for excellence in books for children. *Journal of American Indian Education, 34*(2), 1-9.

Sando, J. S. (1972). White-created myths about American Indians. In J. Henry (Ed.), *The American Indian reader* (pp. 130-134). San Francisco: American Indian Educational Publishers.

Seymour-Smith, C. (1986). *Macmillan dictionary of anthropology.* New York: Macmillan.

U.S. Department of Commerce, Bureau of the Census. (1992). *1990 census of population, general population characteristics, United States* (DCESA Publication No. 1990 CP-1-1). Washington, DC: U.S. Government Printing Office.

U.S. Pharmacopeial Convention. (1995). *United States pharmacopoeia dispensing information.* Rockville, MD: Author.

Wideman, J. E. (1995). Russell Means. *Modern Maturity, 38*(5), 68-79.

Winthrop, R. H. (1991). *Dictionary of concepts in cultural anthropology.* New York: Greenwood Press.

RECOMMENDED RESOURCES

Children's Literature

Baylor, B. (1975). *The desert is theirs.* New York: Aladdin Books. Macmillan. A simple text describing characteristics of the Southwest's deserts, plants, animals and peoples, especially the Papago (Tohono O'Odam) people, who have made the desert their home for centuries. Primary level.

Baylor, B. (1976). *Hawk, I'm your brother.* New York: Aladdin Books. A story of a Papago (Tohono O'Odam) boy who sees himself as a hawk soaring above the desert. To realize his dream, he nurses an injured hawk back to flight. Primary level.

Blood, C. L. (1984). *The goat in the rug.* New York: Simon and Schuster. A Navajo story in which a goat, who lived among the people, turned itself into a rug. Primary level.

Bruchac, J. (1995). *A boy called slow.* New York: Putnam. A story about the childhood of Sitting Bull, the distinguished Lakota holy man who led his nation on the Great Plains between 1831-1890. Primary level and up.

Bruchac, J. (1995). *Dog people: Native dog stories.* Golden, CO: Fulcrum Publishing. A story set 10,000 years ago, when children and dogs had especially close relationships. Each of these stories is based on Abenaki culture and features outdoor adventure, in which children and dogs together find a way to survive. Intermediate level.

Clark, A. N. (1992). *There still are buffalo.* Santa Fe, NM: Ancient City Press. An informative and sensitive account of the relationship between the buffalo and American Indian peoples of the Great Plains. Primary level and up.

Goble, P. (1987). *Buffalo woman.* New York: Macmillan. A legend of a man, woman and boy (a buffalo family) who lived in harmony with the Buffalo nation on the Great Plains. Primary level and up.

Goble, P. (1993). *Beyond the ridge.* New York: Macmillan. A sensitive and fascinating story of an elderly American Indian woman's natural death. It describes American Indian beliefs associated with the afterlife journey. Primary level and up.

Goble, P. (1991). *Iktomi and the boulder.* New York: Orchard Books. Iktomi, a traditional American Indian trickster, attempts to fight and defeat a boulder with the assistance of flying bats. This is a traditional story that attempts to explain why small stones cover the Great Plains. Primary level and up.

Goodman, R. (1992). *Lakota star knowledge.* Rosebud, SD: Sinte Gleska University. An explanation of how American Indians of the Great Plains used star knowledge to guide their journeys in life and death. It shares elders' spiritual and historical knowledge. Intermediate level and up.

Martin, R. (1993). *The boy who lived with seals.* New York: Putnam. This tells the legend of a Chinook boy who was raised by a family of seals along the Northwest Pacific coast. Primary level and up.

Monroe, J., & Williamson, R. A. (1993). *First houses: Native American homes and sacred structures.* Boston: Houghton Mifflin. This book contains stories and legends associated with American Indian houses and sacred structures from many different nations. Intermediate level and up.

Powell, M. (1993). *Wolf tales: Native American children's stories.* Santa Fe, NM: Ancient City Press. These seven wolf stories from different American Indian nations incorporate folklore to explain the relationship between animal people and Native people. Primary level and up.

Raczek, L. (1995). *The night the grandfathers danced.* Flagstaff, AZ: Northland Publishing Company. A young woman at Ute Mountain learns respect for elders and cultural customs. Primary level and up.

Roop, P. (1994). *Ahyoka and the talking leaves*. New York: Morrow. A story of how Sequoyah communicated the meaning and importance of living creatures to her daughter. Intermediate level and up.

Simms, T. E. (1989). *Otter boy*. Rosebud, SD: Sinte Gleska University Printing. An animal people story that teaches traditional values during the celebration of the autumnal equinox. The story takes place before humankind became Homo Sapiens. Primary level and up.

Velardi, P. (1993). *Old father storyteller*. Santa Fe, NM: Clear Light Publishers. A book that retells six warm "grandfather" stories about the Santa Clara Pueblo culture of the Southwest plateau country. Intermediate level and up.

White Deer of Autumn. (1991). *Ceremony in the circle of life*. Hillsboro, OR: Beyond Words Publishing. A story of Little Turtle, a young boy visited by Star Spirit, who introduces him to his heritage and explains his relationship to all things in the Circle of Life. Primary and intermediate level.

Wolfson, E. (1993). *From the earth to beyond the sky: Native American medicine*. Boston: Houghton Mifflin. An interesting look into the process and power of American Indian medicine. Intermediate level and up.

Wood, N. (1995). *Dancing moons*. New York: Bantam Doubleday Dell Books for Young Readers. Wood's carefully crafted poems and heartfelt meditations speak of enduring truths. This book reveals the beauty, mystery and wonder at the core of life. Upper level and up.

Professional Literature

Allen, P. (1992). *The sacred hoop: Recovering the feminine in American Indian tradition*. Boston: Beacon Press. This book describes the history of women in American Indian culture.

Berkhofer, R. F., Jr. (1978). *The white man's Indian*. New York: Vintage. Presents literary images of American Indians from the time of Columbus to the present. This work provides a well-documented perspective through history, philosophy and literature. An excellent resource for teachers.

Bruchac, J. (1991). *Keepers of the animals*. Golden, CO: Fulcrum Publishing. A book that presents science, legend and Native culture through stories and activities for children. This volume has a wildlife theme.

Bruchac, J. (1991). *Keepers of the earth*. Golden, CO: Fulcrum Publishing. A book that presents science, legend and Native culture through stories and activities for children. This volume has an ecology and environment theme.

Bruchac, J. (1994). *Keepers of life*. Golden, CO: Fulcrum Publishing. A book that presents science, legend and Native culture through stories and activities for children. This volume has a special emphasis on the discovery of plants.

Cahape, P., & Howley, C. B. (1992). *Indian nations at risk: Listening to the people* (Contract No. RI-88-062016). Charleston, WV: ERIC Clearinghouse on Rural and Small School Education. This document summarizes papers that describe American Indian education in the past, and how it might be improved. The papers were commissioned by the Indian Nations at Risk Task Force of the U. S. Department of Education.

Debo, A. (1984). *A history of Indians in the United States*. Norman, OK: University of Oklahoma Press. Many American Indian scholars consider this work to be the best, most complete and most sensitive interpretation of Native history. An excellent resource for teachers.

Deloria, E. C. (1978). *Dakota texts*. Vermillion, SD: University of South Dakota Press. This book contains stories that were recorded directly from Native storytellers who lived on the Standing Rock, Pine Ridge and Rosebud reservations in South Dakota. These stories have also been described as parables.

Eastman, C. A. (1980). *The soul of the Indian: An interpretation*. Lincoln, NE: University of Nebraska Press. The author describes his nation's spiritual and cultural customs to his grandchildren. Such explanations provide readers with new insights into the lives of both Native and non-Native people.

Evers, L. (1986). *Yaqui deer songs—Masobwikam: A Native American poetry*. Tucson, AZ: University of Arizona Press. This book presents Native philosophy through mythology, folklore and poetry.

Harvey, K. D. (1994). *Indian country: A history of Native people in America*. Golden, CO: Fulcrum Publishing. The origins and anthropological development of American Indian people in North America are summarized in this excellent resource for teachers.

Reyhner, J. (1994). *American Indian/Alaska Native education* (Fastback No. 367). Bloomington, IN: Phi Delta Kappa Educational Foundation. Provides an overview of American Indian/Alaska Native self-determination policy, and how it has been used in teacher education to serve at-risk Native students.

Reyhner, J. (Ed.). (1994). *Teaching American Indian students*. Norman, OK: University of Oklahoma Press. This book of papers explains American Indian education and ethnic identity. It emphasizes cultural characteristics, and suggests how teachers might respond to children through various school disciplines.

White Deer of Autumn. (1992). *Native people, Native ways series: Native American book of change; Native American book of knowledge; Native American book of life; Native American book of wisdom*. Hillsboro, OR: Beyond Words Publishing. American Indians have traditionally passed wisdom and information to the next generation through stories. These volumes contain representative stories.

[1] Vine Deloria, Jr. is Yankton Dakota Sioux, and a professor and lawyer.

[2] Russell Means, a Oglala Lakota Sioux and a Native leader, activist and film star.

[3] Prior to the selection of children's literature with Native images, the authors recommend a review of the following report:

LaBonty, J. (1995). A demand for excellence in books for children. *Journal of American Indian Education, 34*(2), 1-9.

EARLY CHILDHOOD EDUCATION: ISSUES OF ETHNICITY AND EQUITY

EDITH W. KING
University of Denver

ABSTRACT

In this article attention is placed on what is considered personal and cultural knowledge versus school knowledge; so that educators can begin to question classic concepts of early learning. Included are the accounts of thoughtful, perceptive adults which help us to recognise that the foundation for traditional education of young children was almost totally based in Western tradition.

Defining Ethnicity

What is ethnicity? In recent years ethnicity has come to play an important role in everyday living. It influences almost everyone. It affects our behaviour in the social spheres of our lives. Consider that ethnicity can affect how we spend our money, how we vote, even where we live or where we go out to dine. We use ethnicity as a filter for forming our identities, opinions and attitudes toward others. Sociologists acknowledge that ethnicity is central to many peoples' images and concepts of self-identity. Furthermore, sociologists recognise that individuals function on a continuum of ethnic affiliations ranging from non-recognition of one's ethnicity in daily life to an almost complete identification with an ethnic group in all activities, choices, and designations in daily actions.

Since the rise to prominence of this concept in the 1960s, ethnicity has been defined by numerous social scientists as: *a sense of peoplehood and commonality derived from kinship patterns, a shared historical past, common experiences, religious affiliations, language or linguistic commonalities, shared values, attitudes, perceptions, modes of expression and identity.*

Some Important Issues That Sociologists Have Addressed About Ethnicity

Why has ethnicity arisen as an important issue in our daily lives? The persistence of ethnicity and one's ethnic identification in contemporary, highly diverse societies is due to both negative and positive factors. When the primary reason for group affiliation is hostility from the majority group, it is inevitable that ethnicity seems more to confine and constrict the individual than to provide opportunities and enhance the quality of life. But people are usually drawn to ethnic identification because of the advantages it offers. The ethnic group can be a buffer between the individual and the broader society; individuals use ethnicity as a filter for forming their opinions, tastes, values and habit patterns. Ethnic affiliations also help organise social, economic, political, and religious interaction, both among individuals and among groups.

The Social Construction of Ethnicity

In exploring the concept of ethnicity or one's ethnic identity, we inevitably encounter questions about the "reality" of the social

From *Education and Society*, Vol. 14, No. 1, 1996, pp. 25-32. © 1996 by James Nicholas Publishers. Reprinted by permission.

world in which the individual exists. It seems appropriate, here to cite the theory of the social construction of reality and to apply it to the meaning of ethnicity and ethnic identity. The leading theorists on the topic of the social construction of reality are Peter Berger and Thomas Luckmann, whose ideas and insights help clarify the significance of the social construction of ethnicity and ethnic identity.

Berger and Luckmann contend that the reality of everyday life presents itself to us as a world we share with others. We share a common sense about what is reality and, therefore, our everyday life is characterised by a taken-for-granted reality. But human beings are unique among living creatures, for they can experience and exist in several provinces of meaning or taken-for-granted realities. These can be enclaves within the paramount reality. The theatre provides an excellent metaphor for coexisting realities. To this point Berger and Luckmann tell us:

> The transition between realities is marked by the rising and falling of the curtain. As the curtain rises, the spectator is "transported into another world" with its own meanings and an order that may or may not have much [to do] with the order of everyday life. As the curtain falls, the spectator "returns to reality." (Berger and Luckmann, 1966; 25).

So it is with ethnicity and an individual's ethnic identity. Within the ethnic group, the taken-for-granted world calls for conduct, use of language, referents, mutual affinities and antipathies that are implicit and unspoken. These ways are shared with others of the same ethnic and racial affiliations. The same individual functions within the majority society in the taken-for granted reality of the supermarket, the street traffic or the daily newspaper. Common habit patterns take over to guide conduct. A person pays the price posted and does not bargain with the cashier at the supermarket; goes on the green light and halts on the red light, not chancing the traffic just because no cars are apparent; and comprehends the news story on the front page about rising food prices. We accept and function within cultural continuities even from childhood. Our view of reality and of the world helps us to make sense of our experiences. We interpret social events in the light of meanings we attach to them. Here our ethnicity or our ethnic identification and ethnic affiliation come forth to interpret the meaning of everyday occurrences.

Often, growing up in the ethnic enclave, ghetto or barrio socialises children into the belief that all the world is Mexican American or Jewish or Italian or Puerto Rican. It is useful to realise that children hold these conceptions quite naturally and logically. Biographies and personal histories reveal how the chance factors of everyday life can affect people's conceptions of the ethnic and social world that surrounds them. Examples of the type of socialisation that lulls a child into believing that most of the existing society that she or he will ever encounter is made of people of the same ethnicity or race as the child, are revealed in these statements compiled from experienced teachers' accounts of their childhood socialisation. Following are some excerpts from adults recalling childhood impressions and remembrances of experiences that influenced their attitudes toward various ethnic groups:

. . . As a young child I had limited contact with people of colour. I knew that they existed because I would see them on the buses, or at the shopping malls, or at the movies when I would go. I never really thought too much about them though, because I never met a person of colour, nor did I ever have an opportunity to speak with one.

. . . An ethnic experience that I remember was when we went out to eat once at a Chinese restaurant. I was totally amazed to see a room full of Chinese people. The food was totally weird to me, and watching the people using chop-sticks, kept me mesmerised during the entire meal.

. . . I am a product of the South. In the 1950s my town was a racially segregated city. It was two cities in one. The blacks lived in an area referred to as "coloured" town and rarely mingled with the white population except when catching the bus. In "coloured" town were churches, schools, small stores—all the essentials to keep the blacks from mingling with the whites. On Saturdays on Main Street there were no blacks doing their weekly shopping[,] only crowds of white people. Blacks did not buy their shoes at Thompson's or ice cream at the Dairy Queen. Although my neighbourhood was only three blocks from "coloured" town, I never visited that area of town nor did any of my friends. It was off limits to us. Sometimes our parents would drive blacks home from their jobs cleaning our houses or yards, but we were never invited to ride along. (King, Chipman and Cruz-Janzen, 1994; 106–107).

These comments demonstrate the power of the social construction of ethnicity on an individual's attitudes, opinions and actions.

Remembering and Recounting Early Experiences for the Social Construction of Ethnic Identity: In the United Kingdom and in the USA

Earlier in this chapter a theory of the social construction of ethnicity was elaborated and some brief anecdotes or recollections were cited. Here now are two more detailed and in depth accounts of mature women recalling the social construction of ethnic, social class, and gender identity in the early childhood years of their lives. The intricate intertwining of the social forces of ethnicity, social class, and gender are evident in the stories of these two women, one of them, currently living in the United States, is of Mexican American ethnic affiliation; the other woman is a citizen of Britain of Panjabi and British affiliation.

My Socialization: The Account of a Mexican American Woman. The wind howled in the distance. Thunder rattled the windows, raindrops pelted the roof. My mother screamed in agony, writhing in pain. The rickety old bed trembled beneath her weight. The house was small, two bedrooms. There was nothing out of the ordinary about it, it was just a house. A small house in a small village in the state of Zacatecas in Mexico. My brother and two sisters were sleeping on one bed, oblivious to my mother's pain and my imminent entrance into their lives. It was 2:00 AM on a hot summer's night and I entered the world screaming and kicking at the medicine woman. I entered a country that I would never call my home, because at one month of age I was taken to the United States of America. My green card temporary passport to enter the USA did not even have a picture on it because I was so small. During my childhood in the United States, I was socialised into my Mexican culture, and acculturated into my American culture (see pp.—for definitions of terms used here). Each culture had different roles and expectations for my ethnic affiliation, my social class level and my gender. For the longest time, there was a battle going on inside me, one culture expected the opposite of the other. In time, I learned to synthesise both into the person I am today.

My Social Class Background: My father had nineteen brothers and sisters. Of those nineteen children, twelve survived. My grandfather was a farmer. He had been orphaned when he was six years old, both his parents having died of diseases. My grandfather was very handsome, his complex-

ion was white, like a Spaniard. He had blond hair and blue eyes. My grandmother was beautiful, she was dark-skinned with distinct Aztec Indian features. Neither of my grandparents had any formal schooling. They brought their children up in a three room cabin. One room was for storing feed for the animals; another room served as the kitchen; the third room was a bedroom where everyone slept. When many of my father's brothers and sisters married, their spouses and children would live with my grandparents, too. Their lives were filled with hardships.

By third grade my father, one of the many children, had to drop [out] of school to help his father on the ranch. At times, the family did not have enough food; neither could they afford shoes or warm clothes for their many children. My father wore his brothers' hand-me-down clothes all of his childhood and adolescence. My mother's family was in similar circumstances. Her father was a farmer. They had ten children with my mother being the oldest. My mother dropped out of school in the sixth grade because her mother needed her help caring for the rest of the children. At the age of eleven, my mother found herself caring for her siblings doing the cooking and cleaning for a family of twelve. So at the age of sixteen my mother married my father who was just eighteen and they went to live in my paternal grandfather's log cabin along with too many other people.

After a number of years of marriage my parents came to the United States looking for work and a better life for their children. They worked hard all of their lives to provide for us their six children, all those things that they never had. My father worked as a cook for quite sometime; then he got a job working in a steel mill. He has worked there for twenty years. My mother got a maintenance job cleaning offices. Now she is a supervisor with an office maintenance company. They both provided us with everything that we needed. We had a house, a yard, clothes, toys, food, and love. We were never without the necessities of life. But, one day I realised that our family now living in America, was considered poor! This came about because at my elementary school I made friends with a little Anglo girl named Sandra. Sandra was the daughter of a city council man. I would visit her big, beautiful house. I can still see it in my mind today. I could not believe that she and each one of her sisters had their own bedroom. I had to share my bedroom with my three sisters. She had a bicycle of her own. I had to share mine with my sisters. She had many beautiful dresses. I had to wear the dresses that belonged to my sisters. I felt inferior to Sandra because she seemed to have so many more things than I did. Also, it was at this young age, seven years old, that I began to feel ashamed of my parents. They were not "important" like other children's parents seemed to be in our neighbourhood and community. My parents spoke with an accent and my father wore "guaraches", Mexican sandals. I was mortified when one day, my father showed up at school wearing his "guaraches." As I was writing about this incident I remembered two other incidents that made me realise that my family was considered poor. I remember having to take home applications for free lunch. My mother would fill them out and have us return the forms to school. I was embarrassed when the teacher gave me an application in front of the class. I was also embarrassed when I had to return it. I felt ashamed because I thought that my classmates would think that we were really poor, when we weren't. Also, I recall that one Christmas, a food basket arrived at our house from my school. My school had collected food items to give to poor families during the holiday season. I was so angry that this basket of food arrived at MY house because I thought that then other people would label us as "poor." I took in the images around me, on television, at school; and I thought less of myself and my family because of this.

The Social Construction of Ethnic Identity:

As every other person in the world, I have also been socialised, a lifelong process of internalising the values of one group of people. I have been socialised to be a part of two different cultures; the Mexican and the American cultures. It has been a difficult road, a clash between the values and attitudes of one culture, and those of another.

My socialisation into the Mexican culture occurred first. We lived in "little Mexico", as we have fondly nicknamed our part of town. It was filled with brown people, speaking Spanish. Spanish was my first language. From the time that I was born until I entered kindergarten, everything and everyone around me was Mexican. Except for "Sesame Street" on the television, I did not know that any other world existed. It was not until I entered the public school that I began to encounter the dominant American society in which I actually lived. In my Mexican world of those pre-school years the family was most important. We did everything together. The reason that my two brothers and three sisters and I most often got punished was for fighting with each other. We have a very large extended family now living here in our city in the United States. I grew up with many cousins. I remember the family parties. We would laugh, eat, watch our parents make fools of themselves, play, fight, and stay up until we couldn't stand it any more. A cohesiveness exists within the Mexican family that cannot be easily broken;

but this cohesiveness has both negative and positive consequences. A negative consequence is that such close family ties tend to cause a dependence on one's family and, in my opinion, many Mexican parents bring up their children to be dependent on them. In my family, my parents did everything for us. My mother cooked and cleaned for all of us, never expecting any help from her children.

The dominant American cultural values disapprove of dependence. Many people in the United States believe that the Mexican family is dysfunctional because it encourages dependence on others. I think that it makes life a little harder because you learn to expect people to do things for you. It is harder for you to get out on your own if that is what you really want to do. What happens many times in the Mexican culture is that young ladies and young men do not leave their homes until they are married and are ready to start their own family. However, they are still dependent on the family to help them with child care or other needs. From what I have seen in the American culture, many American parents expect their children to be fully independent by the time that they are eighteen years old.

It has been a struggle. My Mexican culture is constantly clashing with my American culture. If I had to choose today, I would be American. I grew up here, it is what I know. When I am around Mexicans, which is almost always, I realise how different I am. But then, when I am around Americans, I realise that I am very different from them, too. I just can't be one or the other. I am both. I have been socialized with the values and attitudes of both cultures. It is lonely sometimes because you feel different from everyone else. It is like you are standing on the border of both countries. One foot is in the United States and the other foot is in Mexico, but neither country claims you. Yet, it is also nice to be different sometimes because it makes you feel unique. There is no one else like me. I have accepted it!

(Maria del Carmen Salazar; excerpts from unpublished project for the seminar, "Diversity in Education", Univ. of Denver, 1995)

Biculturalism in Britain: One Mother's View

Writing in an article in the British journal, *Multicultural Teaching to Combat Racism in School and Community* (Vol. 13, No. 1, Autumn, 1994), Vinod Hallan, an administrator of an Equal Opportunity Program in the Midlands of England, clarifies her own social construction of ethnic identity, through the experiences of returning to India with her young son to visit the members of their family that remained there.

As a British person I have lived 33 of my 40 years in England, so I should not have been surprised when, on a recent educational visit to the USA, I was constantly referred to as "our English guest" or "our English visitor." I was amazed at how much they admired my English and confused when, on a formal occasion, I received the compliment: "you English always dress so well."

I was puzzled because in all my 33 years in England nobody had ever referred to me in those terms. In England I am always referred to as Indian. Why was my "Englishness" so prominent in the USA and so unrecognised here? . . .

The real surprise came last Christmas when, having left at the age of seven, I returned to India for a holiday. Indian people are able to recognise what they call "Non-Residential Indians" (NRIs) especially the English NRIs, from a distance. My eight year old son, who is not fluent in Panjabi, suddenly found himself in an environment which he did not fully comprehend, where customs and traditions were not always familiar. There was a different emphasis on food, particularly towards vegetarianism, and fast food was a rarity. He was constantly looking for the "safe" and familiar. The street games played by the children of his age were new to him, and, as he spoke little Panjabi and no Hindi, and they spoke only Hindi and no English, it was clear from day one that to stay within the bounds of the safe, he would be spending most if not all of his stay, with me and my parents or with other English speakers. He spent his spare time watching English language broadcasts on cable TV, MTV and BBC Asia, and after the first few days he was missing his Big Mac, chips, and bacon sandwiches, and he was bored.

In my son I was witnessing an amplification of my "Englishness" and a reduction of my "Indianess." As he was only fluent when communicating in English, it was no surprise when some of my relatives began to call him "Angrez"—the Englishman. But here lies the dilemma experienced by English people whose parents originate from outside Europe, particularly those who do not have a white skin and therefore do not "blend in" with most of the British population. In England he is seen as an outsider, an Indian, but in India he is seen as an outsider, the "Angrez", so where does his ethnic identity lie, and what epithet correctly describes his ethnicity?

Many Asian and African-Caribbean people do not like the tag "ethnic minority group" as it places them at a disadvantage. They feel that ethnic minority groups are subordinated segments of society whose characteristics are held in low esteem by the dominant group, conjuring up notions of culturally deficient people whose history, customs and values are of little consequence. Their perceptions are reinforced by fascist political parties, insensitive media and ethnocentric institutions, to an extent where some young black children deny their own colour and firmly believe themselves to be white. The conclusion that I am beginning to draw from this is that black people need to explore new terms which more accurately describe their ethnicity, terms which establish them as part of the "mainstream" where their "Britishness" is recognised first and only then their additional cultural heritage, in a similar way to American citizens who describe themselves as American-Irish, American-Italian, or African-American and where the extended experience of more than one culture is recognised, valued and accepted. For, contrary to popular belief, few black children are torn between two cultures; the majority are bilingually advantaged and bi-culturally proficient. Is this really surprising? Children who are raised in a pluralised society, particularly those whose parents were immigrants, not only acquire the behavioural and social patterns of their parents' ethnic group but also those of the host society. This is most likely to occur with children from a minority ethnic group, is also common among children of mixed marriages, and majority group children who live with minority group children. They have the advantage of being able to function in two different cultures by switching from one set of values to another. It is not surprising therefore that individuals who are biculturally or even multiculturally competent find the existing ethnic identity tags limiting and in many case inaccurate. Ethnicity has been described as a set of beliefs, attitudes and behaviour which distinguishes one cultural group from another. For many of our youngsters their beliefs, attitudes and behaviour spans more than one culture, and so do not readily fit into an accepted ethnic group. Educationalists are no different to the rest of society. Generally they are only proficient in one culture and language, and have direct experience of only one ethnic group. Children who are bi-culturally proficient quickly learn that these people can only function in one particular part of their repertoire, similar to the way the bilingual children learn that some people can only understand and function using a limited part of their own total language ability. In school, I have seen five year olds switch from speaking Panjabi to speaking English, simply by turning their heads from their parents to the teacher.

For my own son I would like to think that there will be a time, in the not too distant future, when he will be able to describe his ethnicity in his own terms, and that people will accept him for what he thinks he is, rather than what they think he should be.

(Excerpted from Vinod K. Hallan. "Whose Ethnicity Is It Anyway", *Multicultural Teaching,* Vol. 13, No. 1, Autumn, 1994, pp. 14–16).

Some Conclusions

Educational sociologists and curriculum theorists have analysed the construction of knowledge, categorising this knowledge so that it brings to our attention new ramifications for what is learned in schools. In this article attention has been raised to consider what is personal and cultural knowledge; school knowledge; and popular knowledge so that educators can begin to question classic concepts of learning. Through the accounts of thoughtful, perceptive adults, educators can recognise that the grounding and philosophy for traditional education of young children was almost totally based in Western European culture and tradition, with little regard for those children and their families whose traditions, heritage, language and customs stemmed from other cultures. The outmoded conception of readiness in the early childhood curriculum, where the teacher plays a passive role merely waiting for the student to develop physically and intellectually, takes no regard or concern for what may have happened to the individual in the family setting or the broader society. Given the crises and traumas in our modern world, this is naive and inappropriate. We no longer exist in an unchanging and safe society. Further, the conventional wisdom that proffers a curriculum model assuming children grow and develop in the same way, at the same time and they all should be able to function in the mainstream or majority society is errant. Additionally, at the beginning of this century the conventional image of the teacher of young children was a loving, gentle WOMAN, but at the close of this century is this conception still appropriate? Those of us who are committed to the vision of equality of educational opportunity in our society and for a worldwide society are asking now at the close of the 20th Century—just what has diversity brought? What will the future hold? Can this vicious rise of racism, sexism, classism, homophobia be contained? Is equity for all our children an attainable goal in the 21st century?

REFERENCES

Allport, Gordon. *The Nature of Prejudice.* Garden City, N.J.: Doubleday Anchor Books, 1954.

Banks, James A. *Multiethnic Education: Theory and Practice.* Needham Hts., Mass: Allyn and Bacon. (1994, 1988, 1981).

Barth, Frederick. (editor) *Ethnic Groups and Boundaries.* Boston: Little, Brown, 1969.

Berger, Peter and Thomas Luckmann. *The Social Construction of Reality.* New York: Anchor Books, 1966.

Fishman, Joshua. *Bilingual Education: An International Sociological Perspective.* Rowley, Mass: Newbury House, 1976.

Hallan, Vinod. "Whose Ethnicity Is It Anyway?" *Multicultural Teaching.* Volume 13, No. 1, (Autumn, 1994) pp. 14–16.

King, Edith. *Teaching Ethnic and Gender Awareness.* 2nd edition. Dubuque, Iowa: Kendall/Hunt. 1990.

King, Edith W., Marilyn Chipman, Marta Cruz-Janzen. *Educating Young Children in a Diverse Society.* Needham Hts. Mass.: Allyn and Bacon, 1994.

Salazar, Maria del Carmen. Unpublished project for seminar, "Diversity in Education", Denver, CO. University of Denver, 1995.

Address for Correspondence: *Professor Edith W. King, College of Education, University of Denver, 2450 S. Vine Street, Denver, Colorado, 80208 USA.*

NAEYC Position Statement: Responding to Linguistic and Cultural Diversity—Recommendations for Effective Early Childhood Education

Adopted November 1995

Linguistically and culturally diverse *is an educational term used by the U.S. Department of Education to define children enrolled in educational programs who are either non-English-proficient (NEP) or limited-English-proficient (LEP). Educators use this phrase,* linguistically and culturally diverse, *to identify children from homes and communities where English* is not *the primary language of communication (Garciá 1991). For the purposes of this statement, the phrase will be used in a similar manner.*

This document primarily describes linguistically and culturally diverse children who speak languages other than English. However, the recommendations of this position statement can also apply to children who, although they speak only English, are also linguistically and culturally diverse.

Introduction

The children and families served in early childhood programs reflect the ethnic, cultural, and linguistic diversity of the nation. The nation's children all deserve an early childhood education that is responsive to their families, communities, and racial, ethnic, and cultural backgrounds. For young children to develop and learn optimally, the early childhood professional must be prepared to meet their diverse developmental, cultural, linguistic, and educational needs. Early childhood educators face the challenge of how best to respond to these needs.

The acquisition of language is essential to children's cognitive and social development. Regardless of what language children speak, they still develop and learn. Educators recognize that linguistically and culturally diverse children come to early childhood programs with previously acquired knowledge and learning based upon the language used in their home. For young children, the language of the home is the language they have used since birth, the language they use to make and establish meaningful communicative relationships, and the language they use to begin to construct their knowledge and test their learning. The home

language is tied to children's culture, and culture and language communicate traditions, values, and attitudes (Chang 1993). Parents should be encouraged to use and develop children's home language; early childhood educators should respect children's linguistic and cultural backgrounds and their diverse learning styles. In so doing, adults will enhance children's learning and development.

Just as children learn and develop at different rates, individual differences exist in how children whose home language is not English acquire English. For example, some children may experience a silent period (of six or more months) while they acquire English; other children may practice their knowledge by mixing or combining languages (for example, "Mi mamá me put on mi coat"); still other children may seem to have acquired English-language skills (appropriate accent, use of vernacular, vocabulary, and grammatical rules) but are not truly proficient; yet some children will quickly acquire English-language proficiency. Each child's way of learning a new language should be viewed as acceptable, logical, and part of the ongoing development and learning of any new language.

Defining the problem

At younger and younger ages, children are negotiating difficult transitions between their home and educational settings, requiring an adaptation to two or more diverse sets of rules, values, expectations, and behaviors. Educational programs and families must *respect* and *reinforce* each other as they work together to achieve the greatest benefit for all children. For some young children, entering any new environment—including early childhood programs—can be intimidating. The lives of many young children today are further complicated by having to communicate and learn in a language that may be unfamiliar. In the past, children entering U.S. schools from families whose home language is not English were expected to immerse themselves in the mainstream of schools, primarily through the use of English (Soto 1991; Wong Fillmore 1991). Sometimes the negative attitudes conveyed or expressed toward certain languages lead children to "give up" their home language. Early childhood professionals must recognize the feeling of loneliness, fear, and abandonment children may feel when they are thrust into settings that isolate them from their home community and language. The loss of children's home language may result in

the disruption of family communication patterns, which may lead to the loss of intergenerational wisdom; damage to individual and community esteem; and children's potential nonmastery of their home language or English.

NAEYC's position

NAEYC's goal is to build support for equal access to high-quality educational programs that recognize and promote all aspects of children's development and learning, enabling all children to become competent, successful, and socially responsible adults. Children's educational experiences should afford them the opportunity to learn and to become effective, functioning members of society. Language development is essential for learning, and the development of children's home language does not interfere with their ability to learn English. Because knowing more than one language is a cognitive asset (Hakuta & García 1989), early education programs should encourage the development of children's home language while fostering the acquisition of English.

For the optimal development and learning of all children, educators must **accept** *the legitimacy of children's home language,* **respect** *(hold in high regard) and* **value** *(esteem, appreciate) the home culture, and* **promote** *and* **encourage** *the active involvement and support of all families, including extended and nontraditional family units.*

When early childhood educators acknowledge and respect children's home language and culture, ties between the family and programs are strengthened. This atmosphere provides increased opportunity for learning because young children feel supported, nurtured, and connected not only to their home communities and families but also to teachers and the educational setting.

The challenges

The United States is a nation of great cultural diversity, and our diversity creates opportunities to learn and share both similar and different experiences. There are opportunities to learn about people from different backgrounds; the opportunity to foster a bilingual citizenry with skills necessary to succeed in a global economy; and opportunities to share one's own cherished heritage and traditions with others.

Historically, our nation has tended to regard differences, especially language differences, as cultural handicaps rather than cultural resources (Meier & Cazden 1982). "Although most Americans are reluctant to say it publicly, many are anxious about the changing racial and ethnic composition of the country" (Sharry 1994). As the early childhood profession transforms its thinking,

the challenge for early childhood educators is to become more knowledgeable about how to relate to children and families whose linguistic or cultural background is different from their own.

Between 1979 and 1989 the number of children in the United States from culturally and linguistically diverse backgrounds increased considerably (NCES 1993), and, according to a report released by the Center for the Study of Social Policy (1992), that diversity is even more pronounced among children younger than age 6. Contrary to popular belief, many of these children are neither foreign born nor immigrants but were born in the United States (Waggoner 1993). Approximately 9.9 million of the estimated 45 million school-age children, more than one in five, live in households in which languages other than English are spoken (Waggoner 1994). In some communities, however, the number of children living in a family in which a language other than English is spoken is likely to be much larger. Head Start reports that the largest number of linguistically and culturally diverse children served through Head Start are Spanish speakers, with other language groups representing smaller but growing percentages (Head Start Bureau 1995).

The challenge for teachers is to provide high-quality care and education for the increasing number of children who are likely to be linguistically and culturally diverse.

Families and communities are faced with increasingly complex responsibilities. Children used to be cared for by parents and family members who typically spoke the home language of their family, be it English or another language. With the increasing need of family members to work, even while children are very young, more and more children are placed in care and educational settings with adults who may not speak the child's home language or share their cultural background. Even so, children will spend an ever-increasing amount of their waking lives with these teachers. What happens in care will have a tremendous impact on the child's social, emotional, and cognitive development. These interactions will influence the child's values, view of the world, perspectives on family, and connections to community. This places a tremendous responsibility in the hands of the early childhood community.

Responding to linguistic and cultural diversity can be challenging. At times the challenges can be complicated further by the specific needs or issues of the child, the family, or the educational program. Solutions may not be evident. Individual circumstances can affect each situation differently. There are no easy answers, and often myths and misinformation may flourish. The challenges may even seem to be too numerous for any one teacher or provider to manage. Nonetheless, despite the complexity, it is the responsibility of all

educators to assume the tasks and meet the challenges. Once a situation occurs, the early childhood educator should enter into a dialogue with colleagues, parents, and others in an effort to arrive at a negotiated agreement that will meet the best interest of the child. For example,

• A mother, father, and primary caregiver each have different cultural and linguistic backgrounds and do not speak English. Should the language of one of these persons be affirmed or respected above the others? How can the teacher affirm and respect the backgrounds of each of these individuals?

• The principal is concerned that all children learn English and, therefore, does not want any language other than English spoken in the early childhood setting. In the interest of the child, how should the educator respond?

• An educator questions whether a child will ever learn English if the home language is used as the primary language in the early childhood setting. How is this concern best addressed?

Solutions exist for each of these linguistic and cultural challenges, just as they do for the many other issues that early childhood educators confront within the early childhood setting. These challenges must be viewed as opportunities for the early childhood educator to reflect, question, and effectively respond to the needs of linguistically and culturally diverse children. Although appropriate responses to every linguistically and culturally diverse situation cannot be addressed through this document, early childhood educators should consider the following recommendations.

Recommendations for a responsive learning environment

Early childhood educators should stop and reflect on the best ways to

ensure appropriate educational and developmental experiences for all young children. The unique qualities and characteristics of each individual child must be acknowledged. Just as each child is different, methods and strategies to work with young children must vary.

The issue of home language and its importance to young children is also relevant for children who speak English but come from different cultural backgrounds, for example, speakers of English who have dialects, such as people from Appalachia or other regions having distinct patterns of speech, speakers of Black English, or second- and third-generation speakers of English who maintain the dominant accent of their heritage language. While this position statement basically responds to children who are from homes in which English is not the dominant language, the recommendations provided may be helpful when working with children who come from diverse cultural backgrounds, even when they only speak English. The overall goal for early childhood professionals, however, is to provide every child, including children who are linguistically and culturally diverse, with a responsive learning environment. The following recommendations help achieve this goal.

A. Recommendations for working with children

Recognize that all children are cognitively, linguistically, and emotionally connected to the language and culture of their home.

When program settings acknowledge and support children's home language and culture, ties between the family and school are strengthened. In a supportive atmosphere young children's home language is less likely to atrophy (Chang 1993), a situation that could threaten the children's important ties to family and community.

Acknowledge that children can demonstrate their knowledge and capabilities in many ways.

In response to linguistic and cultural diversity, the goal for early childhood educators should be to make the most of children's potential, strengthening and building upon the skills they bring when they enter programs. Education, as Cummins states, implies "drawing out children's potential and making them more than they were" (1989, vii). Educational programs and practices must recognize the strengths that children possess. Whatever language children speak, they should be able to demonstrate their capabilities and also feel the success of being appreciated and valued. Teachers must build upon children's diversity of gifts and skills and provide young children opportunities to exhibit these skills in early childhood programs.

The learning environment must focus on the learner and allow opportunities for children to express themselves across the curriculum, including art, music, dramatization, and even block building. By using a nondeficit approach (tapping and recognizing children's strengths rather than focusing the child's home environment on skills yet unlearned) in their teaching, teachers should take the time to observe and engage children in a variety of learning activities. Children's strengths should be celebrated, and they should be given numerous ways to express their interests and talents. In doing this, teachers will provide children an opportunity to display their intellect and knowledge that may far exceed the boundaries of language.

Understand that without comprehensible input, second-language learning can be difficult.

It takes time to become linguistically proficient and competent in any language. Linguistically and culturally diverse children may be able to master basic communication skills; however, mastery of the more cognitively complex language skills needed for academic learning (Cummins 1989) is more dependent on the learning environment. Academic learning relies on significant amounts of information presented in decontextualized learning situations. Success in school becomes more and more difficult as children are required to learn, to be tested and evaluated based on ever-increasing amounts of information, consistently presented in a decontextualized manner. Children learn best when they are given a context in which to learn, and the knowledge that children acquire in "their first language can make second-language input much more comprehensible" (Krashen 1992, 37). Young children can gain knowledge more easily when they obtain quality instruction through their first language. Children can acquire the necessary language and cognitive skills required to succeed in school when given an appropriate learning environment, one that is tailored to meet their needs (NAEYC & NAECS/SDE 1991; Bredekamp & Rosegrant 1992).

Although verbal proficiency in a second language can be accomplished within two to three years, the skills necessary to achieve the higher level educational skills of understanding academic content through reading and writing may require four or more years (Cummins 1981; Collier 1989). Young children may seem to be fluent and at ease with English but may not be capable of understanding or expressing themselves as competently as their English-speaking peers. Although children seem to be speaking a second language with ease, *speaking* a language does not equate to being *proficient* in that language. Full proficiency in the first language, including complex uses of the language, contributes to the development of the second language. Children who do not become proficient in their second language after two or three years of regular use probably are not proficient in their first language either.

Young children may seem to be fluent and at ease speaking a second language, but they may not be fully capable of understanding or expressing themselves in the more complex aspects of language and may demonstrate weaknesses in language-learning skills, including vocabulary skills, auditory memory and discrimination skills, simple problem-solving tasks, and the ability to follow sequenced directions. Language difficulties such as these often can result in the linguistically and culturally diverse child being overreferred to special education, classified as learning disabled, or perceived as developmentally delayed.

B. Recommendations for working with families

Actively involve parents and families in the early learning program and setting.

Parents and families should be actively involved in the learning and development of their children. Teachers should actively seek parental involvement and pursue establishing a partnership with children's families. When possible, teachers should visit the child's community (for example, shops, churches, and playgrounds); read and learn about the community through the use of books, pictures, observations, and conversations with community members; and visit the home and meet with other family members.

Parents and families should be invited to share, participate, and engage in activities with their children. Parent involvement can be accomplished in a number of ways, including asking parents to share stories, songs, drawings, and experiences of their linguistic and cultural background and asking parents to serve as monitors or field trip organizers. Families and parents should be invited to share activities that are developmentally appropriate and meaningful within their culture. These opportunities demonstrate to the parent what their child is learning; increase the knowledge, information, and understanding of all children regarding people of different cultures and linguistic backgrounds; and establish a meaningful relationship with the parent. The early childhood educator should ensure that parents are informed and engaged with their child in meaningful activities that promote linkages between the home and the early care setting.

Encourage and assist all parents in becoming knowledgeable about the cognitive value for children of knowing more than one language, and provide them with strategies to support, maintain, and preserve home-language learning.

In an early childhood setting and atmosphere in which home language is preserved, acknowledged, and respected, all parents can learn the value of home-language development and the strength it provides children as they add to their existing knowledge and understanding. Parents and teachers can learn how to become advocates regarding the long-term benefits that result from bilingualism.

Parents and teachers recognize the acquisition of English as an intellectual accomplishment, an opportunity for economic growth and development, and a means for achieving academic success. There are even times when parents may wish for the ability, or have been mistakenly encouraged, to speak to their children only in English, a language of which the parents themselves may not have command. The educator should understand the effects that speaking only in English can have upon the child, the family, and the child's learning. The

teacher must be able to explain that speaking to the child only in English can often result in communications being significantly hindered and verbal interactions being limited and unnatural between the parent and the child. In using limited English, parents may communicate to children using simple phrases and commands (for example, "Sit down" or "Stop"); modeling grammatically incorrect phrases (for example, "We no go store"); or demonstrating other incorrect usages of language that are common when persons acquire a second language. From these limited and incorrect verbal interactions, the amount of language the child is hearing is reduced, and the child's vocabulary growth is restricted, contributing to an overall decrease in verbal expression. When parents do not master the second language yet use the second language to communicate with their child, there is an increased likelihood that the child will not hear complex ideas or abstract thoughts—important skills needed for cognitive and language development. The teacher must explain that language is developed through natural language interactions. These natural interactions occur within the day-to-day setting, through radio and television, when using public transportation, and in play with children whose dominant language is English. The parent and the teacher must work collaboratively to achieve the goal of children's learning English.

Through the home language and culture, families transmit to their children a sense of identity, an understanding of how to relate to other people, and a sense of belonging. When parents and children cannot communicate with one another, family and community destabilization can occur. Children who are proficient in their home language are able to maintain a connectedness to their histories, their stories, and the day-to-day events shared by parents, grandparents, and other family members who may speak only the home language. Without the ability to com-

municate, parents are not able to socialize their children, share beliefs and value systems, and directly influence, coach, and model with their children.

Recognize that parents and families must rely on caregivers and educators to honor and support their children in the cultural values and norms of the home.

Parents depend on high-quality early childhood programs to assist them with their children's development and learning. Early childhood programs should make provisions to communicate with families in their home language and to provide parent–teacher encounters that both welcome and accommodate families. Partnerships between the home and the early childhood setting must be developed to ensure that practices of the home and expectations of the program are complementary. Linguistic and cultural continuity between the home and the early childhood program supports children's social and emotional development. By working together, parents and teachers have the opportunity to influence the understanding of language and culture and to encourage multicultural learning and acceptance in a positive way.

C. Recommendations for professional preparation

Provide early childhood educators with professional preparation and development in the areas of culture, language, and diversity.

Efforts to understand the languages and cultural backgrounds of young children are essential in helping children to learn. Uncertainty can exist when educators are unsure of how to relate to children and families of linguistic and cultural backgrounds different from their own. Early childhood educators need to understand and appreciate their own cultural and linguistic backgrounds. Adults' cultural background affects how they interact with and/or teach young children. The educator's background influences how children are taught, reinforced, and disciplined. The child's background influences how the child constructs knowledge, responds to discipline and praise, and interacts in the early childhood setting.

Preservice and inservice training opportunities in early childhood education programs assist educators in overcoming some of the linguistic and cultural challenges they may face in working with young children. Training institutions and programs can consider providing specific courses in the following topic areas or include these issues in current courses: language acquisition; second-language learning; use of translators; working with diverse families; sociolinguistics; cross-cultural communication; issues pertaining to the politics of race, language, and culture; and community involvement.

Recruit and support early childhood educators who are trained in languages other than English.

Within the field of early childhood education, there is a need for knowledgeable, trained, competent, and sensitive multilingual/multicultural early childhood educators. Early childhood educators who speak more than one language and are culturally knowledgeable are an invaluable resource in the early childhood setting. In some instances the educator may speak multiple languages or may be able to communicate using various linguistic regionalisms or dialects

spoken by the child or the family. The educator may have an understanding of sociocultural and economic issues relevant within the local linguistically and culturally diverse community and can help support the family in the use and development of the child's home language and in the acquisition of English. The early childhood teacher who is trained in linguistic and cultural diversity can be a much-needed resource for information about the community and can assist in the inservice cultural orientation and awareness training for the early childhood program. The bilingual educator also can be a strong advocate for family and community members.

Too often, however, bilingual early childhood professionals are called upon to provide numerous other services, some of which they may not be equipped to provide. For example, the bilingual professional, although a fluent speaker, may not have the vocabulary needed to effectively communicate with other adults or, in some instances, may be able to read and write only in English, not in the second language. In addition, bilingual teachers should not be expected to meet the needs of *all* linguistically and culturally diverse children and families in the program, especially those whose language they do not speak. Bilingual providers should not be asked to translate forms, particularly at a moment's notice, nor should they be required to stop their work in order to serve as interpreters. Bilingual teachers should not serve in roles, such as advising or counseling, in which they may lack professional training. These assignments may seem simple but often can be burdensome and must be viewed as added duties placed upon the bilingual teacher.

Preservice and inservice training programs are needed to support bilingual early childhood educators in furthering educators' knowledge and mastery of the language(s) other than English that they speak, and training should also credit content-based courses offered in lan-

guages other than English. Professional preparation instructors must urge all teachers to support multilingual/multicultural professionals in their role as advocates for linguistically and culturally diverse children. Early childhood professionals should be trained to work collaboratively with the bilingual early childhood teacher and should be informed of the vital role of the bilingual educator. Additionally, there is a need for continued research in the area of linguistic and cultural diversity of young children.

D. Recommendations for programs and practice

Recognize that children can and will acquire the use of English even when their home language is used and respected.

Children should build upon their current skills as they acquire new skills. While children maintain and build upon their home language skills and culture, children can organize and develop proficiency and knowledge in English. Bilingualism has been associated with higher levels of cognitive attainment (Hakuta & García 1989) and does not interfere with either language proficiency or cognitive development. Consistent learning opportunities to read, be read to, and see print messages should be given to linguistically and culturally diverse children. Literacy developed in the home language will transfer to the second language (Krashen 1992). Bilingualism should be viewed as an asset and an educational achievement.

Support and preserve home language usage.

If the early childhood teacher *speaks* the child's home language, then the teacher can comfortably use this language around the child, thereby providing the child with opportunities to hear and use the home language within the early childhood setting. Use of the language should be clearly evident throughout the learning environment (e.g., in meeting charts, tape recordings, the library corner). Educators should develop a parent information board, using a language and reading level appropriate for the parents. Teachers should involve parents and community members in the early childhood program. Parents and community members can assist children in hearing the home language from many different adults, in addition to the teacher who speaks the home language. Parents and community members can assist other parents who may be unable to read, or they can assist the teacher in communicating with families whose home language may not have a written form.

If the early childhood educator *does not speak* the language, he or she should make efforts to provide visible signs of the home language throughout the learning environment through books and other relevant reading material in the child's language and with a parent bulletin board (get a bilingual colleague to help review for accuracy of written messages). The teacher can learn a few selected words in the child's language, thus demonstrating a willingness to take risks similar to the risks asked of children as they learn a second language. This effort by the teacher also helps to validate and affirm the child's language and culture, further demonstrating the teacher's esteem and respect for the child's linguistic and cultural background. The teacher should model appropriate use of English and provide the child with opportunities to use newly acquired vocabulary and language. The teacher also must actively involve the parent and the community in the program.

If the teacher is *faced with many different languages* in the program or classroom, the suggestions listed above are still relevant. Often teachers feel overwhelmed if more than one language is spoken in the program; however, they should remember that the goal is for children to learn, and that learning is made easier when children can build on knowledge in their home language. The teacher should consider grouping together at specific times during the day children who speak the same or similar languages so that the children can construct knowledge with others who speak their home language. The early childhood educator should ensure that these children do not become socially isolated as efforts are made to optimize their learning. Care should be taken to continually create an environment that provides for high learning expectations.

Develop and provide alternative and creative strategies for young children's learning.

Early childhood educators are encouraged to rely on their creative skills in working with children to infuse cultural and linguistic diversity in their programs. They should provide children with multiple opportunities to learn and ways for them to demonstrate their learning, participate in program activities, and work interactively with other children.

To learn more about working with linguistically and culturally diverse children, early childhood educators should collaborate with each other and with colleagues from other professions. To guide the implementation of a developmentally, linguistically, and culturally appropriate program, collaborative parent and teacher workgroups should be developed. These committees should discuss activities and strategies that would be effective for use with linguistically and culturally diverse children. Such committees promote good practices for children and shared learning between teachers and parents.

Summary

Early childhood educators can best help linguistic and culturally diverse children and their families by acknowledging and responding to the importance of the child's home language and culture. Administrative support for bilingualism as a goal is necessary within the educational setting. Educational practices should focus on educating children toward the "school culture" while preserving and respecting the diversity of the home language and culture that each child brings to the early learning setting. Early childhood professionals and families must work together to achieve high-quality care and education for *all* children.

References

Bredekamp, S., & T. Rosegrant, eds. 1992. *Reaching potentials: Appropriate curriculum and assessment for young children.* Vol. 1. Washington, DC: NAEYC.

Center for the Study of Social Policy. 1992. *The challenge of change: What the 1990 census tells us about children.* Washington, DC: Author.

Chang, H.N.-L. 1993. *Affirming children's roots: Cultural and linguistic diversity in early care and education.* San Francisco: California Tomorrow.

Collier, V. 1989. How long: A synthesis of research on academic achievement in second language. *TESOL Quarterly* 23: 509–31.

Cummins, J. 1981. The role of primary language development in promoting educational success for language minority students. In *Schooling and language minority students: A theoretical framework,* eds. M. Ortiz, D. Parker, & F. Tempes. Office of Bilingual Bicultural Education, California State Department of Education. Los Angeles: Evaluation, Dissemination, and Assessment Center, California State University.

Cummins, J. 1989. *Empowering minority students.* Sacramento: California Association for Bilingual Education.

Garciá, E. 1991. *The education of linguistically and culturally diverse students: Effective instructional practices.* Santa Cruz: National Center for Research on Cultural Diversity and Second Language Learning, University of California.

Hakuta, K., & E. Garciá. 1989. Bilingualism and education. *American Psychologist* 44 (2): 374–79.

Head Start Bureau, Administration on Children, Youth, and Families, Department of Health and Human Services. 1995. *Program information report.* Washington, DC: Author.

Krashen, S. 1992. *Fundamentals of language education.* Torrance, CA: Laredo Publishing.

Meier, T.R., & C.B. Cazden. 1982. A focus on oral language and writing from a multicultural perspective. *Language Arts* 59: 504–12.

National Association for the Education of Young Children (NAEYC) and National Association of Early Childhood Specialists in State Departments of Education (NAECS/

SDE). 1991. Guidelines for appropriate curriculum content and assessment in programs serving children ages 3 through 8. *Young Children* 46 (3): 21–38.

National Center for Education Statistics (NCES). 1993. *Language characteristics and schooling in the United States, a changing picture: 1979 and 1989.* NCES 93-699. Washington, DC: U.S. Department of Education, Office of Educational Research and Improvement.

Sharry, F. 1994. *The rise of nativism in the United States and how to respond to it.* Washington, DC: National Education Forum.

Soto, L.D. 1991. Understanding bilingual/bicultural children. *Young Children* 46 (2): 30–36.

Waggoner, D., ed. 1993. *Numbers and needs: Ethnic and linguistic minorities in the United States* 3 (6).

Waggoner, D. 1994. Language minority school age population now totals 9.9 million. *NABE News* 18 (1): 1, 24–26.

Wong Fillmore, L. 1991. When learning a second language means losing the first. *Early Childhood Research Quarterly* 6: 323–46.

Resources

Banks, J. 1993. Multicultural education for young children: Racial and ethnic attitudes and their modification. In *Handbook of research on the education of young children,* ed. B. Spodek, 236–51. New York: Macmillan.

Collier, V. 1989. How long: A synthesis of research on academic achievement in second language. *TESOL Quarterly* 23: 509–31.

Collier, V., & C. Twyford. 1988. The effect of age on acquisition of a second language for school. *National Clearinghouse for Bilingual Education* 2 (Winter): 1–12.

Derman-Sparks, L., & the A.B.C. Task Force. 1989. *Anti-bias curriculum: Tools for empowering young children.* Washington, DC: NAEYC.

McLaughlin, B. 1992. *Myths and misconceptions about second language learning: What every teacher needs to unlearn.* Santa Cruz: National Center for Research on Cultural Diversity and Second Language Learning, University of California.

Neugebauer, B., ed. 1992. *Alike and different: Exploring our humanity with young children.* Redmond, WA: Exchange Press, 1987. Reprint, Washington, DC: NAEYC.

Ogbu, J.U. 1978. *Minority education and caste: The American system in cross cultural perspective.* New York: Academic.

Phillips, C.B. 1988. Nurturing diversity for today's children and tomorrow's leaders. *Young Children* 43 (2): 42–47.

Tharp, R.G. 1989. Psychocultural variables and constants: Effects on teaching and learning in schools. *American Psychologist* 44: 349–59.

Special Topics in Multicultural Education

Each year we try to focus in this section of this volume on selected special topics that have been of particular interest to those who work in multicultural settings. Topics are also chosen if they have a direct bearing on issues of equality of educational opportunity.

Every teacher needs to be sensitive and concerned about the cultural heritages of their students. Linguistic minority rights need to be taken seriously. Children deserve compassionate and insightful understanding, especially children of minority linguistic and cultural backgrounds. The essays in this unit speak eloquently to this point. Hatred and prejudice must be addressed in schooling in order that future generations of children will understand the necessity of love and acceptance of diversity in society. The family and cultural backgrounds of children must be accepted by all of us.

Issues relating to interethnic and intercultural perceptions need to be dealt with as part of a response to xenophobic reactions to immigrants and migrants.

Educators who work in the area of multicultural education are concerned with research into how students can succeed in school and transcend the impact of socioeconomic inequality and feelings of powerlessness as well as with documenting the causes of school failure. How at-risk minority students can overcome feelings of low self-esteem and develop workable strategies for solving their problems in school are matters of great importance. The students of each racial, cultural, or religious minority group have had their own special historical and sociocultural experience with "mainstream" school curriculum. Multicultural education seeks to help all students to locate or situate their lives in the context of their developing individual identities within a pluralistic social order.

The essays in this unit are relevant to courses in educational policy studies, multicultural education, and cultural foundations of education.

Looking Ahead: Challenge Questions

In what ways can texts used in schools be critically reviewed for cultural and gender biases?

Name several ways for a teacher to empower students. How does a teacher develop a sense of social consciousness in students?

What should every American student know about the Holocaust? Is anti-Semitism still a major problem in America? What can be done to combat it?

How can teachers best respond to the needs of linguistic minority children?

What can be done to help children retain their cultural heritages?

What is the best relationship between teachers and the parents of their students?

Of Kinds of Disciplines and Kinds of Understanding

BY VERONICA BOIX
MANSILLA AND
HOWARD GARDNER

The authors show how, despite sharing a verbal symbol system, understanding in history and understanding in literature pose different challenges to the mind. They address the question, Why should this matter to educators?

THE HOLOCAUST, the systematic mass murder of European Jewry by the Nazis, has transformed humanity's image of itself. It has engendered caution about prevailing nationalisms, about conceptions of race, and about the reaches

VERONICA BOIX MANSILLA is a researcher at Project Zero, Harvard Graduate School of Education, Cambridge, Mass., where HOWARD GARDNER is a professor of education and co-director of Project Zero. Gardner is also an adjunct professor of neurology at Boston University School of Medicine. They would like to thank Facing History and Ourselves National Foundation for inspiring their selection of the example used in this article, as well as the Louise and Claude Rosenberg Jr. Family Foundation, the Ross Family Charitable Foundation, the Spencer Foundation, and the Organization of American States for supporting its preparation.

Illustration by Kris Hackleman

History and literature represent distinct kinds of understanding that cannot be merged uncritically.

of state power. Contemporary efforts to guard civil liberties and human rights around the world are rooted to a significant degree in this horrendous chapter of human history.

The Holocaust has also challenged students, scholars, and educators. Historians, novelists, poets, and artists have sought to make sense of this most ghastly episode of modern times.[1] Educators have tried to draw important lessons from this period as they develop history curricula. Teachers recognize the importance of examining the Holocaust with their students in the hope that they will come to understand it.[2] And yet, in all of our minds the question lingers: What does it *mean* to understand this episode in depth?

In the Holocaust and in our cultural responses to it, issues of identity, morality, political power, state and society, dehumanization, media, and art are intricately intertwined. A deep understanding may emerge only after one has approached this complex nexus of topics through multiple domains and symbol systems. Educators combine historical or political accounts with poetic, pictorial, or sculptural renderings of the experiences of the victims.

But to be effective, we believe, this multidisciplinary approach must not mix these domains and their symbol systems haphazardly; rather, it must honor the specific contributions of each domain to a fuller understanding of the experience.[3] What role does each of these artistic or disciplinary entry points play in understanding? How does creating a monument or writing a poem demonstrate our understanding of the Holocaust? What kinds of understanding can one draw from reading a historical account or a fictional story? And how do these forms of understanding relate to, and differ from, one another?

In this article we focus on history and literature — two domains that use language in different ways — to examine the specific kinds of understanding they elicit. We deliberately use two linguistic domains in order to underscore the importance of the ways symbols are used in each case. If differences in understanding emerge between the "neighboring" domains of history and literature, then we may assume that even greater distinctions exist between those disciplines that use more disparate sets of symbols.

We begin by portraying the multidimensional nature of disciplinary understanding as we have come to formulate it in our own research. We compare understanding in each domain, illustrating our analysis with an important piece of historical work and a highly acclaimed novel. In the end, we examine the educational implications of recognizing the specific qualities of disciplinary understanding in history and literature.

Understanding: A Multidimensional Task

Understanding refers to an individual's ability to use knowledge in novel situations — e.g., to solve problems, fashion products, or create stories — in ways akin to those modeled by knowledgeable practitioners in specific domains. Students demonstrate their understanding when they are able to go beyond accumulating information and engage in performances that are valued by the communities in which they live. For example, they demonstrate their understanding of the Holocaust when they can compare and contrast it with current policies of genocide in Bosnia, when they can empathize with particular aspects of the survivors' experiences, and when they can offer plausible explanations of why and how it happened. In this *performance-centered* view, understanding is not merely a representation of the world in our minds or a set of loosely organized actions. Rather, understanding is the ability to *think with* knowledge, according to the standards of good practice within a specific domain, such as math, history, ceramics, or dance.[4]

Understanding *within* a discipline, such as history or literature, is in itself a multidimensional enterprise. As such, it goes beyond the specific mastery of one or more symbol systems or the recall of a series of facts. To demonstrate understanding, students need to be able to use important concepts, findings, or theories. However, they also need to appreciate the carefully crafted methods and criteria that knowledgeable people have developed to build a comprehensive historical account or to write a compelling novel. They need to communicate according to the specific rules of their chosen genres of performance — oral presentation, written text, theater perform-

ance. And, at best, they need to appreciate the purposes that inspire the writing of a historical account or a fictional work, and they need to be able to use samples of such work to orient their own actions or perceptions of the world.[5]

Two dimensions of understanding underlie our description: 1) understanding of domain-specific *knowledge* and 2) understanding of the *disciplinary modes of thinking* embodied in the methods by which knowledge is constructed, the forms in which knowledge is made public, and the purposes that drive inquiry in the domain. Our main thesis here is that history and literature represent distinct kinds of understanding that cannot be merged uncritically without the loss of important contributions.

One Holocaust: Two Key Texts

To illustrate this point we examine Daniel Goldhagen's *Hitler's Willing Executioners* and William Styron's *Sophie's Choice*.[6] In his study of Nazi Germany during the Holocaust, Goldhagen posits the provocative thesis that the killers who participated in the Holocaust were not primarily members of the SS or fervent supporters of the Nazi party, as most previous interpreters had proposed. Instead, Goldhagen argues that anti-Semitism was deeply pervasive in German society even before Hitler rose to power. Ordinary Germans regarded Jews as a demonic people who had to be exterminated. Germans were predisposed to an active and voluntary participation in this process. Unlike other historians, Goldhagen does not attribute the actions of the German people to Nazi coercion, or to brutal social pressure, or to the anonymity afforded by a bureaucratic system.[7] Instead, he proposes that the common people willingly joined in the brutalization and murder of Jews. To bolster his dramatic and controversial thesis, Goldhagen examines the murderers' world views and values, their institutional means of killing — police battalions, "work camps," and death marches — and the broader social contexts in which the participants in the mass murders lived.

Sophie's Choice examines the experience of a Polish Holocaust survivor through the lens of a young American writer from the South who is determined to render her story. The novel foregrounds three characters: Sophie; Stingo, the writer; and Nathan, Sophie's emotionally unstable lover. Looming in the background is a character from the past based on Rudolf Höss, commandant of Auschwitz. In the novel readers confront the Holocaust as Sophie reveals, bit by bit, the pieces of her story. Toward the end, she bares her most painful secret: the anguish of having been forced to send her daughter to her death in order to save her son. Styron chooses Stingo, the writer, as the narrator whose consciousness determines what and how much of Sophie's anguish — loss of her children, her friends, and her health — will be revealed at each moment in the text. The Holocaust serves as a background against which readers interpret the characters' beliefs and conduct.

Needless to say, Goldhagen's and Styron's books share some features: their use of linguistic symbol systems, their reference to historical facts, and their intention to uncover "truth." However, under closer scrutiny, these two pieces are seen as emerging from different disciplinary enterprises; their value in helping us understand the Holocaust depends more on the ways in which they differ than on the ways in which they are similar. Language, facts, and aesthetics not only carry different weights but also play dramatically different roles in each domain. Shorn of these disciplinary distinctions, students' understanding is likely to be reduced to propaganda or stereotypical opinion. We illustrate this point by comparing these two works through our principal dimensions of understanding.

Understanding in History and Literature

Understanding knowledge. Understanding the Holocaust as a historical phenomenon entails integrating what we can determine about specific events and the particular world views of people involved in them with more general interpretations of events during the period. For example, Goldhagen examines the intricacies of life in the "work camps" and the process by which members of the police battalions were selected. He draws our attention to the superficiality of the ideological and military training that police battalion members received, in order to support his broader thesis — that the mass murder of Jews was driven by the already existing anti-Semitism of the German people. In his account,

factual information alone would be devoid of historical significance if it were detached from the broader thesis he is putting forth. Conversely, his interpretations would become mere opinions if they were devoid of the facts that give them substance.[8]

In history, such expressions as "final solution," "police battalions," or "Nazi regime" correspond to a world that existed in Germany in the 1930s and 1940s. Although the past is only indirectly accessible to historians, and historical narratives are necessarily interpretations, historical accounts aim to mold our present interpretations to a past that we know existed. Historical narratives strive for comprehensiveness and clarity. They seek to describe and explain what happened and why, in a mode of discourse that is as accessible and unambiguous as possible. Given these features of knowledge in the domain, students demonstrate their understanding of the Holocaust when they are able to integrate findings about different agents, goals, contexts, and circumstances into one or more comprehensive and unambiguous interpretations or when they are able to test broad interpretations against the details and evidence that are relevant to those claims.

Unlike history, which aims at portraying what the world was like in the past, literature aims at expressing aspects of human experience. In *Sophie's Choice*, the past operates as a frame, not as Styron's object of study. The novel is about the experiences of guilt, silence, and survival. But it is also about the sensuality of youth and the discovery of writing. For poets and novelists, the Holocaust provides a diabolical stimulus for speculating about the experience of dehumanization or the motives of evil and for pushing fictional and poetic language to its expressive and evocative limits, surpassing the more strictly constrained descriptive language of history. Understanding the Holocaust through literature entails exploring the themes and experiences created by the writer and appreciating his or her sensitive use of language in portraying events that drive many observers to silence.

Understanding disciplinary modes of thinking. Unlike novelists, historians consider past events as central to their work. They aim to capture events in as fair a manner as possible. Goldhagen's convictions about the Holocaust emerged from careful interpretations of texts, documents, and eyewitness reports of the period, leavened by accounts or interpretations proposed by

other historians in more recent times. For example, he examined materials amassed during the investigations of Nazi crimes. He used documentation compiled by the German justice system as well as records of extensive interrogations of the perpetrators themselves, surviving victims, and bystanders. He treated these sources cautiously, recognizing such limitations as memory's natural deficiency and the perpetrators' desire to conceal information. Confronted with euphemistic sources that were often fragmentary, he sought to uncover people's actual intentions, world views, and contexts and test them against competing accounts of similar data.

Despite the power of the questions that historians bring to sources, the intricacies of the selection of documents, or the ideologies that inspire them, historians' recourse to original documents marks the dividing line between history and fiction. Unlike novelists (who may pilfer from or radically alter original source materials), historians aim at reconstructing the past. Through the critical examination of documents, historians' imaginations are subject to the limits of what once was.[9] In contrast to novelists' imaginations, historians' imaginations are rigorously constrained by the evidence they extract from available sources. Goldhagen's text of 622 pages dedicates 22 pages to a framing introduction and 225 pages to notes and references. In a novel, such appendages could only be seen as ironic.

How do novelists produce worthy pieces of literature? For novelists, past events constitute only an instrumental aspect of their work. Unlike historians, they are not concerned with issues of evidence. Instead, they engage in such procedures as portraying and developing fictional characters, producing the effects of verisimilitude, and developing texts that are enriched by ambiguity and invite multiple interpretations.

For example, prior to depicting Höss' tenure at Auschwitz, Styron examined Höss' autobiography, consulted a series of testimonies from the war-crime trials, and visited the site of the death camp. However, Styron feels no commitment to keep facts unmodified. For the sake of enhancing the dramatic power of his narrative, Styron imaginatively creates Commandant Höss' motives, dialogues, and gestures. Rather than portray him as a public figure, Styron emphasizes the private man, surrounded by his wife, children, and friends. He spices up his character with periodic attacks of migraine — a carefully crafted strategy to complete the picture of a privately human Höss. Novelists are primarily concerned with the internal *coherence* of their narratives, rather than with the *correspondence* between their accounts and the data of the past. To be sure, Styron's novel honors the stability of settings and characters throughout. It establishes a "sense of truth" by referring successively, though in nonrepetitive ways, to settings, images, and characters that were previously introduced to the reader. While the trustworthiness of historical narratives relies chiefly on the proficient use of primary sources, the believability of novels rests, in part, on this effect of déjà vu embedded in their structure.[10]

Like most novels, *Sophie's Choice* is polysemous: its symbols invite multiple interpretations. Unlike historical accounts, novels benefit from such allusiveness. For example, Sophie explains that she is slowly becoming human again as she learns how to cry when she listens to music. She associates her humanity with a deep sense of guilt and a certain skepticism about the possibility of human redemption. In describing her feelings when listening to "The Redeemer," Sophie confesses, "I know that my body will be destroyed by worms and my eyes will never see God." Styron chooses language that mimics the Genesis story of Adam and Eve and the loss of paradise. Sophie's Holocaust is for Styron both the story of a fictional individual and an emblem of the human species.[11] Literary writing relies on its ability to play with ambiguity, to invite the reader to grasp multiple layers of meaning, uncover multiple themes, and allow his or her imagination to proceed along idiosyncratic paths. In contrast, the theses put forth in historical accounts seek to avoid ambiguity in order to convince readers of a given interpretation of the past.

In moving from the unprocessed historical record to chronicles and stories, scholars like Goldhagen organize events in time and into the components of a "spectacle" with a discernible beginning, middle, and end.[12] Historians' definitions of the periods they cover emerge from a dynamic interaction between milestone events in the past and the interpretive frameworks that historians bring to their study.

For example, Goldhagen portrays a process that he calls the evolution of a European Eliminationist Anti-Semitism mentality. He marks its beginning in the earliest days of Christianity and its end in the Second World War. On the one hand, the beginning and ending dates are determined by milestones in the past, such as Chris-

tianity's consolidation of its hold over the Roman Empire. On the other hand, they are defined by Goldhagen's framework, in which German anti-Semitic beliefs need to be explored beyond the particular circumstances of Nazi Germany. In *Sophie's Choice* Styron unfolds the story from Stingo's arrival in Brooklyn, New York, to his reflections after the deaths of Sophie and Nathan. Such a time frame is an expression of Styron's imaginative design. The survivors of the Holocaust continue to live with their experiences after Goldhagen has ended his account, and the events of the Nazi regime continue to reverberate in the present, but Stingo ceases to live after page 562.

Narratives are a natural way for historians to represent the unfolding of events over time.[13] But unlike novelists, historians see narrative only as a tool to enhance the quality of their reports, not as their primary focus. Historians have learned about the ways in which the stories they produce shape and are shaped by canonical narrative codes long studied by linguists and discourse analysts.[14] For historians, compelling narratives function to convey their reconstructions of the past. For novelists, compelling narratives are the end product and center of their endeavor. Unlike understanding a history text, understanding a novel is primarily a matter of appreciating the ways in which narratives themselves are crafted (e.g., the use of metaphors, the creation of a character, the continuity of a scene, and so on).

In sum, when students are challenged to grasp the *disciplinary modes of thinking* on which historical and literary accounts of the Holocaust are based, they engage in two very different enterprises. Sources, layers of meaning, narrative structures, correspondence with facts, and coherence not only have different relevance in each domain, but also have different functions.

Students demonstrate their understanding of the Holocaust as a historical phenomenon when they are able to interpret historical claims critically — not as transparent manifestations of the past or idiosyncratic inventions of a creative historian, but as the product of an intricate process of inquiry and marshaling of evidence. They demonstrate their understanding of history when they are able to write accounts that satisfy the standards of evidence and the norms of reference and citation that are institutionalized in historical writing.

In literature, students demonstrate their understanding of *Sophie's Choice* when

they critique or produce a piece of fiction — e.g., showing how figurative language can convey dehumanization in evocative ways, demonstrating the role of symbolism in conveying the maturation of the protagonist, or illustrating how the structure of the work conveys important themes and contrasts. In this case, reporting the sources of evidence or clarifying the main thesis of the work would diminish the qualities of suggestiveness and speculation embedded in literary performances.

The Payoff for Education

So far we have described what expert historians, writers, and critics perceive to be the central features of their tasks. We have shown how, despite sharing a verbal symbol system, understanding in history and understanding in literature pose different challenges to the mind. But the question remains: Why should this matter to educators?

Here it becomes relevant to consider the developing mind. By the time students encounter a topic like the Holocaust, they have already developed a series of beliefs and theories about the past, about this particular episode, and about knowledge — all of which are likely to reflect the "unschooled mind" at work.[15] For instance, students create imaginative accounts of the past on the basis of only a few events they may have encountered in earlier grades, in the media, or in everyday life (e.g., Jews lived in ghettos, or Germans hated Jews). Often students interpret historical sources literally and build stereotypical portraits of historical actors.[16] In literature, students often expect a story to end on a happy note and characters to be depicted as unambiguously good or evil. Transforming these intuitive but inadequate beliefs requires careful instruction. Only in this way can students progressively replace their sometimes too imaginative versions of the past with the evidence-based historical ones that are held as trustworthy by their culture. And only in this way can students grasp the hidden symbolism in literary texts, enjoy the process of sharpening human experience through language, and appreciate the formal structures that shape powerful meanings.

Students also bring their unique combinations of intelligences to their encounter with a topic; they might favor musical, bodily, logical/mathematical, or linguistic modes of thinking.[17] In order to motivate them to pursue their studies, educators face the challenge of devising a variety of "entry points" that honor each student's idiosyncratic ways of representing the world. Some students might be inclined to draw a Jewish scene in the ghetto as it is portrayed in a particular source; others might prefer to write a poem from the point of view of one of the characters; still others might be inclined to use their

> *To demonstrate* historical *understanding, students have to place the scene in a broader context and interpretive frame.*

bodies to mimic the physical and ideological postures of those in the scene.

Such entry points invite students to use symbol systems that they find comfortable and familiar as they engage in complex tasks.[18] In doing so they open up the possibilities for deeper understanding. Their limitation lies in the fact that they only partially represent understanding in history or literature. For example, drawing or mimicking a scene requires that students go beyond the literal meaning of the text to grasp the situation depicted, to assess its plausibility, to interpret the point of view from which it is described. By using familiar symbol systems, such as drawing or body language, students may be encouraged to engage in these complex interpretive tasks. Visual representations or mimicking may "take us to the scene," but they tell us little about the broader historical interpretations in which these situations must be inscribed. The metaphoric language of poetry resonates with our personal experience, but it is still too ambiguous to meet the standards of historical description and explanation.

To demonstrate full-fledged *historical* understanding, students have to place the scene in a broader context and interpretive frame. Why did it happen? What did it mean to the people at the time? What would these people soon find out? Ques-

tions of this sort invite students to produce historical accounts that integrate facts and interpretations, accounts that are respectful of the characteristics of past times and are grounded in carefully marshaled evidence. To demonstrate full-fledged *literary* understanding, students have to grasp the essential aspects of human experience embodied in the scene and use figurative language to portray them in a novel, a short story, or a poem. What does this incident say about human experience? What does it symbolize? How can the story be told? Questions of this sort invite students to produce literary accounts that hold multiple layers of meaning and play with the expressive limits of language.

There is one vital reason for stressing the distinctions between these two modes of presentation. The recent success of docudramas, of historical fiction, and of various movies, such as *JFK* or *Nixon*, has had the effect of blurring the boundaries between what happened, what might have happened, and what has clearly been invented by a writer, director, or actor. Such blurred genres actually revel in collapsing history and literature, truth and fiction. Young students can only be confused by such a mixing of modes of knowing. Indeed, at their most extreme, these blurrings encourage the creation of myths, including the frightening myth that "there was no Holocaust."

Ideally, after approaching the Holocaust through "entry points" that are tuned to their individual intellectual profiles, students will come to produce historical and literary accounts that are exemplary "exit points" of a course or a project. At best, these final performances or demonstrations of understanding will fully show students' mastery of knowledge and disciplinary modes of thinking in each domain.

What forms of representation should these performances take? As Elliot Eisner reminds us, different forms of representation allow us "to construct meanings that might otherwise elude us."[19] In searching for generative final performances for their students, teachers face an important challenge: the challenge of assessing different forms of representation for what students gain and what they lose in the process of building deeper understanding in distinct domains. By viewing understanding as both the ability to *use knowledge* and the ability to *engage in disciplinary modes of thinking*, we have sought to provide an initial framework that may facilitate such nuanced assessment.

1. See Lawrence Langer, "Fictional Facts and Factual Fictions: History in Holocaust Literature," in Randolph L. Braham, ed., *Reflections of the Holocaust in Art and Literature* (New York: Columbia University Press, 1993).

2. See *Facing History and Ourselves: Holocaust and Human Behavior Resource Book* (Brookline, Mass.: Facing History and Ourselves National Foundation, 1994).

3. For a careful analysis of the challenges and possibilities of cross-disciplinary curricula, see College Board and the Getty Center for Education in the Arts, *Connections: The Arts and the Integration of High School Curriculum* (New York: College Board Publications, 1996).

4. David Perkins, "What Is Understanding?," in M. Stone Wiske, ed., *Teaching for Understanding: A Practical Framework* (San Francisco: Jossey-Bass, forthcoming).

5. For a detailed analysis of "dimensions of understanding," see Veronica Boix Mansilla and Howard Gardner, "Assessing Qualities of Understanding," in Wiske, op. cit. See also Veronica Boix Mansilla, "Bridging Meaning and Rigor in Teaching for Understanding," paper presented at ATLAS Seminar, Cambridge, Mass., 1995.

6. Daniel Goldhagen, *Hitler's Willing Executioners: Ordinary Germans and the Holocaust* (New York: Knopf, 1996); and William Styron, *Sophie's Choice* (New York: Vintage Books, 1992).

7. See Michael Marrus, *The Holocaust in History* (Hanover, N.H.: University Press of New England, 1987). See also Charles Maier, *The Unmasterable Past: History, Holocaust, and German National Identity* (Cambridge, Mass.: Harvard University Press, 1988).

8. See Bernard Bailyn, *On the Teaching and Writing of History: Responses to a Series of Questions* (Hanover, N.H.: Dartmouth College, 1994). See also Neil R. Stout, *Getting the Most out of Your U.S. History Course* (Lexington, Mass.: D. C. Heath, 1994).

9. Paul Ricoeur, *Time and Narrative, Vol. 2* (Chicago: University of Chicago Press, 1985), pp. 142-43.

10. See Michael Riffaterre, *Fictional Truth* (Baltimore: Johns Hopkins University Press, 1990).

11. Styron, pp. 93-94.

12. Hayden White, *Metahistory: The Historical Imagination in Nineteenth-Century Europe* (Baltimore: Johns Hopkins University Press, 1973).

13. Louis Mink, "Narrative Form as a Cognitive Instrument," in Eugene Golob, Brian Fray, and Richard Vannin, eds., *Historical Understanding* (Ithaca, N.Y.: Cornell University Press, 1987).

14. See William Cronon, "A Place for Stories: Nature, History, and Narrative," *Journal of American History*, March 1992, pp. 1347-76.

15. Howard Gardner, *The Unschooled Mind: How Children Think and How Schools Should Teach* (New York: Basic Books, 1991); and Howard Gardner and Veronica Boix Mansilla, "Teaching for Understanding in the Disciplines and Beyond," *Teachers College Record*, Winter 1994, pp. 198-218.

16. See Peter Lee, Rosalyn Ashby, and Alaric Dickinson, "Children's Understanding of History," paper presented at the Second International Seminar on History Learning and Instruction, Las Navas, Spain, June 1994.

17. Howard Gardner, *Frames of Mind* (New York: Basic Books, 1983).

18. Howard Gardner, *Multiple Intelligences: A Theory in Practice* (New York: Basic Books, 1993).

19. Elliot W. Eisner, "Forms of Understanding and the Future of Educational Research," *Educational Researcher*, October 1993, p. 6.

THE DISAPPEARANCE OF AMERICAN INDIAN LANGUAGES

Abstract It has been reported that only 206 Native American languages remain; this is a third of the original number, and of these approximately 50 are near extinction. Why are these languages disappearing? What are the various issues involved in ensuring that Native American languages are sustained and nurtured? What are the socio-cultural factors which make it so difficult for Native American cultures as well as languages to exist? Are there some success stories of language maintenance instead of shift? Possible solutions are offered to the question of the disappearance of these minority languages.

Barbara J. Boseker

Barbara Boseker has a joint appointment as Professor of Special Education and Education at Winona State University, Winona, Minnesota. She was formerly Program Development Specialist for the Wisconsin Native American Teacher Corps on the Menominee Reservation. She also served as the evaluator for the Fargo Public Schools' Title IV Indian Education grant for 5 years.

The Problem

It has been estimated that there are perhaps 6,000 languages in the world of which as many as 90% are being lost (Diamond, 1993) with up to half no longer being learned by children. By some time in the next century all but a few hundred languages could be dead or dying (Diamond, 1993: 81). Although the vast majority of people use the so-called 'major' languages, sometimes called 'world' languages, such as Mandarin, Hindi, English, Spanish, Portuguese, or Russian, most of the world's language diversity is in the so-called 'minor' languages with small numbers of speakers. The median number of speakers of these 'smaller' languages may only be some 5,000.

Languages with the most secure futures are the official languages of the world's sovereign states, which now number 170 or so. However, most states have officially adopted English, French, Spanish, Arabic, or Portuguese, leaving only about 70 states opting for other languages (Diamond, 1993); languages with over a million speakers might be secure as well, whether or not they are the official languages of a sovereign state. Official languages of sovereign states plus languages spoken by large numbers of people might number 200 out of the world's 6,000 languages. Are we to lose the other 5,800?

It has been estimated that at the time of their 'discovery' by Columbus the Americas had more than 1,000 languages. Of the 187 Indian languages surviving in North America outside Alaska, 149 are already moribund (Diamond, 1993) and even Navajo, with the largest number of speakers (approximately 100,000) and with its own Navajo language radio station, has a doubtful future because most Navajo children now speak only English (Diamond, 1993).

Case Studies

Let us examine some case studies of indigenous American languages which are disappearing. The last speaker of Cupeno, a southern California language, Roscinda Nolasquez of Pala, California, died in 1987 at the age of 94 (Diamond, 1993). Alaska has 20 Eskimo and Indian languages. Eyak, spoken by a

Table 1 Alaskan languages

Language	N speakers	Age of youngest speaker	Estimated date of loss
Eyak	3 (now 1)	Seventies	2000
Han	20	Thirties	2030
Holikachuk	25	Fifties	2015
Haida	100	Fifties	2015
Tanana	100	Fifties	2015
Ingalik	100	Thirties	2030
Tanacross	100	Teens	2055
Upper Kuskokwim	140	Children	2055
Tsimshian	200	Fifties	2015
Ahtna	200	Thirties	2030
Tanaina	250	Teens	2055
Upper Tanana	250	Teens	2055
Koyukon	700	Thirties	2035
Kutchin	700	Teens	2055
Aleut	700	Twenties	indefinite
Alutiiq	1,000	Teens	2055
Siberian Yupik	1,000	Children	indefinite
Tlingit	2,000	Forties	2030
Inupiaq	5,000	Teens	2055
Central Yupik	14,000	Children	indefinite

(*Source*: Senate Select Committee 1991: 19)

few hundred people on Alaska's south coast, had declined by 1982 to two native speakers, Marie Smith (age 72) and her sister Sophie Borodkin (Diamond, 1993). Sophie Borodkin died last year at the age of 80. The Eyak children speak only English. Seventeen other native Alaskan languages are dying, in that not a single child is learning them and that they have fewer than 1,000 speakers each. Of the original 20 indigenous Alaskan languages, only two are being learned by children: St Lawrence Island (Siberian) Yupik, with 1,000 speakers, and Central Yupik, with 10,000 speakers (Diamond, 1993; Senate Select Committee on Indian Affairs, 1991).

Table 1 is a list compiled by Michael Krauss, the Director of the Alaska Native Language Center, in 1980 and presented to the US Senate Select Committee considering a bill supporting indigenous languages in 1991. The list consists of Alaskan languages which are being lost, their current number of speakers, and the estimated date of their extinction.

The worst thing about this loss is that it was totally unnecessary: Alaskan mother tongues could have been supplemented instead of replaced by English. All Alaskan indigenous languages are now written, with excellent writing systems, but 'there is *not one* Alaskan school district... which has a program of bilingual education that is designed realistically to reinforce the home language, or to allow the children to become speakers of an Alaska Native language' (Senate Select Committee, 1991:113).

Indigenous languages have disappeared not only in the United States, but also in Canada. In November 1990, 'the Standing Committee on Aboriginal Affairs of the Canadian Parliament published a report stating that of the fifty-three native languages still spoken in Canada, only three appeared to have a secure future and more than forty were in danger of prompt extinction' (Abley, 1992: 4).

A case in point is the Huron language, which was not even on the Canadian Parliament list. By the early twentieth century the Huron language was all but extinct since the Hurons collapsed as a nation more than three hundred years ago. The Huron people divided into three fragments in the mid-seventeenth century. One fragment lived outside Quebec City, another was assimilated by the Iroquois, who were victorious over the Huron, and a third fragment settled near Detroit. In the nineteenth century the US government shipped the Detroit group out of Michigan to 'Indian Territory', soon to become Oklahoma. On the Oklahoma reservation Huron continued to be spoken into the 1960s or even later. It is strongly suspected that the language is now dead in the United States (Abley, 1992).

The Canadian branch of the Huron, however, are attempting to revive their language. The 1,500 survivors who speak French as a mother tongue plan to resurrect Huron, using the revivals of Hebrew and Cornish as models (Abley, 1992). Huron is fortunately well documented, thanks to the efforts of early Jesuits. The Huron adults hope to establish an informal club and relearn the language together. They then intend setting up an immersion school for their children modelled on that of the Mohawk several hundred miles away. The Mohawk language, too, was in the process of extinction and its future is also still uncertain.

In another area of Canada, Snowdrift, Northwest Territories, the Chipewyan language is also in danger of extinction. Snowdrift is situated on the eastern side of Great Slave Lake, accessible only by air and water. It is a community of three hundred people, over 90% of whom are Native Indian, or Dene. Due to its isolation, the Chipewyan language survives here relatively fluently in comparison to other Athapaskan or Chipewyan communities (Rodriguez & Sawyer, 1990). However, even in Snowdrift where the language is heard to a much greater extent than in most other

Dene communities, the actual knowledge of the language is much less than expected. The youth use not the language of the elders but a more contracted and changed form. Because of a lack of 'modern' vocabulary in Chipewyan, English was substituted for 'important' transactions such as giving directions (Rodriguez & Sawyer, 1990). Thus English has changed the mother tongue language to a greater degree than hoped for by those interested in language retention. Complicating the situation is employment in the Northwest Territories. Although there is employment for people who are fluent in both English and Chipewyan, most positions require literacy in English. Thus there is a conflict between those who want to teach mother tongue literacy, which has limited use for employment, and English, which assures a job.

The Bureau of Indian Affairs (BIA) faced the same policy decision in the Arctic in the 1930s and 1940s. At that time those who wanted the indigenous cultures preserved encouraged mother tongue usage only without encouraging learning English as well. But it was the Arctic people who spoke English who obtained the jobs in Anchorage, Vancouver and Seattle. Thus those [who] wanted strict 'preservation' of the Arctic cultures 'as is' actually did a disservice (Jenness, 1962, 1968). We should learn from this sad era that preservation does not mean fossilisation. Some communities have difficulty deciding which language they want used in the early grades because they see a conflict between learning English for jobs and learning the mother tongue for retention of the culture. The solution lies in a truly bilingual school system, offering competent instruction in both, but there 'is little evidence that serious bilingual policies are being attempted in the NWT' (Rodriguez & Sawyer, 1990:112). It is doubtful if either oral or literate mother tongue language will survive for any practical use through the next few generations, and the languages may be lost by default.

I was on the Stockbridge-Munsee Reservation in Wisconsin when the last native speaker of Munsee, a 90-year-old tribal elder, died. The Munsee had been moved from Massachusetts in a previous century by the expansion of white settlement from east to west and acquired the name of the Stockbridge-Munsee from the fort in Massachusetts where they had been housed in an earlier era. Since the Stockbridge-Munsee had no reservation, the Menominee of northern Wisconsin generously offered them a corner of their reservation, where the remaining Stockbridge-Munsee live today. It may be argued that when the last Munsee speaker died, the Munsee culture died with him.

How Did Native American Languages Disappear?

What happened to the language diversity of the Americas? Certainly many languages died when their speakers died. Columbus killed the Arawak Indians of the Caribbean and with them their language. Similarly, white Californians killed the Yahi Indians between 1853 and 1870 (Diamond, 1993). When Native Americans were not slaughtered, they often died from disease; indeed, it has been estimated that Native Americans died in greater numbers from diseases such as smallpox, measles and whooping cough than from outright slaughter. It is now known that even when Native Americans surrendered and came into the forts and agencies, they were purposely issued blankets with the smallpox virus on them so that they would hopefully acquire the disease and die.

For those Native Americans who were not slaughtered or who did not die from disease, there was the US government forced policy of assimilation. Indian children were forced into boarding schools where they would be 'civilised' by separation from their parents and through the use of English. This English-only policy was resisted strongly by the missionary schools which had operated bilingually. President Ulysses S. Grant condemned the missionaries for teaching in native languages, and the federal government threatened to cut off their funding. It was at this point in 1879 that the US BIA school system originated with coercive English instruction (Crawford 1990); Indian children were placed in boarding schools often far from their reservations and certainly away from their parents' influence.

When I was working on the Menominee reservation, several Menominee women told stories of how the boarding school teachers washed out their mouths with soap if they dared utter a word of Menominee. Indeed, Crawford (1990) reports that this practice was so common that the word 'soap' was often the first word Native American children learned in English. (The same thing happened in my own high school in Milwaukee, Wisconsin, where at South Division High School I myself observed my classmates, Mexican-American students, being dragged by teachers into the bathrooms if they dared speak Spanish. This same high school now takes pride in its bilingual programmes!) The BIA boarding schools soon became notorious for escape attempts, corporal discipline, and gender segregation.

The usual sequence of events of a language minority facing the onslaught of a majority language is that the minority young adults tend to become bilingual and their children monolingual in the majority language. 'Eventually the minority language is spoken only by older people, until the last of them dies' (Diamond, 1993: 82). Even before the death of the language, the minority language has degenerated through loss of grammatical complexities, loss of vocabulary, and incorporation of foreign vocabulary and grammar (Diamond, 1993).

Success Stories

One of the most well-known stories is the Rock Point Community School in the middle of the Navajo Nation in Northeast Arizona (see Spolsky, cited in Reyhner, 1990). The school is completely bilingual and operated through local community control under Public Law 638, the Indian Self-determination and Assistance Act. In 1988, 43% of the Rock Point students were dominant Navajo speakers while only 5% were dominant English speakers (Reyhner, 1990). When students begin kindergarten, two-thirds of their instruction is in Navajo while the remainder of their time is spent learning oral English. By second grade students are receiving half their instruction in English and half in Navajo. By the time students reach the intermediate level (grades 4, 5 and 6), 15–30% of their instruction is in Navajo with the rest in English. By seventh and eighth grade, students have one period of Navajo studies plus a quarter of Navajo writing each year. In ninth to twelfth grades, students have a half-year of Navajo studies plus a quarter of Navajo writing each year. 'Eighth graders and seniors must give graduation speeches in Navajo and/or English' (Reyhner, 1990: 105).

The bilingual programme at Rock Point can be described as being both a co-ordinate and a maintenance bilingual programme (Reyhner, 1990): instruction in the two languages is kept separate but complementary. Concepts introduced in Navajo are reviewed in English, but not repeated in each language and some teachers teach only in English, others only in Navajo.

The Rock Point curriculum is an example of what Cummins (cited in Reyhner, 1990) has called an additive rather than a subtractive educational programme. A subtractive programme is one that seeks to replace native language and culture with the English language and culture causing minority students to fail; an additive programme seeks to teach English language and culture in addition to the native language and culture creating the conditions for success. What Cummins advocates is consistent with the 'both/and' curriculum, currently considered the most appropriate for Native American students, which advocates teaching both modern aspects of the curriculum (such as computer science) and the traditional (such as incorporating traditional Indian beadwork in art classes), thus preparing Native American students for jobs in the next century as well as honouring and preserving their cultures of the past.

To obtain enough Navajo language teachers, most of the Rock Point elementary teachers were hired locally without college degrees; by now, however, many have earned degrees through on-site college programmes. Teachers without four-year college degrees are required to take 12 semester credits each year leading to appropriate education degrees. In my opinion, this is the only way to achieve language maintenance in isolated areas.

Teaching materials in the mother tongue are another problem. Bernard Spolsky found from his detailed study of Rock Point school in 1973 that there was a 'good bit' of Navajo language material around, but not enough 'to fill out a first grade year of reading' (Spolsky, cited in Reyhner, 1990: 108). Materials in Navajo are more available now, but teachers and students must still rely on their own efforts in materials production. Students learn to type both Navajo and English in the computer class and then use the Macintosh computers at both the elementary and secondary levels to publish school newspapers. The newspapers and booklets so developed are then used as reading material by other students.

Another key to success at Rock Point is strong parental involvement. There is a parent advisory committee that observes the school several times per year, sponsors cultural events, and serves community dinners. Students also participate during clanship week every year wearing slips of paper showing the clans of their mother, father, grandmothers and grandfathers, greeting each other with traditional kinship greetings in Navajo. As a result of parental support, student attendance rates are above 94% of school days attended, and parent conference attendance rates are above 80% (Reyhner, 1990). This is an extraordinary achievement when many other schools are finding parental participation a formidable task.

I can speak with experience of the importance of parental and community involvement. In my evaluation of the Title IV Indian Education Program in Fargo, North Dakota, Public Schools, a strong parental support group has been one of the factors in the excellent attendance of Indian children in Fargo schools (a 92% rate of school days attended) and an exceedingly low drop-out rate (zero drop-outs of Indian students by 1989) (Boseker, 1991).

The Isleta Headstart Computer Program is another success story. Isleta Pueblo is 12 miles south of Albuquerque, New Mexico, and Isletan is a dialect of Tiwa, a language spoken by only four New Mexican tribes (Donahue, 1990). In the 1950s and 1960s Isletan was threatened by technology and urbanisation as Isletans bought cars and took jobs in nearby Albuquerque. Many left their pueblos and took residence in government-subsidised housing tracts on the outskirts of Albuquerque. By the early 1980s Isletan had become a language almost solely reserved for rituals (Donahue, 1990).

Ted Jojola, a University of New Mexico professor who is Isletan and who chairs the UNM's Native American studies department, applied for a grant from Apple Corporation. Through Jojola's efforts, Apple Computer's Wheels for the Mind Foundation granted the Isleta Headstart Program three Macs and two printers. One difficult problem was that Isletan, an almost solely oral language, had never really been written, and the sounds can only be approximated by the English alphabet. A technical problem which emerged was to create programs that integrated sound and video, which became difficult because of the amount of memory needed. None the less, the computer program at the pueblo's Headstart school for four and five year olds began in 1985 and was one of the first of its kind in the United States (Donahue, 1990). Isletan children feed disks into their Macintosh computers that teach them Isletan words for various body parts as well as displays and names of animals (rabbits, pigs, and cows) that roam on Isleta's many farms. The computers helped the Isletan children develop self-esteem (a very serious educational concern for children in the United States today, especially Native American children) before they entered the Albuquerque Public Schools, which are filled with Anglo children whose parents work at high tech jobs such as Sandia labs. Pepper (1976) found that Native American children have some of the lowest self-images in the United States and that their anxiety level is the highest. Indian children used to be intimidated by the Anglo children, but now the Isletan children have technical skills and confidence as a side benefit of working with computers.

Having worked with Native American communities for many years, I can vouch for the grave difficulties which some Native American children have with the competitiveness of American schools. Co-operation, not competition, is a traditional Native American ethic still stressed in Native American childrearing. When I worked in Teacher Corps on the Menominee reservation in Wisconsin, Menominee teachers and teacher aides would constantly ask for ideas and activities which emphasised the ethic of cooperation. The Menominee felt that their children flourished in the spirit of co-operation. If the usage of computers provides the self-esteem Native American children need to face the immense competitiveness of Anglo schools, then this is an added benefit in addition to preserving their language.

The Zuni of New Mexico have followed the Isleta with a similar programme. Through a grant again from Apple, the Zuni have bought Macs, printers and modems which have been used to develop a written version of Zuni, which was until quite recently solely an oral language (Donahue, 1990). The Zuni Literacy Project has been compiling a Zuni/English dictionary and creating a series of filmstrip-like 'storybooks', which use sound and static visual images to tell stories in Zuni (Donahue, 1990). The Zuni have written five storybooks and English definitions for 700 Zuni words and the dictionary has been put to use in a middle school Zuni language class. Like the Isleta, the Zuni hope to create audible videos of Zuni folk tales, a much more technical challenge. The Acoma and San Juan pueblos of New Mexico have also developed Macintosh computer programs that help teach their mother tongues to youngsters.

Another road to success is the development of instructional programs such as the Ogwehowe:ka? Program for second language instruction using the languages of the eight Native American nations located in New York State: Mohawk, Onondaga, Seneca, Oneida, Cayuga, Tuscarora, Shinnecock and Unkechaug (New York State Education Department, 1988). 'Ogwe'o:weh' means 'the real people/the original beings' in Seneca, and 'ogweho:weh' means 'the real people/the original beings' in Onondaga, Oneida, Cayuga, and Mohawk. 'Ogwehowe:ka?' and 'Ongwehonwe:neha:' include all the characteristics pertaining to the way of life of 'the real people/the original beings'. In the syllabus for the program, 'Ogwehowe:ka?' refers specifically to the languages of the eight nations. The purpose of the syllabus is to encourage functional communication in the listening and speaking skills.

The emphasis of the Ogwehowe:ka? Program is not just on linguistics but on a holistic way of life stressing the creator, mother earth, community, nature, and values. The program has three goals: (1) functional communication in Ogwehowe:ka? languages with emphasis on listening and speaking, (2) sharing and understanding the holistic way of life, and (3) an appreciation of the heritage of the Ogweho:weh people. The Ogwehowe:ka? languages have been oral traditions until recent times. The program also shifts second language instruction from an approach which stresses the linguistic aspects of language to one that stresses the skills of functional communication.

Literacy is perceived by the eight nations using this syllabus in a way different from that encapsulated by the dominant society culture definition of 'ability to read and write'. These nations consider 'literate' to mean the ability to 'speak the native language(s), be totally knowledgeable of the "way of life", read all elements comprising the natural environment and the universe, read the lunar cycles, live within cycles and natural laws of nature, recognise purpose of everything comprising natural environment and universe, (and) respecting and being grateful for all of the Creator's gifts' (New York State Education Department, 1988: 54). This refocusing of what is a literate person truly acknowledges the need for linguists and educators to heed the cultural aspects of language learning, not merely the linguistic.

By no means are these success stories the only achievements of Native American language preservation. They do represent, however, solid bilingual programmes (Rock Point), newly innovative programmes (use of computers on Isleta and Zuni reservations), and the incorporation of cultural values (Ogwehowe:ka? Program).

The Future

The future in terms of preserving and protecting Native American languages lies beyond merely linguistics. From my work with Native American people, it would appear to me that the future of their languages is intertwined with the future of Native American cultures as a whole. The cultures as a whole are endangered, perhaps never more so than today with what traditional Indians see as an assault on their values. This assault is accompanied by the English language onslaught and influences such as Las Vegas style gambling on reservations, which as a result of the Indian Gaming Regulatory Act of 1988 pose new threats to cultural and linguistic heritage.

The Indian Gaming Regulatory Act basically states that if gambling is allowed in any form in a state, even bingo in a church basement, Native Americans in that state are allowed to set up gambling casinos of their own. Some traditional Indians view the Las Vegas style gambling on reservations today as antithetical to everything that is Indian. For example, Erma Vizenor, a colleague of mine who is a member of the White Earth band of the Ojibwe of Minnesota and who practices traditional Ojibwe values, feels that Indian reservation gambling is a scourge because when a person gambles, someone else has to lose in order for the gambler to win. That violates the fundamental Native American principle of sharing. On the other hand, the dependent relationship between Native American peoples and the US government is ceasing as a result of the revenue from the casinos. In my own state of Minnesota, Indian people are getting off welfare roles and increasing their own self-esteem through the jobs they have created for themselves in the gambling industry. Future developments in this area are anticipated.

According to some sources (Devenish, 1970; Pepper, 1976) Native American children actually perform as well as or better than whites in the early grades in school. Young Indian children often find school intriguing but it is when they reach the pre-adolescent level that they often fall behind. In terms of school achievement, between 64% and 74% of Native American students score below the national norm on standard achievement tests. Some Arizona data indicate that Indian students lag two to four grade levels behind the national norm (Boseker, 1991). It is at the pre-adolescent level that all children are discovering who they are. Native American children, too, are learning their identities and with those identities their estimate of themselves. And in America that means learning that the dominant society denigrates everything that Indian cultures stand for, including language. I believe that incorporating Native American values in one's teaching is paramount (see Boseker & Gordon, 1983; Gordon & Boseker, 1984). Some Native Americans feel that by incorporating Native American language and culture in the public schools, absenteeism of Indian children is reduced and academic achievement improves. 'That ties heavily into the self-esteem and the feeling of comfort in the schools, as the students realise that their languages and cultures are just as important as the English language and culture', said one Native Alaskan educator, testifying at US Senate hearings on indigenous language preservation (Senate Select Committee, 1991: 60).

Once Indian children fall behind they may never catch up; the ultimate result can be school drop-outs. The national drop-out rate for Native Americans is 60%; in some parts of the United States it is as high as 85% (Boseker, 1991). Currently, in the state of Minnesota, which has the highest high school graduation rate in the United States, 88% of ninth graders will receive a high school diploma in four years compared with only 52% of Native American ninth graders; Minnesota Native American students thus have a 48% drop-out rate, and this is in a state in which some glimmers of hope occasionally appear. For example, a recent advertisement asked for a part-time Ojibwe language teacher in one of Minnesota's school districts (District #317, Deer River), and in summer 1993 Moorhead State University is offering a course in beginning Ojibwe.

Possible Answers

The 1990 Native American Languages Act, signed into law by former President Bush on 10 October 1990, is at least a start in that it actually encourages the use of Native American languages. Furthermore, Senate Bill 2044, signed by former President Bush in October 1992, allocates $2 million a year for Native American language studies (Diamond, 1993); although this is not a large sum of money, it is a beginning.

There are other feasible developments. According to the report which accompanied Senate Joint Resolution 379 to establish a US policy for the preservation, protection, and promotion of indigenous languages, academic credit should be granted to Indian children for proficiency in an indigenous Native American language in the same way that it is granted for foreign languages (Senate Select Committee on Indian Affairs, 1988). For example, students in the remote villages of Alaska currently have the choice of Russian, Spanish or Japanese, all taught via the satellite system. One Native Alaskan student reported to the US Senate that she was in her second year of taking Spanish via satellite from Spokane, Washington (Senate Select Committee, 1991). Why not offer Yupik as the fourth 'foreign' language? A 1988 Senate Select Committee report also recommended that indigenous languages may be used as a medium of instruction as well as an official language in their traditional territories.

Increased usage of radio and television as modes of indigenous language transmission is also feasible. For example, in Bethel, Alaska, KYUK public radio and television has been on the air for 20 years. The station serves some 56 villages and transmits for 18 hours a day, three hours of which is in the Yupik language. KYUK offers two newscasts in Yupik, 30 minutes at noon and fifteen minutes at 6.30 p.m. One Native American broadcaster from the Yupik news department, John Active, envisions a Yupik 'classroom of the air' for 20 minutes on the radio after the news at noon and again at 6.30 p.m., teaching the Yupik language to both speakers and non-speakers (Senate Select Committee, 1991). Such efforts need to be supported, not cut back as John Active fears will happen.

Teaching materials will need to be produced, such as the many materials which have been developed in Yupik for kindergarten through twelfth grade in Alaska, and those available for Cree, which were developed in Canada. Much can be said about the use of videotape formats for the storage of and access to materials. For example, in the 1970s when I was a member of Teacher Corps on the Menominee Reservation, I established a videotape library which contained, among other things, videotapes of Menominee elders telling legends in Menominee accompanied by an English translation; cultural aspects, such as childrearing practices, were also recorded. (That videotape library is today located on the Menominee Reservation in Keshena, Wisconsin).

Fluent mother tongue speakers need to be hired as language teachers, then paid and treated as professionals by the school districts. I had experience of this particular problem in Teacher Corps. Often the people who knew most about how to teach the Indian children on the Menominee Reservation were the Native American teacher aides who were not certified. I personally witnessed experienced Menominee teacher aides being supplanted by inexperienced certified personnel, simply because the certified personnel held teaching licences and the aides did not. Thus career ladders need to be established so that experienced Native American teacher aides can achieve their licensures and 'legitimise' themselves. (One of the major components of Teacher Corps was the establishment and development of career ladders.)

Teaching methods must also be modified. From study after study (Pepper, 1976; Collier, 1979; Rodriguez & Sawyer, 1990) and from my own experience, Native Americans prefer a 'watch then do' approach. This means that teachers must help, wait, watch, help again, and wait some more, rather than the shorter, quicker, 'in and out' or 'cover the curriculum rapidly' modes used by non-Native American teachers. I have elsewhere (Boseker & Gordon, 1983; Gordon & Boseker, 1984) emphasised the importance of 'wait-time'—the time a teacher pauses after asking a question and also after a student's response. Increased wait-time is actually thinking time, giving both the speaker and the listener time to think or engage in speculative thinking; it has been shown that extended wait-time encourages higher-level thinking rather than simple recall (Rowe, 1978). Winterton (1976) found that extended wait-time results in: (1) significantly longer student responses, (2) significant increase in number of student-student comparisons of data, (3) more active verbal participation of usually low-verbal students, (4) decrease of students failing to respond, and (5) students tending to contribute unsolicited but appropriate responses and to initiate appropriate questions.

Finally, computer-assisted multimedia interactive programs could be developed because most schools, even in the most remote villages of Alaska, have access to computers. Indeed, the use of computers is per-haps the most important recent leap in language preservation.

The above are just some possibilities which could be instituted immediately. Other ideas, such as videodiscs, need to be pursued.

Conclusion

The tragic loss of Native American languages must stop. As linguists and educators we must support Native American people in every way possible in their efforts to preserve their cultural and linguistic heritage. As linguists and educators we have all learned that children do not suffer in any way from bilingualism: study after study has shown that when children continue to develop both languages, they are linguistically and cognitively enhanced (Cummins, 1990). Finally, language maintenance rather than language shift is also a human right guaranteed by United Nations Resolution 2200, Article 27, of the International Covenant on Civil and Political Rights. As one North Carolina Native American woman, Janice Jones Schroeder, whose tribe has lost all semblance of its native language after 500 years of white contact, said in testimony before the US Senate:

> I view the speaking of our language as a human right, given to us by the Creator. He chose what group and what individuals should be in those groups to speak the languages, as he gave the birds the individual songs, the animals of the woods, he gives us our languages. No one has the right to take those away. (Senate Select Committee, 1991: 49)

References

Abley, M. (1992) The prospects for the Huron language. *Times Literary Supplement* no. 4662, 7 August.

Boseker, B. J. (1991) Successful solutions for preventing Native American dropouts. *International Third World Studies Journal and Review* 3, 33–40.

Boseker, B. J. and Gordon, S. L. (1983) What Native Americans have taught us as teacher educators. *Journal of American Indian Education* 22, 20–4.

Collier, M. (1979) *A Film Study of Classrooms in Western Alaska*. Fairbanks: Center for Cross Cultural Studies, University of Alaska.

Crawford, J. (1990) Language freedom and restriction: A historical approach to the official language controversy. *Proceedings of the Ninth Annual International Native American Language Issues (NALI) Institute*. Choctaw, Oklahoma: Native American Language Issues Institute.

Cummins, J. (1990) ESL in the 21st century: From demographics to methodology. Speech to the Seventh Midwest Regional TESOL Conference, St Paul, Minnesota.

Devenish, R. (1970) *The North American Indian, Part III: The Lament of the Reservation*. New York: McGraw-Hill (16 mm film produced for J. K. Hoffman Presentations).

Diamond, J. (1993) Speaking with a single tongue. *Discover* 14, 78–85.

Donahue, B. (1990) Computer program helps revive ancient language. *Winds of Change: A Magazine of American Indians* 5, 20–5.

Gordon, S. L. and Boseker, B. J. (1984) Enriching education for Indian and non-Indian students. *Journal of Thought* 19, 143–8.

Jenness, D. (1962) *Eskimo Administration: I. Alaska*. Montreal: Arctic Institute of North America.

—— (1968) *Eskimo Administration: V. Analysis and Reflections*. Montreal: Arctic Institute of North America.

New York State Education Department (1988) *Ogwehowe:ka? Native Languages for Communication, New York State Syllabus*. Albany, NY: New York State Education Department.

Pepper, F. C. (1976) Teaching the American Indian child in mainstream settings. In R. L. Jones (ed.) *Mainstreaming and the Minority Child* (pp. 133–58). Reston, VA: Council for Exceptional Children.

Reyhner, J. (1990) A description of the Rock Point Community School bilingual education program. *Proceedings of the Ninth Annual International Native American Language Issues (NALI) Institute*. Choctaw, OK: Native American Language Issues Institute.

Rodriguez, C. and Sawyer, D. (1990) *Native Literacy Research Report*. Salmon Arm, BC: Native Adult Education Resource Centre.

Rowe, M. B. (1978) *Teaching Science as Continuous Inquiry*. New York: McGraw-Hill.

Senate Select Committee on Indian Affairs (1988) *Establishing as the Policy of the United States the Preservation, Protection, and Promotion of the Rights of Indigenous Americans To Use, Practice and Develop Native American Languages, and for Other Purposes* (28 September) Washington, DC: Congress of the United States, Senate Select Committee on Indian Affairs.

—— (1991) *Alaska Native Languages Preservation and Enhancement Act of 1991* (19 October). Washington, DC: Congress of the United States, Senate Select Committee on Indian Affairs.

Winterton, W. (1976) The effect of extended wait-time on selected verbal response characteristics of some Pueblo Indian children. PhD thesis, University of New Mexico.

Barbara Boseker has a joint appointment as Professor of Special Education and Education at Winona State University, Winona, Minnesota. She received her doctorate from the University of Wisconsin-Madison and was formerly Program Development Specialist for the Wisconsin Native American Teacher Corps on the Menominee Reservation. She also served as the evaluator for the Fargo Public Schools' Title IV Indian Education grant for five years.

Parental Involvement

Column Editor: Dr. Aurelio Montemayor, Intercultural Development Research Associates, TX

Parents as First Teachers:
Creating an Enriched Home Learning Environment

by Abelardo Villarreal, Ph.D.

By the end of the first semester of second grade, Emilio was so fed up with his performance in school that he decided to play sick every morning. His teacher blamed Emilio and his parents for his poor performance, and his parents angrily accused school personnel for the inadequate education that he was receiving. At the losing end of this dichotomy was Emilio and his future.

Unfortunately this is not uncommon. Ill-defined roles and responsibilities for school personnel and parents and an inadequate instructional program for Emilio kept his educational well-being in abeyance. Numerous articles have been written to help school personnel reform their practices to assume a more responsible role in the education of all children and, in particular, the children who speak a language other than English or who share a different culture (TEA, 1994; Díaz-Soto, 1991; Villarreal, 1993). Although schools are still struggling to become more responsive to all students, this lack of success is not always due to lack of information (Cárdenas, 1995).

Parents, on the other hand, decry the lack of access to information for them to play their part as children's first teachers (Schoonmaker, 1992). The purpose of this article is to provide school personnel with insights for use in parenting workshops on enriching learning opportunities during their children's formative years (ages three to five).

Parenting involves taking responsibility seriously, taking advantage of every opportunity to enhance children's learning, and providing children with challenges. Children absorb life experiences indiscriminately. To a large extent, these life experiences form children's character, feelings and values, and they provide the window through which they will view the world (Scott, 1992; Villarreal, 1993). In other words, through interaction with their children and the experiences that they provide them, parents can influence and guide children's growth and development.

By age five children will be exposed to school life. Parents can either provide learning experiences haphazardly or unknowingly (with good intentions, but with little knowledge and no plan) or they can conscientiously plan for quality experiences to occur and exercise their obligation in a more responsible manner. There are three major tasks that parents can do to improve the learning environment at home. These tasks are discussed below.

Task 1: Learn More About How Children Learn

Parents who have been successful in their role as the first teachers of children share a similar philosophy about children's learning. This philosophy is defined by eight key assertions about parenthood and learning (Bredekamp, 1987). The following outlines these major thoughts that are instrumental for parents to be successful as children's first teachers.

A. *Children are always ready to learn.*

Children have an inborn capacity to learn (Forman and Kuschrer, 1983). They start learning from the time that they are in the mother's womb. The fact that children ask many questions or are eager to touch all that they see is an expression of their readiness to receive input from the environment. This innate willingness to learn could be nourished or weakened by childhood experiences from the environment. Parents must be vigilant and expose their children to the "right experiences."

What Parents Should Do
- Turn as many everyday life experiences as possible into learning opportunities.
- Model learning from everyday experiences.
- Talk about the importance of learning as a self-initiated activity.

What Parents Should Avoid
- Interact with children only when they ask a question ("I don't have time to talk").

B. *Children have a curiosity for learning.*

Children test the world. When the child jumps from a chair the first time and finds out that it hurts, he or she has learned the consequences of such an act. The responsibility of the parent is to teach the child that risks need to be calculated. Killing curiosity for learning will have serious consequences later in life.

What Parents Should Do
- Take advantage of children's questions to extend learning.
- Capitalize on children's interest in selecting learning experiences.
- Plan the home physical environment with children's needs and desires in mind.
- Purchase toys that are specifically designed to stimulate children's thinking and creativity.

What Parents Should Avoid
- Leave children's learning to chance.
- Tell children you are too busy to answer their questions.

C. *Children learn from their environment.*

Children learn from all aspects of the environment (Greenman, 1988; Penny-Velázquez, 1993; Adame-Reyna, 1995). The environment is represented by people and objects that surround them. Every experience, whether it is a positive or negative experience, will teach children something. Some experiences that can be used to teach new concepts and develop appropriate behaviors are the following: (1) child sees a mountain and asks about it; (2) child is involved in a fight with another

From *NABE News*, February 1, 1996, pp. 13-17. Originally from *IDRA Newsletter*, April 1995. © 1995 by the Intercultural Development Research Association. Reprinted by permission.

child; (3) sister is reading a book and child sits next to her; (4) child receives a ball of clay; (5) child accompanies parent to the doctor's office; and (6) child watches a cartoon on television.

What Parents Should Do
- Expose children to experiences that teach social, academic and motor skills.
- Capitalize on children's interest in selecting learning experiences.
- Allow children to actively interact with the environment; allow them to explore and ask questions.

What Parents Should Avoid
- Expose children to experiences that focus only on one set of skills.
- Only expose children to experiences interesting to parents.

D.   *Children thrive in an environment of love and respect.*

Children need to feel secure in order to take risks and take advantage of a learning experience (Scott, 1992; González-Mena, 1991; Allen and Mason, 1989). Children are unique individuals whose feelings evolve from their experiences with other people and with the environment that surrounds them. These feelings form the basis for children's self-esteem, love, and an appreciation and an acknowledgment of one's uniqueness.

Feelings can facilitate or hinder learning. Feelings that facilitate learning are based on love and respect. Children who feel a sense of belonging and feel like worthwhile individuals who have unique qualities and characteristics experience love and respect. Parents have the responsibility to sustain an environment full of love and respect and to nourish children's self-esteem when confronted with a hostile or unfriendly environment (Bredekamp, 1987; Scott, 1992; Adame-Reyna, 1995).

What Parents Should Do
- Show love for all their children equally.
- Celebrate the uniqueness of each child.
- Respect children's views of the world.
- Ask and value children's opinions.
- Provide opportunities to excel and experience positive feelings about themselves.
- Model respect for other's beliefs and values.
- Expect children to respect other's beliefs and values.

What Parents Should Avoid
- Be partial to some of your children.
- Criticize children for their actions and behaviors.
- Impose your will without an explanation for your action.
- Demean children because of their actions or beliefs.

E.   *Children have a potential for acquiring language.*

Children learn from their parents or the persons with whom they live. Children have an innate capacity to process and use language (Sosa, 1993; Strickland, 1990; González-Mena, 1991). The process for learning a language is complex, requiring at least 12 years to formalize itself. In homes where the language is Spanish, children will become proficient in Spanish. If children live in an environment where a wide variety of languages are used, they will become very proficient in those languages. Parents, siblings and other adults who spend considerable time with the children become language models.

Parents should make sure that children are exposed to effective language users. Talking and reading with children develops their control of the language. Once children have mastered one language, they can learn a second one quickly. For example, children who have mastered the Spanish language well, have been exposed sufficiently to the English language at the appropriate time, and are not forced to learn the new language, can become proficient users of both Spanish and English. Parents should ensure that children are not prematurely forced to learn a new language.

What Parents Should Do
- Talk to children as often as possible.
- Engage children in conversations.
- Ask for their views about certain topics of interest.
- Increase children's vocabulary on different topics.

What Parents Should Avoid
- Use language to request children's compliance only.
- Criticize children for the way they express themselves.
- Turn down an opportunity to explain or respond to a question.
- Expect children to listen passively.
- Dominate a conversation with children.

F.   *Children can communicate ideas in many different ways.*

Children are versatile individuals who have learned to communicate ideas through language, behaviors and actions (Gandini, 1993; Greenman, 1988). Many have learned that they can communicate ideas on paper. That is, children have learned that people's scribbles communicate an idea. Children who are ready to discover the excitement those scribbles represent begin to scribble themselves. Soon, their scribbling begins to communicate a feeling or an action. When asked, children will talk about the scribbling. Parents can help children master this form of communication by reading and providing them opportunities to scribble and talk about their masterpieces. Displaying their work guarantees acknowledgment of children's unique qualities and characteristics.

What Parents Should Do
- Provide opportunities to communicate ideas through speech or writing.
- Show children ways they can communicate ideas.
- Encourage children to use acceptable behavior.
- Redirect unacceptable behavior.
- Provide opportunities to appreciate art and music.

What Parents Should Avoid
- Criticize or demean cultures or languages that are different from theirs.
- Pressure children to react or respond in one specific way.

G.   *Children can acquire a love and desire for reading.*

Reading is the most efficient way of acquiring information. Reading is a skill that children can develop from a very early age (Strickland, 1990; Greenman, 1988). Children who are exposed to print at a very early age tend to become better readers and learners when they go to school. They develop a thirst for information and knowledge. Parents can help their children by talking about the beauty of reading, by getting books for them to own, and by reading signs, labels and a range of items that have print on them.

What Parents Should Do
- Stress the importance of comprehending what is read.

- Provide opportunities to select topics or books to read.
- Read to children starting at an early age.
- Have print materials (newspapers, books, letters, forms and in whatever language) at home at all times.
- Read all labels and signs to and with children.
- Expose children to different literature styles at an early age.

What Parents Should Avoid
- Ask children to conform with your selection of reading materials only.
- Force children to begin decoding works when they are not ready.
- Criticize children for not liking to read.
- Compare children to other children's accomplishments.

H. Children learn in different ways.

Adults and children use the senses to learn (Forman and Kuschrer, 1983). Some learn by seeing. Others learn by hearing, reading or touching. Some of us are better at learning by using one particular sense or another. For example, some of us can learn better if the reading is accompanied by pictures. Reading about how to put a model together may be sufficient for some. While other children may learn better if presented with a "hands on" activity. Parents should keep this information in mind and determine which is the preferred way of their children to learn. Provide more opportunities for children to learn in their preferred way.

What Parents Should Do
- Provide learning opportunities using all the senses.
- Teach that some questions do not have a right or wrong answer.
- Provide opportunities for problem solving using the different senses.
- Provide with opportunities to role play.

What Parents Should Avoid
- Teaching children to learn only by reading and memorizing materials.
- Teach that one way of learning is better than another.

Task 2: Establish a Vision and Goals

A vision is a mental picture of an event that has not yet occurred. A mental picture allows us to define what children would be able to do within a period of time. Getting there does not happen automatically; parents have to make sure that support is available to help them to get to that point. After hearing about a successful learner who entered school at age five, a parent decided to write down his vision for his three-year-old. The vision went like this:

My son will know about many things. He will be able to talk about them and express his desire to know more about certain things. He will not be afraid to ask if he is unsure of things. He will not be afraid of making mistakes. He will show respect and love for

---

Contract with My Children

During the next six months, I (we) will try out the following five activities:
1.
2.
3.
4.
5.

I (we) will find out if I (we) have been successful if my children do the following:
1.
2.
3.
4.
5.

Signed:_____ Date: _____

---

others and will always be happy. He will be highly dominant in Spanish, the language that we speak at home. He will be in the process of learning English in a meaningful manner and not feel frustrated or hurried to learn English immediately.

I challenge parents to do the same. Write or share with someone else a vision that will guide you and your children through the journey of childhood life.

The parent proceeded to write his goals in meeting this responsibility. Goals are like guideposts that define responsibility in making a vision a reality. His goals were:

- Strive to learn more about how children learn by reading articles, books or watching informational television programs.
- Take advantage of every opportunity to engage my children in learning.
- Create a home environment conducive to learning.
- Instill in my children a desire for learning.

These goals served him and his children well. The parent planned activities to ensure that goals were met and the vision was realized.

Task 3: Reflect and Plan an Enriched Learning Home Environment

The third major task is to take stock, reflect and plan the improvement of the home learning environment. The chart on the facing page provides a checklist with activities that promote a positive home learning environment. Parents can use this checklist to reflect on what has been occurring at home. All ratings of "never" or "sometimes" merit some attention by parents. After

Parents as First Teachers Checklist

Rate each item according to the degree that it is practiced in your household, by writing the appropriate number in the blank to the right of the statement. Use the following codes: Always = 1   Sometimes = 2   Never = 3

1. I take advantage of as many learning opportunities for my children as possible. _____

2. I model by taking advantage of as many learning opportunities as possible. _____

3. I talk about the importance of learning from every experience with my children. _____

4. I take advantage of my children's questions by extending learning. _____

5. I capitalize on my children's interests in selecting learning experiences. _____

6. I plan my home physical environment with my children's needs and desires in mind. _____

7. I purchase toys that stimulate children's thinking skills. _____

8. I expose my children to experiences that develop social, academic and/or motor skills. _____

9. I respect my children's views of the world. _____

10. I ask children for their opinions. _____

11. I acknowledge my children's efforts. _____

12. I praise my children's accomplishments. _____

13. I model respect for other's beliefs and values. _____

14. I expect my children to respect others' beliefs and values. _____

15. I talk to my children as often as possible. _____

16. I engage in conversations and discussions with my children. _____

17. I ask for my children's views about certain topics. _____

18. I strive to increase my children's vocabularies in many different topics. _____

19. I provide opportunities for my children to express their ideas in different ways. _____

20. I model how ideas can be expressed in different ways. _____

21. I acknowledge my children's use of acceptable behavior. _____

22. I redirect my children's use of unacceptable behavior. _____

23. I provide opportunities for my children to appreciate art and music. _____

24. I probe to ensure that my children understand the importance of comprehending what is read. _____

25. I provide opportunities for children to select topics or books to be read. _____

26. I read to my children constantly. _____

27. I have print material available at home. _____

28. I read all labels and signs with my children. _____

29. I expose my children to classic literature. _____

30. I provide my children opportunities to use the different senses to learn. _____

31. I teach my children that some questions do not have a right answer. _____

32. I provide my children opportunities for problem solving using the different senses. _____

33. I provide my children opportunities to role play. _____

using the checklist, parents may identify those activities that they propose to improve upon during the next six months. On this form, parents can write down their commitments to improve the learning environment. They can share this contract with their children and other adults and ask them to "check on them" periodically. They should post this contract on the refrigerator or a place where they will see it often. Repeat this process every six months.

Parents as effective teachers play several roles. First, they are good listeners. They listen to everything that children say, and they observe the environment that surrounds them. They respect what children have to say. There are no absurdities; whatever is said is said with a reason. Parents look for the message and question children when the message needs clarity. A good listener promotes the use of language by children. Children appreciate and are prompted to use language when they know that others listen and do not criticize them. One of the major responsibilities of a parent is to initiate conversations and take every opportunity for their children to use language.

Secondly, parents who are resourceful promote learning in many different ways. They have print available for children to see. They model the use of print to communicate ideas. A resourceful parent creates opportunities for learning.

Resources

Adame-Reyna, Ninta. "What Parents Can Do for Their Children's Mathematics Learning," *IDRA Newsletter* (San Antonio, Texas: Intercultural Development Research Association, February 1995).

Allen, JoBeth and Jana M. Mason. *Risk Makers, Risk Takers, Risk Breakers: Reducing the Risks for Young Literacy Learners* (Heinemann Educational Book, Inc., 1989).

Bredekamp, Sue (editor). *Developmentally Appropriate Practice in Early Childhood Programs Serving Children From Birth Through Age 8* (Washington, D.C.: National Association for the Education of Young Children, 1987).

Cárdenas, José A. *Multicultural Education: A Generation of Advocacy* (Needham Heights, Mass.: Simon & Schuster Custom Publishing, 1995).

Díaz-Soto, Lourdes. "Understanding Bilingual/Bicultural Young Children," *Young Children* (January 1991).

Forman, George E. and David S. Kuschrer. *The Child's Construction of Knowledge: Piaget for Teaching Children* (Washington, D.C.: National Association for the Education of Young Children, 1983).

Gandini, Lella. "Fundamentals of the Reggio Emilia Approach to Early Childhood Education" *Young Children* (November 1993).

González-Mena, Janet. *Tips and Tidbits: A Book for Family Daycare Providers* (Washington, D.C.: National Association for the Education of Young Children, 1991).

Greenman, Jim. *Caring Spaces, Learning Places: Children's Environments That Work* (Redmond, Wash.: Exchange Press, Inc., 1988).

Penny-Velázquez, Michaela. "Yo Escribo: Promoting Interactions in the Early Childhood Classroom," *IDRA Newsletter* (San Antonio, Texas: Intercultural Development Research Association, August 1993).

Schoonmaker, Mary Ellen. "When Parents Accept the Unacceptable," *Early Childhood Education* (Guilford, Conn.: the Dushkin Publishing Company, 1992).

Scott, Bradley. "Providing for Strong Roots: The Teacher and Human Relations in the Preschool" *IDRA Newsletter* (San Antonio, Texas: Intercultural Development Research Association, April 1992).

Sosa, Alicia S. *Questions and Answers About Bilingual Education* (San Antonio, Texas: Intercultural Development Research Association, 1993).

Strickland, Dorothy S. "Emergent Literacy: How Young Children Learn to Read and Write," *Educational Leadership* (March 1990).

Texas Education Agency. *First Impressions: Primeras Impresiones* (Austin, Texas: Texas Education Agency, January 1994).

Villarreal, Abelardo. "The Challenge for Site-Based Decision Making Council: Making Quality Preschool Accessible to Language Minority Students," *IDRA Newsletter* (San Antonio, Texas: Intercultural Development Research Association, June 1993).

Abelardo Villarreal is the director of the IDRA Division of Professional Development.

Reprinted with permission from IDRA Newsletter, April 1995.

Editor's Note: *NABE is pleased to announce the appointment of Dr. Aurelio Montemayor as editor of the new regular* **Parental Involvement** *column.*

Confronting White Hegemony

By Rebecca Powell

As a person of European descent and a beneficiary of White privilege, I have often found it difficult to talk about racism. For one thing, there is a certain legitimacy to the argument that Anglos cannot completely understand the ramifications of racism in our society. While some of us have experienced oppression in various forms, our cultural experiences do not allow us to comprehend fully the magnitude and pervasiveness of the problem. In addition, as numerous scholars have pointed out, the Anglos have always been the "unmarked" group in our society, and consequently are seen as an exemplar against which other groups are judged. (See, for instance, Frankenburg, 1993; McIntosh, 1988; and Sleeter, 1994.) In other words, we as European Americans tend not to "see" our whiteness; it is perceived as both neutral and normative, and persons of color are subsequently "marked" as different from the Western European standard.

Implied within discussions of race is cultural hegemony, or the ascribed social and economic dominance of a particular group based upon the possession of certain cultural characteristics. A child's socioeconomic status, for instance, is a primary

Rebecca Powell is an associate professor of Graduate Education at Georgetown College, Kentucky, and works with the Alliance for Multicultural Education in Kentucky.

determining factor in school success, yet the ways in which we are shaped by classism—like the ways in which we are racially constituted—often remain elusive. Therefore, in this article I focus on what I have chosen to call "White hegemony," *i.e.*, the conferred dominance of Whites through the perpetuation of a White cultural ideology. Accompanying White hegemony is the inability of many Euro-Americans to accept persons who differ in significant ways from the standards that govern acceptable cultural behavior in mainstream thought, *i.e.*, those individuals who diverge from what many consider to be a normative White, middle-class, heterosexual society.

It is important to point out at the outset of this discussion that we are all culturally defined, and therefore we are constrained by our own limited experiences. As cultural beings, we hold certain assumptions that have been formed by who we are, both as individuals and as members of particular groups (race, class, religious affiliation, etc.). Therefore, to suggest that one is "not prejudiced" (as many Euro-Americans often do) is simply erroneous. In effect, we are inevitably biased, and hence it becomes crucial that we identify and interrogate our cultural assumptions so that we might examine how they affect our relationships with others and our expectations of the children we teach.

Admittedly, acknowledging our own biases as members of the dominant group, and then acting on those insights, is a difficult and painful journey. However, it is precisely because our whiteness is generally regarded as unproblematic, precisely because Anglo, middle-class society is seen as normative, that we as European American educators must examine critically our own conceptions of diversity.

In this article, I examine how White hegemony is socially enacted, and the ways that schools—as institutions within a racially- and hierarchically-ordered society—tend to obscure its existence. A primary role of multicultural education, I will suggest, is to make Whites aware of their own cultural identity and the values associated with that identity. The observations I make in this article concerning Whites' perceptions of race and class privilege stem from my work with Anglo teachers, both as a researcher and a full-time instructor of graduate education, as well as from my own personal struggles with the institution of racism and other oppressive forces in our society.

Manifestations of White Hegemony

Racism is both socially and historically constructed. Hence, the ways that it becomes expressed in our society are often contradictory, revealing traces of a West-

From *Multicultural Education*, Winter 1996, pp. 12-15. © 1996 by Caddo Gap Press, Inc. Reprinted by permission of *Multicultural Education*, the magazine of the National Association for Multicultural Education.

Implications
for
Multicultural
Education

ern colonial legacy as well as remnants of more recent movements. In her book entitled *White Women, Race Matters* (1993), Ruth Frankenberg suggests that historically there have been three primary discourses or "moments" relating to race difference: (1) "essentialist racism," in which race difference is defined primarily in terms of biological inequity; (2) "color evasiveness" and "power evasiveness," which suggests that we are all basically the same, and that economically we all have an equal opportunity for success; and (3) "race cognizance," which acknowledges difference but links it to larger social, historical, and political forces. In this article I adapt Frankenberg's framework in order to accommodate a discussion of cultural hegemony and its realization through the views of White educators. It should be noted, however, that our perspectives are complex and often conflicting, and one's views on racial and/or social difference will frequently contain elements of more than one discourse.

Essentialist Position

Arguments that imply a certain biological and/or cultural inferiority of persons of color have been popular in past decades. For instance, in the field of education, such notions were popularized with the publication of "scientific" studies that supposedly "proved" that persons of non-

Western descent statistically had lower I.Q.'s, as measured by standard intelligence tests, than their Western counterparts. While most educators today dismiss such arguments as being scientifically invalid and clearly inaccurate (*The Bell Curve* [1994] being one notable exception), a deficit discourse continues to dominate discussions of educational failure.

In the educational literature, for instance, the term "at risk" is frequently used to refer to students from historically underrepresented groups. For some educators, this term implies that these students do not possess the characteristics necessary for acquiring academic competence, and are therefore "at risk" of failure. Consequently, special or compensatory programs must be designed that will enable these students to adapt to an institution that has primarily been structured to serve a White, middle-class population (Cuban, 1989).

Generally, the essentialist position takes on an expression of what might be termed "undesirable otherness," *i.e.*, that persons who diverge from White, middle-class normative behaviors are "tainted" in certain ways. In other words, the unmarked belief system serves as an invisible prototype against which all difference is measured, and those who do not possess the desired "cultural capital" are seen as being "culturally deprived." Educational failure

is attributed to certain indicators that are linked with non-White and/or lower class populations, *e.g.*, single parenthood, the apparent devaluing of education, etc. Rarely are schools implicated for their failure to become integrated with, and their subsequent alienation from, the communities they serve. Nor is the social elitism of students from primarily White, professional backgrounds seen as problematic. Rather, limited achievement is attributed to characteristics that deviate from a White, middle-class standard.

It is also important to note that educational failure is not always defined in terms of actual academic success. Rather, it is often seen as a rejection of mainstream norms, *i.e.*, the unwillingness on the part of certain groups to "buy into" the system. For instance, Anglo teachers in my graduate classes frequently complain that the (primarily lower-class) parents of the children they teach are not involved in their children's education, as evidenced by their unwillingness to attend parent-teacher conferences. The assumption is that these parents "just don't care" about their children's schooling. The continuation of a deficit model for the explication of educational failure—which inevitably leads to a "blame the victim" mentality—is hardly surprising for, as I will discuss at the end of this article, schools are designed to promote a hegemonic ideology.

Within our educational institutions,

Western Anglo, middle-class standards are seen as normative, and hence, desirable. In other words, individuals who "fit" this category in terms of race and cultural behavior (*e.g.,* language, dress, aspirations, etc.) are "unmarked," in contrast to the "Other" categories that become "marked" as racially, culturally, or socially "different." Such views are consistent with a colonial discourse, in which the cultural behaviors and expectations of the dominant group are viewed as natural and hence appropriate and even superior to those of subordinate groups. This normative conceptualization determines how we define success, both in schools and in society. Hence, the goal of education becomes one of helping our students to become "successful," in terms of a traditional White, male, heterosexual, and middle class conceptualization of success (MacLeod, 1987/1995).

Color-Evasive and Power-Evasive Positions

Arguments that tend to evade race and social class privilege are often intertwined with essentialist arguments. Teachers frequently claim to be "color blind," maintaining that they "treat all of their students the same." I am reminded of a story recounted to me by an African-American colleague, whose son was having difficulty in a particular (Anglo) teacher's class. During the ensuing parent-teacher conference, the teacher suggested that she was not acting in a prejudicial manner because she simply "did not see color."

While this perspective may appear commendable in that it seemingly is based upon a commitment to equity, the tendency to ignore color actually results in maintaining the status quo. For ignoring racial difference generally means that we also ignore issues associated with race, such as the marginalization of persons of color in our classrooms through promoting a predominately White, mainstream perspective. Hence, as Frankenberg suggests, color evasion leads to power evasion. Believing that "we are really all the same" negates the institutionalization of racism; it denies that race has, and continues to be, pervasive in the structuring of relationships in our society. Put simply, race does matter, and as long we as members of the dominant race claim "not to see color," we exempt ourselves from confronting the reality of White privilege.

In many ways, the color evasive perspective reflects an emphasis upon individualism in our society. In the book *Habits of the Heart* (1985), Bellah et al. argue that individualism has become ingrained in contemporary American thought. That is, the underlying ideology is individualistic versus sociocentric; what is good for the individual is generally regarded as good for all of society. Such individualism, I would contend, is manifested in Anglos' limited understanding of issues associated with diversity. Racism, classism, etc. are regarded by most European-Americans as problems associated with certain individuals (*e.g.,* "He's obviously prejudiced, but I'm not"; "Persons on welfare are just lazy," etc.), rather than as problems created by structural inequalities inherent in a competitive economic system. Hence, our responsibility as individuals is

> "...it is precisely because our whiteness is generally regarded as unproblematic, precisely because Anglo, middle-class society is seen as normative, that we as European American educators must examine critically our own conceptions of diversity."

limited to monitoring our own behavior so that we are satisfied that we are treating all persons equally.

Associating oppression solely with individual bias perpetuates our "color-blindness" as Whites, for it allows us to deny our collective racial and social identities as members of a privileged group. Helms (1993) suggests that the development of a White consciousness is crucial for overcoming racism and other forms of social injustice. She writes:

> ...institutional and cultural racism are so much a part of the White (or Black) individual's world that he or she is often blind to their presence. Thus, the White person's developmental tasks with regard to development of a healthy White identity...require the abandonment of individual racism **as well as the recognition of and active opposition to institutional and cultural racism**. Concurrently, the person must become aware of her or

his Whiteness, learn to accept Whiteness as an important part of herself or himself, and to internalize a realistically positive view of what it means to be White. (p. 55) (Emphasis mine)

Helms suggests that it is only when Whites reach the final stage of racial identity formation (Autonomy) that it is possible to abandon both personal and institutional racism.

Reducing oppression to an individual problem, rather than seeing it as a societal problem that affects us all, exempts us from seriously confronting the inequities that are associated with advanced capitalism. In a society that is hierarchically structured, attributing success solely to individual merit enables us to deny the existence of institutional discrimination, both in schools and in the marketplace. In other words, our focus on individual achievement in schools, coupled with a failure to interrogate dominant characterizations of "success" and "goodness," allows us to evade issues of power while simultaneously perpetuating the myths of meritocracy and cultural superiority. It also allows us to regard the curriculum as "neutral" rather than as "racial text" (Castenell & Pinar, 1993)—one that reinforces White dominance while marginalizing the perspectives of others.

Certainly, being vigilant of our own individual response to cultural difference is both important and necessary. What is lacking here, however, is a conceptualization of racism—and other differences associated with power and status—as collective or social problems, *i.e.,* as problems that affect us not just as individuals, but as a society. By continuing to view ourselves as non-prejudiced, we essentially exonerate ourselves from the responsibility to help eradicate oppression, thereby reinforcing it through our silence. (After all, the argument goes, we are not directly contributing to it.) Further, reducing social issues to individual concerns enables us to "blame the victims" for their own failure by associating it with a lack of initiative. Accepting this system of meritocracy while simultaneously denying our contribution to injustice allows us to feel justified in reaping the benefits of cultural privilege; we earned it (so the argument goes) through our own volition.

Multicultural Education: Moving Toward Race Cognizance

In our democratic society, racial and class dominance is rarely achieved through force; rather, it is essentially an unconscious process whereby power is maintained through conformity to certain ideals. McLaren (1989) defines hegemony as "the moral and intellectual leadership of a dominant class over a subordinate class achieved not through coercion...but rather through the general winning of consent of the subordinate class to the authority of the dominant class" (p. 174). He further states that the dominant culture

> is able to "frame" the ways in which subordinate groups live and respond to their own cultural system and lived experiences; in other words, the dominant culture is able to manufacture dreams and desires for both dominant and subordinate groups by supplying "terms of reference"...against which all individuals are expected to live their lives.

These "dreams and desires" are perpetuated and reinforced through an ideology that espouses social and economic success—success as defined by those in power (historically White, upperclass, heterosexual males).

As institutions that continue to promote dominant standards, schools provide a testament to the pervasiveness of the hegemonic ideology. Even in communities where there are few opportunities for upward mobility, educators rarely challenge the validity of the American Dream, believing it can be attained by all who work hard and seek "the good life." Absent in this view is a comprehensive understanding of the institutionalization of oppression and the role that teachers play in sorting students for their future places in society.

As MacLeod (1987) suggests, the hegemonic ideology is actually "a 'false consciousness,' an apparently true but illusory set of views that disguises and distorts the true workings of the capitalist system" (p. 113). Hence, those in our society who are "unmarked" in terms of race, class, ethnicity, and other identifiable characteristics, provide the "terms of reference" for society and are rewarded both socially and economically. Similarly, those who are "marked" as "different" from the dominant norm are seen as deficient and therefore less worthy of society's limited rewards.

In this article, I have argued that the competitive economic arena leads to, and is sustained by, the myths of cultural superiority and individual merit. I would further argue that multicultural education can offer an important, and perhaps even

critical, response to the hegemonic ideology by cultivating a democratic vision—a vision that is characterized by equity, justice, and national unity. As Bellah *et al.* suggest, the construction of a national community requires that we establish common goals—goals that embrace multiple perspectives and are, at least in principle, attainable by all members of our society. Common goals can only be developed if we are open to diverse perspectives and are willing to challenge our own cultural assumptions.

Further, realizing the goal of equity requires that we acknowledge the ways in which behaviors that are seen as "normative" and "neutral" are both racially and socially constructed. Thus, I would suggest that a primary objective of multicultural education should be to examine the beliefs and characteristics of White culture, so that we can make visible the taken-for-granted assumptions that dominate mainstream thought. In other words, Anglos must work toward race cognizance in order to achieve a comprehensive and realistic understanding of their own identity, and education must assist in this process. It is only through acknowledging our unearned privilege and examining the ways in which that privilege functions to oppress others that we can ever hope to eradicate racism.

Multicultural education holds the promise for creating a more just and equitable society. Yet it is important to recognize that, in a society that has been structured to a large extent by racism, classism, and other forms of inequity, cultural differences have profound political implications that cannot be ignored. Thus to view multicultural education as merely learning about other cultures is overly simplistic and, in many ways, serves to reinforce, rather than to challenge, the status quo. Cultural hegemony is enacted every day in real classrooms with real students—through what we define as "important knowledge," through what we consider to be "appropriate behavior," through the expectations we hold for our students. Unless we are willing to confront the reality of White hegemony, schools will continue to be structured primarily around White, middle-class norms, and "marked" cultures will continue to be marginalized. We must recognize that cultural hegemony is a system that is embedded in our society—one that relegates unearned privilege to particular groups and reduces the life chances of others. As a social system, White hegemony cannot be eradicated through individual acts alone, but will require collective action and a commitment on the part of all educators to challenge it, and not just recreate the conditions that sustain it.

References

Bellah, R.N., Madsen, R., Sullivan, W.M., Swidler, A., & Tipton, S.M. (1985). *Habits of the heart: Individualism and commitment in American life*. New York: Harper & Row.

Castenell, L.A., & Pinar, W.F. (Eds.) (1993). *Understanding curriculum as racial text: Representations of identity and difference in education*. Albany, NY: SUNY Press.

Cuban, L. (1989). The "at-risk" label and the problem of urban school reform. *Phi Delta Kappan, 70*, 780-801.

Frankenberg, R. (1993). *White women, race matters: The social construction of whiteness*. Minneapolis, MN: University of Minnesota Press.

Helms, J.E. (Ed.). (1993). *Black and white racial identity: Theory, research, and practice*. Westport, CT: Praeger.

Herrnstein, R.J, & Murray, C. (1994). *The bell curve: Intelligence and class structure in American life*. New York: Free Press.

MacLeod, J. (1987, 1995). *Ain't no makin' it: Leveled aspirations in a low-income neighborhood*. Boulder, CO: Westview Press.

McIntosh, P. (1988). White privilege and male privilege: A personal account of coming to see correspondences through work in women's studies. Working Paper Series #189. Wellesley, MA: Wellesley College Center for Research on Women.

McLaren, P. (1989). *Life in schools: An introduction to critical pedagogy in the foundations of education*. White Plains, NY: Longman.

Sleeter, C. (1994, Spring). White racism. *Multicultural Education, 1*. 4-8.

ARE YOU WORKING WITH PARENTS?

Family and Cultural Context: A Writing Breakthrough?

Susan Evans Akaran and Marjorie Vannoy Fields

It was the second semester in my kindergarten class in Kotlik, Alaska. I had been trying to get the children to write stories instead of merely labeling pictures, but I was getting nowhere. "Tell us about your drawing," I said to Sasha after he had done a beautiful drawing. We had been practicing this activity for about a week and a half. At this point Sasha was supposed to tell us about his story, and the class was going to help him write it. But it wasn't working.

"What is happening in your picture?" I tried again after getting no answer.

"Mouse, girl, bed, stairs . . ." was the child's response.

"What is the girl doing?" I asked.

After many attempts on different days and with different children, I finally got sentences like "The girl is eating an apple in bed" and "He is harpooning the seal." But these were still labels for pictures, not stories. Even the children who could write easily were not writing down their stories. Why was this? These children tell stories all the time. Their

Susan Evans Akaran, B.A., is a primary teacher in Kotlik, Alaska, for the Lower Yukon School District. She recently received her Early Childhood Endorsement through a distance-delivery program.
Marjorie Vannoy Fields, Ed.D., is a professor of early childhood education at the University of Alaska Southeast in Juneau. Marjorie is the author of several books and articles in the field and is a former member of the NAEYC Governing Board.
The first person "I" in this article is Susan Akaran. Marjorie Fields was her mentor in the process described and her editor in writing about it. Photographs courtesy Susan E. Akaran.

Yup'ik (Eskimo) culture has a rich oral history through storytelling.

I decided that I needed to expose the children to more story writing so they would understand what a story is. However, since school began I had modeled writing for the children and taken dictation of their stories, descrip-

In winter, daylight in Kotlik looks like this.

tions of events, and ideas. Why wasn't it working? I began to think about what was relevant and meaningful to these children in this community (Bredekamp & Rosegrant 1992). I decided that my students did not see story writing as either relevant or meaningful; they saw no link between their own oral language and the written language activities at school.

The Yup'ik culture is enriched and passed on through oral stories of the old days and of new happenings. Elders from the community visit our school each year to share some of the old stories. However, the Yup'ik language is an oral language; only recently have outsiders come and put it into writing. This new form of the language is not usually written or read by the remaining fluent Yup'ik speakers. Reading and writing in Yup'ik are done mostly in school programs trying to reestablish a language that is nearly extinguished.

But instruction in Yup'ik is not the answer (NAEYC 1996); my students' first language is English, not Yup'ik. As in other places, these children have lost their own language as a result of educational practices common when their parents and grandparents were in school: punishing

Child's story—Sasha and Evan. Susie let us go on her sled. We use a sled so we can carry heavy stuff and light stuff. We carry mail, boxes, tanks, and people. Skidoos break down. We can go hunting, go Emmonak and drive to school with them.

Background: Kotlik is a very small and isolated Alaska Native American village. There are no roads in or out, therefore the river boat for summer travel and the sled pulled by snow machine for winter travel are essential. The use of both sled and skidoo illustrates how people combine the traditional and the new cultures.

Native American children for speaking their own language, and sending them away from their homes to boarding schools. Along with learning English, my students' families also developed bad feelings and mistrust toward schools.

Bridging the gap between school and home is a big job, but I thought it might be the missing piece to my puzzle. My thinking turned to ways of enlisting parents as partners and putting an emphasis on the oral language used at home (Bredekamp & Rosegrant 1995). I wanted to relate the school writing activities to children's home environment. A plan took shape: How about making a class book of stories told to my students by their family members?

Because we were studying animals, and animals are so significant to this culture, it dawned on me that this might be just the thing to make the connection. I sent a letter home to parents asking that they tell their children a story about a personal adventure involving animals (see Figure 1). The plan was for the children to retell the story at school for me to record. When all of the stories were recorded and children had illustrated them, we would compile them into a book.

Figure 1. The Project

- Parents tell their child a story.
- Children retell stories at school.
- Children illustrate stories.
- Children share stories with the group.
- Stories are made into books.
- Children write letters to parents.
- Stories are shared with parents, and books are taken home.

Because we were studying animals, and animals are such a big piece of what makes this culture thrive, it dawned on me that this might be just the thing to make a connection. How about involving family members in sharing some of their own stories? I sent home a letter to the parents asking that they tell a story to their child. The child would then bring the story back to me and retell it. We would compile all of the stories and make a book of them.

𝔖𝔭𝔢𝔠𝔦𝔞𝔩 ℌ𝔬𝔪𝔢𝔴𝔬𝔯𝔨 𝔄𝔰𝔰𝔦𝔤𝔫𝔪𝔢𝔫𝔱

We are collecting stories. Please tell your child a true story about animals. It could be a hunting story, a traditional story, or a personal experience. Tomorrow I will ask your child to tell me your story. We will put the story in a special class book, and your child will illustrate his or her page. We hope to get everyone a special copy of our book at the end of the year. Thanks for your help with this project.

Animal Tales

by the 1996 Kindergarten Class

Figure 2. Some of the Stories We Recorded and Illustrated

Seal Hunting

Once we were going to our camp. We were playing on the sand. We heard somebody shoot and we hear boats. We go chase the seal and my mama almost hit it. I get my spear and I hit it on it's brain. It float in salty water.

Eagle

My grandma saw a big eagle and she run and she hide and that big eagle circle her and she hide and she circle her. She go in her tent. The eagle go.

About the Whale

That bear was trying to bite me. I take BB gun and next I shoot it on the leg. I bring it down to our camp. Next we cut it up. We make it to parka. We put zipper. We throw the body away. We let the whale eat it.

The Bear

We saw a bear track. My dad saw a fox and he shoot it. We go get it. We bring it to our house. When we bring it to our house, we cut it. We save the skin.

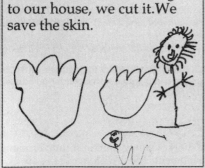

Hunting

Me and my dad catch three ptarmigans and we cook them. We go take a ride. We catch and we eat those ptarmigans. We go home.

That Moose

When my dad see moose trail, he go run after them. Those moose run away.

Although I encourage my students to write independently, I decided to take dictation from them for this activity so that I could use it as a modeling tool.

I sent the letter home to six families a day rather than to everyone simultaneously. This method had two purposes: to allow for alternative stories if a family did not respond right away and to keep me from being overwhelmed with too many stories all at once. As the children came in with their stories, I went to them, one by one, and wrote the stories in big print, using a laptop computer (see Figure 2). I thought that this process demonstrated respect for the child involved. The computer also facilitated the editing process: we read and reread each story until the child decided that it sounded right. The children were fascinated to see their stories in big print.

I copied and bound 30 books over the weekend. On Monday I read the book to the class, and they were thrilled! Each child took a copy of the book, and they all practiced reading their stories to one another and to the group. Their interest continued all week, in contrast to their interest in other writing projects, which the children had ignored after completion. I suggested that they share the books with parents during our quarterly open house. The class was excited. Each child wrote a letter inviting his or her parents and grandparents to come. Six children volunteered to read to the whole group, while others read individually with their parents.

The highlight for me was the reading by a child who had been identified as having special needs. He surprised me by saying that he wanted to read his story aloud to the whole group. He hid under the easel until I asked him if he was ready to share. He immediately stood up, got a copy of the book, and began to read his story in a loud, clear voice. Although he was not actually able to track the words, he knew what a reader does (Fields & Spangler 1995). He stared at the page with his undivided attention, eyes moving from left to right, and spoke the words as if he were reading them. He told the story as he remembered it, which amazed the audience, who all know him well.

During the remainder of the school year, my students—at all levels of reading ability—continued to read and study the books. Many of the children told me they read

Child's story—William and Matthew. This is a boat. It has a steering wheel. It has a tank and tools and spears. In summer we go riding to catch mukluk (seal). Now it's winter. There's no water. The water is frozen.

Child's story—Leeandy and Joseph. This is a mukay house. The stove is made of iron. Fire is in the stove and heat go out of the chimney. People sit down and splash water on the stove. They cool off by the door. When they are done, they wash up with clean water and scrubber.

Background: The mukay (steam bath house) is an important part of the traditional culture and continues to be since the village does not have running water.

Child's Story—Sharon O. and Wilma. They got woods. The Kindergarten people is behind the logs. People get logs 'cause they need for the stove, when they get cold. They get 'em from the water. Us get big woods at far away.

Background: This photo shows the heating system but as the story indicates, there are no trees in the vast tundra of Alaska.

The teacher made this doll so that the children could have a doll that looked like them.

their own copies at home, and I did see the books sitting out as if recently read when I visited their homes informally. In addition, children continued their enthusiasm for bookmaking. They began to make their own books, with less guidance from me. During literacy center time I would hear them ask one another, "How do you spell that?" "What letter is that?" "What are you writing?" "Where is the picture to go with it?" "Is that true or pretend?" A whole new world of writing, creating, and sharing ideas emerged. The children's journal writing also became more focused on ideas and stories.

As I read to my class, the words *author* and *illustrator* took on new meaning. The children wanted to know more about these people: Who wrote these books? What do they look like? Where did they get that idea? How did they know that? They related to authors as people like themselves—clear evidence that they had come to see themselves as writers.

References

Bredekamp, S., & T. Rosegrant. 1992. *Reaching potentials: Appropriate curriculum and assessment for young children.* Vol 1. Washington, DC: NAEYC.

Bredekamp, S., & T. Rosegrant. 1995. *Reaching potentials: Transforming early childhood curriculum and assessment.* Vol 2. Washington, DC: NAEYC.

Fields, M., & K. Spangler. 1995 *Let's begin reading right: Developmentally appropriate beginning literacy.* Columbus, OH: Merrill.

NAEYC. 1996. Position statement: Responding to linguistic and cultural diversity—Recommendations for effective childhood education. *Young Children* 51 (2): 4–12.

For further reading

Brock, D. R., & E. L. Dodd. 1994. A family lending library: Promoting early literacy development. *Young Children* 49 (3): 16–21.

Cohen, L. E. 1997. How I developed my kindergarten backpack program. *Young Children* 52 (2): 69–71.

Garcia, E. E. 1997. Research in review. The education of Hispanics in early childhood: Of roots and wings. *Young Children* 52 (3): 5–14.

Greenberg, P. [1969] 1990. Reading: A key to their future: A freedom. In *The devil has slippery shoes: A biased biography of the Child Development Group of Mississippi—A story of maximum feasible poor parent participation,* 154–170. Reprint, Washington, DC: Youth Policy Institute.

Gutwirth, V. 1997. A multicultural project for primary. *Young Children* 52 (2): 72–78.

Helm, J. 1994. Family theme bags: An innovative approach to family involvement in the school. *Young Children* 49 (4): 48–52.

Johnston, L., & J. Mermin. 1994. Easing children's entry to school: Home visits help. *Young Children* 49 (5): 62–68.

Manning, M., G. Manning, & G. Morrison. 1995. Letter-writing connections: A teacher, first-graders, and their parents. *Young Children* 50 (6): 34–38.

Soto, L. D., 1991. Research in review. Understanding bilingual/bicultural young children. *Young Children* 46 (2): 30–36.

For Vision and Voice:
A Call to Conscience

We look forward to the near-term future of multicultural education with a degree of optimism, yet aware that there are serious challenges before us. Concern in the American public regarding immigration is at a fairly high level. Yet this concern was present in all earlier decades in American history when rates of immigration were running at as high levels as they are now. We all agree that there is much work to be done to accomplish the goals of multicultural

education. There is, however, great hope that these goals will be achieved as our population moves steadily toward becoming ever more unique as a multicultural civilization. The United States is becoming less and less like western Europe and more and more a unique multicultural civilization. The next 30 to 40 years will bring that vision into reality.

The vision for the future of our schools must include a belief in the worth and dignity of all persons. That vision must take into account the ever more culturally pluralistic nation that the United States is becoming. As part of this effort, we should consider the French revolutionary concept of fraternity. Fraternity and its female counterpart, sorority, refer to brotherhood and sisterhood, suggesting that people bond together as brothers and sisters who care for and are committed to one another's well-being. We need to communicate that sense of caring to young people, and the teaching profession could use a good dose of fraternity and sorority as well. Teachers need to work together in solving problems and supporting each other's professional efforts, sharing their experience, knowledge bases, and expertise. We need to learn to team together and teach together more than we have in the past, and we need to have the professional autonomy (independence of professional judgment) to be able to do so at our own discretion and not because someone told us to.

The future of teaching and learning from a multicultural perspective should include more emphasis on cooperative learning strategies that encourage students to develop a sense of community and fraternity, which will transcend competition.

There needs to be more democratization of the day-to-day governance structures of schools so that competent teachers can enjoy the same levels of personal professional autonomy that their colleagues in teacher education enjoy. A multicultural vision of the future of education will embrace the concept that the strengths and talents of all students need an optimum, best possible development. The problems and weaknesses of all students need resolution and assistance. We will have a commitment to the optimum educational development of each student. We need to see young people as a treasured human resource whose needs for safety, health, and cognitive and affective development are to be met by our best efforts as educators. A multicultural vision of our educational future will include an acceptance by educators of an ex-panded conception of their responsibility to their students to include a commitment to teach student's optimum development as a person; we will see our clients whole. We will be more than concerned about their intellectual development, although this is our primary role; we will see schooling as having a therapeutic mission as well as an intellectual one. Diverse cultural backgrounds and learning styles will be accepted and nurtured as brothers and sisters in a shared national community of educational interests.

The future will also see less dependence on standardized, system-wide, behavioral objectives and more emphasis on permitting teachers at the local school level to develop models for assessing whether their students are achieving their educational goals. There will be more informal, teacher-customized approaches to evaluation of student learning and less reliance on rigid statewide standardized learning objectives. Individual school faculties will be permitted to modify their schools' learning objectives for their students, and students will receive more individualized assessment and feedback on their progress in school.

Finally, a multicultural vision of the future of education will include a strong commitment to develop a powerful, critical sense of social consciousness and social responsibility between teachers and students. The educational settings of society are important terrain in the struggle to reconstruct public life along more egalitarian, just social policy lines. A multicultural vision of our educational future will encourage teachers to adopt a pedagogy of liberation that champions the development of critical social awareness among students and that empowers them to evaluate critically all that they may experience.

Looking Ahead: Challenge Questions

What might be the benefits if schools permitted teachers more autonomy in how they assess their students?

What can teachers do to help students develop a sense of social consciousness and social responsibility?

How can teachers help students develop their talents and develop a vision of hope for themselves? How can teachers help students to develop a sense of public service?

What are the most important challenges confronting multicultural educators as we enter the new century before us?

Multicultural Education and Technology:
Promise and Pitfalls
Jim Cummins & Dennis Sayers

Jim Cummins is at the Ontario Institute for Studies in Education; Dennis Sayers is at the University of California, Davis.

It is common to observe that "change is the only constant" to highlight the rapidity of technological change that characterizes the Information Age in which we are now immersed. The implications of these technological changes for education are hotly debated in many countries. In this paper we wish to address one aspect of this debate: the implications of technology for multicultural education.

We will draw from the analysis in our book *Brave New Schools: Challenging Cultural Illiteracy through Global Learning Networks* (Cummins & Sayers, 1995) in which we examine the potential of global learning networks, operating for example through the Internet, to promote intercultural literacy and critical thinking. We suggest that E.D. Hirsch's (1987) call for schools to develop students' **cultural literacy** represents a regression to monocultural myopia and is part of the renewed discourse of intellectualized xenophobia that has escalated in the United States and elsewhere during the past decade. In order to prepare students for the changing cultural, economic/scientific, and existential realities of the 21st century, schools must adopt a pedagogy of **collaborative critical inquiry** that draws on the lin-

All artwork and student writing is from Orilleros, the De Orilla a Orillas newsletter.

guistic and cultural resources that students bring to school to analyze critically the social conditions and power structures that affect their lives and the world around them. We argue that technology can contribute significantly to this form of pedagogy through its power to link distant classrooms for purposes of collaborative projects focused on issues of mutual concern.

In order to contextualize the issues, we will briefly review the ongoing debates in the United States context on (a) cultural diversity and multiculturalism and (b) technology and education. Then we will outline the cultural, economic/scientific, and existential changes that will determine the nature of the society that our students will graduate into and presumably should define the directions for current educational reforms. Finally, we will examine the potential role of computer-mediated learning networks to promote the kind of multicultural awareness and critical literacy and that our society desperately needs if democracy is to survive as anything more than a meaningless ritual.

The Culture Wars

During the past decade, the alleged dangers of cultural diversity have been highlighted by academics concerned that the rapid growth of diversity endangers the coherence and unity of the United States. These authors have articulated a form of intellectualized xenophobia intended to alert the general public to the

infiltration of the "other" into the heart and soul of American institutions. Cultural diversity has become the enemy within, far more potent and insidious in its threat than any external enemy. Most influential was E.D. Hirsch's (1987) *Cultural Literacy: What Every American Needs to Know* which argued that the fabric of nationhood depended on a set of common knowledge, understandings, and values shared by the populace. Multilingualism and multiculturalism represented a threat to cultural literacy and, by extension, nationhood:

> In America, the reality is that we have not yet properly achieved **mono** literacy, much less multiliteracy....Linguistic pluralism would make sense for us only on the questionable assumption that our civil peace and national effectiveness could survive multilingualism. But, in fact, multilingualism enormously increases cultural fragmentation, civil antagonism, illiteracy, and economic-technological ineffectualness. (1987, p. 92)

Hirsch's "cultural literacy" represented a call to strengthen the national immune system so that it could successfully resist the debilitating influence of cultural diversity. Only when the national identity has been fortified and secured through "cultural literacy" should contact with the "other" be contemplated, and even then educators should keep diversity at a distance, always vigilant against its potent destructive power.

From *Multicultural Education,* Spring 1996, pp. 4-11. © 1996 by Caddo Gap Press, Inc. Reprinted by permission of *Multicultural Education,* the magazine of the National Association for Multicultural Education.

It is in this context that we can understand statements such as the following from Arthur Schlesinger Jr. (1991) in his book *The Disuniting of America*:

> In recent years the combination of the ethnicity cult with a flood of immigration from Spanish-speaking countries has given bilingualism new impetus....Alas, bilingualism has not worked out as planned: rather the contrary. Testimony is mixed, but indications are that bilingual education retards rather than expedites the movement of Hispanic children into the English-speaking world and that it promotes segregation rather than it does integration. Bilingualism shuts doors. It nourishes self-ghettoization, and ghettoization nourishes racial antagonism.... Using some language other than English dooms people to second-class citizenship in American society....Monolingual education opens doors to the larger world.... institutionalized bilingualism remains another source of the fragmentation of America, another threat to the dream of 'one people.' (1991, pp. 108-109)

The claims that "bilingualism shuts doors" and "monolingual education opens doors to the wider world," are laughable if viewed in isolation, particularly in the context of current global interdependence and the frequently expressed needs of American business for multilingual "human resources." Schlesinger's comments become interpretable only in the context of a societal discourse that is profoundly disquieted by the fact that the sounds of the "other" have now become audible and the hues of the American social landscape have darkened noticibly.

This discourse of diversity as "the enemy within" has fueled the anti-immigrant sentiment of California's Proposition 187 and the movement to make English the official language of the United States. It is also broadcast into classrooms in ways that affect (and are intended to affect) the interactions between educators and culturally diverse students. With xenophobic rhetoric swirling all around the classroom, educators are required to challenge this discourse and the power structure it represents if they are to create a climate of respect, trust, and belonging in their interactions with culturally diverse students.

Perspectives that promote multicultural awareness (*e.g.*, Darder, 1991; Delpit, 1992; Gates, 1992; Gay, 1995; Nieto, 1996; among many others) tend to occupy the much more limited public space of educational textbooks and peri-

odicals, leaving the newspaper editorials and syndicated columns largely unopposed in preaching to the general public about the dangers of diversity. The media rarely, if ever, bring their readers' attention to the contradiction between the fear of diversity at home and the documented need of American business negotiating in the international marketplace for greater cultural awareness and linguistic competence.

The Promise and Threat of Technology

Business leaders and politicians tend to see the effective use of technology as one of the major means for improving education. Some go further in suggesting that the private sector is better positioned than the public school system to use technology effectively. They argue for the privatization of education as a means of boosting student outcomes while simultaneously generating profits for private investors. Technologically based instructional delivery will require fewer expensive humans, thereby realizing profits based on the same per-pupil expenditure as conventional schooling. In Douglas Noble's words: "Corporate leaders view schools as the last major labor-intensive industry ripe for colonization and modernization. Public schools, finally, represent for them an expensive public monopoly overcome by bureaucratic inefficiency and abysmal productivity" (1994, p. 65).

By contrast, progressive educators (*e.g.*, Apple, 1993; Olson, 1987, and many others) have tended to be highly suspicious of computers and technology in general. Canadian educators, Maud Barlow and Heather-Jane Robertson, for example, express their concerns about what they term the "disinformation highway" as follows:

> To reach young people, as consumers, as future workers, as the social architects of tomorrow, business is looking to the powerful medium-of-choice for kids, high technology. Information is increasingly delivered not by books and teacher lectures but by computers and telecommunications (which are less easily regulated to reflect the consensus standards set by boards, parents, and governments). Technology is becoming the way to bypass the system and go directly to students with a message. While this is as true for environmentalists, labor groups, and others trying to persuade young people to their view, no other sector will have as much financial access as corpora-

Student illustrations from the Orillas Proverbs and Tolerance Project: A comparative Oral History and Folklore Study. **Above:** People who live in glass houses should not throw stones. *El que vine en una casa de vidrio dehe abstenuse de tirar piedras.*—By Rubén Dávila. 5th grade. Truman School, New Haven, CT.

tions to ride the highway into the schools. (1994, pp. 89–90)

We share the concerns of many critics of the regime of technology. However, the dismissal of technology in general, and of the "information superhighway" in particular by many progressive educators ignores the fact that it is here to stay and will play a determining role in the life of every student who graduates in the next millennium. The same critics who dismiss the educational potential of technology as a "corporate plot" have no hesitation using the print medium (books, journals, etc.) to publicize their views and theories despite the fact that the publishing industry is likewise controlled by and largely serves the interests of the corporate sector. Rather than abandoning the field to narrow corporate interests, it seems imperative to us to articulate how powerful a teaching and learning medium the information highway can be when aligned with a pedagogy of collaborative critical inquiry.

The Changing Realities of the 21st Century

In *Brave New Schools* we argue that the changing cultural, economic/scientific, and existential realities that we are currently experiencing highlight the importance of promoting students' capacity for collaborative critical inquiry into social issues of immediate relevance to their lives. Briefly stated, the **cultural** changes are reflected in dramatically increased population mobility brought about by both economic crises and political conflicts in many parts of the world. To illustrate, in the United States the Asian American population is expected to quadruple by 2038 (to 32 million) while Latinos will account for more than 40 percent of population growth over the next 60 years and become the nation's largest minority group by 2013. African Americans will double in number by the year 2050.

These changing cultural realities have immense relevance to educational restructuring. Increased diversity at home and globalization internationally highlight the importance of promoting intercultural understanding and additional language competence in schools. Bilingual and multilingual individuals are essential to maintaining cohesion within our societies and cooperation between social groups and nations. They are also likely to be more attractive to employers faced with providing service to a culturally and linguistically diverse clientele in societal institutions (hospitals, seniors' homes, airports, schools, etc.) as well as to those engaged in international trade. As Australian historian Robert Hughes (1992) has expressed it: "In the world that is coming, if you can't navigate difference, you've had it" (p. 100).

The **economic and scientific changes** are reflected in the explosion of information that individuals, communities, governments and business are dealing with on a daily basis. Both within the workplace and in our daily lives, we are increasingly required to get access to information and reduce it to manageable proportions through critical analysis of what is relevant and what is not. We must then be able to use the information for problem-solving in collaboration with others in the domestic and international arenas who will likely be from different cultural, racial, religious, and linguistic backgrounds.

The clear implication for any school that aspires to prepare students for anything beyond low-level service employment is that students must be given the opportunity for collaborative critical inquiry within the classroom. Unfortunately, large-scale classroom data from the United States (*e.g.*, Goodlad, 1984; Ramirez, 1992) suggest that most schools are still locked into traditional schooling patterns that emphasize transmission of information and skills rather than the generation of knowledge through critical inquiry.

By **existential realities**, we are referring to the increasing sense of fragility that characterizes our relationship to both our physical and social environment. A perusal of virtually any North American newspaper will quickly show the prominence of issues related to poverty, crime, racism, diversity of all kinds, environmental deterioration, global conflict, famine, etc.

Despite these changed existential realities, many schools appear dedicated to insulating students from awareness of social issues in domestic and global arenas rather than communicating a sense of urgency in regard to understanding and acting on them. In most schools across the continent, the curriculum has been sanitized such that students rarely have the opportunity to discuss critically, write about, or act upon issues that directly affect the society they will form. Issues such as racism, environmental

Como se sienten las niñas y los niños porque no hablan el ingles

These are pages from the "New Places" report published by third grade Mexican and Zapotec students who arrived at their California Schools not knowing English. "New Places" is an international research project sponsored by *Project Orillas* on making schools better places for newcomers.

Left: Front Cover—"How boys and girls feel when they don't speak English."
Right: Recommendations—"Treat all children equally. Speak in the child's language so that the children don't feel inferior."

Soluciones para los niños afectados.

Que las maestras aprendan español

Traten a todos los niños y niñas igual

Que los traten en su idioma para que ellos no se sientan inferior.

pollution, genetic engineering, and the causes of poverty are regarded as too sensitive for fragile and impressionable young minds. Still less do students have the opportunity to cooperate with others from different cultural and/or linguistic groups in exploring resolutions to these issues.

A major reason why schools try to maintain a facade of innocence in relation to social and environmental issues is that such issues invariably implicate power relations in the domestic and international arenas. Promoting a critical awareness of how power is wielded at home and abroad is not a task that society expects educators to undertake. In fact, renewed demands for a core curriculum and for imposition of "cultural literacy" can be interpreted as a way of controlling the information that students can access so as to minimize the possibility of deviant thoughts.

It is hardly surprising that issues related to how power is wielded and consent is manufactured in our society are on the taboo list of what is appropriate to explore in schools. However, there are major financial and social costs associated with this attempt to limit critical literacy. Students whose communities have been marginalized will increasingly perceive the omission of these fundamental issues as dishonest and hypocritical, and this will reinforce their resistance to achievement under the current rules of the game. The continued exclusion of culturally diverse students from the learning process at school is pushing us toward a society where everyone loses because every dropout carries an expensive price tag for the entire society. By contrast, a focus on critical inquiry, in a collaborative and supportive context, will encourage students to engage in learning in ways that promote future productive engagement in their societies. The research, critical thinking, and creative problem-solving skills that this form of education entails will position students well for full participation in the economic and social realities of their global community.

In summary, an analysis of the changing cultural, economic/scientific, and existential realities highlights the importance of collaborative critical inquiry as the core pedagogical orientation required for schools to prepare students for both economic and democratic participation. Why is this form of pedagogy so rare in our schools in comparison to traditional transmission-oriented pedagogy?

Despite its obvious relevance to the economic and democratic health of our societies, collaborative critical inquiry is not encouraged in most educational systems for the simple reason that critical

literacy reduces the effectiveness of indoctrination and disinformation. James Moffett (1989) has expressed clearly our ambivalence in regard to critical literacy and multicultural education, both of which permit alternative cultural and social perspectives to be considered:

> Literacy is dangerous and has always been so regarded. It naturally breaks down barriers of time, space, and culture. It threatens one's original identity by broadening it through vicarious experiencing and the incorporation of somebody **else's** hearth and ethos. So we feel profoundly ambiguous about literacy. Looking at it as a means of transmitting our culture to our children, we give it priority in education, but recognizing the threat of its backfiring we make it so tiresome and personally unrewarding that youngsters won't want to do it on their own, which is of course when it becomes dangerous....The net effect of this ambivalence is to give literacy with one hand and take it back with the other, in keeping with our contradictory wish for youngsters to learn to think but only about what we already have in mind for them. (1989, p. 85)

How can participation in computer-mediated learning networks contribute to the promotion of critical literacy and multicultural awareness?

Promoting Critical Literacy and Multicultural Awareness through Global Learning Networks

Sister class exchanges through global learning networks are by no means a new phenomenon. The French educator Célestine Freinet originated interscholastic exchanges in 1924 using the printing press to "publish" students' writings and exchange them and "cultural packages" with distant classes. By the time of Freinet's death in 1966, the Modern School Movement, which he founded, involved 10,000 schools in 33 countries. These schools carried out collaborative projects using the regular postal service to exchange materials and maintain contact.

Although computer and telecommunications technology dramatically facilitate interscholastic exchanges, the basic pedagogical underpinnings of global learning networks are no different than those

implemented by Freinet many years ago using much less sophisticated technology. Students involved in both historical and current learning networks engage in collaborative critical inquiry and creative problem-solving. The issues they focus on have social as well as curricular relevance. Learning takes place in the context of shared projects jointly elaborated by participants in the network rather than from textbooks. Students at the present time also have access to the enormous range of informational resources available through the Internet and World Wide Web.

There are currently a significant number of national and international networks that promote student exchange and inquiry into issues of both social and academic relevance (Cummins & Sayers, 1995). As one example, the multilingual *Orillas* project links students in the United States, Puerto Rico, Mexico, Canada, and Argentina on a regular basis (Sayers, 1994; Sayers & Brown, 1987). Within this network, sister classes engage in two kinds of exchanges: (a) monthly culture packages of maps, photos, audio and videotapes, schoolwork and local memorabilia; and (b) collaborative projects planned jointly by teachers in different sites that involve interdependent, cooperative activity in small groups at both sites. These collaborative projects fall into several categories: (1) shared student publications (*e.g.*, newsletters); (2) comparative/contrastive investigations (*e.g.*, surveys of each community regarding topical social issues such as pollution); (3) folklore compendiums and oral histories (*e.g.*, collections of proverbs, children's rhymes and riddles, songs, etc); (4) cultural explorations (*e.g.*, students in the sister classes alternately playing the roles of anthropologist and cultural informant in order to explore each other's culture).

The common element of all networking projects that focus on social and cultural inquiry is the emergence of a community of learning that thrives on incorporating alternative perspectives in its search for understanding. Such networks potentially challenge the "cultural literacy" of socially approved interpretations of historical and current events by virtue of their incorporation of alternative perspectives on these events. These alternative perspectives derive from both the sister classes and the use of a much wider range of sources for research inquiry than just the traditional textbook. Critical literacy rather than cultural literacy is the goal. For example, the *Kids from Kanata* project links urban and rural First Nations (Native) students (and teachers) with non-

Native students (and teachers) across Canada to explore and share the experience of living in Canada from very different geographic and cultural backgrounds. Students and teachers participating in this network undoubtedly have far greater opportunity to develop an understanding of the roots of First Nations protests in recent years than students who are not involved in this kind of exchange.

At the heart of *Brave New Schools* are eight portraits that we present in Chapter 2 of teachers, parents, and students who are engaged in various global learning networks. These projects address a variety of issues that have immediate social relevance; for example:

◆ the impact of war and ethnic conflict on children and adults who have become refugees;
◆ understanding the different cultural realities experienced by deaf and hearing children from different countries;
◆ confronting inter-ethnic conflict between Latino and African American students;
◆ promoting intergenerational learning among children, adults, and extended families;

◆ exploration and critical analysis of proverbs from different cultures;
◆ researching the Holocaust and other genocides as a way of furthering an end to intolerance;
◆ promotion of global awareness through collaboration in raising money to build village wells in Nicaragua;
◆ publication of an international students' magazine, *The Contemporary,* that focuses on controversial issues of global importance.

In the third portrait, we describe a long-distance collaboration initiated by a Spanish-speaking bilingual teacher from San Francisco and her African-American colleague. The two teachers together sought ways to confront the growing inter-ethnic prejudice in their school between newly-arrived Latino children of Mexican heritage and the African-American students. To do so, they established a "distance team-teaching" partnership with a bilingual teacher in New York City who worked with Spanish-speaking students from the Caribbean. Their rationale, according to Kristin Brown of *Orillas,* who helped locate a suitable partner class to work with in confronting intergroup prejudice, was straightforward:

Since the partner classes in New York would include Spanish-speaking Latino students of African descent, we would be linking San Francisco's Latino students with faraway colleagues who in many ways were like them—students who spoke the same mother tongue and shared the experience of learning English as a second language—but whose physical attributes and pride in their African heritage more closely resembled their African-American schoolmates. In this way we hoped to provide a bridge between the African Americans and the Latinos who saw one another everyday at school but whose interactions were distorted by fears and deep-seated prejudice. (Cummins & Sayers, 1995, p. 36)

The two classes in San Francisco and their New York colleagues shared videos and other projects for a year, including an exchange of folkgames from Mexican, Caribbean, and African-American cultures.

How do these interchanges work to reduce prejudice among these children? Research suggests these attitudes change through a process similar to the way in

Student Report from the Orillas "New Places Project: An International Research Project on Making Schools Better Places for Newcomers

We are an ESL Classroom at Channel Islands High, in Oxnard, California—Mexican and Filipino immigrant students that live in this new place from 2-3 years. We're all struggling to learn the English language.

What We Hoped and Dreamed
Easy life style, freedom, the quality of life better than our own country, opportunity for work, college, and university; equal rights for all the people...

What our New Place was Really Like
Violent, racist, discrimination, low paying jobs for our parents, very expensive to live, crime and drugs, gangs that kill, difficult to survive in school, my people don't have equal rights, Prop. 187 is frightening, we Mexican women are pressured to move on and get married because our parents can't afford to support us...

What Helped Make our New Place Better
Students for Cultural and Linguistic Democracy, a student activist group, and Mr. Terrazas took many risks to establish the following historical events to make our new place better and more just and equal for all immigrants and oppressed students and parents.

Bilingual and Migrant Program: We did not develop this program, but it sure supports and teaches us English and academics in our native Language. Our bilingual program teachers are excellent with lots of love and sensitivity related to a bicultural existence.

Bilingual and Migrant Open House: This is ours! This is totally student centered and directed. We Voice with power, dance, sing, role play problem posing issues, educate our parents, and rise the political, social, and economics consciousness of our people and community. This is really our welcome place and we are proud of it. Our 9th year!

Students Voicing at Teacher and Communib Conferences: Students for Cultural and Linguistic Democracy have been going to and planning conferences since 1992. We've just worked hard to organize our district's first Educatating Our Raza Awareness Conference, which will involve over 350 students and parents.

Students and Teachers Co-authoring a Book: Our students and our teacher have just co-authored a book called Reclaiming Our Voices: Bilingual Education and Critical Pedagogy & Praxis. This books tells about real struggles and experiences immigrant students go through in new places.

Project Orillas: Sharing and caring with students from other places has made us understand that we are not alone in our struggles. We have learned a lot by just listening to each other over telephone voice box, computer modem, and telephone video. Orillas has introduced us to communication technology at it's highest form.

We hope our research will make better, just, and safe NEW PLACES for all students.
—Guillermo Terrazas and English 103 ESL 1st and 2nd period.

which cooperative learning works to reduce prejudice (Sayers, 1994). As Gordon Allport (1954) first proposed in his classic *The Nature of Prejudice*, dramatic reductions in prejudice can occur when children from different ethnic and racial backgrounds work interdependently in small groups. At a local level, cooperative learning helps break down barriers between "ingroups" and "outgroups" as a result of positive interdependence in achieving a common goal. In the same way, global learning networks can promote significant changes in attitude when two distant classes work cooperatively.

Was prejudice reduced as the San Francisco teachers hoped? There were definite signs it was. The parents of two African-American students in San Francisco **demanded** that their children be allowed to learn Spanish by studying with the children in the bilingual education class. Also, for the first time ever, Latina girls have joined the Girl Scout troop, originally organized by African-American and European-American mothers at the school. Who were the new recruits? Every single girl in the bilingual class that worked on the global learning project.

As a context for dialogue, intercultural learning networks provide an opportunity to find a voice, to have a say and to be heard in terms of learning goals shared with another distant group whose voices are equally valued. Above all, it is a dialogue about finding common ground for working with distant partners, about negotiating a joint site for meaning construction and the definition of identity. It is about jointly posing a significant problem of mutual interest to be investigated locally; about deciding on a basis for comparison of what is being learned; about discovering and refining comparable tools of study; and about sharing and comparing the outcomes of parallel locally-based studies and helping one another transform learning into action. It is about developing a working knowledge of what it means to "think globally and act locally."

Conclusion

We have argued that computer and telecommunictions technology has the potential to act as a catalyst for the development of both intercultural understanding and critical literacy. The emergence of electronic communities of learning potentially threatens the hegemony of "official knowledge," as encapsulated in textbooks, because it is much more difficult to pre-script and neutralize the content of communication across cultural and national boundaries. Only issues that relate directly to students' lives and to the world around them are likely to sustain long-term meaningful collaborative projects. In short, global learning networks represent a powerful tool to deconstruct the sanitized curriculum that most students still experience within the classroom and to prepare students to function within the cultural, economic/scientific, and existential realities of the 21st century.

References

Allport, G. (1954). *The nature of prejudice*. Reading, MA: Addison-Wesley Publishing Company.

Apple, M. (1993). *Official knowledge: Democratic education in a conservative age*. New York: Routledge.

Barlow, M. & Robertson, H. (1994). *Class warfare: The assault on Canada's schools*. Toronto: Key Porter Books.

Cummins, J. & Sayers, D. (1995). *Brave new schools: Challenging cultural illiteracy through global learning networks*. New York: St. Martin's Press.

Darder, A. (1991). *Culture and power in the classroom: A critical foundation for bicultural education*. New York: Bergin & Garvey.

Delpit, L. D. (1992). Education in a multicultural society: Our future's greatest challenge. *Journal of Negro Education*, 61, 237-249.

Gates, H.L., Jr. (1992). *Loose canons: Notes on the culture wars*. New York: Oxford University Press.

Gay, G. (1995). Bridging multicultural theory and practice. *Multicultural Education*, 3 (1), 4-9.

Goodlad, J.I. (1984). *A place called school: Prospects for the future*. New York: McGraw Hill.

Hirsch, E.D., Jr. (1987). *Cultural literacy: What every American needs to know*. Boston, MA: Houghton Mifflin Co.

Hughes, R. (1993). *Culture of complaint: A passionate look into the ailing heart of America*. New York: Warner Books.

Moffett, J. (1989). Censorship and spiritual education. *English Education*, 21, 70-87.

Nieto, S. (1996). *Affirming diversity: The sociopolitical context of multicultural education*. 2nd ed. New York: Longman.

Noble, D. (1994). The regime of technology in education. *Our Schools, Our Selves*, 5 (3), 49-72.

Olsen, P. (1987). Who computes? In D.W. Livingstone (Ed.), *Critical pedagogy & cultural power* (pp. 179-204). South Hadley, MA: Bergin & Garvey.

Ramirez, J.D. (1992). Executive summary. *Bilingual Research Journal*, 16, 1-62.

Sayers, D. (1994). Bilingual team teaching partnerships over long distances: A technology-mediated context for intra-group language attitude change. In C. Faltis, R. DeVillar, & J. Cummins (Eds.), *Cultural diversity in schools: From rhetoric to practice*. (pp. 299-331). Albany, NY: State University of New York Press.

Sayers, D., & Brown, K. (1987). Bilingual education and telecommunications: A perfect fit. *The Computing Teacher*, 17, 23-24.

Schlesinger, A. Jr. (1991). *The disuniting of America*. New York: W.W. Norton.

What is Orillas?

By Kristin Brown, Enid Figueroa, & Dennis Sayers

De Orilla a Orilla (Spanish for "from shore to shore") is an international teacher-researcher project that has focused on documenting promising classroom practices for intercultural learning over global learning networks. Since 1985, Orillas has employed modern telecommunications to promote and extend an educational networking model first developed by the French educators Célestin and Elise Freinet in 1924.

Following the Freinet model, Orillas is **not** a student-to-student penpal project but rather **clusters** of class-to-class collaborations designed by two or more partner teachers who have been matched according to common teaching interests and their students' grade level. Orillas has been an international clearinghouse for establishing long-distance team-teaching partnerships between pairs or groups of teachers separated by distance, forming "sister" or "partner" classes with a focus that is both multinational and multilingual (including primarily Spanish, English, French, Portuguese, Haitian, and American and French-Canadian Sign Languages).

The collaborating teachers make use of electronic mail and computer-based conferencing to plan and implement comparative learning projects between their distant partner classes. Such parallel projects include dual community surveys, joint math and science investigations, twinned geography projects, and comparative oral history and folklore studies. Often teachers in Orillas electronically publish their students' work over the Internet.

Research on Orillas has focused on those networking activities which effect social change, validate community traditions in the schools, and promote anti-racist education and linguistic human rights, while allowing teachers to explore the classroom practicalities of teaching based on collaborative critical inquiry. Robert DeVillar and Chris Faltis in Computers and Cultural Diversity judged Orillas "certainly one of the more, if not the most, innovative and pedagogically complete computer-supported writing projects involving students across distances" (SUNY Press, 1991, p. 116). In their recent book Brave New Schools, Jim Cummins and Dennis Sayers write that "Orillas remains-after more than a decade-the leading global learning network project working to explore and expand the theoretical and practical boundaries of multilingual, intercultural learning" (St. Martin's Press, 1995 p. 23).

How to Participate

Parents or teachers should contact Orillas if they are interested in participating in learning projects over global learning networks that:

1. Promote bilingualism and learning another language.
2. Validate traditional forms of knowledge, such as the oral traditions associated with folklore, folk games, proverbs, and learning from elders through oral history.
3. Advance anti-racist multicultural education.
4. Develop new approaches to teaching and learning that encourage students, parents, and communities to take action for social justice and environmental improvement.

This year, Orillas established a new relationship with I*EARN (the International Education and Resource Network), a nonprofit organization with the goal of "youth empowerment to make a difference to the planet and its people." As a result of the Orillas-I*EARN collaboration, students and teachers in both networks now have extended opportunities to participate in partnerships and project work in Latin America and globally.

Orillas operates over various networks; thus, cost for participation ranges from no-cost to low and moderate cost, depending on the type of service provider available to a parent or teacher. For more information, or an annotated list of articles and research reports on Orillas, contact Kristin Brown, Enid Figueroa or Dennis Sayers.

Kristin Brown—<krbrown@iearn.org> 5594 Colestine Road, Hornbrook, CA 96044

Enid Figueroa—<efigueroa@igc.apc.org> Box 23304 University Station, San Juan, PR 00931

Dennis Sayers—<dmsayers@ucdavis.edu> 351 East Barstow Avenue, Fresno, CA 93710

Kristin Brown is the co-founder and co-director of Project Orillas. Currently, she is ith International Program Director for I*EARN.
Enid Figueroa is the co-founder and co-director of De Orilla a Orilla. She coordinates the project form the Department of Education at the Rio Piedras Campus of the University of Puerto Rico.

Invisibility: The Language Bias of Political Control and Power

Marta I. Cruz-Janzen

Marta I. Cruz-Janzen is presently at the University of Denver completing her dissertation toward a Ph.D. in Curriculum Leadership with a focus on equity and diversity. She is co-author of Educating Young Children in a Diverse Society *(Allyn and Bacon, 1994).*

Often people say, "We don't see color, we only see children." For quite some time I didn't understand what was so disturbing about this statement until one day when I asked a White woman in Atlanta for bus directions. Although I asked her repeatedly she acted as though I was invisible. I knew she heard and understood me, and I remember the bewildered look of both Blacks and Whites. An African-American woman finally pulled me aside, and told me that "Black folks don't ask White folks for help in public."

I felt naked, violated, stripped of all dignity as a member of humanity, vulnerable and helpless, wanting to run away in shame. I still vividly recall withdrawing deeply within myself for answers and protection. If you really want to hurt people, treat them as if they are invisible, and thus, excluded and rejected.

We have learned the power of invisibility, which clearly conveys the message that one is not worthy of membership within a group. We use invisibility when we punish children by banishing them to a "time-out area" or ignoring them for unacceptable behaviors. Fear of exclusion and rejection is strong within us all and leads to the adoption of behaviors deemed desirable for group acceptance and membership. Long-term invisibility has deep consequences for it violates the human integrity of those excluded.

If we don't see people of color, regardless of age, we are denying their rich and unique experiences. We are essentially denying their humanity and telling them that they do not exist. We are attempting to convince ourselves that we are not uncomfortable with their physical differences and that perhaps ignoring these differences will make them disappear.

This discomfort with racial diversity stems from internalized stereotypic images of "typical" Americans that have been sustained throughout our history and which ignore anyone not of White European ancestry. People of color cannot melt into America's mythical "melting pot" but we sometimes do attempt psychological assimilation.

Unfortunately, children of color often get the message that something is indeed wrong with their physical appearance. We, too, lead them to believe that ignoring their own unique differences will somehow make the differences all go away. The tragic outcome of this is that ultimately we betray children of color for they soon learn that their physical differences stay with them, that others around them do notice and are really uncomfortable with them. We betray they if we do not prepare them for the real world by instilling in them a sense that they too have a unique richness worth sharing.

Invisibility can be experienced in various ways besides blatant acts of discrimination and racism. People of color and women have been invisible from textbooks, curricula, decision making, positions of authority and respect, and economic and political power. As equity advocates, we discuss the six **"Forms of Bias in Curricular Materials and Classrooms"** (Grayson, 1990): Invisibility, Stereotyping, Imbalance/Selectivity, Unreality, Fragmentation/Isolation, and Linguistic.

As teachers and equity advocates, we rarely address "The Language Bias of Political Control and Power" inherent in our everyday vernacular. The opening statement above has less to do with the children's skin color than with their lower status as humans— their invisibility and worthlessness—and the politics of control and power that perpetuate their condition. Acknowledgement of people of color is tantamount to acknowledgement of their lesser status and the need for their inclusion as valued members of humanity. Doing so would represent a direct threat to the established dominant White structure.

Knowledge is power and those who control the knowledge also control the power. American education is very political and designed to maintain the status quo of White male power and White supremacy. It teaches what is valued and not valued in our society. We need to understand how knowledge reflects the social, economic and political context of those in power along with their self-preservation interests. We also need to understand how this becomes reflected through our vernacular and knowledge gaps.

For female students and students of color it is not just what they are taught, but what they are not taught, that hurts them.

For female students and students of color it is not just what they are taught but what they are not taught that hurts them. A school dropout once told me that "Education is for White people. It is about what White people have done and can do. It is about what we haven't done and can't do. It is about what Whites have done to us and for us. I am tired of hearing that we were slaves, field and laundry workers, or servants; that we had to sit on the back of the bus and drink from separate fountains. I am tired of seeing us as lazy, criminals and drunks."

Here are some examples of invisibility. Children learn:

1) Commander Perry, a White man, was the first person to reach the North Pole. They do not learn that Matthew Henson, an African-American man who was a skilled sleigh driver and Perry's ground breaker, reached Camp Jessup first.

2) Thomas Edison, a White man, invented the lightbulb, but they do not learn that Lewis Lattimer, an African-American man, invented the carbon filament that made the lightbulb possible.

3) Eli Whitney, a White man, invented the cotton gin, but they do not learn that the idea came from Catherine Littlefield Green, a Southern White woman who could not patent her invention and invited Whitney to help her develop and promote it.

4) Lewis and Clark explored the Northwest Territory, but they do not learn that Sacajewea, a 17-year-old Shoshoni woman with a newborn baby on her back, led Lewis and Clark across the Rockies to the Pacific and back.

5) Children learn about the human sacrifices of the "heathen" Aztecs in religious ceremonies, but they do not learn about the extermination of the Aztecs at the hands of Europeans in the name of Christianity. Nor do we teach them about the wasteful slaughter of buffaloes on the Western Plains as a systematic plan to starve and exterminate American Indians. We do not

discuss the symbolic eating of the "Body of God" and the drinking of "His Blood" in some ancient religious ceremonies that prevail today.

Examples of such knowledge gaps are almost unlimited, representing not only invisibility, but also the relegation of women and people of color to positions of powerlessness and feelings of worthlessness. Invisibility is a clear statement of political control and power for it teaches that only White males have done anything worth mentioning and that all others are not as good. American education teaches people of color and women that they are sub-beings less deserving of human respect or consideration. That they are forced to learn schools' curricula about others and not themselves further reinforces their feelings of hopelessness and powerlessness to control their own lives and destinies.

Powerlessness creates feelings of vulnerability in a hostile and threatening environment. When individuals feel threatened they withdraw from the situation in search of a safe haven. It is an instinctual human survival mechanism. The safe haven could be physical, as when students drop out of school, but most often it is buried deep within students' subconscious, as when they withdraw emotionally and psychologically from the learning experience.

Female students and students of color internalize these messages of hopelessness and worthlessness. Gloria Ladson-Billings (1995) calls it "self-condemnation" and writes that "members of minority groups internalize the stereotypic images that certain elements of society have constructed in order to maintain their power" (p. 57).

America's language of control and power recognizes only five racial/ethnic categories: White, Black, American Indian, Hispanic and Asian. Of these, only Hispanic is considered an ethnic category because it purports to encompass persons of all racial groups. Yet, we are very cognizant of the fact that American society is comprised of more groups than those five, and that there is much diversity within each.

The census categories group all European Americans, with the exception of White Hispanics, together as Whites with everyone else in distinct and isolated subgroups. White Americans have excluded White Hispanics, who are also EuropeanAmericans, from American history and institutions because of a historical dislike for Spaniards. American history is written by the same English, German, Dutch and French people who were enemies of Spain for centuries (Cerio, 1991; Duncan, 1991).

The politics of race and racism have long been part of America's historical heritage. In light of this, it should be no surprise that White America extends its racist ideologies to its definitions of other groups. The term "Hispanic," from Hispania or Spain, was created by the U.S. government supposedly to identify speakers of the Spanish language or persons who, regardless of race, could trace their ancestry back to a Spanish-speaking country, and thus, to Spain. Yet, it does a lot more than that. For one, it claims to represent all Latinos including Brazilians and other Latin Americans who neither speak Spanish nor trace their ancestry to Spain. So why isn't the more accurate term "Latino" used?

Moreover, the term "Hispanic" creates a contradiction for Latinos of color, relegating them to invisibility through subliminal denial of the Black and Indian mestizos or mestizaje that also comprise one of the most salient characteristics of Latino culture and history.

The term "Hispanic" represents outright exclusion of White Hispanics from the White-European American culture and power structure. It is punishment for the "mestizaje" that took place over centuries of Moorish domination of Spain. It is a denial of the mestizaje that also took place over centuries of intermarriage in America.

Miscegenation has occurred between White EuropeanAmericans and American Indians, AfricanAmericans, and others since the beginning days of our nation, yet it is strongly denied and overlooked. One drop of "Black blood" has always meant being identified as 100% Black in America. The opposite axiom has never even been considered.

It is estimated that between 75 and 90 percent of all AfricanAmericans can claim White/European ancestry due to miscegenation (Hodgkinson, 1995; Steel, 1995). It is further estimated that one percent, or millions, of White Americans have some Black ancestry (Funderburg, 1994). Yet, the popular assumption has been that you are Black even if you have White blood but you cannot be White and have Black blood. Clearly the hidden message is that somehow the blood types of Whites and Blacks are different, with Black blood being inferior. This is related to White EuropeanAmericans' (Western Civilization) need to maintain their superiority, survival and growth through the maintenance of racial purity and prevention of racial mixture (Banks, 1995).

Most White Americans think of Americans as being White, relegating everyone else including American Indians, to invisibility and foreign status within their own country. "People come in all colors" is a popular American expression, yet it is most often used to define Latinos in reference to their mestizaje and implied lack of White racial purity. White Hispanics are not considered racially pure enough to be included as White Americans. "It is no accident and no mistake that immigrant populations . . . understood their 'Americanness' as an opposition to the resident Black population. Race, in fact, now functions as a metaphor so necessary to the construction of Americanness that it rivals the old pseudo-scientific and class-in-

formed racisms whose dynamics we are more used to deciphering . . . Deep within the word 'American' is its association with race" (Morrison, 1992, p. 47). As a Black Latina I have often traveled outside this country and have been told that I "do not look American."

The power of the "majority" versus the "minority" or "minorities" is all encompassing. For one, it signifies that there is only one majority and many minorities in America. Even when combined, American minorities remain the minority. Our language of select control and power lets minorities know that they are small, isolated and therefore powerless. The thought of uniting all minorities within one inclusive category, such a "People of Color," is unthinkable and recent attempts to use this term have been met with criticism. Conceptually it represents a threat to the "Divide and Conquer" principles of White European-American dominance.

White Europeans continue coming to the U.S. as immigrants; yet Latino and immigrants of color are more often referred to as "aliens."

We really do not need to search too far for examples. There are many persistent power-laden expressions in common usage that are unequivocally designed and allowed to stand which reinforce the invisibility and inferior status of women and people of color.

• The lack of a "Biracial/Multiracial" category in the U.S. census reflects the need of America's power elite to define Americans as White and perpetuate the isolated racial/ethnic categories that subjugate all others to inferior minority status. This exclusiveness denies persons of color entry into the power elite and further denies America's mestizaje for fear that significant numbers of Americans, including Whites, may claim biracial/multiracial ancestry.

• White Europeans continue coming to the U.S. as immigrants, yet Latino and immigrants of color are more often referred to as "aliens." We do not often hear of German, English or Dutch aliens. Alien not only means foreign and still lacking citizenship, it also means not belonging to the same government. Thus the word "alien" implies a threatening, unsympathetic outsider. We don't have to deal with the plight of fellow Puerto Ricans if we think of them as foreigners. The connotation is prevalent that Puerto Ricans, with

Spanish as a national language and a diverse culture, are foreigners to the U.S.

• Puerto Ricans did not come to America—America came to them with forced citizenship in 1917 and military service during World War I. Puerto Ricans asked for a plebiscite to determine how many wanted U.S. citizenship but the U.S. Congress ignored their request (U.S. Commission on Civil Rights, 1976).

• Puerto Ricans living in the continental U.S. are referred to as immigrants but they really are migrants. Puerto Ricans, as U.S. citizens, migrate within their own country without the need for passports or any other legal documents.

• We focus on Indian cultures of the Southwest to the exclusion of Native American Indians from other areas (Harvey, 1994). Clear in our minds remain the manufactured Hollywood images of the "drunken, ignorant and savage" Southwest Indians who were repeatedly defeated, decimated and forced from their lands by U.S. settlers and troops. We do not have to deal with the needs of today's Native American Indians if we make them invisible and turn them into sub-beings existing only in the past.

• We focus on the "romantic," friendly, and spiritual Indians still living in tepees, migrating after buffaloes, worshipping the land and spirits, attired in ceremonial clothes and feathers, while ignoring that they too have moved on to the 20th century. In reality, American Indians attend schools, live in urban areas off the reservation, hold jobs and are leaders today.

• We continue allowing the dehumanization of American Indians through sports team names such as "Braves," "Redskins," etc. We would not make reference to "White Skins," "Black Skins," etc.

• "Squaw" is one of the most debasing referents for American Indian females. Many books, state roads and counties still use the term officially. The equivalent of this word within other American cultures is much too inappropriate for use even in this essay; yet, it is considered acceptable for American Indian females.

• To "discover" something clearly means that no one else knew about it. To claim European discovery of America makes American Indians nonexistent.

• European Americans claim to have "colonized" the Americas. Although by definitional standards it was an invasion, and our curricula continue to ignore the American Indian perspective.

• It is erroneous to assume that all American Indians and Asian/Pacific Americans are the same. Each category represents many diverse groups with unique cultures, languages, religions, physical attributes, etc. Yet, the language makes those differences invisible and forces conformity within one of the categories defined by the dominant group.

• Continued reference to Asian/Pacific Americans as "Orientals" reflects the days when Europe ruled and considered itself the center of the world. Orient means to the east of Europe and includes many countries. Use of this term continues to set White Europeans apart and to insist on their control and superiority.

• We say that Asians have "slanted" eyes with the connotation that they are abnormal, mysterious and not fully trustworthy. We do not need to bother ourselves with the diversity of Asian/Pacific Americans if we define them as the same and assume that they all act, look, speak and think alike.

America's dominant White European culture defines everything from families and matrimony, education and success, to the concepts of time and ownership. It defines human classifications and relationships between people. These definitions are validated within their own cultural context with very little concern for whether they are harmonious with those of other cultural groups in our society. In essence, they become the standards of achievement and compliance by which everyone else will be measured—standards that often lead to the failure, dehumanization, and continued exclusion of women and people of color. American's dominant White European elite clearly conveys and exerts its power and control over the rest of society through language that excludes, rejects and relegates all others to an invisible and subhuman status.

References

Banks, J.A. (1995). The Historical Reconstruction of Knowledge About Race: Implications for Transforming Teaching. *Educational Researcher*. March 1995, pp. 15–25.

Cerio, G. (1991). The Black Legend: Were the Spaniards That Cruel? *Newsweek*. Special Issue, 1991.

Duncan, D. E. (1991). Spain: The Black Legend. *The Atlantic*. Vol. 268, No. 2, August 1, 1991.

Funderburg, L. (1994). *Black, White, Other*. NY: William Morrow and Co.

Grayson D. (1990). The Forms of Bias in Curricular Materials and the Classroom. Adapted from D. Sadker & M. Sadker, *Sex Equity Handbook for Schools*. (2nd Ed.) 1982. NY: Longman.

Harvey, K. D. (1994). Native Americans: The Next 500 Years. University of Denver.

Hodgkinson, H. (1995). What Should We Call People? *Phi Delta Kappan*. October 1995.

Knopp, S. L. (1995). Critical Thinking and Columbus: Secondary Social Studies. 3440 State Street Road, Eau Claire, WI 54701.

Ladson-Billings, G. (1995). Toward a Critical Race Theory of Education. *Teachers College Record*. Vol. 97, No. 1, Fall 1995.

Morrison, T. (1992). Playing in the Dark: Whiteness and the Literary Imagination. Cambridge, MA: Harvard University Press. In J. A. Banks, The Historical Reconstruction of Knowledge About Race: Implications for Transformative Teaching. *Educational Researcher*. March 1995.

Steel, M. (1995). New Colors. *Teaching Tolerance*. Spring 1995.

U.S. Commission on Civil Rights. (1976). *Puerto Ricans in the Continental United States: An Uncertain Future*. A report. October 1976.

Turning the Tide:

A Call for Radical Voices of Affirmation

Bakari Chavanu

Bakari Chavanu is a teacher at Florin High School in Sacramento, California.

Reading essays by the Black feminist thinker, writer, and teacher, bell hooks, in which she speaks of the "awareness of the need to speak, to give voice to the varied dimensions of our lives..." (1989. p. 13) reminds me of my younger days in high school when I fortunately became aware of a distinctive existence of the Black voice in literature and consequently in my own life.

Bused, but not necessarily integrated, into a traditional white high school during the mid 1970s, I reflect now—as I didn't realize then—how this forced integrated school was unprepared for a different culture of students who came loaded with our own distinctive experiences and ignorance to the purpose of attending a predominantly white institution. But as far as I could tell, the first year of integration was not met with physically violent resistance on the part of White students or their parents. I even doubt that myself or the other Black students attending the school at the time were aware of Little Rock or what blood had been shed for us to attend. We were simply indifferent to attending because we could not go to one of the predominantly Black schools on the northeast side.

As I look back on it, high school was a kind of senseless four years of my life. The image of fellow students sleeping at their desks during class constantly comes to mind. So many of my Black peers in my graduating class made conscious and unconscious decisions to not take school seriously. We participated in forms of reckless indifference—skipping classes, refusing to do course assignments or homework, talking back to instructors, and laughing off three-day suspensions which to us meant a vacation. We came to school with little or no missions to fulfill.

I don't wish to make blanket generalization about every Black student at this forcibly integrated school. Some Black students, depending largely on their family background or where they grew up, actually made good grades and wound up, like myself, attending college (albeit through much trial and error and certainly not by design). One year, the school even elected a Black male as student body president; however, many of us didn't make much of it because we knew his light skin and growing up in the white community surrounding the school gained him quite a few votes.

There were also a handfull of Black teachers and a Black vice-principle. We brought with us our amateur Michael Jacksons, Stevie Wonders, Roberta Flacks, all-pro ball players, and theatrical jazz dancers. But when I say the physical resistance to our presence at John Marshall was not met with violent resistance, I don't mean such was true in the curriculum of the classroom.

As a literature and writing teacher today, I am keenly aware of the cultural silence that exists in most classrooms. When I look back on my high school years, I am painfully aware of how important voice is to culture. Fundamentally, little has changed since I sat behind a classroom desk over ten years ago. The literature curriculum back then rarely spoke powerfully or meaningfully to any students, especially us Black students. Many of us just didn't know that we existed in books which again served to remove us from any sense of purpose in attending an integrated school. In fact, as with the vast majority of Black and other minority students today, the literature and school curriculum was downright insulting and harmful in ways many teachers and society will never understand.

But it was in my junior year that I stumbled across the voice of a writer who helped change forever my sense of Blackness and how much larger life was than the bus ride to John Marshall. It was probably on a Sunday afternoon listening to the Black radio station that I heard an album recording of Nikki Giovanni reading one of her poems set to jazz music—no better way to capture the mind of a teenager.

For the first time, I really heard poetry and felt the presence of a Black voice which was not singing, even though Black singing voices were also important to me. (Even today, Black music remains unconsidered as an important form of communication worth studying.) I grasped hold of Giovanni's words as something valuable, new, bold, and culturally me. The next day I went out and purchased her album. Later, reading a book of her poems and her "extended autobiographical statement on my first 20 years of being a Black poet," titled *Gemini* (1971), lead me to other Black literary voices and, above all to an appreciation of reading.

Unfortunately, my experience is something not easily brought to students. Teachers who care about wanting their students to love reading and writing relish moments when a student takes hold of a book without being motivated by grades or the promise of a diploma. I value deeply the importance of my students discovering the power the written word and the power of their own individual and cultural voices. As bell hooks points out, however, so much in the American hegemony serves to silence voices of women, the working class, and non-European people. "Silence," she understands and clarifies, "is the condition of one who has been dominated, made an object; talk is the mark of freeing, of making one subject" (1979).

Black students who are met with literary core works like *Huckleberry Finn*, *To Kill a Mockingbird*, or even *Of Mice and Men* don't hear powerful Black voices. They hear passive, stuttering voices dominated by a white power structure. It is no wonder that so many Black students are captivated by Malcolm X. For them, he is subject, speaking his mind—boldly, intelligently, and with conviction. Rarely, if ever,

From *Multicultural Education*, Fall 1995, pp. 23-24. © 1995 by Caddo Gap Press, Inc. Reprinted by permission of *Multicultural Education*, the magazine of the National Association for Multicultural Education.

do students hear radical voices in the classroom—voices that speak to the joys, frustrations, and aspirations of the Black community.

Today, with the conservative control of education, students hear what I call politically passive voices in and outside the classroom. Teachers and the curriculum they are compelled to teach are either silent in their ignorance of the cultures in their classroom, or they are too passive or reluctant, for fear of reprisal, to share voices that may not belong to the dominate mainstream America—the white elite.

Today, for sure, a well developed and complex tradition of literature by people of African, Native American, and Asian descent is grounded and growing so much so that you have to step over it to avoid it. These post-colonial voices must be heard by all students if we are going to challenge them to see American society and the world as it really is. Far too many institutions—including education—exist to confuse and make students complacent about the issues and systems of the domination historically maintaining hundreds of years of race, class, and gender oppression.

I witnessed with dismay, for instance, how easily my students, taking their perspectives from the media, espoused the propaganda that the "riot" in Los Angeles was nothing more than hoodlums gone out of control. Only when I read to them a quote by Malcolm X (1991, p 29) about the motivations and tactics behind urban rebellions did they stop to rethink the message they received from the television.

The work of Malcolm X, Giovanni, and other Black writers and cultural workers I now realize were for me when I was growing up voices that constructively challenged the status quo and how the world, especially the Black world, is traditionally viewed. Theirs was and continues to be a voice of affirmation. As June Jordan has pointed out, "affirmation of Black values and lifestyle within the American context is, indeed, an act of protest" (1974).

How can students witness or hear about the racism and other forms of injustices they see acted out and are so often impacted by and not feel a sense of rage, indifference, or an innate feeling of protest? If and when they are silent about what they see around them, it is only because they are never led to constructively confront, dialogue, study, and reflect on the

various forms of resistance struggles to dismantle oppressive infrastructures of racism, poverty, sexism—road blocks in so many people's lives. What they confront day after day are silent voices—passive, indifferent, and many times hostile.

In her essay on "coming to voice," hooks concludes by saying:

> To understand that finding a voice is an essential part of liberation struggle—for the oppressed, the exploited a necessary starting place—a move in the direction of freedom, is important for those who stand in solidarity with us. That talk which identifies us as uncommitted, as lacking critical consciousness, which signifies a condition of oppression and exploitation is utterly transformed as we engage in critical reflection and as we act to resist domination. (1979, p 17)

More teachers must become role models who "engage in critical reflection," even when it means often teaching against the grain. During the last presidential election, I was asked by my students the inevitable question of who I would vote for. I had avoided the question more than a few times when it was previously asked, until I thought I had the time to explain my response. I told them I didn't plan on voting. Many of them appeared shocked. How could I be a role model, one of them retorted, if I, myself, did not vote? I emphatically said that voting was not the only way to voice your opinion; that in fact not voting made a statement.

What they were getting from me was an oppositional view that for some of them was new and to others demonstrated outright contempt for the "democratic" process in America. But I understood before answering the question that the dominate ideology under which they were being taught did not put an emphasis on the radical tradition that had brought about various reforms in this country (very few fundamental changes in this country have been initiated in the voting booth). Nor had they been made aware of alternative political parties and their agendas. Again they were simply co-opted by the mainstream elite. I informed them that I was not advocating that voting is a waste of time, but that they should be as knowledgeable as they can of the various ways change comes about, and thus not to automati-

cally, at such a young age, resign themselves to just one option.

As the struggle increases to expose, clarify, and dismantle forms of domination in this country and throughout the world, I think students growing up in oppressive/exploitive cultures will increasingly feel alienated and indifferent toward public education. They will, as many of my minority students have done in my classroom, speak out and make interrogations about the absence or silence concerning the cultural experiences that have shaped their lives and the people of their communities. Lecturing them about meeting the challenges of the "real world" in which they must learn to fit into rather than change will motivate only a minority of Black students—and perhaps that is by design in a system that has maintained itself on the back of fundamental inequalities.

I believe students really want to learn. But they must be heard. They must be exposed to various voices, especially literary and critically conscious voices speaking to the world they see falling apart around them. Frederick Douglas must be read along side Mark Twain. The voices of the civil rights, Black power, and African liberation movements must be understood and made just as important as the American revolution, the death of John F Kennedy, and the concept of America as the leader of the free world. Contemporary Black feminist or womanist writers—indeed female writers and cultural workers in general—must be equally a part of a core curriculum as the works of Jane Austin. Radical voices worldwide must play a part in making education truly multicultural and meaningful for all students.

References

Giovanni, Nikki. 1971. *Gemini*. Indianapolis, IN: Bobbs-Merrill Co.

hooks, bell. 1989. *Talking back: thinking feminist / thinking black*. Boston, MA: South End Press

Jordan, June. March, 1974. On Richard Wright or Zora Neale Hurston: Notes toward a balancing of love and hatred. *Black World*. p. 5.

X, Malcolm. 1991. *Malcolm X talks to young people*. New York: Path Finder Press.

Index

Credits/Acknowledgments

Cover design by Charles Vitelli

1. The Social Contexts of Multicultural Education
Facing overview—© 1998 by PhotoDisc, Inc. 30-31—Illustrations by Catharine Bennett.

2. Teacher Education in Multicultural Perspective
Facing overview—© 1998 by PhotoDisc, Inc. 56—Illustration by Kay Salem.

3. Multicultural Education as an Academic Discipline
Facing overview—© 1998 by Steve Takatsuno. 78, 80—Illustrations by Bill Dillon.

4. Identity and Personal Development: A Multicultural Focus
Facing overview—© 1998 by Cleo Freelance Photography.

5. Curriculum and Instruction in Multicultural Perspective
Facing overview—© 1998 by Cleo Freelance Photography.

6. Special Topics in Multicultural Education
Facing overview—Stock Boston photo by Bob Daemmrich. 206-207, 209—Photos by Susan Evans Akaran.

7. For Vision and Voice: A Call to Conscience
Facing overview—United Nations photo by Y. Nagata.

ANNUAL EDITIONS ARTICLE REVIEW FORM

■ NAME: _____ DATE: _____

■ TITLE AND NUMBER OF ARTICLE: _____

■ BRIEFLY STATE THE MAIN IDEA OF THIS ARTICLE: _____

_____

■ LIST THREE IMPORTANT FACTS THAT THE AUTHOR USES TO SUPPORT THE MAIN IDEA:

_____

_____

_____

_____

■ WHAT INFORMATION OR IDEAS DISCUSSED IN THIS ARTICLE ARE ALSO DISCUSSED IN YOUR
TEXTBOOK OR OTHER READINGS THAT YOU HAVE DONE? LIST THE TEXTBOOK CHAPTERS AND
PAGE NUMBERS:

_____

_____

_____

_____

_____

■ LIST ANY EXAMPLES OF BIAS OR FAULTY REASONING THAT YOU FOUND IN THE ARTICLE:

_____

_____

_____

_____

■ LIST ANY NEW TERMS/CONCEPTS THAT WERE DISCUSSED IN THE ARTICLE, AND WRITE A SHORT
DEFINITION:

_____

_____

_____

_____

*Your instructor may require you to use this ANNUAL EDITIONS Article Review Form in any
number of ways: for articles that are assigned, for extra credit, as a tool to assist in developing
assigned papers, or simply for your own reference. Even if it is not required, we encourage
you to photocopy and use this page; you will find that reflecting on the articles will greatly
enhance the information from your text.

We Want Your Advice

ANNUAL EDITIONS revisions depend on two major opinion sources: one is our Advisory Board, listed in the front of this volume, which works with us in scanning the thousands of articles published in the public press each year; the other is you—the person actually using the book. Please help us and the users of the next edition by completing the prepaid article rating form on this page and returning it to us. Thank you for your help!

ANNUAL EDITIONS: MULTICULTURAL EDUCATION 98/99
Article Rating Form

Here is an opportunity for you to have direct input into the next revision of this volume. We would like you to rate each of the 38 articles listed below, using the following scale:

1. **Excellent: should definitely be retained**
2. **Above average: should probably be retained**
3. **Below average: should probably be deleted**
4. **Poor: should definitely be deleted**

Your ratings will play a vital part in the next revision. So please mail this prepaid form to us just as soon as you complete it.
Thanks for your help!

Rating	Article	Rating	Article
	1. Moving from an Obsolete Lingo to a Vocabulary of Respect		20. Decentering Whiteness: In Search of a Revolutionary Multiculturalism
	2. Saving Public Education		21. Opening the Closet: Multiculturalism That Is Fully Inclusive
	3. Melting Pot, Salad Bowl, Multicultural Mosaic, Crazy Quilt, Orchestra or Indian Stew: For Native Peoples, It's Your Choice! Or Is It?		22. The Making of a Hip-Hop Intellectual: Deconstructing the Puzzle of Race and Identity
	4. The Challenge of Affirmative Action: Strategies for Promoting the Goal of Diversity in Society		23. Becoming Multicultural: Focusing on the Process
	5. How to Teach Our Children Well (It Can Be Done)		24. Meeting the Needs of Hispanic Immigrants
	6. A New Vision for City Schools		25. Is English in Trouble?
	7. Home Was a Horse Stall		26. "Let Me Take You Home in My One-Eyed Ford": Popular Imagery in Contemporary Native American Fiction
	8. Multicultural Education Requirements in Teacher Certification: A National Survey		27. Success for Hispanic Students: A 14-Year Veteran of Teaching Them Describes His Experiences
	9. Cultural Diversity and the NCATE Standards: A Case Study		28. Creating Positive Cultural Images: Thoughts for Teaching about America Indians
	10. Faculty Fear: Barriers to Effective Mentoring across Racial Lines		29. Early Childhood Education: Issues of Ethnicity and Equity
	11. What Matters Most: A Competent Teacher for Every Child		30. NAEYC Position Statement: Responding to Linguistic and Cultural Diversity—Recommendations for Effective Early Childhood Education
	12. Teaching Teachers: Graduate Schools of Education Face Intense Scrutiny		31. Of Kinds of Disciplines and Kinds of Understanding
	13. Recognizing Diversity within a Common Historical Narrative		32. The Disappearance of American Indian Languages
	14. The Challenges of National Standards in a Multicultural Society		33. Parents as First Teachers: Creating an Enriched Home Learning Environment
	15. Multicultural Education and Curriculum Transformation		34. Confronting White Hegemony: Implications for Multicultural Education
	16. Multiculturalism and Multicultural Education in an International Perspective		35. Family and Cultural Context: A Writing Breakthrough?
	17. Bridging Multicultural Theory and Practice		36. Multicultural Education and Technology: Promise and Pitfalls
	18. Acquisition and Manifestation of Prejudice in Children		37. Invisibility: The Language Bias of Political Control and Power
	19. Race and Class Consciousness among Lower- and Middle-Class Blacks		38. Turning the Tide: A Call for Radical Voices of Affirmation

(Continued on next page)

ABOUT YOU

Name _____ Date _____

Are you a teacher? ❑ Or a student? ❑

Your school name _____

Department _____

Address _____

City _____ State _____ Zip _____

School telephone # _____

YOUR COMMENTS ARE IMPORTANT TO US!

Please fill in the following information:

For which course did you use this book? _____

Did you use a text with this *ANNUAL EDITION*? ❑ yes ❑ no

What was the title of the text? _____

What are your general reactions to the *Annual Editions* concept?

Have you read any particular articles recently that you think should be included in the next edition?

Are there any articles you feel should be replaced in the next edition? Why?

Are there any World Wide Web sites you feel should be included in the next edition? Please annotate.

May we contact you for editorial input?

May we quote your comments?

ANNUAL EDITIONS: MULTICULTURAL EDUCATION 98/99

BUSINESS REPLY MAIL

| First Class | Permit No. 84 | Guilford, CT |

Postage will be paid by addressee

Dushkin/McGraw·Hill
Sluice Dock
Guilford, CT 06437